FROM CRANMER TO SANCROFT

Reverendissimus in Christo pater GULIELMUS SANCROFT Providentia
Divina Archi Episcopus Cantuariensis totius Angliæ Primas & Metropo-
litanus Serenissimo Regi CAROLO II do a secretioribus Consilijs.

William Sancroft (1617-93), Engraving by Daniel Loggan, 1680.
(*National Portrait Gallery*)

From Cranmer to Sancroft

Patrick Collinson

hambledon
continuum

Hambledon Continuum

A Continuum imprint
The Tower Building,
11 York Road, London SE1 7NX

80, Maiden Lane
New York, NY 10038
USA

First Published 2006

ISBN 1 85285 118 X

A description of this book is available from the
British Library and from the Library of Congress.

Distributed in the United States and Canada
exclusively by Palgrave Macmillan,
a division of St Martin's Press.

Printed in Great Britain by
MPG Books Ltd, Bodmin, Cornwall

Contents

Acknowledgements

The author and publishers are grateful to the following for permission to reprint articles which appeared originally in the following places:

1. *The English Religious Tradition and the Genius of Anglicanism*, ed. Geoffrey Rowell (Ikon Productions, Wantage, 1992).

2. *Religious Dissent in East Anglia*, ed. Elisabeth Leedham-Green, (Cambridge Antiquarian Society, Cambridge, 1991).

3. *Studies in Church History*, 23, ed. W.J. Sheils and D. Wood (Oxford, 1989).

4. *International Calvinism, 1541–1715*, ed. Menna Prestwich (Clarendon Press, Oxford, 1985).

5. Published as *The Puritan Character: Polemics and Polarities in Early Seventeenth-Century English Culture* (Clark Library, UCLA, 1989).

6. *Puritanism: Transatlantic Perspectives on a Seventeenth-Century Anglo-American Faith*, ed. F.J. Bremer (Massachusetts Historical Society, Boston, Massachusetts, 1993).

7. *Voluntary Religion: Studies in Church History*, 23, ed. W.J. Sheils and D. Wood (Blackwell, Oxford, 1986).

8. This appears here for the first time.

Introduction

On several previous occasions, including the writing of the prefaces to two earlier collections of essays, I have made clear my desire to be discharged of any further debt to the study of Protestantism and Puritanism in post-Reformation England. It is now nearly fifty years since my teacher, Sir John Neale, said that he liked to think of me spending the rest of my life on this subject, as he had devoted his to the study of Elizabeth I and the politics of her reign; and at the time I thought that an absurd suggestion. But now, aged seventy-six, I find myself in the position of the painter Lowry who, on Radio 4 in the late sixties, said that he had done enough and would do no more. ('But you must be a very wealthy man Mr Lowry.' 'I'm a dammed poor man if you want to know.') I resemble (in this respect at least) Philip Larkin, whose company I shared at breakfast in All Souls in 1981, who said the same thing, in response to a polite question about his current poetic output. 'I've done enough.' Would that all ageing historians were possessed of the same wisdom.

I have not given up on history entirely. I retain an active and fertile interest in the politics of what I have called the Elizabethan Monarchical Republic. The once accepted notion of 'Tudor Despotism', at least as applied to any of the years after Henry VIII, that Stalin of his century, was in his coffin, appears to me deeply mistaken. Social historians (sometimes called the 'new' social historians) and historians of the political process have converged and collaborated in fruitful recognition of how intricate and interactive, across and below the levels of social hierarchy, was the management of affairs in Elizabethan England. It was not Elizabeth I who paid the bills and did the strenuous work required to pull down the beams and the crucifixion statuary which stood on those beams in eight thousand parish churches, nor her courtiers and privy councillors. It was the church wardens, in their nameless thousands. In the many years which passed while Elizabeth remained unmarried and heirless, those same thousands knew that their futures lay, or ought to lie, in their own hands. If the queen was not willing to determine the future on her own account, she ought to do it on their account. What else was she for? Those with the education to do so articulated a loyalty to something they called the commonwealth, and to their native country, which was often in unwelcome tension, if not conflict, with their duties as subjects. These were citizens as well as subjects.

Much other recent work has concerned the literary reverberations of that aroused sense of citizenship, and membership, of the commonwealth of England. I have written on John Stow and William Camden, harvesting six years of a Special Subject taught in the Faculty of History of the University of Cambridge called 'Perceptions and Uses of the Past in Sixteenth-Century England'. For several years, in parts of the world as various as Stratford-upon-Avon, California, Wellington New Zealand, Zurich and Geneva, I maintained a strenuous engagement with the literary scholars who marched, not always in orderly rows, behind Stephen Greenblatt's banner of 'New Historicism'. The historical nature of 'texts', and the textual character of much historical documentation, is not something I question. I began to think in those terms in 1988, when I sat at the feet of Lisa Jardine as she lectured on 'Reading Shakespeare Historically', and she at mine as I taught a course to historians on some major figures in Tudor literature: Skelton, More, Spenser, Sidney, and, yes, Shakespeare. My quarrel with the so-called New Historicists was, and insofar as they have not mended their ways, still is, that their method is not really historical at all. Meanwhile I was engaged, as Neale had been in his day, with the endlessly baffling and fascinating Queen Elizabeth I, and with Mary Queen of Scots. My Elizabeth was the longest article of all in the *Oxford Dictionary of National Biography*. But having managed that I decided that I wanted no more to do with the woman and returned to the publishers Blackwells a cheque for £1000 which had been my advance for a full-scale biography. I bowed out of that part of the historical landscape by editing for a new and scholarly edition of John Nichols's *Progresses of Queen Elizabeth* Nichols's materials relating to Mary Queen of Scots and, fittingly, the death and funeral of Elizabeth. At about that time I harvested years of teaching Martin Luther and the European Reformation in Sydney with a little book on the Reformation intended for the lay reader: the first of my books to have been translated into both metropolitan Portuguese and the Portuguese of Brazil. What next? I want very much to write a book about what happened to my wife's parents, Geoffrey and Helen Selwyn, and to her in the Kenya of the early 1930s: a tragic story resembling, in its encapsulation of colonialism in all its effects, George Orwell's *Burmese*

Days. The book might be called *Black and White Mischief.* It is certainly a more interesting and important story than tales of white mischief in Kenya's so-called Happy Valley. A version has already been published in the *London Review of Books.*

But, on this occasion, back to Protestantism and Puritanism; or, as the Bible tastefully puts it, the dog returns to its vomit. The end-posts consist of essays on two archbishops, Thoms Cranmer and William Sancroft. The Cranmer piece was originally a lecture given in Keble College Chapel as part of a series on 'The Genius of Anglicanism'. The invitation had been extended by Geoffrey Rowell, now bishop of Gibraltar. It was the first and still the only time that I had entered that extraordinary and richly decorated shrine, which Cranmer would probably have found disquieting. Diarmaid MacCulloch had yet to publish his definitive biography of Cranmer, and, in the light of that great book and of important work by Ashley Null and David Selwyn, it was necessary to make some changes. The essay on Sancroft (not previously published) began life as a lecture delivered in Emmanuel College Cambridge on the 300th anniversary of his death, in 1693, on the invitation of the then master of Emmanuel, Sancroft's successor, Lord St John of Fawsley. Later I did much more work on Sancroft for the *History of Emmanuel College* which I co-authored with Sarah Bendall and Christopher Brooke. What an extraordinary life, and even more extraordinary in its documentation! Sancroft seems never to have thrown anything away. His papers, preserved in hundreds of volumes in the Bodleian library, include schoolboy exercises and, at the other end of his life, the successive summonses sent from the House of Lords across the river to Lambeth, requiring his attendance in the sequel to the Revolution of 1688; in between, not only the copious record of his governance of the Church as archbishop, a subject on which Robert Beddard is expert, but the love-letters Sancroft exchanged in his youth with his room mate (or 'chamber fellow') Arthur Bownest.

But the bulk of this collection consists of a number of essays on what the late A.L. Rowse, in reviewing my very first book for the *English Historical Review*, and managing to dispose of it in a dozen lines, called the 'thoroughly rebarbative' topic of Puritanism. 'Godly Preachers and Zealous Magistrates in Elizabethan East Anglia' was a paper read to the first of a series of conferences on the subject of religious dissent in East Anglia. It followed and drew upon the extensive local research in my native county of Suffolk and neighbouring Essex which occupied much space in my monstrous 1957 doctoral thesis 'The Puritan Classical Movement in the Reign of Elizabeth I', and was dealt with more summarily in the 1967 book, *The Elizabethan Puritan Movement*. This work came to its final fruition in volume 10 of the Church of England Record Society, which I co-edited with John Craig and Brett Usher: *Conferences and Combination Lectures in the Elizabethan Church*. This was an edition of the minutes and other papers generated by the conference of Puritan ministers meeting in and around Dedham in Essex in the 1580s, and the polemical reverberations of a dispute which arose in the weekly Monday 'combination' lecture preached by the godly ministers of the locality at Bury St Edmunds in Suffolk in the early 1590s. A colleague remarked that with this stout volume the subject of East Anglian Puritanism was well and truly Dedhamed and Buryed.

'Shepherds, Sheepdogs and Hirelings' was a paper read to the Ecclesiastical History Society in its 1988 Summer Conference. It demonstrated how far the values generally associated with a broadly defined Puritanism had penetrated the post-Reformation Church of England as reflected in sermons and treatises formally and ostensibly dealing with the pastoral ministry of the Church, but almost reducing that ministry to the function of preaching. It was a curtain-raiser for the forthcoming monograph on preaching in the early seventeenth century, soon to be published by my brilliant former pupil, Arnold Hunt. At the time I was about to become Regius Professor of Modern History at Cambridge. My immediate predecessor, Sir Geoffrey Elton, was present and warned me, as was his wont, that the paper was too long (anything that ran up to the wire of sixty minutes was intolerable to Geoffrey), and that I must not subject my Cambridge students to so much material: a lesson I have yet to learn and it seems never will.

'England and International Calvinism' was written in response to an invitation from the late Menna Prestwich to contribute to an Oxford University Press collection of essays on what we were just beginning to call International Calvinism. The book was given an almost inappropriate title. It was more a collection of studies of Calvinism in a variety of national and cultural contexts than an analysis of what might, by simple inversion, and without too much anachronism, be called the Calvinist International(e). In the years since Prestwich's volume was published, the remarkable and precocious cross-national character of Calvinism has been more effectively addressed in work by David Trim, on its military aspects, by Ole Grell on the fields of charitable relief, education and medicine, and by Andrew Pettegree, Philip Benedict, Mark Greengrass, and others. But I hope that I led the way in demonstrating that the internationalist imperative to assist and sustain 'the best reformed churches' and their often embattled and imperilled members, whether French and Flemish asylum-seekers, or the city of Geneva itself, or, in the 1620s, the Calvinists of the overrun Palatinate, belonged above all to those advanced and highly committed English Calvinists who came to be known as Puritans.

The fifth, sixth and seventh essays in this collection grapple with some problems and even contradictions in the character and trajectory of this Puritanism. 'The Puritan Character' plays, which I think is the appropriate word, with the suggestion that Puritanism as a stereotype was dependent upon Anti-Puritanism; that the stigma of 'Puritan' was, in the eye of the beholder, telling us more about those who deployed the abusive term than about those to whom it was applied, or at least about the two halves of a stressful relationship in a cultural context which thought and acted in terms of binary opposition. The essay contains the admittedly rather extreme statement that to have some idea of a typical 'Puritan' it is necessary to know as little as possible about actual and particular Puritans, who varied in a thousand ways from the simple and crude type. The use of 'character' was an intentional reference to the popular and mischievous literary genre of the Theophrastan character, in which a variety of human types was reduced to invariably negative stereotypes. In a companion essay, contributed to a Cambridge University Press collection of literary-historical essays called *The Theatrical City*, I spoke of the 'invention' of Puritanism, a process which began in the theatrical backlash against the stagey libels of the Puritan satirist Martin Marprelate, and which led with rapidity to such familiar characters as Malvolio and Zeal-of-the-Land Busy and the other 'saints' pilloried in Ben Jonson's city comedies, *Bartholomew Fair* and *The Alchemist*. The stage Puritan, who did so much to reify the popular perception of Puritanism, turned his, or her, eyes heavenward, appeared to be excessively religious, but in reality was avaricious, sexually predatory and, above all, seditious. All this annoyed and provoked no end the leading historian of Puritanism and its opposite tendencies, Peter Lake. Lake was and is in reaction against the fashionable tendency to reduce history to language, the new nominalism. It was not necessary to invent Puritans. They really existed, whether you called them that or not. But Lake and I have, I think, found common ground in the recognition that even if 'Puritan' was a stereotypical stigma, a matter of construction as much as of simple observation and description, it was a badge soon accepted by the so-called Puritans themselves. As T.S. Eliot famously told us, mankind cannot accept too much reality.

Lake is no less dissatisfield with the argument of the two remaining essays to be discussed in this Introduction, 'Sects and the Evolution of Puritanism' and 'The English Conventicle'. Both pursued a little further arguments first advanced in the 1981 book of my Ford Lectures, *The Religion of Protestants*. This was that in the early seventeenth century Puritanism was less a movement of alienation from and active opposition to the Church of the Elizabethan and Jacobean settlements than the most vigorous tendency within it. 'Sects and the Evolution of Puritanism' arose from an invitation from Frank Bremer to contribute to a conference held at his University of Millersville, Pennsylvania, on Puritanism as 'a transatlantic faith'; a meeting for which Peter Lake produced a paper 'Defining Puritanism - Again?' I was asked to talk about 'Puritanism and the Evolution of Sects', but chose to invert the title. Puritanism was not, in the terms of a cliché originally borrowed from Bossuet and a host of other anti-Protestant polemicists, an intrinsically centrifugal force, for ever balkanising and even atomising the one true Church. Its conscious thrust was centripetal, its opposite not only the 'popish' prelacy of the bishops but the sectarianism of pre-Reformation Lollards, the mid-sixteenth century 'Freewillers', and the Elizabethan and post-Elizabethan Separatists, whom mainstream Puritans, almost without exception, vigorously opposed. Ernst Troletsch proposed a grand anatomy of christian ecclesiology, and sociology: church-type and sect-type Christianity. Puritanism straddled the two types, and struggled with them. It was ideologically church-type, only circumstantially sect-type.

'The English Conventicle' was an attempt to explain how Puritanism, to the satisfaction of Puritans if not of their opponents, was contained within an established Church which required the at least outward conformity of all its members. There was public religion, the religion of the parish church; and private religion, the religion of informal meetings of 'the godly', often for the purpose of mutual edification through the exercise of sermon repetition, repeating the sermons originally heard in church. The church authorities called such meetings 'conventicles' and, in post-Restoration times, legislated against them. Those who frequented 'conventicles' denied that they were schismatic. But schismatic many of them became, circumstantially, in the new religious climate which began with the accession of Charles I in 1625 and continued after his execution in 1649, a revolutionary and counter-revolutionary climate.

Peter Lake, especially in two very substantial books, *The Boxmaker's Revenge* and *The Antichrist's Lewd Hat* has insisted on the intrinsically destructive and internecine character of what he might want to call the Puritan virus. These people came not to bring peace but a sword. They were trouble-makers. As for Patrick Collinson, has he by now forgotten what he himself wrote about Puritanism all those years ago, especially in *The Elizabethan Puritan Movement*? Well, historians are entitled to change their minds, or at least to adjust their perceptions. But no, he has not forgotten. It is not that he is confused but that the people we both study were themselves confused and distracted, on the horns of an inescapable dilemma. This dilemma continued long after the thick slice of history in which I have taken an active interest, into the days of Archbishop Sancroft, and beyond. At least as late as the triumph of Liberalism in the General Election of 1906, Puritans and their children and grandchildren, Dissenters and Nonconformists, could never make up their divided minds on whether their divinely inspired mission was to take over and make over English society, or to withdraw from it into an alternative version of what it was to be English, and Christian. Archbishop Cranmer, with a little more imagination, might have foreseen that that was how the contradiction, in many ways, of Protestantism and a National Church might work itself out, and ultimately unravel.

August, 2005
Trinity College, Cambridge

1

Thomas Cranmer and the Truth

To entitle this essay 'The Truth About Thomas Cranmer' would be presumptuous. For what is that? Even the partial truth of outward appearance is shrouded, not least by that composed, uncommunicative portrait by Gerlach Flicke, emblematic and not intended to reveal the man behind the episcopal rochet. In much the same way, the great and the good and the unspeakable of the eighteenth century are hardly recognisable as creatures of flesh and blood under their great wigs, which are a form of disguise. And what do we know of anyone to whom we are first properly introduced in middle age? You do not have to be Sigmund Freud to find that unsatisfactory. One of Cranmer's modern biographers devotes more pages to his last twenty-four hours than to the first forty years. What is now the definitive *Life* needs only thirty-seven pages out of nearly seven hundred to deal with those forty largely hidden years.[1] By the end of his life, those years were so remote from Cranmer himself that he could no longer remember whether his first wife's name was Black or Brown, although he did recall marrying 'one Joan'.[2]

What little was written by contemporaries contains only fragments of apparently authentic description: few flies in this amber.[3] We hear about Cranmer's total baldness in old age, offset by a free-flowing, snow-white beard, full enough to offer some protection for his chest, but grown, it appears, for an ideological reason: a Protestant beard, more emblematics. We know that Cranmer never used spectacles; and that 'my lord bitt his lippe, as his maner was when moved'. So his secretary reported, no doubt as reliable a witness as Cardinal Wolsey's gentlemen usher and biographer, George Cavendish.[4] What was that meant to tell us? Apparently something about a capacity for self-control, unusual and remarkable in sixteenth century. Such a man was perhaps more liable to do violence to himself than to others. Contemplating Cranmer, the Elizabethan martyrologist John Foxe wondered whether overmuch patience might not be a vice.[5] But then we remember that Thomas More described King Richard III 'knawing on hys lippes' (according to Polydore Vergil, Richard

'dyd continually byte his nether lyppe'), so we wonder what that was
supposed to be emblematic of; and we finish up wondering whether we
have learned anything truthful about the man, Thomas Cranmer.[6]

Cranmer *and* the truth is another matter, the subject of almost everything
that posterity has had to say about him. There is, of course, but one truth,
not a Protestant truth and a Catholic truth, nor, God help us, an Anglican
truth. (There have always been any number of Anglican truths.) But if
posterity had been able to agree on what that truth is, Cranmer might
have been allowed to rest in peace, instead of being so often disturbed,
not least, the fate of all great men, by centenary occasions.[7] 'Truth' was a
word which the archbishop often invoked. We are told that as a young
arts graduate at Cambridge, 'considering what great contraversie was in
matters of religion [he] bent himselfe to trye out the truthe herin'. In that
momentous encounter at Waltham with the king's servants, Edward Fox
and Stephen Gardiner, a conversation which not only made Cranmer's
career but helped to change the course of English history, the future
archbishop, having already confessed his substantial ignorance of the ins
and outs of the king's great matter, was nevertheless prepared to declare
with starting confidence: 'This is moost certayne ... that there ys but one
trueth in it' — a theological rather than a legal truth.[8] (We now know
that Cranmer's ignorance of these matters was exaggerated. He had been
interested for some time in the precedents and texts which would soon
be stockpiled by others, notably by Edward Fox, in order to buttress the
ideological claims summed up in the royal supremacy. We also know
that Waltham was by no means Cranmer's first step into the corridors
of power.)[9] When, many eventful years later, Henry VIII committed to
Cranmer himself the investigation of a conspiracy to bring the archbishop
ro ruin, the king told him: 'For suerlie I reken that you will tell me the
trueth'.[10] Writing about a certain heretic, a man who was about to die for
his beliefes, Cranmer noted that he had denied transubstantiation, and
therein 'I think he taught but the truth.'[11]

As late as 1548, Cranmer publicly endorsed the view that to deny the real
presence in the eucharist (not necessarily by the mode of transubstantiation)
was 'deceitfull'. 'Suche men surely are not trew Christyans'.[12] Yet it
appears that Cranmer, more privately, had abandoned belief in the real
presence two years earlier. Presently, arguing the eucharistic toss with
Bishop Stephen Gardiner, Cranmer asked: 'Doth not God's word teach a

true presence of Christ in spirit? . . . Was it not a true presence that Christ in these places promised?'[13] So Peter Brooks has identified Cranmer's mature, post-1546, doctrine of the Lord's Supper as one expressive of a true presence, something other than Christ's literal, carnal presence.[14] Yet, as he wrote in his final recantation, when Cranmer was 'come to the end of his life', 'whereupon hangeth all my life past': 'now is time and place to say truth', whereupon he renounced his heretical doctrine of the sacrament; only to reaffirm it in the final and theatrical renunciation of his recantations, with remorse for having acted 'contrarye to the truth which I though in my heart.'[15] The truth about Thomas Cranmer? He renounced his recantations only when he knew that they would not save his life.

It would not be quite right to say that Cranmer was the only archbishop of Canterbury in all history to have been addicted to the truth, or even to have set so much store by the truth: only that an almost obsessional concern with truth was the hallmark of Cranmer's century. Never, perhaps, in all history was the possession of the truth more fiercely contested, or regarded as so precious a prize. The challenge to the once-received truth of custom and tradition, Martin Luther's challenge, made it so, together with all the counter-challenges which followed. Truth without the provocation of falsehood is inert and lifeless. Bishop Latimer declared from the pulpit: 'It is a goodly word "Peace", and a fair thing Unity . . . [But] peace ought not to be redeemed . . . with the loss of truth; that we would seek peace so much, that we should lose the truth of God's word.' (The Elizabethan Catholic controversialist Thomas Stapleton made the same point more pungently, quoting perhaps some old adage: 'Truth purchaseth hatred'.) 'Therefore', pronounced Latimer, 'whereas ye pray for agreement both in the truth and in uttering of the truth, when shall that be, as long as we will not hear the truth, but disquiet with crafty conveyance the preachers of the truth, because they reprove out evilness with the truth. And, to say the truth, better it were to have a deformity in preaching, so that some would preach the truth of God': seven 'truths' in one peroration.[16]

Sixteenth-century historians, in the heat of controversy about the truth of every kind of thing, from the origins of the British peoples to the fate of the little princes in the Tower, constantly invoked the old trope about truth the principal adornment of history, truth the daughter of time. William Camden wrote, in his apologia for his history of the reign of Elizabeth: 'Which Truth to take from History, is nothing else but, as it were, to pluck out the Eyes of the beautifullest Creature in the World'.[17] The Protestant ecclesiastical historian and martyrologist John Foxe claimed to 'open the plain truth of times lying long hid in obscure darkness of antiquity'. So it was that Foxe's Protestant readers took it as axiomatic that his 'Book of Martyrs' was true, 'a book of credit', whereas by the same token his Catholic critics exposed it as a tissue of lies, 'so many lines, so many lies'. The merits of the book were discussed on the basis of truth and on no other basis, there being no half-truths. Foxe himself scouted the polite convention of Renaissance historiography, which left the final judgment to the reader. Take it or leave it was his uncompromising message.[18] Bishop John Aylmer made an audacious claim for the English Reformation. Our countryman and brother John Wyclif begat Jan Hus, who begat Luther, who begat truth. Since Christ was equivalent to truth, that was as much as to say that Christ had been 'as it were' born a second time in England, and Aylmer was not afraid to state explicitly this ethnocentric heresy.[19]

The century had turned before Francis Bacon in his essay *Of Truth* wrote his famous line: 'What is truth? said jesting Pilate; and would not stay for an answer'. But the sixteenth century was already familiar with Bacon's answerless question. It appears that when Thomas More turned historian, he found that history could not be easily made to square with the truth, or to serve the purposes of truth. For in the tragical history of Richard III, we have to ask what was true and what was false amidst so much hearsay, so much treachery, some of it benign, as when More's old master, Bishop Morton, suborned the duke of Buckingham. George Cavendish sat down to write what he claimed would be the true history of his master, Cardinal Wolsey ('therefore I commyt the treuthe to hyme that knowyth all truethe'), but to have confronted all the truth, not least about his own falsehoods in the circumstances of Wolsey's fall, seems to have alarmed and disgusted Cavendish.[20] Later in the century, Sir Philip Sidney found that only fiction ('poetry'), not 'true' history, could be trusted to vindicate and exemplify those ultimate truths which are moral and fruitful. The historian was hopelessly tied 'not to what should be, but to what is, to the particular truth of things'. If one wished to see virtue extolled and vice punished, 'truly that commendation is peculiar to Poetry, and far off from history'.[21] Neither the historian of the sixteenth century nor the biographer of Thomas Cranmer is likely to disagree, although we might want to point out to Sidney that we are often at a loss to know what were the particular truths of things, what in truth was. Enough for us to determine those things, if we can, and let morality look after itself.

The divines, with their sound training in logic, knew about such things. Having first defined truth as 'Christ himself, the word of God', Thomas Becon added: 'There is also a civil truth or verity . . . and that is when with that which is said the thing agreeth, and when we find words agreeing with the thing itself': in other words, there is the truth of what is, a mundane truth, and there is the higher truth of what ought to be, not at all one and the same thing.[22] Meanwhile, those living (and dying) in the real world of what is (and they included the author of that poetic fiction *Utopia*) found that often the survival not only of themselves and their values but of the truth itself depended upon economies with the truth so drastic as to leave little of the truth intact: to such an extent that a study of these agonies of the sixteenth-century conscience is called not Valiant for Truth but *Ways of Lying*. To lie might be the only way to hang on to the truth.[23]

And there was always Pilate's question, asked not in a mocking and cynical vein but with desperate and conscientious urgency, and by no inhabitant of the sixteenth century with more urgent conscientiousness than by Thomas Cranmer. A few years after his violent death, Bishop Jewel would pen some disturbing sentences:

> The philosopher telleth us, truth and falsehood are nigh neighbours, and dwell one by the other; the utter porch of the one is like the porch of the other; yet their way is contrary; the one leadeth to life; the other leadeth to death; they differ little to the shew . . . Thereby it happeneth that men be deceived . . . they call evil good, falsehood truth . . .[24]

This was the world inhabited by the mind and conscience of Thomas Cranmer, not least in those last twenty-four hours. Only that branch of improving fiction which is hagiography would portray Cranmer as an utterly true man or even (to speak in modern terms) as a consistent man. Was he true to his own self? Few men have made their ends with so many undefended, unexplained, unresolved inconsistencies as this archbishop who stood so much upon the truth. At his consecration, Cranmer took a solemn oath to the pope, preceded by a protestation that the oath would not be binding. On trial, Cranmer said that that was routine procedure. Perhaps so. Cranmer dissolved Henry VIII's marriage to Ann Boleyn, referring to an impediment involving Henry's dealings with Ann's sister:

something that he had known all about when he had blessed the union in the first place. He abandoned colleagues and friends when all pleas on their behalf (which are not to be overlooked) failed, and it became necessary to abandon them. At the downfall of Thomas Cromwell, we are told that 'there would have byn laied thousands of powndes to hundrethes in London, that he should have . . . byn sett upp in the Tower beside his frende the Lorde Crumwell'.[25] (Canny punters would have kept an eye open for the rogue card, Henry VIII.) But while Cromwell and others died, Cranmer lived, an archbishop expressing less regret for all that spilled blood than the poet Wyatt — but perhaps biting that nether lip.

Cranmer was one of that small minority in any generation to change their religion, denouncing as error what had been stoutly maintained as the truth, and in Cranmer's case not as an innocent child or half-formed adolescent but in middle life. In his late thirties, Cranmer still believed in the pope, and even more in the Catholic doctrine of the magisterial authority of church councils. Reading the attack mounted on Luther by Bishop John Fisher, the presiding genius over the university of those younger years, Cranmer filled the margins with observations which leave us in no doubt about the loyal and traditional Catholic sentiments which in the 1520s still moved the future Protestant archbishop. In the 1530s, the pope had been expunged from Cranmer's creed (by law), but not yet the doctrine of the real presence of Christ's body and blood in the sacrament of the altar, which he would discard only in the 1540s.[26]

So on sleepless nights, if there were any, Cranmer may have remembered that he had consented to the death of a man who believed only what he himself now believed. He would know that St Paul had shared that experience, the blood of the first Christian martyr, Stephen, on his hands. At Cranmer's trial the prosecutor was careful to remind him of that embarrassing circumstance. The trial ended in a series of recantations, no less than five, followed by that renunciation. Less dramatically, Cranmer's first Prayer Book of 1549 presented 'the truth' so artfully that it was almost a piece of equivocation in itself. That may have been intended to deceive (or should we say help?) 'the simple sort', although they were not deceived down in Cornwall. And someone as lacking in simplicity as Stephen Gardiner *chose* to be deceived, declaring that the 1549 rite was 'not distant from the Catholic faith in my judgment'.[27] So in our our own age learned scholars have been misled into believing what is most unlikely:

that Cranmer changed his doctrine of the eucharist (which is to say, his religion) between 1549 and 1552.[28] To explain, even to comprehend, these apparent inconsistencies it is necessary to know the sixteenth century and to know it well; but to know the twentieth century also helps, not least in order to have some empathy for those sad recantations. To have served with the Gloucesters in Korea and to have been brainwashed (something that happened to one of my friends, with damaging and lasting consequences) might help any biographer of Archbishop Cranmer. One might almost say that not to have gone through something like would be a handicap.

We may now ask what this archbishop, founder of the Chruch of England and of Anglicanism as we have known it, has to do with the truth? To enquire what Cranmer had to do with the truth, rather than with a series of compromises with the truth, is in effect to ask whether the Church of England, which he really founded, is a true church. Bishop Stephen Gardiner was not one to mince his words. He told Cranmer that by his example one might think that 'our religion is nothing but an agreement made for the time being, and then changeable as occasion arise'.[29] Well, we have heard something like that before, and not long ago. Ambivalent Cranmer is the ghost of Church of England which is still with us, not merely its remote founding father.

But was he ambivalent? Jasper Ridley has sliced through these problems with a surgical instrument, his scalpel the sixteenth-century principle that to be a true man it was sufficient to be a true subject, obedient to one's lawful prince. Truth consisted in obedience. When Cranmer told Henry VIII that he had always believed the best of his wife, Ann Boleyn, until obliged to believe otherwise, when he assured the king that he had always believed Cromwell to have been the truest servant he ever had, even when Cromwell was en route for the block, he was not saying that he had changed his intellectual opinion about those great persons with whose active assistance the cause of religious reform had been advanced. He meant that he now had no choice, in all conscience and obedience, but to alter his private opinion and to join in the general denunciation. Students of modern Chinese history might have less difficulty in understanding and perhaps condoning Cranmer's actions than ourselves. Cranmer made no attempt to resist the *coup d'état* of the summer of 1549 which toppled Somerset and brought Northumberland's conciliar

regime to power, although at the time it must have appeared that this
political upset would strike a fatal blow at everything in which Cranmer
most profoundly believed. When, under Mary, Cranmer recanted, it was
less from intellectual wavering, still less from mere fear, than out of the
conviction that perhaps the prince could constrain mind and conscience,
even in matters of faith. Ridley writes:

> If the known facts of Cranmer's life are impartially examined, nearly all the
> apparent contradictions disappear and a consistent personality emerges. Like
> most of his contemporaties . . . Cranmer believed in royal absolutism. He
> believed that his primary duty as a Christian was to strengthen the power of
> the King, and was prepared if necessary to sacrifice all his other doctrines to
> accomplish this.

Thus far Jasper Ridley. Obedience simplified everything, for the historian
and biographer, just as it simplified nearly everything for Thomas
Cranmer.[30]

For those who have explored the entrails of Tudor politics, this will not
do. Tudor England was not a despotism, still less a kingdom inhabited by
the willing slaves of a despot. To be sure, no one should underestimate
the force of obedience in the England of Henry VIII, as not only a
constitutional but a theological necessity. Notoriously, William Tyndale
wrote in his book on the subject (a book written as a disaffected exile)
that the king was 'in this world without law; and may at his lust do right
or wrong, and shall give accounts but to God only'; that princes were 'in
God's stead' and 'may not be resisted: do they never so evil, they must
be reserved unto the wrath of God'. Only if princes were to countenance
evil must the subject disobey and say 'we are otherwise commanded of
God'. But they must on no account offer resistance.[31] And who was to
say, with authority, what was evil, or what was error, since truth and
error were such close bed-fellows? Cranmer went further than Tyndale.
'All Christian princes have committed unto them immediately of God,
the whole cure of their subjects, as well concerning the administration of
God's word for the cure of souls, as concerning the ministration of things
political and civil governance'.[32] So what happened to Tyndale's principle
of passive obedience where matters of faith were concerned if your king
was also your bishop, the curate of your soul? For that was what Henry
claimed to be, looking to the Old Testament for precedents. One might
say that if the leitmotif of the Lutheran Reformation was salvation by

faith alone, the corresponding foundational principle for the Henrician Reformation was salvation by obedience alone.[33] It was obedience rather than faith which Henry's Great Bible of 1539 was intended to arouse in those exposed to its text, or so according to the graphics of its engraved title page. The Bible is transmitted to the people from the pulpit, and the people respond with 'Vivat Rex!', 'Long Live the King!'. Where preaching wanteth, Archbishop Grindal later warned Henry's daughter, obedience faileth.[34]

Nevertheless, Ridley's scalpel was too sharp, the surgery too neat. In reviewing his life of Cranmer, Peter Brooks invoked Sir Isaiah Berlin's fable of the hedgehog and the fox.[35] According to Ridley, Cranmer was one of history's hedgehogs, curled into the protective ball of one commanding idea; but according to Brooks a fox, an improbable survivor who owed that survival to his political dexterity. Witness the adroitness with which, with more that a little help from Henry VIII, he turned the tables on his accusers in the so-called Prebendaries' Plot of 1543, which could so easily have unseated him.[36] At that dangerous moment something more than a hedgehog-like obedience was needed.

But Dr. Brooks's fox is not the solution to all our problems. The sixteenth century knew all about foxes, of course. Almost the only thing known about England on the Continent was there were no wolves in that country, which was the subject of the only recorded conversation in which Sir Philip Sidney took part, in Prague.[37] But if no wolves, or so the saying went, all the more foxes. Everyone in the age of the Renaissance knew about crafty, foxy Ulysses, not least William Shakespeare when he wrote *Troilus* and *Cressida*, a play badly misrepresented by E.M.W. Tillyard when he credited that character with a hedgehog-like obsession with cosmic order and degree.[38] Dr. Andrew Perne, the famous (or infamous) master of Elizabethan Peterhouse, told Gabriel Harvey when they met at the funeral of Sir Thomas Smith that he was a fox for having gained possession of part of Smith's much-coveted library. Not while you are still around, said Harvey. I can't claim to be more than a mere cub.[39] The ecclesiastical fox *par excellence* was Perne's patron and Cranmer's arch-rival and theological enemy Stephen Gardiner, the principal target of polemical pamphlets with titles like *The Hunting of the Romish Foxe*.[40] For foxes symbolised covert popery, which was the point of calling Perne a fox.

No one in the sixteenth century would have called Cranmer a fox. Rather, unless Henry VIII was himself lying like a fox, Cranmer was the youthful George Washington, constitutionally incapable of telling lies. Henry told the archbishop's political enemies: 'I accompte my Lord of Canterbury as faithfull a man towardes me as ever was prelate in this realme'. 'O Lord', he is supposed to have said to Cranmer at a moment of supreme danger, 'What manner of man be you! What simplicity is in you!' Cromwell remarked: 'You were borne in a happie howre I suppose . . . ffor, do or sey what you will, the kyng will alwaies well take it at your hand . . . [His Majestie] will never give credite againste you . . .'[41] It is of course possible that Henry saw in Cranmer an Israelite indeed in whom there was no guile when there was considerable guile. Perhaps this spider at the heart of a courtly web of dishonesty and intrigue needed the dream, however fantastic, of a man who was sincere and true. The wisdom of serpents can coexist with the harmlessness of doves. The Bible says so.[42] And what Peter Brooks meant when he identified Cranmer as a fox was that, far from succumbing in passive and unthinking obedience to Henry VIII, he worked resourcefully with the vast and capricious power of that monarch, not merely to survive but in order to promote his cause of reformation, tapping the huge energy of the royal supremacy to erect a reformed Church of England.

So much for Cranmer the politican, the survivor, the teflon prelate. But theological infidelities, theological falsehoods, are presumably less venal than political. Did Cranmer the theologian play fast and loose with the truth? What do we say of an archbishop who must have knowingly authorised, if he did not himself expressly effect, the deft conjuring trick which altered in a small but critically important respect the sense of the more or less official *Catechism*, published in the second year of the reign of Edward VI, three editions within one year? This *Catechism* was a translated adaptation of a Latin text of German provenance, deriving from Martin Luther's *Little Catechism* and the work of Cranmer's wife's uncle, the Nuremberg reformer Andreas Osiander, but linked in its Latin version with another German name, that of Justus Jonas.[43]

In the first English edition, the account of the Lord's Supper was faithful to its Lutheran original. 'For he doth not only, with his bodily mouthe receave the bodye and bloude of Christ, but he doth also beleve the wordes of Christ, whereby he is assured, that Christes bodye was gyven to death for us, and that his bloude was shed for us'. But in the third edition, which appeared within weeks of the first, the Lutheran doctrine of the real presence was deftly jettisoned in favour of a formulation consistent with South German-Swiss, proto-Reformed doctrine, dispensing with the real presence as either Catholics or Lutherans affirmed it. This was done by omitting the two words 'only' and 'also': a good example of how theology in the age of the Reformation was exploited by and almost subordinated to grammar.[44] Now no longer 'he doth not only with his bodyly mouthe receave the bodye and bloude of Christ . . . but he doth also beleve the wordes of Christ', but 'he doth not with his bodyly mouthe receave the bodye and bloude of Christ but he doth believe the wordes of Christ.' Was this honest? Was it true? It was not the case that Cranmer had changed his mind on the subject of the real presence in the summer of 1548, between two editions of the *Catechism*. If we combine his own testimony with evidence supplied Nicholas Ridley and Sir John Cheke, it appears that Cranmer's conversion in this respect had happened two years earlier, in 1546.[45] An economist, or Chancellor of the Exchequer, who changed his position on, say, monetarism, so drastically and yet so insidiously, would not retain much professional or political credibility, especially if he had lost his faith two years before so shyly disclosing the fact. Cranmer had more to do in that summer than write new recensions of the *Catechism*. But what was done was done in his name. Why should we buy a used church from such a churchman? Since the *Catechism* was addressed to children, his theological opponents might be forgiven for thinking in terms of millstones, and of being cast into the depths of the sea.

What needs to be said at this point is that Cranmer was not the only prominent Tudor churchman to wonder, if not what he should believe, what it was proper and feasible to confess. Truth and error were too close for comfort, and at moments of confessional instability they could look like nearly identical twins, or the two charming ladies of *The Beggar's Opera*. How happy, according to circumstances, one might be with either. In Cranmer's own university, the balance of judgment even in Edward's reign still tipped towards traditional, Catholic belief. That was the gound on which the Lady Margaret Professor and first Master of Trinity, John Redman, stood, and such was his intellectual authority that for minds and consciences less robust it was sufficient to believe as Redman believed. Even the king found himself in this position, for Redman was one of the authors, perhaps the principal author, of that supposedly definitive theological statement of Henry's later years known as *The King's Book*. Yet under the radically Protestant regime headed by the duke of Northumberland, not even Redman was safe, and it was not necessarily safe to stay with Redman. Redman chose this moment to die, and he was questioned about his beliefs on his deathbed, amongst others, by the schoolmaster of Westminster and future dean of St Paul's, Alexander Nowell, and by the Master of Christ's, Richard Wilkes, a known proponent of the new learning.[46]

Asked by Wilkes whether we receive Christ with our mouth in the sacrament, Redman reportedly 'paused and dyd holde his peace a lytle space, and shortely after he spake, sayinge, I wyll not saye so, I can not tel, it is a hard question'. Pleased with this answer, Wilkes went on. 'Mayster Doctor yf I shulde not trouble you, I wolde praye you to knowe your mynde in transubstantiacion.' 'Jesu Mayster Wilkes sayeth he, wyll you ask me that?' 'Syr sayde I, not yf I shulde trouble you, no, no. I wyl tel you sayth he'. It appeared that both Redman and his Trinity colleague, John Young, also present, were wavering on transubstantiation, had perhaps already surrendered the point. Once they would have burned for the doctrine, themselves or others. Now they didn't know. Young said: 'A man shall knowe more and more by the process of tyme, and readinge and hearinge of others'. Even what he had just heard fall from Redman's dying lips contained food for thought. So, in our own time, minds and consciences have squirmed in Eastern Europe and the former USSR. But, under Mary, it would be more or less officially stated by no less an authority than Bishop Cuthbert Tunstall, who was Redman's uncle, that he had died a good Catholic; while Young became Mary's regius professor of Divinity, presided over the heresy trial of a King's man who was burned on Jesus Green, and after Elizabeth's accession would spend the last twenty years of his life in custody, as an unwavering Catholic recusant.

All the books tell us that Cranmer charted his intellectual and spiritual course according to the principles stated by Young: 'A man shall know more and more by process of tyme, and readinge and hearinge of others'. Usually we are told that Cranmer's glacially slow conversion was unusual, even unique, which it was probably not. Everyone quotes the letter he wrote to the Swiss reformer, Vadianus: 'I have come to the conclusion that the writings of every man must be read with discrimination'.[47] And sometimes this is linked with what we are told in an anonymous near-contemporary account of the archbhishop's working practices: 'He was a slowe reader, but a diligent marker of whatsoever he redd, for he seldome redd without pen in hand, and whatsoever made eyther for one parte or the other, of thinges being in controversy, he wrote it out yf it were short, or at the least noted the author and the place, that he might fynd it and wryte it out by leysure; which was a great helpe to hym in debating of matters ever after'.[48] We may owe if not the Church of England then the Church of England as imagined and even defined by Thomas Cranmer to a mind which would have been awarded an upper second, not a first, in a modern tripos examination.

When public office swallowed up the leisure for such open-ended intellectual pursuits, Cranmer's research assistants continued to apply these same methods on his behalf, providing us with a good example of what is nowadays called 'the archaeology of reading practices', the particular practice in question being that whereby busy men had books read and gutted for them by their intellectual men of business.[49] The evidence survives, in copious quantity, in Cranmer's theological commonplace books preserved among the Royal MSS of the British Library: *Collectiones ex Sancta Scriptura et Patribus*; and also material abstracted from the modern theologians, Luther, Melancththon and Brenz, Zwingli and Oecolampadius.[50]

And then an extraordinary concatenation of emergencies and opportunities brought some of these names to life and to England, enabling Cranmer to continue his dialogue with a spectrum of theological opinion, 'in zhe meat', as a German chairman once said in introducing to his audience the late Professor H. H. Rowley of Manchester. For the political triumph of Protestantism in England coincided with the severe setback in Germany of a conservative religious settlement imposed by the Emperor Charles V after his victory over the political forces of Protestantism in the Schmalkaldic War. This drove into English exile many of the ranking theologians of the emergent Reformed tendency: Martin Bucer and Peter Martyr above all, who were appointed to the two regius chairs in the universities. It was not Cranmer's fault that their Lutheran counterparts declined all invitations to join the party, so that the great debate on eucharistic doctrine and liturgy lost its Lutheran dimension and became a matter of fine-tuning the important but somewhat narrower differences within the non-Lutheran camp of Bucer, Martyr and the Polish comet in this firmanent, John à Lasco.[51]

These are usually represented as footprints of a certain cautious cast of mind, filmed, as it were, in slow motion. But they are not evidence of Cranmer's chronic inability to make up his mind, still less of the wavering instability allegedly manifested around John Redman's deathbed. Put to Cranmer the biblical question: 'How long halt ye between two opinions?' and he might have replied: 'Just so long as it takes'. But it was another matter entirely, having persuaded himself of the truth of matter, to profess it publicly, and yet another to impose it upon the profession of others, and on policy. Hence the complexity of the Prayer Book problem: 1549 and 1552, as at once the expression of public policy, of a nation's belief, embodied in acts of parliament, and of Thomas Cranmer's own belief. His 1544 English Litany was devised, as he himself wrote 'to the intent . . . your hearts and lips may go together in prayer'.[52] This was a conjunction not easily achieved outside and beyond well-worn, time-honoured, almost instinctive forms. As Bishop John Williams was heard to say in the following century, intending his words as criticism of the policies of Archbishop Laud: 'It is well known, how he that will bring a People from custom in God's Worship with which they have been inured, to a Change, must be more than wise; that is, he must be thought to be wise . . .'[53] How Cranmer managed to be as wise as he was in these respects, even to be seen to be wise, is one of the mysteries about him. But in all this complexity and amidst so much public and private camouflage, one thing is reasonably clear. From a relatively early date in his public career (albeit in middle age), Thomas Cranmer had heard, understood and internalised a broadly evangelical, Protestant doctrine of salvation. No other prominent English reformer was in this respect more Lutheran: not because his views and emphases were precisely those of Martin Luther, but that he shared Luther's sense of the utter centrality of the doctrine of salvation, the fundamental significance of the Gospel as something utterly gratuitous. It was this which will prove to have been the most consistent thing about Cranmer, the automatic pilot which kept him on course towards that definitive statement of the English Reformation and of Anglicanism which was the Book of Common Prayer.

It appears that Cranmer's understanding of the matter of salvation moved within essentially Lutheran parameters no later than his German embassy of 1532, when he married his Lutheran wife (a remarkable and radical step in itself, which he would hardly have taken if he could have foreseen the promotion to Canterbury which immediately followed) and had the opportunity to discuss the critical question of justification with his wife's uncle, the preacher Andreas Osiander. This was not the experience of many of his Cambridge contemporaries or, indeed, juniors. Only the ex-Augustinian Robert Barnes, the theological diplomat of the 1530s, took on more of what Cranmer's next successor but one would call a 'Germanical nature'.[54] John Young, who clashed in Edwardian Cambridge with Martin Bucer, said in 1551 (he was then thirty-seven to Cranmer's sixty-two) that 'he dyd repent him that he had so much strived against justification by only fayth': but he would spend the rest of a long life regretting that he had ever leant towards that doctrine. Redman, fifty-two years of age when he died in 1551, the principal author of *The King's Book*, denounced Lutheranism posthumously in a book called *The Complaint of Grace*, written, it was claimed, 'not verie long before he left this transitory lyfe'. The dead Redman, yet speaking, declared that what was needed was not Luther's only faith but 'the pricke of spirituall exhortacions to charitie, humilitie, pacience, hope, godly vertue and wisedome'. Bishop John Fisher had confronted Luther's heresy with the same medicine. As for Andrew Perne, the most notorious turncoat and weathercock of the mid-Tudor Cambridge scene, a mere thirty-two years of age in 1551, there is no evidence that he ever did agree with Luther on the *ordo salutis*. Perne had already rejected transubstantiation and, for a while, continued to do so under Mary. But at heart he was no Protestant and never would be. For a Protestant must believe, at heart, that we are saved entirely of grace through the all-sufficiency of Christ's once-for-all sacrifice, appropriated by faith, and regardless of any voluntary motion or effort.[55] Cranmer was in that primary respect a Protestant. Whether he was an Anglican, or in what sense, is secondary.

Biographers of Cranmer (before MacCulloch), and historians of Anglicanism, for reasons partly understandable and allowable, partly of theological bias, focus on other issues and miss what is the most important of all the facts and circumstances concerning their subject: that he was the most Protestant of all the leading figures in the mid-sixteenth-century Church of England, more Protestant than even Hugh Latimer, not in the sense that he was more opposed to traditional religious belief and practice (although opposed he was, and with a blind vehemence hard for anyone on the other side of the fence, shall we say Professor Eamon Duffy, to stomach), but in the sense that, like Luther, he understood the matter of faith to be the mainspring of religion, in comparison with which almost nothing else mattered. We do not learn that from Latimer's remarkable sermons, which strike out in a number of directions but in their essential moralism have no theological kernel, no sense that there is such a thing as *the* Gospel. It is something we are bound to learn from Cranmer's *Homilies*, the 1547 homilies of Salvation, of Faith, of Good Works, composed by the archbishop and promulgated within months of Henry VIII's death, cancelling, as it were, the theology of Redman's *King's Book*.[56]

Cranmer's profound Lutheranism (in this most proper sense) was something half concealed as long as Henry lived, just as his Lutheran wife was kept out of sight in a metaphorical if not literal box, especially in the last years of the reign, when the church of which he was primate was bound to the *King's Book* and to the Act of Six Articles. On justification the *King's Book* taught:

> And albeit God is the principal cause and chief worker of this justification in us . . . yet so it pleaseth the high wisdom of God, that man, prevented by his grace, (which being offered, man may if he will refuse or receive) shall be also a worker by his free consent and obedience to the same, in the attaining of his own justification, and by God's grace and help shall walk in such works as be requisite to his justification . . .[57]

Hence Stephen Gardiner's indignation at the constitutional no less than the theological impropriety of so precipitately repudiating that doctrine in Cranmer's *Homilies*, published in the name of a nine-year-old child and with his royal father hardly cold in the ground; and equally in Cranmer's version of the *Catechism* of Justus Jonas, which was in truth the work of Cranmer's wife's uncle, Osiander: not so much the King's Book as Osiander's, or Luther's Book.

For repudiation the *Homilies* were, an unambiguously evangelical statement. This has sometimes been doubted, as if these sermons, which are made a kind of appendix to the Anglican Articles of Religion and so remain in some measure still in legal force, teach something other than justification by faith. The *Homilies* do, to be sure, contain evidence of Cranmer's sensitivity to that charge of antinomianism which the stark paradoxes of Lutheran solifidianism, and even of St Paul's doctrine in *Romans*, always attracts. In July 1537 he spent two days grilling the vicar of Croydon, who had alleged in a sermon that those who trusted to be saved by faith and baptism had 'left all good works', such as prayer, fasting and alms deeds.[58] But Cranmer was not so scared of the antinomian bugbear as to compromise his understanding of the Gospel when the change of regime freed him from the constraint of the Henrician formularies.

So those exposed to the Homily of Salvation heard that sinful man 'of necessity' was obliged to seek for a righeousness other than his own, embraced by faith, which was 'taken, accepted and allowed of God', 'for our perfect and full justification'. 'And therefore St Paul declareth here nothing upon the behalf of man, concerning his justification, but only a true and lively faith, which nevertheless is the gift of God, and not man's only work, without God'. 'What can be spoken more plainly, than to say, that freely without works, by faith only, we obtain remission of our sins'. Cranmer called this, as Luther might have done, 'the strong rock and foundation of Christian religion'. To be sure, he declared, faith did not exclude good works, 'necessarily to be done afterwards of duty towards God'. But note the 'afterwards', and what follows. 'But it excludeth them, so that we may not do them to this intent, to be made just by doing of them'. Similarly, we should not be misled by Cranmer's rhetorical skill in the two succeeding Homilies of Faith, and of Good Works, particularly in the delicate rhetorical art of *concessio*. The Homily of Faith is all about good works, for a faith which brings forth no good works is idle, barren, unfruitful, dead. As for the Homily of Good Works, it is all about faith, for good works cannot be performed without faith. But the penitent thief on the cross, a compelling figure for Cranmer even as the moment of his own death approached, provides the bottom line. 'I can shew a man that, by faith, without works, lived and came to heaven; but without faith, never man had life'. 'Faith by itself saved him, but works by themselves never justified any man'.

For a full decade and more before this doctrine was made official, Cranmer had been promoting and protecting it in his advancement of evangelical preaching, as Susan Wabuda has shown:[59] in his own diocese, in his licensing of roving preachers, in those islands under his control in otherwise hostile territory which were the archbishop's peculiars: parishes in London and Essex within Bishop Stokesley's diocese but outside his

jurisdiction, Hadleigh in Suffolk, in a diocese otherwise under the control
of the fiercely conservative Bishop Nix, who was succeeded by the dogged
and equally conservative William Rugg. In 1537 the vicar of Croydon
denounced Robert Barnes, Edward Crome, Richard Champion, 'and many
other soo', who preached that 'faith which justifieth of necessitie bringeth
forth good workes'. At Harwich, the curate closed his pulpit to one of
Cranmer's protégés, complaining of 'new learned fellows and teachers of
new doctryne'. Cranmer's evangelical thrust had its negative, even cruel,
side. The curate of Hadleigh, a former religious called Hugh Payne, whom
the archbishop's formidable troubleshooter Rowland Taylor thrust aside,
had taught that one paternoster said by the injunction of a priest was
worth a thousand paternosters said voluntarily. He had also supported
Katherine of Aragon. Cranmer pursued this man until, bound in irons
and deprived of warm clothing, he died in the Marshalsea Prison.[60]

By the time the *Homilies* were read in the parishes, Cranmer had applied
the full implications of evangelical doctrine to that good work which was
public worship of God and his sacraments. Cranmer knew that sacraments
were God's ways of working, not man's; that the only appropriate human
response was one of reception, with the organ of faith, itself a gift from
God; that the only acceptable sacrifice to be offered to God was one
of praise and thanksgiving, coupled with the sacrifice of our selves, our
souls and bodies. And he had been persuaded that the doctrine of the
real presence in the eucharist was not only not true, as a statement of the
case, but not answerable to the nature of true religion. Stephen Gardiner
understood all this perfectly, pronouncing: 'It is evident to anyone that
these things are so joined and interdependent that whoever has admitted
the doctrine of "only faith" in justification is compelled to reject the
Sacrament of the Eucharist in the way we profess it'.[61]

Nothing could be more clear, nothing less clear, initially, than Cranmer's
great work of liturgical simplification and reconstruction which came
to its first fruition in the Book of Common Prayer of 1549. Gardiner
was partly responsible. From motives which were less than candid, he
chose to endorse the 1549 service as 'not distant from the Catholic faith
in my judgment'. Things precious to this continuing Catholic were 'so
Catholically spoken of', as in the words of the 1549 prayer of consecration,
sanctifying these creatures of bread and wine 'to be to us the body and
blood of Christ'.[62]

For Cranmer (and the prime responsibility was his, this was 'committee work' only in a formal sense) had constructed a service of which a 'Catholic' construction could be made, at least superficially. The Holy Communion, what Cranmer would have preferred to call the Lord's Supper, was said to be 'commonly called the Mass'. Words and formulae consistent with real presence belief were retained: 'The body of our Lord Jesus Christ, which was given for thee, preserve thy body and soul unto everlasting life'. Unlike any other Protestant liturgy, Cranmer's service retained the great prayer of consecration, to all appearances, especially in its 1549 construction and setting, the canon of the Mass, still punctuated in the printed text with those small crosses at 'bless' and 'sanctify', which called for the traditional manual acts. Nothing explicitly forbade the habitual elevations. But the effect was not that those 'creatures' of bread and wine should 'become' the body and blood of Christ but rather that they should 'be' 'unto us' Christ's body and blood; as Cranmer insisted in his book against Gardiner 'that we may so eat them and drink them [those 'creatures'], that we be partakers of his body crucified, and of his blood shed for our redemption'.[63]

If Cranmer's eucharistic liturgy was unique in its retention of a kind of canon, it was no less distinctive in the strength of its Protestant insistence on the once-for-allness of Christ's sacrifice, 'who made there by his one oblation of himself once offered a full, perfect and sufficient sacrifice, oblation and satisfaction for the sins of the whole world'.[64] A careful reading of the 1549 consecration prayer will confirm that Christ's sacrifice is brought to remembrance, not repeated; and that the only sacrifices spoken of as enacted in the service are the sacrifice of praise and thanksgiving, and the sacrifice of the communicants themselves, their souls and bodies, 'to be a reasonable, holy and lively sacrifice'.

In 1549 Cranmer was still constrained: constrained by the need to carry with him his episcopal and other clerical colleagues; constrained politically by the theologically moderate regime of the duke of Somerset; constrained by the difficulty of placing in people's mouths sentiments which were not yet wholly theirs; and, moreover, constrained to an extent which cannot now be exactly measured by Cranmer's veneration for traditional structures and language, a conservative liturgical instinct in evident tension with the reformist thrust of his theology. This last difficulty has led some authorities to the dubious opinion that 1549 was Cranmer's preferred liturgy, because closer to traditional forms, even that he had diminished responsibility for 1552; others to insist (surely correctly) that 1552 was a plainer, truer, expression of what he had always intended. In 1552 the possibility of reading the real presence into the communion service was no longer available. Now it was 'these creatures'; 'take and eat this', 'drink this' 'this', not defined in terms other that those of bread and wine.[65]

So far so good. But as an assessment of Cranmer's theological position, not quite far or good enough. It has been suggested that on the centrality of the Gospel, Cranmer was at one with Luther from an early date in his public career, and that his understanding of the Gospel moved within essentially Lutheran parameters, not that he was exactly a Lutheran in a card-carrying sense in his account of justification and of the relation of faith to works, any more than many German theologians of the sixteenth century whom we do not hesitate to call some kind of Lutherans taught exactly what Luther taught. And how theologically consistent was Luther himself, who always wrote for the occasion, as the spirit moved him, writing little that was systematic?

This issue is somewhat technical and concerns whether Cranmer believed that we are saved by a wholly other, extrinsic, righteousness, merely imputed to us, the doctrine theologians call 'forensic' (and perhaps Lutheranism at its purest); or by the *imparting* of that righteousness to us, so that it becomes an indwelling righteousness, in a sense our own, although not originally nor properly ours but Christ's. The latter possibility resembles the position adopted by the Nuremberg and Königsberg preacher and Cranmer's adoptive uncle, Osiander, which landed him in a fullscale 'Osiandrist' controversy around 1550.[66] The prime evidence is contained in certain notes on justification which survive at Lambeth Palace, in Cranmer's own handwriting: commonplaces collected, according to the archbishop's habitual method, from Scripture, the Fathers, certain schoolmen.[67] Unfortunately these notes are undated and we cannot be sure that they represent the rough work for the great Homilies of Salvation, Faith and Good Works, as some have assumed. In that they are in Cranmer's hand rather than a secretary's they may be very much earlier, representing a transitional stage in his understanding of this subject.[68] Either on that account, or because of the ingestion of patristic and scholastic as well as biblical material, or because that was indeed his settled opinion on the matter which drew him to these texts, Cranmer

here wrote of a justification which continues and increases by means of
charity as well as by faith, although the charity no less than the faith are
ascribed only to Christ. There is also the evidence of the Justus Jonas
Catechism, published on Cranmer's instructions three times in the year
after the *Homilies*. The *Catechism* in its translated version fails to speak
of justification by faith alone, even where *sola fide* appears in the original
Latin, and it teaches that God both imputes and gives unto us the justice
and righteousness of Christ.[69]

So it is rather more clear that Cranmer taught salvation by grace alone
than that he advocated salvation by faith alone, with true Lutheran
starkness. It also appears that for Cranmer saving faith was not far distant
from what the scholastics had called *fides formata*. True, the dying thief on
the cross had saving faith which had no time at all to work as *fides formata*.
But, said Cranmer, if the thief had lived 'and not regarded faith, and the
works thereof, he should have lost his salvation again'.[70] Seventy years
later, that doctrine would have been called 'Arminian', and condemned as
such by perhaps a majority of ranking Anglican theologians, 'Calvinists';
and yet it continued to stand in the Homily of Good Works, which is to
say in the Articles, into the seventeenth century and beyond. The 'beyond'
included John Henry Newman's Tract 90, which attempted, at the cost
of his own defection from Cranmer's Church of England, to square the
circle of Anglican-Catholic difference. But it would be anachronistic to
call Cranmer either an Arminian or a Calvinist.

Alister McGrath, surveying this evidence in the course of a large book
on justification in the history of Christian doctrine,[71] speaks of the general
'theological mediocrity' of the English Reformation, and of Cranmer's
inability to distinguish clearly between the Lutheran doctrine of imputed
righteousness and a more properly Augustinian concept of factitive
righteousness, 'making righteous': to which, with the sole exception of
that most Germanical nature Robert Barnes, he believes that the English
reformers all leaned. However, it is not clear that Cranmer misheard
Luther, and Dr. McGrath may go too far when he says that the English
doctrines of justification 'were quite distinct from those of the mainstream
Continental Reformation'; for that is to make the Continental Reformation
itself, even the Lutheran Reformation, altogether too monolithic. If
Cranmer believed that justification embraced the inner renewal of the
justified man, so did his wife's uncle; and Osiander, while attracting the
combined wrath of Melanchthon and Melanchthon's opponents, the

so-called 'Gnesio-Lutheran' hardliners, believed that his doctrine could be read legitimately out of certain Lutheran premises. This means that Cranmer, and Cranmer's Anglicanism, was at the heart of Protestant Europe, not in some insular limbo.

But it is undeniable that Cranmer placed a distinctive premium on those good works done afterwards, the works and fruits of faith, and that he even defined salvation as perseverance in those faithful works. And that is more than a technical point. For Cranmer's Prayer Book is, as it were, marinated in that understanding of the salvation process, an exercise in the first instance of what it has become fashionable to call 'self-fashioning', but thereafter an instrument for the fashioning of others, indeed of an entire nation. *Credere est orare, orare credere*. This is especially true of the Prayer Book collects, those little gems which are translated and filtrated adaptations of traditional and in no way Protestant prayers. In these supplications, the Prayer Book serves as a manual for a Christian life which must persist in faith and the good works which spring from faith if it is to come safely to its end and attain salvation.

Phrases once familiar to churchgoers can make the point: 'that thou being our ruler and guide, we may so pass through things temporal, that we finally lose not the things eternal'; 'that we loving thee in all things may obtain thy promises'; 'that we, running to thy promises, may be made partakers of thy heavenly treasure'; 'grant . . . that we may so run to thy heavenly promises, that we fail not finally to attain the same'. 'Almighty and everlasting God, give unto us the increase of faith, hope and charity; and that we may obtain that which thou dost promise, make us to love that which thou dost command . . .'

If there was theological tension between these expressions of Cranmer's faith and other versions of Protestantism, soon to be nearly dominant in the later sixteenth-century Church of England, to such an extent that there are difficulties in calling Cranmer's accout of the matter simply 'Anglican', the tension was equally one of tone, mood and proportion. The collects are all between thirty and sixty words in length, whereas the prayers in the Middelburg, Puritan prayer book of 1587, which is such a liturgy as many English Protestants of that generation would have composed without the prompting and restraint of Cranmer and the law, run to as many as two thousands words and more, forty times the length of the average collect, and so not prayers in the same sense at all.[72]

We should not forget that Cranmer's legacy was not simply one of the sublime, quasi-Shakespeareian consensuality of the Prayer Book, warm and comfortable like the service of Choral Evensong on Radio 3, which MacCulloch assures us Cranmer would have gladly abolished,[73] the spiritual equivalent of a pint of warm English beer. The immediate legacy was one of tension, division, and the extreme bitterness of a civil war which, in part, was a war fought for and against the Prayer Book, for and against Archbishop Cranmer's continuing hand on the tiller of the nation's religious consciousness and sensibility.[74] That was a hand which, for all that it was itself guided by an essentially and deeply Protestant mind and conscience, could compose out of a time-worn original such a prayer as the second collect at Evensong, redolent of a cradle-to-grave, static and institutional religious structure, as timeless as the parish church where for generations it would be read; an 'edifying' prayer, but not in the urgently Pauline sense of edification, revived in English Puritanism.[75] 'Give unto thy servants that peace which the world cannot give; that both our hearts may be set to obey thy commandments and also that by thee, we being defended from the fear of our enemies, may pass our time in rest and quietness'. Or does the apparent timelessness of that prayer, like a pebble rounded on the beach by countless tides, sound to us like that only because of the passage of all those generations? It was a revolution for the first of those generations to hear such prayers in their own language. And the language of the collects, like the English of Tyndale's New Testament, was what people then spoke.

Cranmer himself can scarcely be said to have passed his time in rest and quietness; and at the end no man was in more need of the peace which the world cannot give. According to one possible reading of his recantations, this was a man who no longer knew which was the truth which would save him, the error which would damn him. He was, in John Foxe's patterning of history, the most emblematic and representative of the English Protestant martyrs, the last of 'the learned sort' to go to the stake, burned 'about the very middle time' of Mary's reign, so that he was also 'almost the very middle man of all the martyrs'. But, as even Foxe conceded, no martyr needed martyrdom more, to resolve, heal and make amends, in Foxe's unforgiving words, 'to purge his offences in this world', an interpretation of the meaning of martyrdom made of none of Foxe's other martyr characters.[76]

Just as it is hard to quarrel with suicide, so martyrdom removes the martyr beyond our reproach; even such a hesitant, unwilling martyr as Thomas Cranmer, although in the end he ran to the stake. Hence the inestimable value of martyrdom as apologetics. We have pursued the theme of truth by twisting, labyrinthine paths. One symbol of truth and sincerity, in our culture, is the right hand, the hand which composed the Prayer Book, but also signed those dubious recantations. Few of us can be as proud of what our right hands have accomplished, but since we are for the most part private men and women, we may also have less to be ashamed of, or to regret. In any event, none of us is likely to have the opportunity to hold that offending member, the right hand, in the consuming flames, as Cranmer did, oftentimes repeating, 'hys unworthy right hand'.[77]

2

Godly Preachers and Zealous Magistrates in Elizabethan East Anglia: The Roots of Dissent

Professor John Bossy, the distinguished historian of post-Reformation English Catholicism, penned an often-quoted sentence at the end of his seminal article on 'The Character of Elizabethan Catholicism'. 'The history of Elizabethan Catholicism', he wrote, 'is a progress from inertia to inertia in three generations.'[1] By the same token one might say that the history of Protestant Dissent in East Anglia travels full circle from minority enthusiasm to minority enthusiasm in five or six generations. Within the intervening circuit lay the ideal, partly realised in the late Elizabethan and Jacobean periods, of the righteous Commonwealth, comprising godly ministers, zealous magistrates, and willing and tractable people. That interim is the subject of this paper, an episode of anti-dissent enveloped in a more persistent continuum of dissenting history.

The story begins with Lollardy and revolves towards the post-Restoration Dissent of the later seventeenth century: both cottage religions or, as often as not, farmhouse religions, strongly rooted in the microcosmics of the East Anglian landscape. Up-to-date students of religious history, prompted by the writings of Alan Everitt, Margaret Spufford, Keith Wrightson and other social historians of 'mentalité', are asked to consider how far these religious cultures are to be accounted for by the many regional and local differences in the use to which that landscape was put; the as many variations in the relation of the human inhabitants to their environment; and by the social relations of different elements of the population, dictated in part by those environmental, ecological factors, and by many other factors besides.[2]

To speak of Dissent is by definition to speak of minority religion (the majority does not dissent) but not thereby to disparage or belittle it. I digress for a moment in an autobiographical direction. As the product of long and exacting Sundays at Bethesda Baptist Church, Ipswich (the cathedral of the Norfolk and Suffolk Association of Strict and Particular

Baptists)[3] the childhood veteran of Easter conventions at the Railway
Mission in Colchester and the Independent Chapel at Great Barton; briefly
(in 1942) an attender at both an independent evangelical church (mornings)
and a Primitive Methodist chapel (evenings) at Littleport; the son of a
Quaker father who in the first years of this century itinerated all over East
Anglia on a bicycle with the Friends' Evangelistic Band and the Young
Men's Christian Association and an occasional visitor to what is called
the Collinson Room in the Friends' Meeting House in Ipswich; sometime
a teacher in the Sunday School at Eden Baptist Church, Cambridge, and
the brother of the some time Baptist (BU) minister at Swavesey: for
all these and many other reasons I am not likely to underestimate the
strength of East Anglian Dissent or its importance in the formation of that
contradiction in terms (and only a native-born East Anglian is allowed to
say this) East Anglian civilisation.

Consequently I do not need to read Browne's *History of Congregationalism
in Norfolk and Suffolk* to know that a village chapel was called a 'cause'.
'The cause here owed its origin to the efforts of Mr Gooch, a resident
farmer'; 'the cause here was commenced in 1859'.[4] I have been party to
more family conversations than I can number about this or that chapel,
always referred to as a cause, usually in the phrase 'a poor little cause' or
'a struggling cause'. So I know that causes should not be little and poor,
should not have to struggle. I have had my small share in the triumphalism
of Sunday School anniversaries behind that prosperous Doric colonnade
which is Bethesda Ipswich, a flourishing cause. And that is to touch
upon the longest-running continuum in dissenting history; the tension,
contradiction even, between the religious experience of the self-defining
godly remnant or holy huddle and its sense, however presumptuous and
preposterous, of a wider, national and even universal mission, not only
to evangelise but to command and control. This notable anomaly was
the Nonconformist Conscience in political action in the late nineteenth
century and, in the seventeenth century, the rule of the Major-Generals.

The period which I have to look over in contributing to this symposium
is that period when Dissent was not yet Dissent but proto-dissent,
when the aspiration to command and control as well as to evangelise
was still paramount, but when the moral majority (as it were) which
entertained this aspiration was nevertheless a social minority, not only
in an arithmetical sense, which has only a limited relevance to sixteenth-

and seventeenth-century circumstances, but in its own perceptions and emotions. It considered itself a remnant and a minority.

In East Anglia, as in other parts of England and, for that matter, Western Europe, the children of the Protestant Reformation, not merely readers of the Bible but virtual inhabitants of a biblical mental landscape, drew their inspiration and understanding from two strands of discourse which were interwoven in their experience, but interwoven as they moved against each other in almost contrary directions. These strands were two ecclesiologies, both authentically biblical in inspiration. According to the first, the church was equivalent to the whole people in a covenanted relation to God. 'You have not chosen me but I have chosen you', with the added inference, 'whether you like it or not': an idea which the reception of Calvinisim reinforced. This led to the equation of the nation, the church in the sense of the whole circumcised (baptised) community, and Israel as essentially one, the town, be it London or Ipswich, Jerusalem: or rather the reinforcement of that notion, which was older than the Reformation. And since that identification was derived from the prophetical books of the Old Testament, where Israel is castigated for its apostasy, it mattered in a sense not at all that the English nation or East Anglian society failed to live up to these expectations, or to behave as if it really was a chosen and convenanted people of God. That was only to be expected. But the pulpit, with its dire warnings and threats of impending judgement, was by no means complacent, for all that. Yet all these warnings, and even the ultimate dread that God might abandon his people and depart from England for ever ('as sure as God is God, God is going from England', said Thomas Hooker in his farewell sermon to his Chelmsford flock in 1628), were understood to be conditional, to take effect if we fail to repent, part of a divine poker game of cosmic proportions in which, said one Jacobean preacher, we seem to have entered into a contention with the Almighty to see whether we can be more sinful or he more merciful.[5]

The contrary tendency or strand shrank the church for all practical and especially experimental purposes to the pious remnant, that small minority (it was always assumed in those religious milieux which were ancestral to East Anglian Dissent to be a *small* minority) of 'Christians indeed': those who were seen to repent of their sins, to exercise lively faith and (perhaps the critical criterion) to gather with others of the same kind and persuasion in self-selective, exclusive company, various kinds of 'conventicle', sometimes convenanted.[6] 'Be of good comfort *little* flock', Jesus had said, 'it is your Father's good pleasure to give you the kingdom'. These were those few who had found the strait and narrow gate, and path. Calvinism underwrote these attitudes also, with its insistence on selective and prejudicial election.

It is important to appreciate that in the period with which this essay is concerned, which lies behind 1640 and perhaps behind the late 1630s, the cord composed of these two strands held together and took the strain. Separatism was to pull out of the cord one of its two strands. This happened and to an extent which cannot be accurately measured, although the more celebrated episodes of Elizabethan and Jacobean Separatism have provided later Nonconformity with its title deeds, family history and mythology. I believe that the rupture of separation occurred rarely, even exceptionally, and in response to particular circumstances.[7] The ecclesiology and the religious experience of conformable church-goers, the majority (easy to disparage, harder to characterise, equally impossible to measure) also had only one strand to it. But the religious tendencies and, I think that we may dare to say, the religious movement which gave birth to East Anglian Dissent (but which, but for extraordinary events and circumstances of the 1640s, need not have given birth to it) kept the two strands together in a woven cord. The private meetings of the godly few, the conventicle, had a separatist potential and, short of separation, had divisive and socially damaging effects. but it was not, for the most part, actually separatist. Private duties were held not to exclude public, nor vice versa. That is to say that a kind of Dissent, and certainly a religious tendency which was defined by its difference from the religion of 'most people', was contained within the national and parochial church, not erected outside it. That is not necessarily to say that it was tidily or comfortably so contained in all circumstances.[8]

Diarmaid MacCulloch, the historian of Elizabethan Suffolk, has identified Reformed Protestantism itself as it grew up within the still essentially unreformed and Catholic forms and structures of the established church as 'the cuckoo in the nest'. So it remained, until some of the cuckoos left the nest, willingly or unwillingly, and took flight. This is to propose that the Protestant Reformation, for all the strength of its aspiration to unite the nation in religion as never before, created tensions which were not contained or resolved and which opened up cracks which eventually widened and deepened to become established geological features of the ecclesiastical and socio-political landscape. Protestantism in its most prevalent and predominant English form (Calvinist rather than Lutheran or Arminian) and in English conditions (a church which was structurally and liturgically at best half reformed) was not very well suited to serve as the ideological basis for a national church.[9]

Nevertheless, the focus of the remainder of this essay will fall on a period when a Protestantism both evangelical and Calvinist enjoyed a kind of established ascendancy, if not universally in East Anglia then in many East Anglian communities. This was a generally pervasive and politically sustained ascendancy in, for example, south-west Suffolk, a more intensive social and cultural ascendancy amounting to advanced internalisation in certain rural parishes exposed to particularly intense godly pressure, and in such towns as Bury St Edmunds, Ipswich, Yarmouth and King's Lynn.

This ascendancy only begins to be clearly visible in the later 1570s. As a feature of East Anglian politics it can be dated quite precisely from certain events in the region in the summer of 1578, when the Court came to Suffolk and Norfolk on royal progress. Before 1578, evangelical Protestantism in East Anglia was a form of Dissent without effective local political support. After 1578, and certainly by the later 1580s, it was backed up by such effective local political support that it ceased to look much like Dissent, although that was still, according to a number of criteria, what it was. That remained the position up to and into the years of the Civil War.[10]

Before coming to 1578 I will comment briefly on what was locally detrimental to the fortunes of evangelical Protestantism before that date, and this will enable us to identify the forces favouring those fortunes from the later 1570s onwards. But first we must take account of the Lollard tradition, running back at least as far as the 1420s, when there were extensive judicial investigations conducted by Bishop Alnwick and his officers into heretical belief and activity in a number of rural locations in Norfolk and in Norwich itself.[11] There were almost certainly meaningful connections between the Lollardy still actively present in Essex and East Anglia in the early decades of the sixteenth century and the beginnings of an indigenous, locally-supported Protestant movement. It was Lollards who went to hear Thomas Bilney preach in Ipswich in 1528 and who, far from hearing anything new, seem to have been confirmed in what they already believed, for example about the worthlessness of venerating images.[12] It is likely that the groups which Bilney visited and taught on his way to Norwich and to martyrdom were Lollard conventicles.[13] There is more evidence of the convergence of old and new dissenting currents in the villages forming the hinterland of Colchester and in Colchester itself. The three young men of Dedham who walked twenty miles through a frosty night to avenge Bilney's death by burning the famous rood of Dovercourt, and who were hanged for their pains, were probably part of a well-established dissenting current.[14]

But there are difficulties in placing late Lollardy and early Protestantism in simple chronological sequence, the kind of sequence alleged when Browne in his *History of Congregationalism in Norfolk and Suffolk* (going even beyond the sixteenth-century martyrologist Foxe) calls the Lollards of the 1420s 'Protestants' and implies that they were actually primitive Congregationalists. It is by no means clear that the men of Mendlesham who, in the early 1530s, were calling themselves 'Christian Brethren', were Bible-reading, card-carrying Protestants; rather more clear that they were expressing the insubordination characteristic of the mixed economy of high Suffolk, with its weak manorial organisation and lack of gentry control.[15] (But Mendlesham remained a notoriously nonconformist neck of the woods for the remainder of the sixteenth century and beyond.) The evidence of Marian heresy trials in Suffolk, like similar evidence from the Kentish Weald, reveals forms of heresy more radical than orthodox, Edwardian Protestantism, and distinct from it.[16]

Moreover, to inhabit or merely to visit the clothing parishes of south and south-west Suffolk, to investigate the places themselves and their churches, is to be convinced that East Anglian Protestants were the children (literally as well as metaphorically) of late medieval East Anglian Catholics, not only, or especially, of Lollard heretics. The continuities and discontinuities which must be understood lie between the still Catholic clothiers of circa 1510, who beautified these churches and used them to endow propitiatory masses for repose of their own souls and those of their kindred and friends, and their Protestant grandchildren who founded Calvinist lectureships in these self-same churches, doing their best to turn those exuberant edifices into large meeting-rooms for preaching and prayer.[17]

Old Lollards (in their conventicles a model and even a continuous tradition of minority Dissent) and old Catholics both required conversion and absorption into the individualistic belief — but deeply social and corporate religious experience — which constituted the new Protestantism. That depended primarily upon preaching ministers who before the 1570s were in very short supply, except in some parts of Essex: scarce in west Suffolk, and much of Norfolk; almost non-existent in the coastal belt of Suffolk, from Lothingland to the Orwell, where for years the only Protestant sermons were provided by an itinerant preacher called John Laurence, who was not even a minister, although he enjoyed some official, episcopal support.[18]

A marked improvement in this situation waited upon political factors which remained in many respects unfavourable until the 1570s and our critical year, 1578. The early Elizabethan bishops of the region (Grindal of London, Parkhurst of Norwich, Cox of Ely) all had impeccable Protestant credentials (all three had been Marian exiles). But Cox and Parkhurst both contended with daunting political obstacles, and Parkhurst, with no great competence or effectiveness, with the corrupt bureaucracy which he inherited from his predecessors.[19] The eclipse of the all-powerful and religiously conservative house of Howard with the execution of the duke of Norfolk in 1572 left many dependents of the Howards, openly or cryptically Catholic, still influential in the commissions of the peace in both Norfolk and Suffolk. In these circumstances the evangelical Protestant element remained exposed as an unpopular and intransigent minority which drew a sharp and uncompromising line between their own religious convictions and practices and those of Catholics and crypto-Catholics. This line the Elizabethan religious settlement had deliberately blurred. So their ministers refused to wear the white linen surplice or to use the sign of the cross in baptism, or to use unleavened wafers in the communion as the royal injunctions directed. The liturgy was abbreviated to allow more time for preaching, and metrical psalms in the Geneva fashion were sung demonstratively, even provocatively, not only in church but on the way to church. Disapproval of non-preaching clerics, especially unreconstructed 'mass priests' carried over from the Marian and even the Henrician past, was openly expressed. There is evidence that these sentiments and prejudices were entertained and articulated not only, or even primarily, by ministers, but by laity of the kind called

in sixteenth century sources 'gospellers', often 'simple gospellers', and in
the seventeenth century 'private christians', 'notable private christians',
otherwise known as 'professors'. There is also evidence that the evangelical
Protestant movement was in part self-generating and not absolutely
dependent upon the professional ministry. Such people were beginning
to be called Puritans.[20]

The narratives contained in John Foxe's *Acts and Monuments* (or
'Book of Martyrs') are strongly suggestive of the deep roots of popular
Protestantism (or Puritanism) in places like Hadleigh and Stoke by
Nayland. The Hadleigh which experienced the full violence of the Marian
reaction, including the burning of its charismatic preacher, Rowland
Taylor, and two of his lay supporters, was, wrote Foxe, more like a
university than a town of cloth-making and labouring people. At Stoke
in the same years only two villagers (and we are bound to regard them as
a minority of popish dissenters) were prepared to receive communion in
the then authorised, Catholic manner.[21]

When Edmund Freke succeeded John Parkhurst as bishop of Norwich
in 1575 he seems to have received instructions from the highest level
to discipline all nonconformists, the so-called Puritans. Preachers were
silenced and ejected, especially in Norwich itself, and the religious
scene was still further polarised. It was said that the state could not long
continue thus. It must either to papistry or puritanism.[22] Politically a
distinctive Anglican option was not viable. To survive, Freke had to make
friends with some of the more notable Catholics in Norfolk, including Sir
Thomas Cornwallis of Brome, a vigorous sapling reared in the shadow of
the Howards and now shot up towards the sunlight with their extinction,
still young and both well educated and well connected.[23]

Such was the background to the summer of 1578 and that royal progress
through East Anglia which was arranged at very short notice and with
the clear intention (the intention of the Privy Council, to some extent in
general, and probably of Robert Dudley, earl of Leicester in particular)
of redressing the politico-religious balance in the region. The seesaw was
now to be tipped in favour of Protestantism, not to say Puritanism. One
precondition for this calculated high-political initiative was the process
of generational change which had brought into their great inheritances
Protestant Elizabethans, succeeding in estates and county offices their
Henrician and still Catholic fathers, This transition was especially

significant for the parts of west Suffolk around Bury, where Robert Jermyn of Rushbrooke succeeded the Catholic Sir Ambrose Jermyn in 1577 and in 1571 his ally, John Higham, had followed his father Sir Clement, a notable prosecutor and persecutor of Protestants under Mary. Similar processes had begun to shift the balance of power towards Protestantism on the Norfolk bench.[24]

The queen's summer progress of 1578 was made the occasion to honour Jermyn, Higham and other Protestant justices with knighthoods, and to disgrace and degrade a number of Catholics and crypto-Catholics, including Cornwallis. The Rookwoods of Euston, near Newmarket (Edward Rookwood was Cornwallis's brother-in-law) were deliberately and (one suspects) cynically destroyed after an image of the Virgin was discovered as the queen was about to leave the hospitality of Edward Rookwood's roof. Rookwood was subsequently broken by imprisonment and recusancy fines, while his cousin found himself among the gunpowder plotters of 1605. No wonder that 1578 was later looked back to as a watershed in East Anglian history, Jermyn recalling in a letter of 1601 the 'satisfaction' which he and his friends had received at that time from the central government.[25] East Anglian Catholicism was now obliged to retreat into its recusant and separatist ghetto. The region would henceforth experience Protestant government, as well as what Professor Everitt has called 'a dread of popery among Suffolk country folk of exceptional intensity'. 'Perhaps nowhere, except in London, did the dream of the New Jerusalem seem more vivid'.[26]

However, the religious power struggle which had had Bishop Freke at its centre was not so tidily resolved, and it continued for a few more years. It was a struggle to purge the administrative and household personnel of the bishop of Norwich; to bring the Reformation to Lothingland, the hinterland of Lowestoft, a coastal region of strategic importance, which it had so far scarcely touched. It concerned the government of Thetford, where in the early 1580s the town government was still in the hands of conservatives (and illiterates) and where very few sermons were preached. But above all this was a struggle for religious control of Bury St Edmunds and its surrounding parishes. On the one side of these 'Bury stirs' were ranged Bishop Freke and his commissary in Bury, supported by elements in the town which were hostile to the Puritan preachers and their patrons; supported too, and more potently, by the visiting judges of

assize, who proved to be determined opponents of anything resembling
Puritanism. These interests were opposed by Jermyn, Higham, and some
other neighbouring country gentlemen, together with their ally in Bury
itself, Thomas Badby, who had made his home among the ruins of the
great abbey church where he had entertained the queen in 1578.[27]

Simultaneously at the sharp end of the Protestant–Puritan advance and in
the firing-line of the conservative counter-attack were the many preaching
ministers who had begun to move into the west Suffolk parishes, thanks
to the patronage of the Puritan gentry. Jermyn presented to ten livings,
Higham to four, other like-minded patrons to a further thirty. These
preachers may be described as a Cambridge mafia. Of eighty-one Suffolk
clergy connected in one way or another with Puritan Nonconformity in
the 1580s, fifty-one are known to have been at the university in the late
1560s and early 1570s when it formed a kind of crucible of radical and
insubordinate churchmanship, no less than thirty of them at the same
college, St John's.[28]

Some of these preachers were now arraigned at the assizes and even
imprisoned. Bishop Freke drew up articles against their supporters among
the JPs and complained, first to the Privy Council and then to the queen
herself. Although Elizabeth referred the matter back to her Council, the
gentlemen were called up to London to make their answer, a fearful blow
to their credit and credibility. They protested that since they had been
called out of their country 'every street doth sound our disgrace, wrought
by the bishop'. At another moment in the evolution of this 'Suffolk
country cause', Bury witnessed the unusual spectacle of fifteeen of the
'principal men of Suffolk', headed by the lord lieutenant himself, Lord
North, and including seven of the thirteen knights of the bench, waiting
upon the assize judges at their lodging on behalf of their preachers, humbly
asking them to 'handle trifling matters the more kindly' for their sakes.
At the height of this tragi-comedy Jermyn and Higham were suspended
from the Commission of the Peace at a time when they were jointly
serving as deputy lieutenants, an office which put them in charge of the
military resources of one of the richest counties in England at a moment
of national crisis. It made very little sense, indeed less sense than most
episodes in Elizabethan politics.

This was no ordinary storm in a factional tea-cup, the usual stuff of
high county politics in Elizabethan England. The religious factor was

transcendent and served to carry the issues at stake and awareness of them down through the social strata. Without Bishop Freke we should probably never have heard of the Brownists, the label most commonly stuck on separatist schismatics for half a century to come and more, not merely in East Anglia but nationally. For it was in the context of Freke's in many ways misguided and damaging vendetta against East Anglia's godly Protestants that Robert Brown and Robert Harrison, with an immediate background in ministry and schoolmastering in and around Norwich, led the first significant Protestant secession out of the reformed Church of England.[29] Brownists were in evidence in Bury St Edmunds too. Indeed it was a peculiarly offensive attack on the queen's religious policy, made in the form of certain texts from Revelation attached to the royal arms in St Mary's church in Bury, which not only led to the hanging of two Brownists at the assizes (the so-called 'Bury Congregational martyrs') but served to explain how a peer of the realm and seven knights could be standing cap in hand on Angel Hill before two assize judges, one of them very junior.[30] Not that these worthies held any brief for Brownists. They told the Privy Council: 'We abhorre all these, we punishe all these'.[31]

Whenever we have some record of the local reverberations of this struggle for the soul as much as for the political future of East Anglia, we find a cast if not of thousands then of significant tens and scores. Such were the fifty inhabitants of the small parish of Lawshall who had found relief from a decrepit and immoral vicar in his eighties by procuring an 'extraordinary lecture' to be preached in their church over three years, which led to 'a stirring of many . . . to seek the Lord in his word'. Soon the men of Lawshall were moving around the country in a body, hearing sermons in other parishes, behaviour which presently brought some of them before Judge Anderson at the Bury Assizes. A member of the grand jury who indicted them was heard to say that 'he hoped ere long to see all that carried Geneva Bibles hanged'. This was Independency of a kind, for the godly of Lawshall were registering their disapproval both of their vicar and of the lord of the manor, Henry Drury, a Catholic.[32]

But the godly were not much troubled in that way after the mid-1580s. Freke went off to enjoy a quieter life as bishop of Worcester. Sir Robert Jermyn and Sir John Higham became two Nestors of their country, fellow knights of the shire in the 1587 parliament. They were succeeded in the following generation as 'one of the top branches amongst our Suffolk cedars' by the immensely wealthy and godly Sir Nathaniel Barnardiston of Ketton. These Suffolk worthies were matched in Norfolk by Sir Nathaniel Bacon of Stiffkey, and in Essex by the Barringtons of Broad Oak, Sir Francis Barrington, Barnardiston's contemporary, being described as 'truly noble, perfectly religious', 'our Joshua, our Jethro'.[33]

So Puritanism in East Anglia was not destined to collapse into Brownism, at least not for another fifty or sixty years. Through the later years of Elizabeth, and throughout the reign of James, our two-stranded cord held. East Anglian Puritanism combined the characteristics of what the German social theorist, Ernst Troeltsch, distinguished as the two basic ideal types of Christian organisation: simultaneously church and sect.[34] What made this possible and gave the cord the strength to take the strain was the paradigmatic alliance of godly magistracy and ministry: the principle celebrated by the Norwich minister who spoke of 'the magistrates and ministers embracing and seconding one another, and the common people affording due reverence and obedience to them both'.[35] That implies a kind of formal parity of what the Ipswich preacher, Samuel Ward, called 'these two optic pieces'.[36] Of this Ward himself and, in the country, the celebrated John Knewstub, rector of Cockfield for forty-five years, were figures or portents in their own proper sphere, as Jermyn and Barnardiston were in theirs.

The Suffolk ministers, with Knewstub as their acknowledged president, were a formidably well-qualified and essentially Presbyterian body of men, although quite happy to acknowledge the benevolent, if remote, patronage of Freke's more sympathetic and pragmatic successors as bishops of Norwich, such as the Jacobean bishop, John Jegon. They included Nicholas Bownd, author of a best-selling book on *The Doctrine of the Sabbath*, and Robert Allen, who wrote a one thousand page tome called *The Doctrine of the Gospel*, so that, he said, the world should know 'what these things are which the faithfull Ministers of Jesus Christ doe beate their wittes about', a book also designed to demonstrate 'in how many truths, that is in particulars above number, we do agree'. When another of this circle, Mr Walsh of Little Waldingfield, died in 1605, Knewstub preached the funeral sermon, after which 'he with other preachers carried his coffin on their shoulders'. Samuel Fairclough's Thursday lectures at Ketton were preached to 'so great a number of the Clergy, all the Ministers (for many miles compasse) coming constantly to heare them', as well as never less than ten or twenty scholars from Cambridge. According to Robert Reyce's *Breviary of Suffolk* (1618), Bishop Jegon was given to boasting that no bishop in Europe commanded so grave, learned and judicious a ministry, 'especially in this country'.[37]

At Barnardiston and Fairclough's Ketton it was said that 'the Magistracy and Ministry joined both together and concurred in all things for the promoting of true Piety and Godliness', the magistrates and minister having a settled agreement to visit one another at least twice a week. 'They heartily also joined hand in hand to promote both the force and power of Godliness in that Town and Country'.[38] According to a pious legend repeated as late as 1650, when Queen Elizabeth came into Suffolk on that famous progress of 1578, she was met by the ranking gentry, each flanked by his own minister, whereupon she remarked that now she understood why that county was so well governed: magistracy and ministry stood together.[39]

Good government along these lines in Bury St Edmunds meant a severe, even draconian code of bye-laws, publicly displayed in the two parish churches. Here was that 'culture of discipline' described by such historians of Puritan Essex as Keith Wrightson and William Hunt.[40] The penalty for fornication (going somewhat beyond any statute then in force and far beyond the censures of the official church) was to be

> tyed to the poaste for that purpose appointed (having hir haire cutt of if it be a woman) and so remaine tyed to the poaste for the space of one whole daie and a night, and that daie to be the Lordes daie, and after on the markett daie to be whipped, receiving thirtie strypes well layed on till the blood come, the Cunstable seeinge the execution thereof.[41]

Monday was not only market day but lecture day, when the country ministers took it in turns to preach. On other days there were more sermons offered by the equally gifted preachers of the town, who included William Bedell, the future and celebrated bishop of Kilmore in Ireland, and Joseph Hall, later an even more illustrious bishop of Exeter and Norwich. Towards 1600 someone observed: 'Your townsmen of Bury are such diligent hearers of the Word on the Monday exercise that they may easily be singled out from other men'.[42] Bury was not without other amenities, making it a popular shire town and resort for the gentry. There was also that famous grammar school from which presently emerged the most appealing of all the princes of the Jacobean pulpit, Richard Sibbes, author of *The Bruised Reed*. But sermons were at the heart of the town's culture up to the 1630s when Bishop Wren's visitors commented on the dominance of the vast pulpit and reading desk, the women's sighs and men's 'hawkings' which punctuated the incessant preaching.[43] This was a town with the most impeccable of Puritan credentials, and these perhaps made it resistant rather than open to the activities of Mrs Katherine Chidley and other Independent pioneers who, in the late 1640s, signally failed to gather more than a tiny fraction of Bury's population into their scarcely viable separatist congregation.[44] There is no evidence that the religious public which gadded in companies to sermons, riding down from Ipswich to John Rogers' electrifying sermons at Dedham saying 'let's go to Dedham to get a little fire',[45] were disposed to separate from the Church of England; much evidence to the contrary.

A Bury preacher asked in 1600: 'If magistrates and ministers agree not and the people reverence and love them both, what can come of it?'[46] But did 'the people' love and reverence their magistrates and ministers? How many, and which sorts of, people were recruited into the religion of Bible-reading and preaching which to this extent prevailed in early seventeenth century East Anglia? Magistrates, ministers and 'people' are too crude and uninformative as categories with which to inspect the social composition of East Anglian Puritanism; 'the people', that phrase beloved of smooth-talking politicians, particularly so. Was evangelical Calvinism, or Puritanism, a religion of clothiers rather than of weavers, of yeoman farmers, dairy farmers, cheese producers, more than of poor husbandmen and labourers? Was it over-represented in the class from which churchwardens, constables and other petty officers of the commonwealth were recruited, implying a close connection with the processes of social and moral control and the repression of those country disorders in which such officers were professionally interested? Was it a religion of equal interest to both men and women, the young and unattached as well as the mature and settled elements in society? Were the East Anglian Brownists of the 1570s and 1580s, and the more numerous sects of the mid-seventeenth century, supported at a lower social level than non-separatist Puritanism?

Some historians have been readier to answer these questions than others, but some of the more confident answers may prove prejudicial in one way or another. Empirically, the matter has not been taken very far, and indeed, for a social analysis of pre-1640 Puritanism there are evidential limits beyond which all but the earliest stages of such an enquiry cannot be taken. Margaret Spufford's work on seventeenth-century Cambridgeshire, and the research on various forms of rural nonconformity carried out by her gifted pupils,[47] incline us to expect to find a socially cross-sectional distribution of Puritanism and Dissent. From the Spufford school we know enough to be suspicious of two contrary paradigms once widely reflected in the literature. According to the first of these, sectarian Dissent articulated the concerns only of the poorer, disinherited levels of society. We may call that the Nietzscheian paradigm. We tend to find on the contrary (the Spuffordians tend to find) the significant involvement in enthusiastic, minority religion of elements of the upper crust of rural society, those said in contemporary parlance to be 'of ability', or, in the vernacular of a later age, worth a pound or two. But the Nietzscheian paradigm should not be simply turned upside down, as if Puritanism was the same thing as comfortable prosperity or middling wealth, expressing itself in the imperatives of social control. On this score Dr Spufford herself has said some wise and salutary things, including some very influential remarks about 'a society in which even the humblest members, the very poor, and the women, and those living in physical isolation, thought deeply on religious matters and were often profoundly influenced by them'.[48]

To pose the social question somewhat differently, let us return to our metaphor of the cord composed of strands. You will recall that the metaphor was applied to Puritan and proto-dissenting ecclesiology, the cord composed of churchly and sectarian, inclusive and exclusive, strands. But let us now use the cord as a metaphor for the social composition of evangelical Protestantism. The gentry, Jermyn and Barnardiston, were one strand; the ministers, Knewstub, Ward and Bownd, another. But 'the people' were several strands, as various as their statuses and interests. Did this cord also hold, or did it fray and break, succumbing to what a Marxist or perhaps any kind of materialist historian might regard as its internal contradictions? After all, any East Anglian parochial congregation of the early seventeenth century was liable to contain within itself such contradictions as landlords and tenants, wealthy clothiers and struggling weavers, those who paid tithe and the clergyman to whom they paid it.

I think that we have to acknowledge that the parish church itself, and its various components, from the seating arrangements to the modalities for the collection and redistribution of money and other charitable resources, was a mechanism designed to reconcile the otherwise irreconcileable, to effect what Professor Bossy has called the social miracle.[49] The shared experience of Puritanism, a somewhat different religious institution from the parish but overlapping with it, was perhaps another such mechanism. But I think that we must also admit that the contemporary mind was capable of taking a jaundiced view of these arrangements, seeing them as a contrivance to defuse or divert attention from potentially explosive issues, perhaps, that mind might even have said, real issues; and also that the contrivance did not invariably or always succeed.

How often that jaundiced and as it were Marxist view of the social function of religion was taken by those living on the wrong side of the social tracks we cannot tell. But this is what a future archbishop of Canterbury had to say about what purported to be a typical Bury St Edmunds sermon, preached in the critical late 1570s when the future archbishop, young Richard Bancroft, had been drafted in to Bury to shore up the crumbling cause of conformity:

> This application must not touche in anye case the grosse synnes of their good Maisters, either oppression of the poore, enhauncing of Rentes, enclosinge of common groundes, sacriledge, symonye, pride, contempt of magistrates, of lawes, or ceremonyes and orders ecclesiasticall, nor anye suche like horrible synnes wherewith all the most of our precise gentlemen are infected: But all must be applied with a slaunderous invective against the present estate and government of the church ... The Gentlemen looke one at another with smyles and wynkes, as who should saye: This geare fadgeth: they are gyrded indeede.[50]

To be sure that was satire, constructed with a partisan and polemical intent. But the historian ought to take due account of what, in any epoch, lies within the imaginative scope of the satirist.

My best evidence that the social miracle did not always succeed, and that the social cord did not always hold, comes from two sermons in the Puritan tradition, both preached in Jacobean Suffolk, and neither conforming in the least to Bancroft's amusing caricature. In 1603 Thomas Carew of Bildeston,[51] a clothing town, expatiated on that text from the Epistle of St

James which has so often served as a charter for various kinds of Christian Socialism: 'Go to ye rich men, weep and howl.' This was published under the title *A caveat for clothiers*.[52] Why, asked Carew in his Preface, did he direct the doctrine of James's Epistle particularly at clothiers? Because they made up the bulk of the congregation which he was addressing on that occasion; and because clothiers were the least socially responsible of all rich men, quite simply the worst of employers. The sermon itself contained a swingeing attack, as specific in pounds, shillings and pence, and hours, as any nineteenth-century Blue Book, on the unjust economics of cloth production, proving (not merely alleging rhetorically) that in this industry large profits depended upon wholly inadequate wages. Carew was most specific about the piece rates for weavers, less so on the subject of shearmen, with whose working conditions he was less familiar. And yet, he said, he did not seem to have met many prosperous shearmen. But (Carew made an objector ask) aren't our clothiers some of the most charitable benefactors of the poor, especially when they write their wills? Answer: they need to be, but what they give is a miserable pittance in relation to what they derive from their business. And are not clothiers the most religious men in their communities? Carew said: it all depends on what you mean by religion.

Some years later, Bezaleel Carter delivered the regular lecture at Clare and chose to use the occasion to make an equally spirited but more diffuse attack on 'our greatest professors' as the least generous in the charitable distribution of their substance, the worst usurers, extreme landlords, reluctant tithers. According to Carter's by no means original doctrine of Christian Socialism, the wealthy were stewards, not outright owners, of their property, and Christ would hold them to account for their stewardship. 'Though thy goods be thine, yet are they not so thine, but that the poor have a letter of attorney from God to have to their use as well as thy self'. The Clare lecture was habitually attended by Sir Nathaniel Bamardiston, who was both the greatest 'professor' and the richest man in Suffolk. So it is hardly surprising that Carter's intemperate sermon (to his professed and profound embarrassment) was widely interpreted as a personal attack launched against this great man. Carter was locally denounced as 'a turbulent spirit'.[53]

I do not wish to suggest on the basis of two odd sermons that the social cord in early seventeenth-century East Anglia broke, or even threatened to break. Mostly it seems to have held, and for that I give credit to those middling elements in society whom historians of many periods and cultures are learning to call 'brokers'. For this was perhaps the strongest strand in the cord which was pre-Civil War proto-dissent in the eastern counties. These brokers were the substantial, responsible yeomen of the region, called in Reyce's Jacobean chorography of Suffolk 'very many yeomen of good credit and great liberalitie, good housekeepers'. In 1577, one of those specimens, an inhabitant of the yeomen's heartland of high Suffolk, declared that if he might have three or four of the chiefest yeomen in the county he 'wold not care for never a justyce of them all'.[54]

Where the yeomen brokers were enabled, or obliged, to act on their own account and authority, either because, as at Mendlesham in high Suffolk, there were no resident gentry, or, as at Lawshall, because the gentry were excluded from active service by Catholic recusancy or some other disability, they appear in visible action, and often in religious action.[55] But in other places, where their role was more covert, they were doubtless of equal importance as mediators and brokers, taking the part and perceiving the interests of those above and below them in the social hierarchy (as well, to be sure, as their own interests) as occasion served. A gathered dissenting sect could manage without gentry support. It is doubtful whether it could make much headway without middling, yeoman backing, providing not only leadership but those equally essential components of any successful conventicle, accommodation and 'housekeeping'.

Before 1640 the godly among the yeomanry of East Anglia do not appear to have been much interested in gathering dissenting congregations on the model of Brownist separatism but rather in realising the vision of a godly commonwealth and sustaining such a commonwealth in so far as it already existed. As Dr MacCulloch writes:

> It was ... in the world of Protestantism that the yeoman elites of Suffolk were to find an identity and a use for their energies and their organisational ability, in a form that would bring them into harmony with the hopes and beliefs of Puritan county magnates like Sir Robert Jermyn or Sir John Higham.[56]

But what I can be reasonably sure of is that the cords which broke are the cords which have been traced and described in this essay. One of the frayed and broken ends was the migration to New England, most of it in the 1630s.[57] It was from the heartland of evangelical Protestantism, south-west Suffolk, from its advanced but troubled economies (Carew's analysis was after all definitive), that the migration mostly came: 324 from West Suffolk, including nineteen from Bury St Edmunds, forty-two from Lavenham, fifty-four from Sudbury, compared with only seventy-five transatlantic migrants from the whole of East Suffolk.

Another series of broken ends, but also new beginnings, were the gathered, sectarian churches of the 1640s and 1650s.[58] I believe that in a number of cases, especially in Suffolk, these congregations had their beginnings and what I have called their prehistory in the conventicles of the godly, sometimes formally covenanted, which had met in these communities, often for many decades before 1640, and which were the substance and stuffing of the pre-Civil War Puritan establishment in East Anglia: those people referred to at Wymondham in 1646 as 'the godly party', at North Walsham in 1655 as 'the solid Christians', at Cookley in 1647 as 'the saints'.[59]

This is to pose (in conclusion) what Dr Spufford calls 'the most central question' to be asked of the Dissent of the third quarter of the seventeenth century: whether it was simply propagated by gifted leaders and apostles (as the annals of early Nonconformist churches tend to suggest) or sprung from grass roots existing at lower and essentially lay social levels from before the days of the Commonwealth evangelists. Comparing the villages noted for Dissent in the later seventeenth century with those which were prominent in petitioning against Bishop Wren, Spufford favours the second of these possibilities, disclosing a bias towards what she calls 'a grass-roots phenomenon amongst the very humble'. 'From these beginnings,' Dr Spufford writes, commenting on events in Willingham in the 1550s and later in the 1630s, 'a strong and lasting Congregational Church developed under the Commonwealth.'[60] My own instincts are the same, with the important proviso that I do not think that the Puritanism of the earlier seventeenth century was bound of nature and necessity to evolve into a fully separated and gathered Dissent, without the precipitating events and circumstances of the 1640s, 1650s and 1660s.[61]

And of course it would also be a mistake to suppose that all the 'godly party', all 'saints', and 'solid Christians', became full-blown dissenters before 1662 or even after that watershed. The Compton Census of 1676 counts only four to five per cent of Nonconformists nationally, a statistic which Dr Spufford confirms for Cambridgeshire. In 1669 Congregationalists were the strongest sect in Cambridgeshire and yet counted no more than seven hundred members. Baptists and Quakers numbered perhaps six hundred each. Add a pitiful handful of Presbyterians and others and you reach a total dissenting population in this eastern county of some two thousand.[62] Whether the 'solid Christians' of the years before 1640 were as few as five per cent of the total population of East Anglia we shall probably never know. But if they were, then the prehistory of Dissent is not so much a matter of minority to minority in five or six generations as of minority throughout.

3

Shepherds, Sheepdogs and Hirelings: The Pastoral Ministry in Post-Reformation England

The categories of shepherd and hireling are conventional elements of what may be called biblical and ecclesiastical pastoral, the legacy of John's Gospel chapter 10 and the basis of a perennial polemical dichotomy. Preaching at Manchester in 1582 on a text redolent of arable husbandry (Luke 10:2 — 'the harvest truly is great but the labourers are few') the vicar of Warrington strayed out of the cornfield into this pastoral vein: 'Wee must understand that our Savior speaketh not of false Hierlings but of true Pastoures, not of those which beare an ydle name and title of Pastoures'.[1] John 10 had inspired a literary motif running back to Chaucer and Langland which, in what Sir Philip Sidney called 'the old rustic language' of Spenser's *Shepheardes Calendar* (1579), revived in the May eclogue. 'Piers', a good (and, according to Spenser's commentator 'E.K.', Protestant) pastor rebukes 'Palinode' (a papist, or at least a traditional clerical type) for condoning the Maytime sports of the country people, and in the person of Palinode all hirelings:

> Well is it seene, theyr sheepe bene not their owne,
> That letten them runne at randon alone.
> But they bene hyred for little pay
> Of other, that caren as little as they,
> What fallen the flocke, so they han the fleece,
> And get all the gayne, paying but a peece.

Long before the Reformation, it was a commonplace that there were two kinds of priests, good and bad. For hirelings in the post-Reformation Church read double-beneficed men, non-residents, scandalous ministers and, above all, non-preachers.[2] We shall not assume that two clearly cut categories really existed, only that they made a convenient rhetorical and polemical device. Robert Carr, an Elizabethan curate of Maidstone, was variously esteemed according to some inconsistent evidence given under oath, in court. Some had seen him leaving the pub the worse for wear and testified that he was a gamester who played at tables for his dinner or the price of a pint of wine, using 'hot and lowd speaches touching misreckoning', that once when he had gone from the sign of the Star to the King's Meadow to play at bowls he had been too drunk to stand and cast his bowl: a hireling if ever there was one. But others reported that Mr Carr was of good name and fame for both doctrine and living, and 'a good preacher'. Mr Clark, minister of a Romney Marsh parish, was sorely abused by one of his parishioners who railed on him, accusing him of coming in at the window and starving souls. That is evidence of one layman's familiarity with John 10, where the hireling climbs up 'some other way'; but not necessarily of Mr Clark's character and professional standing, since the man who defamed him had been disappointed in failing to secure a profitable lease of some tithes.[3]

Our subject is that portion of the ministry conventionally deemed to be not only good but 'godly', that is, the 'godly preaching ministry', a dominant and even normative model in the post-Reformation Church of England. By the 1570s it was usual for Kentish clergy to call themselves 'minister and preacher of the word', while in Surrey 'minister of the word' was the style used in almost all clergy wills by 1600.[4] The common currency of these terms accompanied the creeping 'graduatisation' of the parish clergy, the process of converting it into a more or less learned profession described by Dr Rosemary O'Day.[5] A secondary consequence of this development was to convert Puritanism from a stridently alien and minority tendency into the dominant religious culture of the Jacobean Church.[6] Dr Helena Hajzyk found that in early seventeenth-century Lincolnshire those professionally competent parsons who set themselves against the godly model, on some such ideological basis as the ideas of Richard Hooker or 'Arminianism', made up a tiny minority of scarcely half a dozen.[7] So this is some indication of what we shall understand by 'shepherd'.

The further difference implied in my title between shepherd and sheepdog is less canonical, if only on account of certain basic differences in the practice of animal husbandry between the biblical Near East and the Christian West. But it was present in the Church nevertheless, as a tension between pastoral care and a coercive discipline with punitive overtones. When Martin Luther defined the Church as the sheep who hear their shepherd's whistle this was an echo of Psalm 23, where the flock is not driven but led.[8] The old and New Testaments are silent on the subject of sheepdogs. So when Protestant controversialists sharpened their pens against the Romish Wolf who menaces the sheep and from whose approach the careless hireling flees, their pastoral borrowed from the more secular metaphors of the hunting field.[9] But Isaiah 56 v. 10 complains of dumb dogs that cannot bark, a text which was often invoked in the denunciation of non-preaching hirelings. The text presumably refers to watchdogs. But the function of sheepdogs too, in pastoral literature, was to bark in urgent warning at the approach of the wolf. The funerary brass of Bishop Henry Robinson of Carlisle, designed in about 1610 by Richard Haydocke, shows such a dog standing stoutly between the wolf and the flock which he refuses to desert, clearly the sheep's faithful friend.[10] And in the September eclogue of *The Shepheardes Calender* we meet Roffyn's vigilant and vocal Lowder: 'Never had a shepheard so kene a kurre, / That watcheth, and if but a leafe sturre.' 'Roffyn' was evidently meant for Spenser's employer, Bishop Young of Rochester. Perhaps 'Lowder' was his chancellor, or generally symbolic of the corrective, even punitive apparatus of the ecclesiastical courts.

Such 'keen curs' 'with wide open throte' remind us that the pastoral ministry could itself be intrusively aggressive as well as protective. Addressing his fellow clergy in Somerset in 1615, Samuel Crooke insisted that it was their proper role as ministers to preside over a 'reformation of manners' (an early use of an expression which was to have a great future), to 'rise up first in the Lord's quarrel', attacking 'the troops of armed and audacious enemies, I meane sinners'. Here were the beginnings of that new symbiosis of spiritual and secular government summed up in the slogan 'magistracy and ministry' and celebrated by Samuel Ward of Ipswich when he spoke of 'these two opticke peeces', 'guardians and tutors of the rest'. Another preacher invoked the sword of the magistracy and the bow of the ministry.[11]

However we cannot state it as a simple and exhaustive fact that the ministry became in this period a crudely coercive instrument of so-called 'social control', all bark and bite. The formal record of the church courts gives one impression, the stray correspondence which accompanied court proceedings but survives more scantily, sometimes stuck between the leaves of act books, another. In one such note Robert Abbot of Cranbrook asked the court at Canterbury to spare one of his more timid parishioners the trauma of public penance: 'I would willingly winne him by more gentle courses if I may'.[12] And the parsons of the twin parishes of Toynton in Rutland wrote to ask that a poor labourer might be relieved of his formal excommunication: 'Who is so pore that he is not able eyther to paye that charges or sustaine the cost that he shall be at in the iourney.'[13] In Durham diocese the clergy were presumably no slower than elsewhere to condemn incontinence. But at Hurworth the rector took the lead in organising public relief for the mother of a bastard, while in Durham city the curates regularly stood as godfathers to illegitimate children.[14]

So much for shepherds, hirelings and sheepdogs, the first and ornamental part of my title. What follows takes a more direct path to the subject, but not a very hopeful one, since I shall propose that it is more difficult to write about the pastoral ministry in this period than at almost any other time in the history of the English church and churches, whether medieval or modern. And that is because of a credibility gap standing between what the ministry was supposed to have consisted of according to nearly all public discussion of the matter at the time and what we know, or may think that we know, it must really have entailed, although that reality is seen through a glass, somewhat darkly. To anticipate much of what follows: public and what we may call abstracted accounts of the ministry in the later sixteenth and early seventeenth centuries (the period in question is roughly 1570 to 1640) were restricted to a remarkable extent to one function and one function only, that of preaching, or preaching and catechising: a bias built into these sources themselves, since often they consist of sermons delivered, for example, at ordinations, or prove as books to have been derived from courses of sermons. Sometimes contemporary commentators, especially those reacting against the prevalent Calvinism of the English church in a more or less Arminian direction, objected to this unbalanced obsession with the pulpit, as if the human body had been reduced to a single organ and that organ the ear. Yet it is sufficiently remarkable that those who insisted that prayer rather than preaching was what the ministry was about should have been so many lone voices crying in the wind. I doubt whether Matthew 21 v. 13 ('mine house shall be called the house of prayer') was much preached upon between 1598, when John Howson took it as his text at Paul's Cross, and 1633, when Walter Balcanquall handled it in the presence of Charles I and asked: can there be too much preaching? 'Yes, there may be too much of anything'.[15] But where were these and similar complaints expressed? In sermons.

Of course we know that the life of a clergyman, even if he called himself 'preacher of the word', consisted of more than preaching. In an often quoted account of his burdens, John Favour, vicar of Halifax, explained that his controversial writings were squeezed into a routine which otherwise included not only preaching on Sundays and lecturing on every other day of the week but also 'exercising justice in the commonwealth' and the 'practising of Physick and Chirurgerie'.[16] There was also a living to be made, collecting tithe and sometimes suing for it, working the glebe and seeking out those supplementary pieces of by-employment and enterprise which earned Ralph Josselin a little more than his 'living' and which made the difference between Micawberish misery and happiness.[17] To dwell only on those ways of spending time which may be deemed professional: we know that they included above all the conduct of common prayer and the administration of the sacraments, weddings, churching women, baptising babies, catechising children, visiting the sick, burying the dead, reproving the wicked and comforting bruised consciences. The minister had a role to play with other parish officers in reporting offences and offenders to higher authority, administering and certifying acts of penance, denouncing excommunicates. He and the material resources at his disposal were involved in parochial charity. Time was spent in study (the night time in Favour's case) and in the company of other clergy, for the purpose of what is now called in universities career development.

One may well imagine that of all these many activities the most significant in the estimation of the laity had to do with the occasional offices, which in anthropological language is to say those rites of passage which are the punctuation marks of all our life-cycles. These occasions, invested as they were with the inevitability of life and death and the capacity to make and break, resolve and dissolve the bonds of human society, brought the parish clergy into the most meaningful and certainly the most earth-bound of their involvements with their flocks. These offices, as well as the sacramental office of ministering communion, interlocked with what John Bossy has identified as the primary social task entrusted to the parish priest or his equivalent throughout the rural parishes of Europe between the fourteenth and seventeenth centuries, that of a settler of conflicts, the principal instrument of what Bossy has elsewhere called the social miracle.[18]

Many of these scenes from clerical life are under-explored, some are unexplored and a few are almost unexplorable. Almost to excess we have studied the formation of the clergy, their recruitment through the multiple processes of higher education, ordination, patronage and preferment, their incomes and livelihood, their quality in terms of residence, moral behaviour and, above all, capacity to preach: which makes the point that academic studies of the post-Reformation clergy reflect the limited concerns of contemporary comment on the subject, as well as the original sources which, as it were, deep-freeze those concerns. These studies embody the static qualities and methods of administrative and prosopographical history and they tell us very little about activity, what the clergy did in a day, a week, or a year. So from a very substantial body of scholarly literature we do not learn about such matters as whether baptism was administered (as the Prayer Book directs) in a congregational context, at the time of common prayer, or more privately at other times, and at which times; whether the clergy visited the sick and dying according to commonly recognised rules and at prescribed times, and what rules and times; or how their pastoral visits to other parishioners interacted with habits and rhythms of hospitality and according to what social conventions; and what, in the absence of a sacramental economy of supreme unction and auricular confession, was said on such occasions. Would the threatened visit of the minister lead to an onslaught on household dirt, as in modern Scotland? I have already had my say elsewhere about the failure of historians to consider the English clergy in this period as a social and collegiate group or 'tribe' (to use a contemporary expression), sharing each other's company not only at synods and what George Herbert called 'clergy councels', but at combination lectures, funeral sermons and concomitant dinners which invariably accompanied these events; or simply over business at market or travelling to and from market. It was emphatically not the case that every parish was a desert island and its incumbent Robinson Crusoe in a Geneva gown.[19]

Some of the neglected corners of the clerical life will not remain in shadow for much longer. Dr Ralph Houlbrooke and Mr Christopher Marsh tell us only a little less about the terminal pastoral ministry than Professor McManners knows about deathbeds in eighteenth-century France.[20]

Other subjects are capable of recovery from sources which are still too little used, but which are also somewhat limited and deceptive in their utility. The occasional offices are illuminated from the church courts both by instance causes between parties and by office causes, which is to say, quasi-criminal prosecutions. Cases detailing a state of hostility between parson and parishioners contain the bias of untypicality which made them criminal, or actionable, in the first place. But normality can sometimes be inferred from abnormality. The vicar of Selling in Kent offended when he conducted the ceremony of 'churching' from his own seat without calling the woman who was to give thanks up to the communion table. The Prayer Book rubric will tell us that that is what he should have done, for it directs the women to kneel 'in some convenient place nigh unto the place where the table standeth', with the vicar standing by. But only the kind of evidence given in this case informs us that in this parish at least churchings were conducted immediately after morning prayer. When the vicar of Wye refused to church women who came to the ceremony wearing kerchiefs 'as the custome hath bene in tymes past', when he failed to meet the dead corpse at the church gate or stile, and when he remained seated throughout the marriage service except to rise to ask who gave the bride in marriage, failing to put the ring on her finger, we can infer normal practice which may not be otherwise recorded. The last detail, for example, confirms that marriages took place, in this parish at least, inside the church (the rubric requiring that 'the persons to be married shall come into the body of the church') and not, as we sometimes assume to have been the case, at the church door.[21]

But depositions in matrimonial causes usually concern marriages which failed to take place, and so they tell us less about weddings, when the minister was present, than about betrothals, from which he was normally absent.[22] Actionable slander not infrequently happened around a child-bed, among a group of gossips, not at christenings, which women, mothers at least, seem not to have attended. It was an unexpected bonus for the historian when the title-tattle at a confinement in Canterbury in 1579 turned to the subject of the vicar of St George's, Mr Saunders, and to the offence which he had occasioned by rebuking the women of the parish for taking their prayer books with them to church in order to follow the service in the somewhat private manner of the old religion.[23] These sources often reveal the parson in Professor Bossy's role of peace-making among quarrelsome neighbours, sitting, as it might be, in a great seat in the church or even on an alebench. But such episodes appear as snapshots, frozen in a moment of time. Outside the record left by a very few diarists it is difficult to reconstruct regular rhythms of activity, or to answer the question once put by a child within my hearing of a certain rhinoceros in the Zoo: 'But what does he do *all day*?'

Yet it is unlikely that these rhythms were a matter of idiosyncratic whim or circumstance. Social pressures, collegial and professional, tended towards a regularity of practice. The Dedham ministers, meeting in monthly conference on the Suffolk-Essex border in the 1580s, sought a common mind on such matters as 'the right use of the lordes daie', the baptism of children born to pregnant brides, and whether all their parishes should administer communion on the same day. Richard Parker, vicar of Dedham and clerk of the conference, wanted to know 'whether a pastor were bound by virtue of his office to visite every particular family in his charge notwithstanding his public teaching; so that if he do it not he omittes a duty'. In response he received a variety of conflicting advice. Yet the point is that the Dedham ministers in principle accepted that they should follow a more or less consistent practice, even if this was made up of case law of their own devising.[24] Much standard pastoral technique must have been acquired in the informal apprenticeship schemes or mini-seminaries conducted in their households by such celebrated divines and preachers as Bernard Gilpin, Richard Greenham, John Cotton and Richard Blackerby.[25] But whatever Elizabethan and Jacobean clerics learned from their colleagues or mentors it was not a lore recorded in instructive manuals for the ministry since there were no such manuals, in stark contrast to the fourteenth and fifteenth centuries when there was an abundance of more or less technical literature bearing such titles as *Oculus Sacerdotis* and the related *Pupilla Oculi*, the *Memoriale Presbiterorum* and John Mirk's *Instructiones*, which remained in print up to the 1530s.[26]

It is an exaggeration to say that no such written advice was supplied to the post-Reformation clergy. There was an Elizabethan and Jacobean literature of exhortation on the ministerial office which bears the same sort of relation to the real circumstances of clerical life as domestic conduct literature, books like Gouge's *Of domesticall duties* or Whateley's *Bride bush*, seems to have borne to marriage and parenthood in the same period.[27] But if anything the scene set by these texts is rather less satisfactory, since Gouge and Whateley dealt with many aspects of family life and in principle with the whole of it, whereas books which profess to be about the ministry have nothing to say about most aspects of their subject, as viewed with any descriptive objectivity. So we can say that the first great age of print saw less matter published on many facets of this subject (of all subjects) than on bee-keeping, or the management of great horses, or the husbandry of hops.

So far I have taken up a prejudicial position against such titles as John Holme's *The burthen of the ministerie* (1592), William Perkins's *Of the calling of the ministerie* (1605), Samuel Crooke's *The ministeriall husbandry and building* (1615), or George Downame's sermon of 1608, *Commending the ministerie*. But let us by all means hear what these teachers have to say. Downame declares that 'the principall burden and chiefe worke of the Ministery . . . is the preaching, that is the expounding and applying of the word to the diverse uses of doctrine, confutation, instruction and reproofe.' So far he says no more than the Council of Trent which defined preaching as '*munus praecipuum*'. But Downame comes close to making it *munus solum*. On the subject of 'the Leiturgie or publike service of God in the Congregation', he found space for just 164 words; on the administration of the sacraments, for 140 words.[28] And on other duties there were no words at all. Charles Richardson, preacher at St Katherine's by the Tower, laid down in *A workeman that needeth not to be ashamed . . . A sermon describing the duty of a godly minister* (1616) that the function consisted first in private study, second in frequent prayer, and third, 'in diligent preaching of God's word'. Only the last of these was a public action and no other public action was mentioned.[29]

Other treatments of the subject are indicative of their contents by their very titles: for example, Stephen Egerton's *The boring of the ear* (1623) and Samuel Hieron's university discourse *The spiritual fishing* (1618), which contains this metaphorical conceit, worthy of Archdeacon Paley himself: 'For as the fishes skippe and play and take their pleasure in the sea, and are unwillingly taken in the net, and labour to get out, and being in the boate would faine, if they could, leape backe into the sea; so naturally we take pleasure in our sinfull wayes'; it being God's contrary purpose 'by man to catch man, and by his ministerie to bring soules into his kingdome'. 'Fishes do die if they be taken; wee can not escape eternall death if we be not caught'.[30] The argument for a preaching ministry consisted in the stark fact that there was no salvation to be had without it. Downame declares: 'The necessitie is that without it ordinarily men cannot attain to salvation, no nor yet to any degree of salvation.' So Edward Dering spoke exaltedly of 'the minister by whom the people do beleeve'.[31] This reminds us that the difference between the pre- and post-Reformation churches lay not so much in the emphasis put upon preaching as in its motive and object. William of Pagula told fourteenth-century priests that 'all their work should be in preaching and teaching', but not because that was the only way that souls could be redeemed.[32]

One of the most substantial treatments of the ministry published within our period was *The faithfull shepherd* by Richard Bernard, some time a radical Puritan plucked back from the brink of Separatism and transported by the great and the good of the Jacobean Church from Nottinghamshire to Batcombe in Somerset.[33] An outsider to this discussion might suppose that a book 355 pages in length and with such a title, written for the benefit of ordinands, 'to further young divines in the studie of divinitie', might deal in a fully-rounded fashion with a whole range of professional and practical skills. Not so. After some preliminary, defensive discussion of the ministry as a worthy calling which gentlemen ought not to despise, distinguishing between the worthy and the unworthy who secured livings 'not to feed Christes flock but only to maintaine themselves with the fleece', the entire contents were devoted to the minister as preacher. Chapter Two 'of a mans fitness to the ministerie' proves to be about his fitness for the pulpit: 'It is fit that there be a comely bodily presence of a Minister, standing up in the face of the Congregation, and in the place of God . . . a comely countenance, sober, grave, modest, . . . a seemly gesture, stable and upright'. There is a long taxonomical chapter dealing with pastoral sociology and psychology and distinguishing between six kinds of people in a typical congregation. But they are defined exclusively in respect of their various responses to the word preached. Book Three has for its subject 'The Public Assembly', but includes nothing about the liturgy and sacraments, or rather only this: 'The Minister and man of God well prepared, the godly order of Divine Service, so called, as it is by the Church appoynted, without giving of offence observed, and as the custome is, after a Psalm sung; then may he ascend up into the Pulpit'. Once there we reach Book Four, 'The Method to be Observed in Preaching', which runs to 200 pages, or almost two-thirds of the entire text.[34] If Bernard's treatise be taken as representative of early seventeenth-century treatments of its subject this literature contrasts not only with the pastoral science associated with what may be called the seminarian approach to priesthood and ministry in more recent times but with what was available for the instruction of apprentice priests up to the 1530s. And what is more, as an ideal it must surely have conflicted with much early seventeenth-century reality.

The exception which may seem to prove the rule is George Herbert's *Priest to the Temple*, the book more familiarly known from its sub-title as *The Countrey Parson*. Here we find distinct chapters on 'The Parson's Charity' and 'The Parson in Circuit', that is, as parochial visitor. 'The Countrey Parson upon the afternoons in the weekdays, takes occasion sometimes to visite in person, now one quarter of his Parish, now another', for there he finds his flock 'most naturally as they are, wallowing in the midst of their affairs'. Sunday afternoons were to be spent 'either in reconciling neighbours that are at variance, or in visiting the sick, or in exhortations to some of his flock by themselves'. Further passages follow on 'The Parson Comforting', 'The Parson in Sacraments', 'The Parson Blessing'.[35] It is clear that here is a different set of values from those of Bernard, in conventional perspective Anglican rather than Puritan or 'godly' values. There is a conspicuous contrast between Herbert's condescension to country habits and customs, 'if they be good and harmlesse', and the contempt expressed for these things by such a Puritan as George Gifford, author of *The countrie divinitie* (1581), or by the Northamptonshire preachers Robert Bolton and Joseph Bentham with their caustic denunciation of so-called 'good fellowship'.[36] Herbert's parson 'condescends even to the knowledge of tillage, and pastorage . . . because people by what they understand, are best led to what they understand not.'[37]

But some words of caution are necessary before we conclude that Herbert furnished what was otherwise lacking from the resources of the early Stuart Church: an instructional manual for an Anglican priesthood. For one thing *The Countrey Parson* is not an instructional manual of any kind but a piece of expanded character literature, as its title proclaims, 'The Countrey Parson, His *Character*'. It is an example of that subtle parody of the Theophrastan character, the idealised and edifying character: written indeed for Herbert's own edification, 'a Mark to aim at' in his ministry at Bemerton and not published until twenty years after the author's premature death.[38] Like the poems comprising *The Temple* (which however were published immediately after the poet's decease by Nicholas Ferrar and which were in their fifth edition by 1638), these were evidently somewhat 'private ejaculations'. We have also to note that Herbert's stress on preaching, if somewhat differently premissed, is not much less than we find among his 'godly' contemporaries. The difference, as I have suggested elsewhere, was that between 'godliness' and 'holiness' and it was not an enormous difference.[39] Nor should we expect any absolute difference in a Calvinist (of a kind) like Herbert, who could write of God's providence in predestination:

> Wherefore if thou canst fail,
> Then can thy truth, and I.

So, says Herbert, 'The Country Parson preacheth constantly, the pulpit is his joy and his throne.' Even his pastoral visits are directed particularly towards those 'whom his sermons cannot, or doe not reach'. Herbert indeed differs from the godly school in nowhere suggesting that sermons are a unique instrumentality for the conversion of souls, so standing in a succession which, as Peter Lake has demonstrated, was not so much Arminian as Hookerian[40] — and both pre-Protestant and a-Protestant. But he was typical and wholly of his time in the didactic assumptions which govern every line of *The Countrey Parson*, including the first two lines : 'A Pastor is the Deputy of Christ for the reducing of Man to the Obedience of God.' *The Temple* was not only metaphorically architectonic (which is sufficiently obvious) and Protestant (something insisted upon since Joseph Summers wrote on Herbert and Barbara Lewalski published her *Protestant Poetics*) but in form a kind of catechism with a close affinity to that fundamentally Pauline and Protestant concept of edification explored by John Coolidge, in which the essentiality of preaching is seen to consist in the fabrication of a living temple out of lively stones.[41]

I have already disclosed my scepticism about the 'mark to aim at', whether of Herbert or of his more puritanical contemporaries, if it is to be taken as a decriptive account of how, in fact, the bulk of the early seventeenth-century clergy understood and acted out their role. Such scepticism is as much in order as when historians reading domestic conduct books doubt whether they provide a realistic description of early modern family life. To say no more, the transcendent totalitarianism of the theory necessarily overlooks the phenomenon known to sociologists as 'routinisation'. Parochial circumstances must have imposed a certain constraining routine on all but the most exceptionally inspired of ministers.

However, before that argument is extended it is necessary to examine with an equally critical scepticism the suggestions of some recent historians that the model of the godly preaching ministry, far from representing the only legitimate expression of valid pastoral care, was utterly antipathetic to many of the social and cultural contexts in which it asserted itself, and perhaps to all save certain favourable urban contexts. Consequently it was bound to fail, since Protestant preaching was intellectualy over-demanding, morally and culturally oppressive, and instrumentally unrelated to the real needs of ordinary people. These were better served by sacraments and sacramentals working on the traditional principle of *ex opere operato*, not to say by magic, and performed by a kind of folk or at least folksy clergy cut from the same homespun as their parishioners.[42]

Perhaps the most extreme statement of this prejudice (for I am not sure that it is much more respectable than a prejudice) was made by Christopher Haigh when he pronounced this verdict on evidence of the failure of the quintessentially godly Richard Greenham to cut much ice in his parish of Dry Drayton: 'If Richard Greenham, of all men, in Cambridgeshire of all counties, could not make committed Protestants of more than a tiny handful of his parishioners, then nobody could and the task was impossible. In Elizabethan conditions . . . the English people *could not* [Haigh's italics] be made Protestants'.[43] But how reliable is the evidence of Greenham's failure? It occurs in what is, in effect, his obituary and consists of these few words in explanation of his withdrawal to London: 'The causes of his Removal were partly the untractableness and unteachableness of that people amongst whom he had taken such exceeding great pains'. The author's motive was to explain why his hero deserted a parochial charge for a more lucrative and comfortable post in London as a lecturer or 'doctor', and this he did partly by reference to an untractable people but also by informing the reader that Greenham had built up a nation-wide practice in the resolving of afflicted consciences which required a London base.[44] Whether the people of Dry Drayton were really so unresponsive remains uncertain[45] (One recalls Thomas Settle's complaint against the inhabitants of Mildenhall 'being frozen in their dregges, which seeme to have made their large Fen their God'.[46]) It is certainly possible and Greenham himself taught as a general principle that 'Ministers should most frequent those places where God hath made their Ministerie most fruitfull: they should heerein be like the covetous man, that where they have once found the sweetnesse of gaining of soules, thither they should be most desirous to resort'.[47] Compatibility was all. It was Dry Drayton's misfortune, perhaps, to be so close to that powerhouse of militantly evangelical Protestantism which was Cambridge University, as it was Greenham's to be stuck with Dry Drayton: two incompatibles who were probably wise to part, with Greenham shaking the dust (or washing the mud) off his feet. But as the basis for a comprehensive indictment of the supposed failure of the godly preaching ministry in its entirety the case is evidentially almost worthless.

That the preacher was liable to fail in his object was a commonplace, the commonplace of the Parable of the Sower on which George Gifford preached in Essex and William Harrison in Lancashire.[48] The parable finds fault with the unsuitable soils on which most of the seed fell, rather than with the seed or the sower. Already in Edward VI's reign Latimer's court preaching had made this point: there was no fault in preaching. 'The lack is in the people, that have stony hearts and thorny hearts'.[49] But the great John Dod was only one of many Jacobean commentators to blame the sower as well, complaining that 'most ministers in England usually shoot over the heads of their hearers'. Richard Bernard insisted that the minister must take stock of his people, 'what sort of people as they bee'. 'For as they bee, so must hee deale with them'. 'He that is a Pastour must informe the ignorant, urge men of knowledge of sanctification, reclaim the vicious, encourage the vertuous, convince the erroneous, strengthen the weak, recall the back-slider, resolve such as doubt, confirme the resolved, and comfort the afflicted'.[50] Elizabethan and Jacobean preachers cannot be accused of underestimating the complexity of this task and it is unreasonable to make a wholly negative assessment of the didactic instincts and methods of the church in this period. Such a basic device as dividing the biblical text into verses implies a realistic sense of how uneducated or poorly educated minds work. As Dr Peter Jensen has remarked of this innovation, it imparted to the Bible 'an oracular, aphoristic nature'. 'The text was to be absorbed piece by piece, word by word'. Whatever its theological consequences, which those nostalgic for a more humanistic, less sententious Protestantism may regard as deplorable, this was not necessarily a mistaken pedagogical method.[51]

Dr Jensen has remarked that those who listened to sermons and read their Bibles 'did so with faculties trained by catechisms'. We should only write off the effectiveness of the instructive ministry when we have carefully considered the almost universal practice of the catechism and found it wanting. Catechising, according to Herbert, was the first point in the parson's repertoire and without it the other two, the infusion of saving knowledge and the building up of knowledge into a spiritual temple, were not attainable. 'Socrates did thus in Philosophy'.[52] Richard

Bernard, who was the author of two catechisms and of a treatise on the subject,[53] wrote in *The faithfull shepherd*: 'Experience shewes how little profit comes by preaching, where catechizing is neglected'.[54] The more obscure Richard Kilby, a curate of Derby who was often too ill or too disorganised to preach and who used a catechising method instead, turned necessity into a virtue and advocated the more extensive and creative use of that medium. The common sort were 'very grossely ignorant', but also 'much neglected', since most sermons were unfit for their 'lowe and small capacities'. 'For ought I know', Kilby went on, such persons had a greater appetite for the things of God than many of higher degree and greater understanding, but they needed to be plainly and briefly taught. Instead of which the often interminable sermon left them wondering: 'When will yonder man have done?'[55]

The flood of published catechisms has been seen as evidence in itself for a perception of pastoral failure,[56] a response to the spectacle of nominal Protestantism and to a kind of crisis in the presentation of the Protestant doctrines of faith and assurance.[57] But in view of the volume of that flood we should perhaps stress the perception and response to failure rather than failure itself. Dr Green counts an astonishing total of 350 catechitical titles printed in the century from 1549 to 1646, and this is far from a complete tally of all catechisms published, let alone unpublished. Some were best-sellers: the More-Dering catechism, over forty editions, Paget-Openshawe, at least thirty-one, Perkins over thirty, Egerton forty-three by 1635 (the earliest surviving edition being the sixteenth), Ball thirty-three by 1645. Some of the titles are indicative of the degree of condescension implicit in the enterprise of exploring the mysteries of religion plainly and economically. In the preface to his catechism, Francis Inman wrote of 'poore servants and laborers . . . aged persons of weake and decaied memories'. 'Yet all these have immortall soules . . . of these care must be had.' William Crashawe's 'North Country Catechism' was called 'milke for babes', Samuel Hieron's west country catechism was 'short for memory, plaine for capacity'.[58]

Bernard's method was admirable and perhaps influential. (We are told that 'diverse painfull and profitable labourers in the Lordes vineyard had their first *initiation* and *direction* from and under him'.[59]) This was his advice: Let the people learne word for word, by rote. 'Interrupt not beginners with interpretations . . . Goe not beyond their conceits; stay somewhat for an answer but not too long; if one know not, help him and encourage him by commending his willingnesse . . . Teach with cheerful countenance, familiary and lovingly'. With exquisite tact William Lyford told his people: 'You first directed and taught me, how to teach you'.[60]

There can be no attempt made on this occasion to measure the degree of success eventually obtained towards the middle decades of the seventeenth-century by these and more advanced methods of indoctrination, such as the almost universal practice of sermon repetition.[61] In the *longue durée* of the English reformation process it would be premature to draw up a balance sheet much earlier than 1640. It may be that many, even most people beneath a certain economic and social level, or below a certain age, remained resistant. The teachers and preachers often said so, but from polemical and rhetorical motives which limit the value of their testimony. No doubt Protestantism in its didactic and demanding presentation was selective and divisive, like education and literacy sowing the seeds of a kind of sectarianism. But to acknowledge that this was not a religion for all should not blind our eyes to its attractiveness for some, like the women at Wye in Kent who on summer evenings came to the house of the curate Mr Gulliforde at eight or nine of the clock until late, 'as yt is sayd, at prayer'; or the 'divers gentlewomen' of that part of Kent who dined with Mr Gulliforde after his Thursday lectures, paying two shillings and sixpence each for the privilege.[62]

   That the religious and even the theological concerns of country and small town clergy were capable of being communicated to some at least of their hearers is suggested by the affair of the Lincolnshire minister William Williams, rector of two rural parishes near Sleaford. This case is the discovery of Dr Helena Hajzyk.[63] Williams was a proto-Arminian who imported into deepest Lincolnshire the anti-Calvinist doctrines taught in Cambridge by Peter Baro and refuted in the Lambeth Articles of 1595. For these opinions, and specifically for a provocative visitation sermon preached at Sleaford in June 1598, Williams was denounced to Bishop Chaderton by his fellow clergy. Dr Hajzyk is fascinated, as well she may be, by the light cast by the cause papers surviving with exceptional richness from this prosecution on Williams's dealings with other ministers of the district, not only at sermons and other clerical gatherings but 'sitting in Sleaford market place upon a seate there', or riding to and from Sleaford and Lincoln. She plausibly suggests that this fierce controversy was the reason not only why Bishop Barlow later refused to sanction a combination lecture at Sleaford but why in 1614 Bishop Neile's visitors reported that at the visitation dinner held in the town there was no talk at all of divinity matters.[64]

But of equal interest in the Sleaford affair is evidence of the intelligent response to Williams's heresies of some of the more substantial townspeople. In August 1598 there was a meeting held in a chamber of the Angel Inn and attended not only by the clergy but by two local gentlemen, a seventy-one year-old mercer, a thirty-three year-old iron-monger, and three self-styled yeomen, aged forty-four, thirty-eight and thirty-four, including the landlord, George Gladwin. On this occasion the company heard Williams affirm baptismal regeneration (which the wife of one of the gentlemen present, Mrs Burton, said he had also taught in two christening sermons which she had heard); and that 'an elected man might fall away from grace totallie', as David did 'in his adulterie and murder'. Everyone knew that the word 'totally' was of crucial significance. The ironmonger, William Barrow, who had often heard Williams 'speake somewhat disdainfullie of God's predestination', told him that no learned man in England was of his opinion, that is, that the elect can fall irrevocably from grace. Williams responded: 'Yea, that there were, for my lord grace of Canterbury was of his opinion'. Everyone present remembered this dramatic and scandalous claim, which related to Williams's direct dealings with Archbishop Whitgift and a number of ranking Cambridge theologians and heads of houses. William Burton of Aldingham put an anxious question: 'Are we not to believe that there ys predestination?' Both Mrs Burton and William Scochie reported that it was generally thought and by some uttered that if Mr Williams were not punished his hearers would have to conclude that his doctrine was right and true. One wonders how many converts to 'Arminianism' Williams made, for he was not punished but managed to have his case transferred to the Court of Arches which left him unmolested and free to preach in and around Sleaford for another forty years.

How 'general' was the concern about predestination voiced by Mrs Burton? How widespread interest in the proposition that baptised children dying before actual sin were regenerated, leading Williams's hearers to believe, or so complained the bishop, that the sacraments confer grace *de facto*? Perhaps quite general, surprisingly widespread, although a majority of the inhabitants of Sleaford below the rank of ironmonger may have cared little for such niceties. It may be that the intensification of the debate about the terms and title-deeds of salvation, together with rising professional standards and collegial pressures, had the effect of spiritually disfranchising the majority. Of the famous Northamptonshire preacher Robert Bolton it was said that 'he prepared nothing for his people but what might have served a very learned Auditory'.[65] (And yet Bolton's published sermons are fine examples of the so-called 'plain style'.) 'Christian Reader', explained the Leicestershire minister Anthony Cade in introducing a published sermon: 'the concourse of many learned Ministers at our Ordinary Monthly Lecture. . .whereunto now also resorted . . . many learned juditious gentlemen required matter of more then ordinary worth and learning. To satisfie whome, if I have layed the grounds of my Sermon more Schoole-like then thou thinkest fitte for the Country, beare with mee . . .'[66] But most Elizabethan and Jacobean sermons were doubtless more 'fit for the country' than for publication and those which were published may give a false impression of the typical level of learned sophistication at which such discourses were pitched.

Nor should we underestimate the sensitivity of the palates of country sermon-tasters. In the early 1580s the Kentish village of Egerton, a religiously serious community on the northern edge of the Weald,[67] was subjected to the irregular ministrations of a hedge priest called Edward Hudson. The inhabitants could easily distinguish between the real MacCoy and the incoherent tale-telling which was Hudson's idea of a sermon. When Hudson expounded the text 'God so loved the world' and went on about kissing and cuddling and 'thank God all love was not lost', assuring the congregation that he would not fob them off with stories of St Francis or of a 'roasted horse', they smelt a rat. John Wythers, a fifty-year-old weaver, Simon Wolton, a thirty-nine-year-old clothier, Ralph Elston, a forty-five-year-old butcher and a young farmer Robert Spycer, were all contemptuous of Hudson's 'fryvolous tales', his 'fond speeches tending to no man's edification', the butcher reporting that 'the sobrest sort of the auditory . . . were much offended at his so light and undiscreet toyes then uttered', when, said another parishioner, 'godly preaching and good information to the edification of Gods people ought to be in the fear of God reverently to be done'. Spycer said that Hudson's speeches were applied 'to no purpose at all'. The butcher knew that Hudson was speaking out of turn when he claimed that whenever he was at a deathbed 'he could have an ayme which way that party should go'. Wolton the clothier was offended in conscience when Hudson taught that the people would be saved whether they had communion or not. And even if the parishioners sympathised with Hudson's nonconformity they knew it was an offence against decorum to refer to the surplice as a 'whore's weed'.[68] At Hawkhurst in the same county a sixty-year old miller, a forty-seven year old clotheir, and a young husbandman were all sufficiently alert after an hour-long sermon on the gospel for the day to know that their curate was digressing from his text in making a gratuitous attack on the sexual mores of the rich, which a local worthy interpreted as a personal attack upon himself. They were able to give an exact account in court of the words in question.[69]

So much for preaching. But what are we to say of the bulk of the minister's vocation, that nine-tenths of the iceberg below the surface of the evidence which was the non-preaching ministry, or at least the ministry when not engaged in preaching? It is a paradox that we are able to say least about that function which competed with preaching as the bread and butter of the job, the reading of common prayer and the conduct of public worship: and it must be a paradox since if we count up the time spent on this activity by a normally conscientious incumbent in a full year, morning and evening prayers, Wednesdays and Fridays and holy days as well as Sundays, the common prayers and readings, litany and ante-communion, we are talking about not less than five hundred hours, in a lifetime's ministry perhaps twenty thousand hours. But this is not a paradox confined to the sixteenth and seventeenth centuries. From the early nineteenth-century Somerset diary of William Holland it is difficult to say much about Holland's inner disposition to what he called 'the Duty', that is, the duty of conducting divine worship in his two parishes. On Sunday, 8 September 1805 the church at Overstowey was 'uncommonly full'. But what Holland found memorable about that day was the unusual quantity of wasps' nests encountered along the road to Overstowey. 'They were burnt out and smoking and the places startled the horse several times.'[70] It is tempting but would be unwise to conclude that 'the Duty' was for Holland as much a routine as his regular Saturday night chore of winding up all the clocks before retiring to bed. But what if it was? Historians (unlike anthropologists) are not best qualified to evaluate routine.

It is not difficult to find Elizabethans of the godly school who took a wholly negative view of liturgy. John Field, the voice of radical Elizabethan Puritanism, can speak for all when he complained not only of certain 'popish dregs' in the Prayer Book sevice but of its inordinate length, 'the quantity of thinges appointed to be reade, saide, songe or gone over', which was 'tedious'.[71] A Norfolk minister claimed to have read the appointed service with all the prayers and chapters, except, he disarmingly explained, when 'by reason of preaching I omitted them'. Radical Puritan practice seems to have discarded nearly everything, Venite, Te Deum, Creed, and Litany, retaining only the lessons, a few prayers, and the psalm, on which the Prayer Book was silent but which was now *de rigueur.*[72]

We are talking about a small minority of incorrigibly Puritan parishes. A more widespread and moderate practice was to read the whole service according to law but to omit certain objectionable ceremonies. In 1605 the vicar of Loughborough reported that kneeling at the communion, the sign of the cross in baptism and the surplice had been disused in the town 'all her Majesty's reign'.[73] At Loughborough it was the people who insisted on these omissions, just as in parishes of a different temper there were popular pressures to have the entire service as printed, whether we attribute that preference to 'Prayer Book Anglicans' or to 'church papists'.[74]

However, conformity, whether partial or complete, by the emphasis placed on legal compliance does not in itself suggest much positive enthusiasm for the liturgy. Elizabethan apologists for the *status quo* of the religious settlement defended ceremony and liturgical practice as things merely indifferent. In Peter Lake's phrase, 'they were there because they were there'.[75] In the diocese of Durham service books virtually disappeared from clerical inventories in this period, in marked contrast to the libraries of pre-Reformation clerics in which they predominated.[76] It appears that few Elizabethan and Jacobean clergy would have listed liturgy among their hobbies or private enthusiasms, or have joined the Henry Bradshaw Society. It was in pronounced and polemical reaction to this apparent contempt for the very principle as well as what Dom Gregory Dix called the shape of the liturgy that Hooker and Howson, and presently Andrewes and Buckeridge, began to insist on the supreme value of worship and prayer as the essential content of public religion, reflecting that churches were properly '*oratoria*', not '*auditoria*'. Hooker gloried in the length of liturgical services and even commended the Roman Church for regarding public prayer as 'a duty entire in itself'.[77] In 1598 Howson proclaimed at Paul's Cross that 'of all religious actions, prayer is reckoned the first and the chiefe', bitterly complaining that 'all the service of God is reduced to hearing of sermons'. In 1633 Walter Balcanquall spoke of a generation of fools who would run miles to hear a sermon 'but for the publike prayers of the Church, they will hardly crosse the street'.[78] But this was reactive and no more part of the main stream than Field's extreme Puritanism. Perhaps less so.

Communion presents an even greater problem, and mystery. Leaving aside the voice of rabid radicalism ('Do they make so much a do for chewinge a peece of bread and drinkinge a cupp of wine?'), [79] the generality of godly practice looks 'low', in the terms of modern churchmanship, but perhaps deceptively so. Dr Jeremy Boulton has established that in some of the larger London parishes communion was offered to householders no more than the canonical minimum of three times a year and perhaps only once, round about Easter, when the sacrament was almost universally received. But there were more select monthly communions for the parish elites, the members of what were now normally closed vestries.[80] That looks more like a social perk than extraordinary devotion on the part of the vestrymen. But it is very difficult to appreciate the spirit and motivation with which the sacrament was both administered and received: again the problem of routine. John Randall of the London parish of St Andrew Hubbert always preached on the subject of the Lord's supper before his monthly administration of it, and the gist of his doctrine was this: 'Nothing concerns your spirituall state more than the reverent and worthy receiving of this sacrament, no dutie more necessarie to be taught, no greater danger then the prophanation and abuse of it'.[81] That was the voice of the moderate Puritan tradition, not of sacramental 'Anglicanism'. Writing of the later seventeenth century, Dr Donald Spaeth suggests that reluctance to receive or to receive more than very occasionally may have implied not disrespect for the sacrament but the reverse: an almost superstitious dread of receiving unworthily, induced by the prohibitive tone of the Prayer Book prefaces and rubrics. That too was the legacy of Protestantism, even of Puritanism.[82]

And so, it may be, with the Prayer Book forms in the perception of the godly ministry. We cannot be sure that they were simply dismissed as a meaningless waste of time. This was a religious culture which took such a grave view of the language of vain and casual swearing that it became a scandal throughout Kent when it was rumoured that the bishop of Dover had said in public hearing 'By God's Soul!'[83] Is it likely that this tradition was indifferent to the language of solemn invocation in the public assembly? To deplore, with the New Testament, 'vain repetitions' was not to despise all repetitions whatsoever. But the devotional mood and temperature of the typical Elizabethan congregation and its president remains an impenetrable subject. Bowing at the name of Jesus and the sign of the cross were widely rejected as popish superstitions. But did English Protestants, like continental Calvinists, remove their hats every time God was named? We know all too little about hat drill in church. Standing to recite the Creed was spoken of in the House of Commons as if it was a rare innovation.[84] Kneeling for prayer on entering one's pew may have been conventional practice, then as now.[85] Yet some denounced it, together with 'putting the hat and hand before the face to pray', declaring that such 'private praying' was a sin. That was not to despise prayer but to insist on the fully corporate nature of common prayer, 'the worship of God in hand'.[86] So much for Puritan 'individualism'. When Herbert spoke of the parson in prayer as 'truly touched and amazed with the Majesty of God before whom he then presents himself' and with himself the whole congregation, this was not a narrowly Anglican in the sense of anti-Puritan sentiment, any more than Hooker went against contemporary standards of 'godliness' in insisting that the people should not repeat the prayers 'as Parrats' but as a reasonable service.

It remains to discuss the ministry in what, in the categories of the seminary, is taken to be the essentials of 'pastoralia', beyond and outside the public assembly and devoted situationally and clinically to the cure of souls. An Essex incumbent can serve to epitomise an alternative and, as it appears, older and more traditional model of the pastoral ministry than the 'godly' school so far discussed, practical, compassionate, and devoted to the unbroken continuum of the Christian community.[87] The question is whether or how far this tradition was suppressed by the superimposition of the godly preaching model. This incumbent, appropriately named Sheppard, was vicar of the obscure village of Heydon for forty-five years, as it happens the most critical forty-five years in the long history of the English Reformation and perhaps in the entire history of English Christianity, since they began in 1541, with the late Henrician Catholic reaction in full swing, and ended in 1586 on the eve of that event which, politically speaking, ensured the survival of Protestantism, the execution of Mary Queen of Scots. Sheppard, who was born in the days of Henry VII, that Indian Summer of the old religion, and lived to hear about the Spanish Armada, was already middle-aged when he came to Heydon as an ex-monk of the Augustinian Priory of Leeds in Kent. If we knew less than we do about this old Henrician it would be easy to dismiss him as one of those dumb dogs and hirelings who continued for too long to obstruct the onward march of Protestant evangelism. In fact, or so Mr Byford suggests on the basis of Sheppard's own record of his achievements, he, and perhaps others like him whose lifespan encompassed 'a series of conforming experiences', helped to ease the transition from the old religious world to a measure of adaptation to the new. 'Silent conformity need not have been the product of indifference'.

Yet the continuities of Sheppard's ministry are more in evidence than the discontinuities and he does seem to have embodied a number of old rather than new pastoral values. Indeed the motivation behind the chronicle of 'beneficiall good deeds' which he recorded in the parish register[88] speaks of a religion of 'good works', the old religion. Sheppard's good deeds included regular repairs and improvements to the church fabric over and above his legal responsibility for the upkeep of the chancel, many acts of charity including the provision of generous dowries for the girls of the village, and the making over of all his glebe land to the poorer inhabitants, together with the provision of causeways, bridges, fences and drainage ditches.[89] He also extended the village hall with the intention of promoting good fellowship among all his neighbours. The total value of these various bequests was £134 15s 4d., a quarter of his entire income as vicar of Heydon, and that before rather than after tax. Forty years after his death, Sheppard was still remembered as 'a liberall man and good to the poore'. He was a preacher but his one surviving sermon suggests that he confined himself to short homilies of a traditional kind, punctuated with many 'now good neybors' and 'therefore good neybors'.[90]

Sheppard may remind us a little of a more famous contemporary, himself initially ambivalent in his response to enforced religious change, the sainted apostle of the North, Bernard Gilpin. According to his biographer, Gilpin overflowed with charitable works, both casually spontaneous and as it were programmed, in the Sheppard style. He also conducted on a more heroic scale a notable ministry of reconciliation and extended hospitality to his parishioners at Houghton-le-Spring not only at Christmas, which was usual, but on every Sunday from Michaelmas to Easter.[91]

This kind of ministry, with its hallmark of active, practical, reconciling love must always have been somewhat exceptional, but as 'a mark to aim at' it is echoed in Herbert's *Countrey Parson*. And the question stands, was it temporarily thrust aside in the interim by the alien and less benign programme of the impatient godly ministry? Dr Haigh thinks so, characterising the post-Reformation Church as 'a more obviously repressive institution', served by university-trained professionals, more clericalist than the old priesthood and determined to replace meaningful ritual with incomprehensible Bible-reading and 'tedious sermons to pew-bound parishioners'. This figure was 'naturally less popular than his priestly predecessor'.[92] Possibly so. Dr Freeman found that in the diocese of Durham there were a hundred more tithe disputes in the five years 1595 to 1600 than there had been in 1577–82 and more than twice as many between 1629 and 1634. But for this trend there may have been more than one reason and Dr Freeman is too cautious to attribute the inflation in tithe litigation to personal or professional unpopularity.[93] More or less popularity cannot be so easily measured. On the one hand we hear the voice of the vicar of Gateshead, writing his will in 1571 and committing his 'deare and loving flocke' to 'the great Shepherd Jesus Christ . . . Fare well once agayne my deare and loving flocke';[94] or, sixty years later Robert Abbot of Cranbrook in Kent, rejoicing with Pauline fulsomeness in his 'deare and loving parishioners . . . my ioy and my crowne!'[95] On the other we hear the bitter recriminations of the rector of the Leicestershire village of Belleau who said that it ought to be called 'Helloe'.[96] No general conclusions are possible on the basis of this teeming and inconsistent evidence.

Nor can we jump to conclusions about discontinuity in traditional pastoral routines from the failure of godly ministers, one-eyed in their obsession with preaching, to mention them. Many recorded lives of ministers in the godly tradition suggest that Herbert's practice of door to door visitation was not as 'Anglican' and exceptional as it may seem.[97] However, if we may presume to confront these elusive topics of popularity, compatibility and effectiveness we must face one clear and easily established fact, not so far mentioned. William Sheppard, who gave away a quarter of his modest substance, was an unreconstructed lifelong celibate. Gilpin, who spent three quarters of his large income on his school and seminary at Houghton and other charities, commended the married state to the clergy — but was himself unmarried, or he could hardly have been as generous as he was. Herbert regarded virginity as a higher state than matrimony and wrote that the country parson was 'rather unmarryed than marryed'; although he was himself, like St Peter, a married man. Apart from other, theological considerations, for it or against it, a married clergy was in practice hard to reconcile with the proverb quoted in the Royal Injunctions of 1559: 'the goods of the Church are called the goods of the poor'. And to be sure, all that the Injunctions required by way of Christian charity was that non-resident incumbents worth no less than £20 a year should distribute a fortieth part of their income to the poor of the parish, which could be as little as eight shillings. And the Canons of 1604, all 141 of them, were utterly silent on the use of ecclesiastical revenues for charitable purposes. The Elizabethan Mr Quiverfull could barely afford to be as generous as the law required, let alone to emulate the example of the solitary Sheppard of Heydon. This the many critics of clerical marriage, sounding off in the public bar, knew very well.[98]

Perhaps the partner of the parson's great double bed offered some pastoral compensation. We know all too little about what clergy wives of this period did or were expected to do in a pastoral way. Perhaps they were for ever diving in and out of cottage doors with baskets on their arms. But at Norton in County Durham the vicar's wife was sheepdog as much as co-pastor. She made it her business to interrogate unmarried mothers in order to identify the fathers of bastard children, which was to take upon herself the office normally assigned to the midwife.[99] And a fleeting snapshot of Mrs Plat, the wife of an Elizabethan vicar of Graveney near Faversham in Kent, is a little daunting. She had taken up residence in the 'cheefest pewe in all the church', historically the property of Judge Martyn and his wife, her former seat being thought 'a blemishe to the church and not thought fyt for any the meanest of the parishioners there to syt, muche lesse for the ministers wife'.[100]

But one source in particular suggests that we should not simply assume that the godly preaching ministry neglected such perennial mainstays of the pastoral function as visitation, reconciliation and even generous charity. I refer to the compilation of the *Lives* of notable divines in the Puritan tradition derived from funeral sermons and put together in the later seventeenth century by Samuel Clarke.[101] Richard Greenham may have been as unsuccessful in converting his parishioners to his own form of religious faith as his obituarist suggests, but according to the same narrative it was not for want of charity. Not only was he generous with his own resources. He persuaded the wealthier villagers to set up and stock a common granary for the poor. He was also said to have worked hard at reconciling his neighbours and acquaintances, preventing them going to law. William Bradhsaw was exercised by the condition of the prisoners kept on the galleys at Chatham. The Suffolk saint John Carter was said to have been 'very diligent in visiting the sick, especially the poorer sort', and to have given more than the total annual revenue of his vicarage to the poor. (Perhaps he had private means.) Part of the folklore relating to John Dod was that when the poor came to buy butter or cheese he commanded his dairy maid to take no money from them. William Whateley, the 'roaring boy' of Banbury, was nevertheless ' a great Peace-maker amongst any of his flock that were at variance'.[102] There is no indication in these sources that the idealised role of the post-Reformation ministry differed in any substantial respect from the standards of a century before, or indeed from those of Chaucer's parson, who was 'a shepherde and noghte a mercenarie', loth to sue for his tithes but ever ready to give to his parishioners from his own small substance.[103] Or, as one of William Sheppard's parishioners reported, years after his death: he 'did not seek to increase his lyvinge by that which to others pertayned'.[104]

So was there nothing new under the sun? There was. Apart from the critical factor of clerical marriage and clerical progeny there was the sacrament of penance, or rather the absence of that sacrament and of the compulsory practice of making and hearing confessions. Other reformation changes made a deal of difference, not least the eradication of the mass and of the concomitant doctrine and practice of propitiatory masses for souls in Purgatory. But in relation to the pastoral ministry in the narrower sense, nothing can have made a greater negative impact than the lapse of the universal obligation to confess to a priest, as the condition both of receiving the sacrament and of remaining an acceptable part of what was still a compulsory christian society.

To be sure, the post-Reformation Church had its surrogates for sacramental confession, even in the absence of that comprehensive 'discipline' which Presbyterian Puritans so ardently desired. The social rationale of the sacrament was partly met by the obligation of parishioners to reconcile themselves to their neighbours before presuming to receive, together with the matching responsibility of the ministry to take an active

and even intrusive role in reconciling the irreconcileable and to repel from
the sacrament those who remained obstinately unreconciled. There is so
much direct evidence from the church courts of clergy performing this
function, especially with the approach of the obligatory Easter communion,
that we are probably entitled to regard it as a normal and nearly universal
office. And in some places the parson's peacemaking role was formalised
as an accepted extra-curial mechanism for ending quarrels. At Gilpin's
Houghton, for example, but after Gilpin's time, it was agreed that all
controversies should be formally referred to the arbitration of some of the
chief inhabitants and of the parson who was to be universal 'umpire'. (But
later it was acknowledged that this 'pious order' had lapsed into disuse.[105])
Jane Freeman brings a challenging charge against the post-Reformation
clergy as fallible peace-makers when she suggests that every one of the
thousands of defamation suits heard in the courts represented another
small failure in the ministry of reconciliation.[106] But defamation suits
were themselves part of a delicate mechanism made up of informal and
formal procedures for damage limitation in social relations which invites
a sensitive anthroplogical as well as legal-historical investigation.[107]

The passing of confession also displaced into the presentment of
offenders to the courts and the forms of public penance often enforced
against those convicted. These too were last resorts for conscientious
clergy anxious to induce christian and moral behaviour by 'gentler' means
stopping short of total social humiliation.[108]

As John Bossy has taught us, confession and absolution were both
public and private business.[109] As private business, the sacrament was
replaced by that form of casuistry dispensed in the reformed Church of
England and called the healing of wounded consciences. Of this ministry
there is abundant testimony, not only in Clarkeian hagiography but in
the correspondence passing between divines and their lay 'patients', as
often as not female,[110] and in such sources as the record kept by Arthur
Hildersham of the sayings and resolutions of Richard Greenham, in
which literary continuity is provided by the repetitive formulae: 'To
one that would know . . . hee gave this advice', 'When one complained
to him . . . he said', 'Unto one that was troubled with unbeleef, he gave
this counsaile . . .'[111]

But none of this was a sufficient substitute for the old sacrament and
discipline of penance, or so many Protestants themselves said. If we refer
back to those pre-Reformation manuals for parish priests we find that

they imply by their organisation that sacramental penance was what nineteenth-century Anglo-Catholics would later insist that it was, the mainspring of the priesthood. The *Oculus Sacerdotis* of William of Pagula begins with a manual for confessors sufficiently comprehensive to include advice for expectant and nursing mothers. The Memoriale Presbiterorum is nothing more nor less than a manual for those hearing confessions. For example, it warns those dealing in this capacity with sailors that 'pen can scarcely suffice to write the sins in which they are involved'.[112]

I do not know how closely acquainted Elizabethan and Jacobean ministers were with the sins of sailors, the special case of ships' chaplains aside. It was as if the great unwashed public said to them: don't call us, we will call you. The difference was critical and perhaps critically damaging. A succession of Protestant and even Puritan writers complained that the loss of the ordinary penitential function had had the effect of tying one of the reformed minister's hands behind his back. Not that they had any ambition to bring back the popish claim to bind and loose with all the abuse inseparable from it. But to abandon the practice of one Christian making confession to another was to throw the baby out with the bath water. Latimer had complained in the time of Edward VI: 'But to speak of right and true confession, I would to God it were kept in England; for it is a good thing.'[113] Nor was this merely the backward-looking opinion of a proto-Protestant born in the year of the battle of Bosworth. The Elizabethan puritan ideologue Thomas Cartwright taught that it was as lawful and convenient to make one's confession to any other man as unto a priest. Yet 'there is none so meete for thy purpose in the behalfe as thine own Curate . . . For he is appointed of God to be heardman of thy soul'[114] And William Perkins later taught that, since it was incumbent upon the minister to confess to God not only his own sins but the sins of his people, his people must first confess their sins to him. 'The want of this is a great fault in our churches' and it made ministers 'accessories to the sinnes of their people'. Perkins went on to condemn auricular confession as a spiritual confidence trick, ' a rack to the consciences of poore Christians'. But he commended the more informal practice of opening one's estate to the pastor, unburdening the conscience and craving his assistance and prayers. 'And the want of it is the cause why a Minister cannot discerne the estate even of his own flocke, nor can complaine to God of their pollutions and confesse their sinnes so particularly as would be good both for him and them'.[115]

In effect Cartwright and Perkins were complaining of the neglect of one essential part of Calvinist discipline, and one committed as much to the eldership and consistory as to the minister alone. But in England the discipline remained in most respects a pipe dream and these pleas were so much hot air escaping between the formalised censures of the church courts on the one hand (what the Separatist John Robinson called 'rattles')[116] and the voluntary resolution of afflicted consciences practised on the other by such physicians of the soul as Greenham. Later the attempt by Laudians to reinstate universal auricular confession along lines closer to Roman practice were no more successful. Anthony Sparrow's words published in 1637, 'he that assents to the Church of England . . . cannot deny the Priest the power of remitting sinnes', were a 'popish' provocation.[117] Anglican rather than Calvinist discipline was closer to coercive social control than to the genuinely pastoral and restorative cure of souls. It was capable of imposing conformity but not of completing and complementing the preacher's work of conversion. For the converted, the logic of conscientious voluntarism tended towards sectarianism and separatism, something as remote as possible from the intentions of the godly ministry and from the fully parochial establishment of religion which has been assumed as the basic 'given' throughout this paper.

Historians are rightly suspicious of monocausal explanations. If we wanted to explain why the Church of England as a pastoral agency eventually found itself ministering to a largish sect rather than to a nation we should have to scan several centuries and a great many distinct factors including, at theological root and so far as this period is concerned, Calvinism in all its implications. But the loss of confession on the Catholic model without the gain of effective Protestant discipline would be high on the list if we had to opt for a single explanation. As Dr Spaeth has pointed out, in the late seventeenth century it was left to individuals and self-selecting groups to decide on the basis of general exhortation whether they were morally fit, or could be bothered, to conduct themselves as fully communicant members of the church or not. How they responded to that challenge, and to the Gospel itself, depended upon the preacher, the effectiveness of his sermon and the response of the hearers, that variety of soils on which English exponents of the Parable of the Sower had so often commented.[118]

The Parable of the Sower was not a suitable foundation on which to erect a national church. Richard Hooker provided a more plausible basis

for what Dr Lake has called a 'broad-botttomed' Christian community,
but Hooker's motivation was itself polemical and so in a sense sectarian,
part of the problem rather than a solution.[119] And in any case Hooker
and the Hookerians were not much read or listened to. In the past I
have been reluctant to agree with Dr Christopher Hill that a voluntarist
plurality and diversity of religious belief, including what Newman in the
nineteenth century called 'Nothingarians', was implicit and imprinted
in Protestantism in its Lutheran title-deeds, since these consequences
were so clearly at variance with everything for which the Protestant
ministry stood. But I suppose that the *longue durée* of the Reformation
proves Dr Hill to have been right after all. The pastoral ministry in post-
Reformation England was a long-term failure, the religious plurality and
secularity of modern Britain its ultimate consequence and legacy.

England and International Calvinism, 1558–1640

In 1569, Jan Van der Noot, a native of Antwerp, had occasion to reflect on his own distracted times, when most European states were full of tumult and, 'more is the pitie', with the shedding of Christian blood. But God had raised up godly princes and certain safe places 'where the elect and faithful have resorted and bene preserved'.[1] Such was the Rhenish Palatinate and its Prince Elector Frederick, a veritable Daniel or Josiah. But Noot was addressing not Daniel but Deborah, for he was one of those who had chosen to take refuge in England, 'a moste safe and sure harborough, where we live (God be thanked) under your Maiesties protection and safegarde in great libertie to serve God in eyther language, the French or the Dutche . . .' And not only in French and Dutch. 'The worde of God is purely preached here in six or seven languages'. Counting on the fingers of two hands, one confirms the accuracy of the arithmetic. In Elizabethan London one could hear Protestant sermons not only in English and Latin but in French, Flemish, Italian and even Spanish. And so Noot congratulated Queen Elizabeth on her blessed state, 'maugre the beards' of her enemies, and designated her 'specially elect of God'.

These were not everyone's perceptions, perhaps not entirely those of the queen with whom they were shared. Noot's fellow-countryman Emanuel van Meteren reported, plausibly enough, that the English were very suspicious of foreigners, 'whom they despise'. Elizabeth's lord keeper, Sir Nicholas Bacon, had once said (admittedly in the aftermath of the fall of Calais): 'That there be in England to many Frenchmen and that it were much better yf ther wer none at all I cannot perceive that anie man denieth'.[2] Nor, from where they stood, were all foreign Calvinists as delighted with the Elizabethan dispensation as Noot. Theodore Beza had to explain to Heinrich Bullinger why Geneva was hated in England and on another occasion exclaimed: 'Quae talis unquam Babylon extitit?' The English church settlement rested primarily on the principles of

autonomy from Rome and royal supremacy, not on the reception of true
doctrine and conformity with the community of Reformed churches.
Consequently, relations between England and the centres of continental
Reform were never secure and always subject to political arbitrariness.
As early as 1568, Bullinger wrote: 'Expectabimus ergo non ex Anglia sed
ex coelo liberationem'.[3] Nevertheless, we may begin by investigating
the substance behind Jan van der Noot's sanguine vision of an England
where Word, sacraments, and discipline were all received in acceptable
forms; where the ruler was an elect instrument of divine purpose; where
the faithful of all nations were welcome; and where a common religious
identity transcended differences of language and national culture.

A recent writer has rightly insisted that 'the English Reformation was
uncompromisingly Protestant' and has demonstrated that at the heart of
its Protestantism was the Swiss or Reformed theology of grace, which
emphasised predestination. This was 'the fundamental theology of English
Protestantism'.[4] From the earliest moment at which one can discern a
formal and political alignment of the English church in this direction,
which is early in the reign of Edward VI, the local fortunes of Calvinism
(as it is distinctly anachronistic to describe the theology and ecclesiology
of the 1550s) and the place of England in international Calvinism were
matters inseparably intertwined. The adoption of Reform on the Swiss–
South German pattern was favoured by the presence in Edwardian
England of the leading non-Lutheran Protestant divines, of whom Martin
Bucer of Strasburg, the Italians Pietro Martire Vermigli (Peter Martyr)
and Bernardino Ochino, and the learned Pole Jan Laski (John à Lasco)
were the most distinguished. It was also aggressively insisted upon by
Englishmen who knew 'the best reformed churches' from the inside, of
whom the most prominent was John Hooper called by the Dutchman
Maarten Micron 'the future Zwingli of England', but in fact a future
bishop and martyr. For a time Hooper had lodgings with Micron who was
one of the founders of the 'Stranger-church' which in 1550 received its
royal charter and the use of the large church building of the Austin Friars.
This foundation was seen by its sponsors as much more than a home for
foreign Protestant refugees. Like Zürich itself, and presently Geneva, it
was an example which both the Church of England and the embryonic
Reformed Church in the Netherlands were encouraged to emulate: a
model church, presided over by a superintendent who was a pioneering
modeller of churches, à Lasco.[5]

With Mary's accession, foreign and native Protestants alike scattered to continental cities of refuge, where the experience of the English exiles completed their assimilation into the Reformed camp at a time of worsening relations with the Lutherans. The colonies at Frankfurt, Strasburg, Zürich, Geneva and Emden were all of seminal importance for the immediate future of the English Church and English Protestantism. Emden, another of Laski's churches and a mother church for the Dutch Reform, was a launching pad for anti-Marian propaganda. Strasburg and Zürich nurtured the episcopal leadership of the future. At Frankfurt there were portents of an alternative churchmanship, critical and opportunistic, the germ of Elizabethan Puritanism. The leading light of this tendency was the first Englishman who can be called a Calvinist (rather than Zwinglian) internationalist: William Whittingham, a future dean of Durham. Whittingham was an expatriated Francophone with long experience in the universities of Orleans and Paris, who was corresponding with Calvin before the death of Edward VI. He was the first Englishman to receive ordination within the non-episcopal, reformed ministry, indeed at the hands of Calvin himself. But he was not, in spite of a hoary tradition, the reformer's brother-in-law.[6] After the 'troubles' of Frankfurt, which were proleptic of later convulsions in the Elizabethan Church, Whittingham's party and its sympathisers, together with their principal pastor John Knox, made a second migration to Geneva, where the church was founded which was joined to the future of English Calvinism by a kind of umbilical cord, and out of which came an invaluable asset of that future: Whittingham's Geneva Bible of 1560.

On Elizabeth's accession, roles were again reversed. Beza could now address the English Church as 'vos Anglos suo tempore dispersos, qui nunc per Dei gratiam estis dispersorum hospites'.[7] In London the Stranger-churches — the Dutch in Austin Friars, the French in Threadneedle Street, together with an Italian and, for a time, a Spanish congregation — were refounded under a modified constitution which placed them more immediately under the surveillance of the bishop of London, now their superintendent *ex officio*. Under the first Elizabethan bishop, Edmund Grindal, a recently repatriated Strasburg exile, this imposed few restrictions on the autonomy of the congregations, although it did help to prevent their infiltration by Anabaptists and other undesirables.[8]

From the outset, Geneva recognised, as any foreign observer would, the strategic importance of Protestant England. Englishmen in Geneva who were reluctant to commit themselves to a still uncertain future under Elizabeth were urged by Calvin himself to return.[9] As for the Stranger-churches, they had a double value both as resources of relief and recuperation for embattled French and Dutch Protestants and as a means of correcting any errant tendency on the part of the English state. Calvin made this second motive abundantly clear when he told Grindal that he deeply regretted the fact that things had not gone as well as all good men had hoped and at first expected, doubtless a reference to the queen's taste for popish ceremonial and her appetite for church lands. On the other hand, there was a real danger that the Stranger-churches would themselves become reservoirs of infection. Geneva had some experience of the proclivity of refugee communities to fall into disarray, prey to doctrinal error and human failing, and especially to that most reprehensible of all weaknesses for a Calvinist, 'ambition'. The best prophylactic against such dangers was to reduce the participation in church affairs of 'the people' and to locate authority with 'the best' in a carefully modelled consistory.

The prime instrument of this policy was Nicolas des Gallars, sieur de Saules, a senior colleague of Calvin who in 1551 had acted as his ambassador to the Edwardian Court and in 1559 had played a signal role in the first national synod of the French Reformed Church, held secretly in Paris. That Calvin was willing to spare the pedigree and diplomatic gifts of such a man, 'non sine acerbo dolore', is some indication of London's importance in his perception. Calvin, Des Gallars and Grindal made a troika. Calvin told the London French that Grindal was their friend and protector. Grindal assured Calvin that Des Gallars had been of the greatest assistance to himself 'and to our own churches'. Des Gallars assured Calvin that without Grindal he would not have been able to cope.

Although Grindal was not always at ease with the ruthlessness with which Geneva imposed its will and its own narrowly conceived orthodoxy, he was mostly willing to serve as its ally and agent. First, Des Gallars was enabled to overcome the resistance to his leadership of rival claimants to the pastorate. Then the authority of the bishop, assisted by Des Gallars' polemical talents, was invoked to suppress a challenge to the consistory of the Dutch church made by the Dutch martyrologist Adrian van Haemstede, assisted by the Italian libertine Giacomo Aconcio (Acontius). Haemstede's offence was to speak up for the Anabaptists as weak and deluded members of Christ, and it was compounded by the very Acontian proposition that the heretical doctrine of Christ's nature entertained by these dissidents was merely circumstantial, not fundamental. There followed a protracted cause célèbre, described by its historian as 'un combat aux frontières de l'orthodoxie'[10] and a matter of international interest and report. Eventually, Grindal had no choice but to rafity the sentences of excommunication passed against Haemstede and his supporters by the Dutch consistory, and to repeat the sentence when Haemstede, having fled to Emden, returned to Austin Friars in the spirit of Michael Servetus' provocative appearance in Geneva in 1555.

In 1561 Des Gallars was a spokesman with Beza at the Colloquy of Poissy and in 1562, after burying his wife and several children in plague-stricken London, he left for Orleans. Further troubles followed in the Dutch congregation, and more battles royal in defence of Calvinist integrity (or, as seen from the other side, in defence of religious liberty) involving the Spanish evangelicals Casiodoro de la Reina and Antonio del Corro. In these episodes Grindal proved a more reluctant executioner. Soon the international Calvinist telegraph would hum with complaints about the complacency of the English bishops. The sentences which counted in these circles were not those pronounced by the bishop-superintendent but the view of Beza that Reina and Corro were probably crypto-Servetan antitrinitarians, which appeared in his published *Epistolae* (1573). This publication contained a chilling reminder of the probable fate of free-thinkers in a truly godly commonwealth, in Beza's endorsement of the public execution of the Heidelberg dissident, Johannes Sylvanus.[11] That Corro was given a hearing in London and Oxford for many years and was protected by powerful patrons is indicative of the qualification which the historian must at once make if he is to call Elizabethan England a Calvinist state. Yet when Des Gallars returned to Geneva from war-ravaged Orleans in 1569, he took occasion to remind Grindal of the notable role which the bishop-superintendent had played in the defence of the truth. In the dedicatory epistle to his edition of the anti-heretical writings of the early Latin Father Irenaeus, Grindal was told that he was Irenaeus reborn: 'Merito igitur te Irenaeo comparo'.[12]

For a Des Gallars or a Beza, heresy was meat and drink. If it had been found not to exist it would have been necessary to invent it. There was no lack of resistance to Calvinism in Elizabethan England. But much of it was

the sullen rejection of ordinary people, instinctive Pelagians who found
predestination an unacceptable proposition and many of whom were still
Papists at heart. This inertia, embedded in what one writer called 'The
Countrie Divinitie',[13] was inarticulate and would be all but inaccessible
to us but for the publicity accorded to it by Calvinist and Puritan critics.
Even in academic circles there seems to have been little investigation of
alternative theologies of a provocative kind, apart from the activities of
Corro at Oxford and, a little later, the teaching of the Frenchman Peter
Baro in Cambridge. So for the time being the talents of an Irenaeus were
not in great demand. What was required was the converting, missionary
energy of a new and Protestant Augustine. In the conservative English
north country, Archbishop Grindal would soon have to take upon him
the role of an apostle. As for international Calvinism, so far as English
involvement was concerned this had more to do with diplomacy, money
and cultural cross-fertilisation (which is to say with Sir Philip Sidney)[14]
than with heresy-hunting.

Perforce, this essay has to be Hamlet without the prince: by which
is meant the Protestant foreign policy[15] first envisaged by Sir Nicholas
Throckmorton, 'the first true Puritan politician', and then, in the 1570s
and 1580s, elaborated by the secretary of state Sir Francis Walsingham
and his staff, under the potent patronage of Robert Dudley, earl of
Leicester. Dr Simon Adams has called this a policy of 'political Puritanism'
defined as 'the advocacy of assistance to the Church abroad, rather than
rapprochement with the Catholic powers or *Realpolitik*, as the guide for
English policy'. The ardent religious conviction at its heart, and one which
Walsingham evidently shared was expressed by the Puritan lawyer and
pamphleteer John Stubbes: 'We have the Lord's right hand on our side
and all the hearts and hands of those of the religion'.[16] 'For the common
cities of God there ought to be a common defence', wrote an anonymous
Puritan diplomat. This apparently naïve ideal, not so much a substitute
for policy as a guiding light through the complexity of policy, was first
attempted in the military expedition of Le Havre (Newhaven) in 1562–63,
frequently advocated in the late 1570s but as constantly frustrated by the
queen's opposition and other factors. Finally it was somewhat ingloriously
allowed its head in Leicester's Netherlands expedition and governorship
of 1585–87, 'primarily a Puritan enterprise' both in inspiration and
participation. At this moment England came closer than at any other

time in history to undertaking that active leadership of the international Calvinist cause which enthusiastic publicists so often attributed to her. Stubbs exclaimed: 'These wars are holy'.

After that it was downhill all the way. For a full half-century there was more of fantasy and nostalgia in 'the Protestant Cause' than substance, given the reluctance of the monarchy to identify with it. Under James I, who favoured eirenical solutions to the problem of European security, much of the political aid which had been rendered to internationally militant Calvinism in Elizabeth's name was withdrawn. Meanwhile, efforts to discover in a succession of aristocrats, from the second earl of Essex through Prince Henry to the third earl of Pembroke, what Dr Adams has called 'an *ersatz* Leicester' were not very successful. In the 1620s the contortions of the duke of Buckingham's dealings with the French Huguenots involved some cynical manipulation of the tattered fragments of the good old cause, as well as what a preacher denounced as 'taking part against our own religion'. Nevertheless, the importance, even the negative importance, of the impossible dream can scarcely be exaggerated. However, this is a subject for the wide screen, too vast to be accommodated in this essay and so, except for these brief remarks, omitted.

Fund-raising in aid of the international Calvinist cause still awaits the historian with the heroic capacity of a Braudel to draw together a mass of scattered evidence and the vision to see the topic whole. We may then discover a motivation, a network, and a methodology reminiscent of the 'third world' charities of our own time, with their particular concerns for refugees, for the sustenance of both persecuted and militant groups in revolutionary situations, for education and the preparation of leadership cadres, and even for the purchase of military hardware and the mounting of guerrilla operations. Until this work has been done, we must make do with a debris of fragments, although the bits and pieces can be so arranged as to suggest regularities and continuities.[17] 'To the afflicted churches, either of the strangers or of our own, tenne pounds', runs the modest will of Robert Smith, servant to the Northamptonshire MP and active Puritan, George Carleton. Learned and impoverished strangers were one of the principal subjects of the posthumous charity of the government attorney Robert Nowell, as distributed by his brothers, the deans of St Paul's and Lichfield. A total of £221. 11s. 4d. was dispensed out of this fund to the Italian, Dutch, and French churches in London and the provinces and to many individual strangers. In disposing of another estate, the London mercer Richard Culverwell, uncle of a famous Puritan preacher, bequeathed a gold chain which he had received from the queen of Navarre and spoke of 'manye other her jewells of greate value' which had come into the possession of others, 'for the furtherance and defence of the Ghospell and suche as sincerely professe the same'. Although Culverwell describes these treasures as 'franckly' given, they seem to have been pledges. In 1582, an agent of the Geneva government estimated that La Rochelle was in debt to the city of London to the tune of £40,000.[18]

An important element in the rhythm of religious life among English Calvinists and Puritans was the public fast, kept as a whole day of humiliation, prayer and preaching and often related to some special 'occasions'. In 1586 in Suffolk these included 'the state of the Frenche church' and two years later the London French related their own fast to the afflictions of the Church, 'tant en France que au pais bas, ensemble l'estat de ce Royaume'. It seems to have been common practice on these special days of assembly to collect money for some specific purpose, perhaps linked with the occasion of the fast. According to a cryptic report from the anti-Puritan sleuth Richard Bancroft, the money collected by Puritans in this way 'for their brethren that travell for them beyond the seas' was forwarded to Culverwell and to the London preacher John Field.

So it was that when a conference of Puritan ministers in the country, the so-called Dedham Classis, received a request from the Threadneedle Street church for aid and relief, it was decided not to make a public collection but 'to deale privately with the best affected'. To gather funds publicly but without due authorisation was sometimes attempted but it was irregular if not illegal. Partly for this reason, partly for reasons of ideological commitment, we can be sure that much of the money raised in the cause of international Calvinism came from the pockets of 'the best affected'. The 'contes des deniers des pauvres' of the French church in London have been preserved for the period November 1572 to December 1573[19] (and no other accounts until the late seventeenth century), presumably because they contain a creditable record of English benevolence in the aftermath of the St Bartholomew massacres, when scores of refugee pastors poured into the south of England. But much of the generosity was that of 'the best affected', including Calvinist notables like the countess of Sussex and Sir

Francis Hastings, brother of the earl of Huntingdon, who brought £10. 4s. 'venant des gentils hommes du conté de Lecestre'; and famous preachers and divines, among them Thomas Cartwright, Thomas Lever, William Whittingham, and old colleagues of Whittingham from the English consistory in Geneva, William Williams, Thomas Wood and John Bodley. We also find the names of the wealthy Puritan goldsmith with whom Cartwright was staying at this time, Richard Martin, and of a young law student called Nicholas Fuller, who was destined to become a vociferous Puritan attorney and parliament man.

In 1582–83, the greatest of all such 'gatherings' was launched in order to relieve the city of Geneva itself from the threat posed by the duke of Savoy, Charles Emmanuel. This was no hole-in-the-corner affair but a public collection supported by the Privy Council and duly licensed. In the diocese of Canterbury, the contributors whose names were recorded were numbered in hundreds (but not in thousands) and represented a cross-section of provincial society.[20] But even in these auspicious circumstances the response had clear ideological overtones, as we learn from almost every page of the journal kept by the agent of the Geneva government, Jean Maillet, who cooled his heels in London from November 1582 until September 1583.[21] Alderman Richard Martin (whom we have already met and whose personal contribution on this occasion was £20) told Maillet that it was the government's opinion that Papists should not contribute but only those whose sympathies were engaged as co-religionists — which was why those who were of that sort contributed more largely, so that they might not appear suspect and of a contrary religion.[22] Evidently subscribing to the Geneva found had some of the same significance as taking the Bond of Association a year later.[23]

The queen had no such need to pretend to a sympathy which she did not feel. When the agent first met the secretary of state, Sir Francis Walsingham warned him not to expect much from that quarter, since he foresaw 'grands empeschements': notably 'la mauvaise opinion' which the queen had always entertained of Geneva on account of John Knox's *First Blast of the Trumpet Against the Monstrous Regiment of Women*. (One of Des Gallar's rivals in Threadneedle Street had suggested in 1560 that Elizabeth might refuse to confirm the appointment of a pastor sent 'by those who have greatly offended her'.) In any case, Walsingham suggested, better wait for the return to Court of the earl of Leicester. When Leicester came he told the agent that his mistress regarded Geneva as 'une lampe qui a servi pour esclairer presque toutes les Églises de l'Europe'. Such words cost nothing. The agent was not granted an audience, but Walsingham reported back that the queen doubted whether the city was in any serious danger and thought that she was probably more in need of money than Geneva was. Walsingham, expecting this outcome, had asked Maillet how much he was looking for. He had replied that beggars could not be choosers.

After delays and elusive promises, the Council placed the responsibility for raising the money on the City and the Church, employing the standard procedure for charitable collections beyond the locality under the device of letters patent. By late April, £1434 had been collected in the province of Canterbury, although some bishops were defaulters, including John Scory of Hereford, whose exile in Emden was now a distant memory. (But Edwin Sandys of York said that he would stake his all, 'engager sa chemise', in the cause.) In these circumstances the agent was tempted to do business with an unofficial committee of leading Puritan ministers, headed by Walter Travers, Cartwright's right-hand man: but was advised that it would be prudent to work through more regular channels. In the event, the church collections produced a satisfying response. A vicar in Hertfordshire pleaded poverty ('I fare full sad') but still sent ten shillings 'to helpe these godlie people, troubled for the gospel of Jesus Christ': 'a widow's mite indeed, since Walsingham himself gave only twenty times as much.[24] Eventually the machinery set in motion managed to raise not far short of £6,000. Subsequently (and there were further collections for Geneva in 1590 and 1603), it became accepted practice for the government to call upon the official Church to arrange voluntary contributions from the faithful, presumably on a parochial basis.[25]

But the success of the 1582–83 operation depended critically on the patronage of Calvinists in the upper echelons of government. Sir Walter Mildmay, who in times past had wished that he could join the English exiles in Geneva,[26] was cordial. Philip Sidney promised that his father would arrange a collection in Wales. The earl of Bedford recalled the hospitality of Geneva in Mary's days and thought that this debt should now be paid. For three hours he enquired minutely into the condition of the city, protested that it was as dear to him as his native country and swore that the representative of such a republic was equal in his estimation to the ambassador of the greatest monarch under Heaven. Back from his estates three months later, Bedford brought more money than he had expected. The 'bonnes gens du pays' had paid two, three, four pounds without compulsion. He had never seen them better disposed. But was it done for Geneva, or for the name of Russell? The Protestant councillors and courtiers all made substantial contributions, from Bedford's £40 and Leicester's £30 to ten pounds each from Sidney, Walsingham, and Mildmay and 20 from Francis Bacon's enthusiastically religious mother. The conservatives, Sir Christopher Hatton, Sir James Croft, Lord Hunsdon, seem to have given nothing. The moral is clear. The response to Geneva in her hour of need had come spontaneously from certain old Geneva hands like John Bodley, who acted as Geneva's banker on this occasion; and from a small Puritan clique. Only the patronage of the Protestant earls stimulated the respectable appearance of a groundswell of national sympathy and support.

The experience of 1582–83 was closely paralleled more than forty years later in the English reaction to the disaster of the Rhenish Palatinate, and in particular to that aspect of the crisis which most engaged the hearts of Calvinists: the destitution of Calvinist ministers and schoolmasters and their wives, families and widows: at least eight hundred souls, not to count 'sundrie thousands of godly private persons' who had fled as refugees from the Habsburg onslaught on their homeland.[27] Between 1626 and 1633, the English contribution to the Palatinate relief fund far outstripped the help which came from the Swiss, French and Dutch, or so the Palatine ministers themselves were prepared to testify to 'the whole sympathyzing Christian world'.[28] The recovery of the Palatinate was the occasion for a charitable collection in 1620 and then, after the failure of the 1621 Parliament to deliver a subsidy or an effectively compulsory 'benevolence', again in 1623.[29] The relief of refugees was a distinct issue and considered wholly an object of Christian charity. Once again, although seventy years separated these events from the reign of Mary, there were those who remembered the Exile and regarded English generosity on this occasion as payment of an old debt.[30] And once more, just as the Puritan preachers of London had concerned themselves with the relief of Geneva in 1582–83, so in 1626 an early initiative was taken by their successors, the ranking godly ministers of this later generation: John Davenport of St Stephen's Coleman Street, William Gouge of Blackfriars, Richard Sibbes of Gray's Inn and Thomas Taylor, lecturer at St Mary Aldermanbury, where John Field had once preached. In a circular letter addressed to 'all godly christians', these ministers dramatised the plight of their Palatine brethren, who would be 'very thankfull for course bread and drink if they could gett it' and called for a 'gathering'. This was to discard the caution which Travers (characteristically) had shown in 1583 and the subscribers to this letter were prosecuted in the High Commission, presumably for their temerity in organising an unauthorised, semi-public collection.[31]

The subscribing ministers said that they knew 'a sure and safe way' to get help into the hands of those for whom it was intended. These men usually did know a way, for Davenport, Gouge and Sibbes were part of that extraordinary Puritan enterprise known as the Feoffees for the Purchase of Impropriations which began operations in this same year, 1626. Another famous cleric associated with both the Feoffees and the Palatinate gathering was the so-called 'patriarch of Dorchester', John White, who had already raised large sums for the Palatinate in his own town and parish. One senses that talent for almost conspiratorial wheeling and dealing which in 1629 would carry over into the Providence Island Company and the Massachusetts Bay Company, enterprises partly inspired by John White's writing. Just as the Feoffees included merchants and lawyers as well as divines, so the Palatinate collection involved the close co-operation of preachers and prominent Puritan laymen, like Alderman Isaac Pennington, whose home in the Whitefriars served as an 'ordinary' for Puritan visitors to the city.[32]

The 'safe and sure' way which the London preachers knew for channeling funds to the Palatine refugees was the Dutch church in London through its *'politicke mannen'*, merchants with appropriate resources and contacts and much experience in fund-raising. (Austin Friars found the vast sum of £33,000 for the relief of its own poor in only sixteen years.)[33] Close cooperation between the strangers and English Calvinists in the Edwardian and Elizabethan tradition continued and was assisted by a partial merging of the two communities. One of the elders at Austin Friars, John de la Motte, had been born in Colchester to Flemish parents. He was a wealthy and pious London businessman who found his way into Samuel Clarke's catalogue of modern English saints, with special commendation for his 'Sympathizing bowels' shown towards the persecutions and troubles 'in France, at Rochel, in the Valtaline, in Bohemia, in Germany: And more particularly in the Lower and Upper Palatinate'.[34] When, in 1628, Charles

I ordered general collections for the Palatine refugees, his proclamation referred to information received from the Dutch church in London. Both on this occasion and in the second collection ordered in 1630 centralised administration and transmission of the funds was delegated to the Austin Friars consistory. According to the refugees themselves, the king had been persuaded to take these steps by the intercession and labour both of the London Dutch and 'cordatiorum quorundam Anglorum'.[35] The archives of the Dutch church, which contain well over a hundred items of correspondence between Austin Friars and the refugee groups, record the diligent thoroughness with which the money was doled out and accounted for, while in England the Dutch consistory was engaged in an endless round of letter-writing to bishops and other clergy, of visits to Lambeth House, and of frequent meetings.[36]

The royal collection was to be commended in every parish in England and Wales and taken up either in church services or from door to door. But once more, as in 1572 and 1583, the names of those who gave generously reads like a selective rollcall of what a seventeenth-century Puritan would have called 'notable private Christians'.[37] In a way the Palatines were drawing attention to this ideologically motivated response to their needs when they pointed out that Camden's *Britannia* told them that there were 8,700 parishes in England and that it seemed unlikely that all of them could have contributed to their uttermost!

Our investigation of Protestant fund-raising has suggested that English Calvinism, like English humanitarianism or English Communism in later generations, was the cause of an inner circle, well known to one another and somewhat estranged from the generality of society. That degree of estrangement is pin-pointed in the stigma of 'Puritan' which, from the 1560s to the 1660s, was commonly attached to such people, indicating not only the unusual warmth of their attachment to religion, but their dissatisfaction with the extent of the reformation achieved in the English Church within the terms of Elizabethan Puritanism, *An Admonition to the Parliament*, composed in 1572 by two young London preachers, Thomas Wilcox and John Field, these questions were put: 'Is discipline meete for Scotland? and can it be unprofitable for this Realme?'[38] This sense of solidarity with the international Protestant community was demonstrated by Puritans in London (and perhaps in provincial towns like Norwich, Colchester, and Canterbury, although this has yet to be investigated) in their active involvement in the affairs of the stranger churches, which they continued to regard as models of the 'church rightly reformed' such as they hoped to see established in England.[39] An obscure London parson, suspended from his cure for nonconformity, wrote plaintively: 'Yt semethe ryghtfull that subjects naturall receve soe muche favoure as the churches of natyonall straungers here with us. But we can not once be harde so to obtayne'. On more than one occasion, Puritan agitators and politicians pointed out that Parliament had no need to look beyond the forms of worship employed in the Stranger-churches in order to find an acceptable alternative to the Book of Common Prayer. The *Admonition to the Parliament* was published only after the failure of a parliamentary bill which would have legalised the use of these liturgies in parish churches.

This led an opponent of the Puritans to complain that all the troubles in the English Church were attributable to the 'strange churches, as well beyond the seas as here among us remaining'. There was some truth in this. In the course of the 1560s, the Geneva pastorate, inspired and taught by Beza, was hardening its attitude with respect to 'the discipline', insisting on the necessity of that element in the life of the church and in the hands of its own officers, and defining it according to a narrow exegesis of certain New Testament texts. Presently Geneva took exception to the view, defended in Heidelberg by Thomas Erastus, that under a Christian magistracy there was no need for discipline in this sense; and found itself at odds with the mentors of Erastus and the true home of 'Erastianism', Zürich. As for England, Beza moved from a cautious familiarity with the Elizabethan bishops, Grindal in particular whom he knew personally, to a largely negative appraisal of English religious conditions as falling victim to 'avarice' and 'ambition'. In this he was encouraged by the pessimistic reports carried to Geneva by Puritan emissaries. The critical shift in his attitudes can be traced through Beza's *Correspondance*, especially with Bullinger in Zürich, and it accompanies a hardening contempt for diocesan episcopacy as lordly 'domination'.[40]

But Beza was not lacking in diplomacy and like Agag he contrived to tread delicately. When the Puritans urged him to intervene directly in the English controversies he declined, knowing that letters from Geneva were more likely to hinder than help.[41] In 1568 he dedicated his New

Testament to the queen and two years later chose Sir Walter Mildmay as the recipient of his *Tractatae theologicae*, apologising for their acerbic tone. When the *Admonition* appeared he attempted to detach himself from 'such very indiscreet proceedings', which were liable to prejudice his own dealings with certain English 'seigneurs'.[42] That was said in a letter to Threadneedle Street. Correspondence between Geneva and the English Puritans was commonly directed through the French church in London, 'a thing they do very frequently', according to one report.[43]

The recipients of these letters seem to have moved in and out of the foreign congregations with ease and familiarity. Some, especially merchants with a command of foreign languages and relevant business contacts, served as officers, For example, that inveterate internationalist John Bodley was an elder of the French church. When Sir Thomas Middleton became Lord Mayor of London in 1613 he had been a member of the Dutch church for more than thirty years.[44] Early in Elizabeth's reign, the communicants at Threadneedle Street were joined by veterans of the English Geneva congregation, Whittingham and his French wife among them, 'et plusieurs aultres englois'. From time to time more distinguished guests flashed what were doubtless calculated signals by ostentatiously taking the sacrament with the French: in 1565 William Cecil's brother-in-law, the diplomat Henry Killigrew, and in 1568 no less a personage than the earl of Leicester. Ten years later, at a time when he was hoping to find an active and commanding role in the Low countries, Leicester heard a sermon from the Dutch minister in Norwich and wrote: 'Me thinkes I hear every day the voyce of that people'.[45]

Grindal had to ask the French to exercise discretion in admitting English visitors to their services, and to distinguish between those who merely wished to make an ecumenical gesture and others who were effectively schismatics and had deserted their own parish churches. Later, with the worsening of conflict in the Church of England, the authorities became increasingly anxious that the stranger churches should not provide a bolt-hole for disaffected Puritans. The strangers, who were glad to welcome English communicants 'a cause qu'ils son unis de fois avec nous', were obliged to give undertakings not to encourage dissidents. On the other hand John King, bishop of London from 1611 to 1621, followed the earlier example of Grindal in instructing the London parish clergy not to give sanctuary to strangers who were in flight from the discipline of their own congregations. In Grindal's time that was regarded in Threadneedle Street as 'acte de levesque remarquable'.[46]

Not only Geneva veterans like Bodley and Whittingham but Puritans who had never crossed the sea and had never met Calvin or Beza seem to have felt more affinity with their foreign co-religionists than with fellow Englishmen who were of a contrary religious persuasion or of none. In 1584 this sense of international brotherhood was demonstrated in the streets of London when the funeral of a Scottish minister, one of a group of Presbyterian exiles, was accompanied by a procession of more than five hundred 'godlie brethren, ministers and citizens', including three French pastors with 'manie Frenchmen'. Old Sir Nicholas Bacon, with his talk of eradicating Frenchmen, would have been flabbergasted. But the twentieth century, which is experienced in its own manifestations of international ideological solidarity, finds itself on familiar ground. In Edinburgh, a Scottish minister who received on consecutive days letter from La Rochelle and from John Field in London wrote to Field: 'It is no small comfort brother . . . to brethren of one natione to understand the state of the brethren in other nationes'. 'Touching the word *forreyne*', wrote William Bradshaw, 'those Churches being all the same household of faith that we are, they are not aptly called forreyne . . . So all Churches and all members of the Church, in what Country so ever they be, are not to be accounted Forreyners one to another, because they are all Citizens of heaven, and we all make one family or body'.[47]

In this essay, English Calvinism and Calvinists have so far been defined narrowly as a partisan cause and a coterie somewhat out of the main stream of English society and drawing closer to the international Calvinist community. But the time has come to acknowledge that there was a more broadly-based reception of Calvinism in the Elizabethan and Jacobean Church of England, amounting to 'the received interpretation of the Church's doctrine'.[48] The 'English Creed', as an Elizabethan author styled the Articles of Religion,[49] was different in form and application from the confessions of faith of the national Reformed churches. So it has often been said that the Church of England is not a confessional church. Nevertheless, the account of salvation, faith, grace and predestination rendered by the Articles was broadly consistent with the Reformed consensus on these matters and directly indebted to specific Reformed sources at some points.[50] The consequence was a public sense, rarely challenged before the time of Archbishop Laud, that the English Church and nation were in essential harmony with other Reformed churches, their sacraments and ministries interchangeable for migrants and foreign travellers. Episcopacy, which other reformed churches lacked, was of the *bene esse* rather than the *esse* of the church.[51]

So English Calvinism was not equivalent to Puritanism. Few Elizabethan religious controversialists referred more frequently to Calvin than the Puritans' most doughty opponent, Archbishop John Whitgift. And Whitgift was only one of many English divines conventionally classified as 'Anglicans' rather than 'Puritans' who expressed their regard for Calvin on many occasions. Yet a distinction may be drawn between intellectual debts of this kind, which admitted Calvin into the controversial arena, and an absorption of Calvinist divinity which was so complete as to structure and furnish a world-view, an intellectual system, and a rule of life. This was the difference between a merely theoretical Calvinism and the applied, practical, and highly combative Calvinism of some puritan divines, and it distinguishes Whitgift from the dominant theological force in late Elizabethan Cambridge, William Whitaker, whose powerful mind turned and spun its syllogisms within the concepts of the exclusive truth and authority of Scripture, the sovereignty of God's predestinate grace, and the Antichristian falsity of the pope's church.[52]

Hence, the extent to which English Protestantism in the age of its maturity can be properly called Calvinist is one of some delicacy and difficulty. 'Calvinist' is a stereotype and too blunt an instrument for any discriminating purpose. English Protestants were not disposed to surrender their theological judgement to some Genevan magisterium. 'Calvin herein grants more than I would grant', was the marginal comment of an unknown reader on a particular point encountered in his reading of the *Institutes* in Thomas Norton's English translation. John Whitgift and his Puritan opponent Thomas Cartwright freely quoted Calvin the one against the other, but each met with the same response: we reverence Mr Calvin but we do not believe anything to be true simply on the basis of his say-so. Later Whitgift warned against giving more credence to the 'bare names and authoritie' of Calvin and Beza than was given to the ancient Fathers; and even declared that the Church of England 'doth in no respect depend upon them'.[53] But these were debating points, and to quote the last remark out of context would be particularly misleading. There was considerable dependence.

But at the same time, the student who has only heard of 'Calvinism' must learn that English theologians were as likely to lean on Bullinger of Zürich, Musculus of Berne, or Peter Martyr as on Calvin or Beza, while they accorded a higher measure of authority to Ambrose, Athanasius, Augustine, Chrysostom and Cyprian, for the apologetics of the Church of England (and not only the English Church) always rested on a patristic foundation. Such names were the missile weaponry of Elizabethan divinity, so much of which was polemical. But if we were to identify one author and one book which represented the centre of theological gravity of the Elizabethan Church it would not be Calvin's *Institutes* but the *Common Places* of Peter Martyr, described by his translator, Anthony Marten, as 'a verie Apostle'. And at least equally influential was Bullinger, whose view of the religious role of Christian magistracy was well adapted to political reality in Elizabethan England.[54]

Even when their purposes were different, Elizabethan Protestant writers were eclectic. To take the martyrologist John Foxe as an example: in the works of religious edification and spiritual comfort which he wrote or edited and brought to the press it would be hard to apply any limiting label and we must pause before defining Foxe as a Calvinist — or anything else. He found much of value in the writings of Martin Luther (although he was not a Lutheran) and especially in those works which reveal Luther as a physician of the wounded conscience. It was due almost entirely to Foxe that Luther lived on in the English religious consciousness, above all as the author of the ever-popular *Commentary on Galatians*.[55]

A generation after Foxe, 'Calvinism', if it meant anything, no longer signified Geneva and the churches that looked to Geneva for guidance but a loose and free alliance of churches, universities, academies, and other intellectual, political and spiritual resources located in France, the Netherlands, south-west Germany, England and Scotland, not to speak of more distant outposts. New names began to count: Beza for one, but also Junius, Danaeus, the Heidelberg doctors and their influential Catechism, Ursinus, and above all Zanchius, called by an early seventeenth-century Oxford professor 'clarissimus superioris seculi theologus'.[56] The very names, let alone the voluminous works, of these second-generation Calvinist theologians are now unknown to all but a few specialists. Yet at the turn of the century they were studied not only in Oxford and

Cambridge but by the erudite country clergy of East Anglia.[57] These authors were all in a sense 'Calvinists', but whether their Calvinism was a legitimate implementation of Calvin's own programme or a departure from the spirit and method of his theology is still a matter of debate.

All this must be borne in mind as we concede that the Church of England was putting down its anchors in the outer roads of the broad harbour of the Calvinist or (better) Reformed Tradition. The anchors sometimes shifted but they did not drag until the late 1620s. The anchor-chains were the magisterial theologians who made themselves masters of the schools and of half the colleges in Oxford and Cambridge in the second half of Elizabeth's reign: in Cambridge, William Whitaker, William Fulke, Laurence Chaderton and in a rather different and more popular vein, William Perkins; in Oxford the formidable John Reynolds, who as an expositor of the Calvinist scheme of grace had cut his teeth on the free-thinking Spaniard, del Corro. Reynolds, as a recent study has emphasised, almost epitomised in his own person the Reformed Church of England, 'not narrowly Calvinist and Genevan, but inspired by a variety of continental protestant centres', expressing 'a hybrid and broadly-based theological tradition'.[58]

As they pursue the developing and changing fourtunes of that tradition into the early decades of the seventeenth century, historians of doctrine encounter and sometimes fail to agree on three related questions which will be briefly rehearsed in conclusion. To what extent was that version of Calvinism which we find elaborated by the prolific English school of 'experimental predestinarians', with its penchant for the concept of covenanting with God ('federal theology'), an original outgrowth with a manifest destiny in North America?[59] What, in its English version, was that radical variant of Calvinism, a sucker as it were growing from the root, known as Arminianism? What was its derivation and at what point did it seriously and successfully challenge the Reformed or Calvinist ascendancy? The final question concerns the nature of that challenge. Was the anti-Calvinist, Arminian backlash a fundamental repudiation of the doctrinal heart of the Reformation itself, a denial of what had been taken for orthodoxy, as its opponents claimed? Or was it little more than reaffirmation of religious and ethical values which were authentically Protestant, entrenched in the Thirty-Nine Articles, and never lacking defenders within the native tradition of the Reformed

Church of England? In this perspective 'Arminianism' was simply a
salutary correction of distortions perpetrated by the extreme Calvinism
which had triumphed at the Synod of Dort (1618). After all, Calvin
himself (unlike Beza) took no exception to the proposition that Christ
died for all men, which later became a hallmark of 'Arminianism'.[60]
Each of these problems could comfortably occupy a large volume and in
a few paragraphs it is possible only to review the present state of these
difficult and still controversial questions.

'Calvin against the Calvinists' has been an attractive slogan, drawing
attention to the significant changes in theological method which are
detectable in the work of Beza, Zanchius and Perkins, and thereafter in
much English and New English divinity. And it makes a useful point
which has some general validity, as indicating the difference which
necessarily exists between a religious founder and the movement which
acquires his name. Calvin had no intention of creating a system of thought
called Calvinism.[61] And his theology was one of equipoise, in which
predestination was not, as it was for later Calvinists, the major organising
principle. Nevertheless, to mean by 'Calvinist' something other than a
follower of Calvin will always seem a trifle perverse, while the extent to
which Calvin's legacy was falsified by his immediate successors has been
exaggerated.[62] It is possible to speak of a 'giant leap' across the 'chasm'
separating Calvin, the biblical humanist, from seventeenth-century
Calvinist scholasticism while regarding Beza as a transitional and bridging
figure, a systematiser but scarcely a Protestant scholastic. The Aristotelian
rot, if that is what it was, seems to have begun not with Beza but with the
Italians Peter Martyr and Girolamo Zanchi.[63]

As for English Calvinism, it may be simple ignorance of concurrent
developments in continental theology which has sometimes led to undue
stress on the particular deviance of the English school. These writers were
such attentive students of the whole body of Reformed divinity that their
treatment of the life of the individual Christian, or of such topics as the
'conscionable' keeping of the Sabbath, sometimes regarded as an English
peculiarity, may represent a practical application of what they had learned
rather than any conspicuous departure from it.[64]

However, those who emphasise a peculiar 'English Calvinism' are right
in one important respect. Calvinist doctrine was far from shaping the
institutional fabric of the English church, as to a large extent it was able to

do elsewhere, where the Reformed religion was not politically established, or where the political establishment was amenable. On the contrary, that fabric thwarted and redirected the forward thrust of doctrine, diverting its implementation away from the objectivity of church order, sacraments and discipline, which before the 1540s English Calvinists were powerless to alter, towards the subjectivity of personal piety. Consequently, English Calvinism both fed into and fed upon that devout anxiety about eternal destinies which Perkins expressed in the title of a casuistical treatise: *A case of conscience, the greatest that ever was: How a man may know whether he be the child of God or no* (1592). More and more the 'practical syllogism' of godly living was brought into play to provide not only the comfort but the instrumentality of assurance. But the intense scrutiny of self and of the difference between true and counterfeit faith may have actually reinforced what threatened among devout Calvinists, and especially Calvinist women, to become an enervating obsession. It also drew ever more odious attention to the conflict between the godly lives of the elect and the profane lives of the reprobate which in the public sector was socially divisive. A reaction against these damaging excesses was readily forthcoming, precisely because the reception of Calvinist doctrine in England had never been so complete as to exclude other theological tendencies which found space to live within the latitude of the Articles of Religion and which were nourished by elements of a more Catholic tradition, preserved in the principal resource of the Reformed Church of England, the Book of Common Prayer.

In England, as in the Netherlands and elsewhere, the worm in the apple was presently identified as 'Arminianism', belief in the potential universality of divine redemption and in the capacity of man's free will to appropriate God's grace or to spurn it.[65] This doctrine was not so much 'the spawn of a papist', as an English critic put it, as a residuum of Lutheran teaching on these matters. In mid-Elizabethan England, a reviving preference for the optimistic evangelicalism of the Lutheran tradition was revealed in the popularity in some quarters of the writings of the Danish syncretist, Niel Hemmingsen.[66] But not only were aspects of the Calvinist scheme of strictly predestinate grace under fire in England some years before the views of Arminius of Leiden became notorious. There was a capacity within the Church of England to set up a more fundamental and broadly based reaction against Calvinism than was implied in the Arminian onslaught on the predestinarians. For the English liturgy implied in its undertones and ethos as much as in any explicitly dogmatic statement the universal availability of grace through the sacraments and the use of petitionary prayer. It surrounded prayer and sacraments with a potential richness of ceremonial devotion which was anything but Calvinist. And it stimulated a revived sense of the ministry of word and sacraments as a holy priesthood, deriving its validity not from the Christian community (as Luther said) or from its political head (as Henry VIII would have it) but from Christ and his apostles, through a divinely commissioned episcopate. An important and provocative aspect of this revived clericalism was to confront directly the material interests of lay society by reaffirming the sacrosanctity of ecclesiastical property. The Arminian disputes in the Netherlands between Remonstrants and Contra-Remonstrants were of a radical nature, but they remained disputes within the Reformed tradition. English 'Arminianism' threatened to step out of that tradition altogether.

The implications of what may be regarded as a portmanteau of religious attitudes[67] may not have reached as far as the total subversion of the Protestant Reformation itself. But it has been said that they threatened the essence of the Protestant religious experience. William Prynne (a lawyer) thought that the very title-deeds of salvation were at stake.[68] Moreover the circumstances of its promotion were such that many, perhaps most, informed Protestants feared a conspiracy to bring back popery in transparent disguise. It used to be thought that the *fin de siècle* attack mounted on Calvinism in late Elizabethan Cambridge heralded the natural wasting of a foreign body in the English Church and a return to sanity in the form of a balanced and normative Anglican theology of the middle way. But this is incorrect. Archbishop Whitgift's ruling in the Cambridge controversy, contained in the Lambeth Articles (1595), was an endorsement of the substance of the position staked out by Whitaker and other Calvinists, although in Whitgift's recension tending to favour the biblical and cautious Calvinism of Calvin himself. After all, as Whitgift assured his brother Hutton of York, these were 'matters never doubted of by any professors of the Gospell during all the tyme of your aboade and myne in the universitie'.[69] If the Lambeth Articles had been officially endorsed and imposed, English Calvinists would have had little more to fear. Although this did not happen, high Calvinism continued to prevail, dominating the universities and the religious press throughout the reign of James I, a monarch who was at ease with the moderate Calvinist consensus,[70] and for much of Archbishop George Abbot's long tenure of the primacy.

This was not necessarily a reflection of free opinion, since both academic debate and scholarly publication were biased by regulation and even censorship. By the same token, when fashions changed it was not a consequence of the natural attenuation and exhaustion of Calvinism. That might have occurred by 1650 but not in 1630. It was a sudden and politically contrived *renversement* which toppled Calvinism from its throne. The contrivers were the so-called 'Arminian' churchmen themselves: principally Richard Neile and secondarily William Laud; the duke of Buckingham who leant increasingly in that direction; and above all King Charles I. As late as 1628 Charles was still viewed as orthodox by the godly Sir Robert Harley and in 1629 he was lauded by the Palatine exiles as 'Orthodoxae fidei strenuus defensor'.[71] But his contrary religious preferences had been clear to those with eyes to see soon after his accession and his actions now represented, according to some observers, an unprecedented invasion of the realm of theological definition by the royal governor. When the issues were debated at York House in 1626, in the presence of Buckingham, it was obvious which way the wind would now blow. Within months further discussion was stifled by the royal declaration which to this day prefaces the Thirty-Nine Articles. Ostensibly this maintained the officially agnostic reticence of the Church of England on 'curious points'. But since its effect was to silence the Calvinist moral majority from preaching on matters considered of vital importance in the salvation of God's elect children, the royal proclamation made the Church safe for William Laud's assumption of ecclesiastical primacy and his implementation of the Caroline ecclesiastical policy in the 1630s. Dr Tyacke has written: 'The Arminians and their patron King Charles were undoubtedly the religious revolutionaries in the first instance'. 'The result was a polarization of extremes unknown since the Reformation'.[72]

But how to characterise one of these two extremes remains a problem. To call it 'Arminian', as contemporaries increasingly did, is to stigmatise, to define the whole in terms of one of its parts and to distract and falsify by importing the name of a foreign theologian whose authority in England was uncertain. 'Anglican' anachronistically obscures the important truth that Calvinists too were members of the Anglican Church who could justly claim to have the weight of recent tradition on their side. And 'High Church' will not do at all, since Calvinists too had occupied the heights and often embraced the principles of *jure divino* episcopacy. As for 'Laudian', this term not only imposes the views of one man on a party whose opinions were by no means monolithic or even coherent. It has led some critics to ask whether the religious reaction and polarisation described by Dr Tyacke was really as drastic as he has suggested, since Laud was careful (if only for tactical reasons) to distance himself from the dogmatic excess of Arminianism in the strict sense and was more overtly concerned with 'decent' and stately ceremonial than with controversial doctrine.[73]

There was a spectrum of theological opinion in the early seventeenth-century church, and some finely adjusted positions with respect to grace and predestination. Many ranking churchmen were deliberately eclectic, the biographer of Laud's bitter enemy Bishop John Williams remarking: 'He that is discreet will make his Profit out of every side, or every Faction, if you like to call it so'.[74] There was a strong polemical disposition to avoid the excesses of both sides in the Dutch controversy and at Dort the English delegation (itself divided on some matters) adopted an eirenical stance which lay between, although by no means midway between, the Remonstrant and Contra-Remonstrant positions. But the centre of gravity, 'orthodoxy', was still Calvinist and the desire of the English delegation at Dort to draw back from the extremities of hyper-Calvinism implied no weakening with respect to that orthodoxy but rather a concern which was as much pastoral as polemical and political to avoid what the bishop of Bath and Wells, Arthur Lake, renowned for his exemplary piety, called 'distasteful accessories'. This would deprive the unorthodox (the Remonstants) of 'all excuse' not to submit.[75]

Yet to conclude that a kind of moderation really prevailed, even after 1626, or that the English Church was swinging back to a traditional *via media* which only external pressures had disturbed, or that Archbishop Laud merely corrected the rudder and set his course by the lodestar of the Thirty-Nine Articles is to be deceived by the subtle conventions of contentious debate. The fact is that there were two sides, both given to the language of moderation and consensus, both deeply dyed in the mentality of divisive faction.[76] Whatever else animated and motivated the Laudians we may confidently attribute to them a perfect hatred not only of Puritanism but of what they chose to call Puritanism, which their opponents defended as the orthodox faith of the Church. The suggestion by Richard Montagu in his book *A new gagg for an old goose* that Popery and Puritanism were Scylla and Charybdis and that the Church of England stood in the gap between them, which was also Laud's view, was totally unacceptable to the religious majority. Earlier in the century, Archbishop Richard Bancroft had been called by a loud-mouthed Scot 'the capital enemy of all Reformed churches in Europe'.[77] Laud really was such an enemy and would have been proud of the label. 'To think well of the Reformed Religion', wrote the earl of Northumberland in 1639 'is enough to make the Archbishop one's enemy.' At Laud's trial it was alleged that in 1634 he had insisted on altering the letters patent for the third Palatinate collection so as to exclude the words 'the true Religion which we together with them do professe' and William Prynne (a hostile witness) alleged that the archbishop had expressed his distaste for a cause which he only supported for the sake of the queen of Bohemia. Laud denied these circumstances, stated that 'we may be, and are of the same religion', though differing in some points; and whether for the sake of the winter queen or from any other motives, actively supported all three collections: 'What I may further do for that cause shall not be wanting'.[78] But what Laud could do to make life unbearable for the stranger churches in his own diocese and in London was also not wanting.[79] Not only Prynne and his kind but that extreme moderate, Lord Falkland of Great Tew, would condemn as both 'unpoliticke' and 'ungodly' the archbishop's evident breach of 'that union which was formerly betweene us and those of our religion beyond the sea'.[80]

Laud's triumph was transient, and where we leave the story the climax of English Calvinism was still to come, in the Westminster Confession of 1647. Thereafter it would fall victim not to sudden assassination but to its own contradictions, and to the morbid processes which eventually overtake all systematic achievements of the human mind and spirit. But before that happened the ancient debt to Geneva was repaid: not so much in money (although relief was as readily available in 1685 as it had been in 1572, 1583, and 1626) as in the currency of that pragmatic, pious divinity of the English Puritan school which had been nurtured in the unusual ecclesiastical conditions prevailing in post-Reformation England and which was to be the perdurable product of English Calvinism. By 1640, English Calvinism was making its way back to its continental source, especially in the works of the most widely read of English divines, William Perkins. In the early seventeenth century, his books were to be found as far afield as Hungary. In 1648 his *The whole treatise of the cases of conscience* was translated into Hungarian, where it joined Bishop Lewis Bayly's best-seller *The Practice of Piety*. By then, Perkins had been translated into Czech, Dutch, French, German and Spanish, and as a posthumously international Calvinist he made his contribution to the next chapter of Protestant history as a father, or rather stepfather, of Pietism.[81]

The Puritan Character : Polemics and Polarities in Early Seventeenth Century English Culture

'Truly,' said Oliver Cromwell at a critical juncture in the Putney Debates of 1647, 'I think it hath pleased God to lead me to a true and clear stating [of] our agreement and our difference. And if this be so, we are the better prepared to go [on]'.[1] Since the problem Cromwell addressed was a small matter of reconciling two incompatible versions of the English constitution, his confidence is awe-inspiring. And, of course, it was misplaced, or perhaps disingenuous. Witness the subsequent execution of some of his Leveller opponents at Cockbush Field and Burford. But if Oliver had been grappling with the even more daunting task of bringing into line the different understandings of Puritanism current among its historians perhaps even he would have thought twice before claiming that God had led him to a true and clear statement of agreements and differences.[2] Nevertheless, these observations on the Puritan character are intended, however presumptuously, to offer a way up and out of the tightly introverted spiral of these debates so that, in Cromwell's words, we may be 'the better prepared to go on'.

 'The Puritan Character' points in the right direction. For what is a *character*? As a literary-generic term deriving from Theophrastus of Athens, it indicates an interest in human *types* in their fascinating variety. But the interest is expressed most properly in an ironically censorious mode, exploiting human frailty, and takes a form not far from what we call caricature. 'If Theophrastus wrote characters of virtues they are not extant', observes one authority,[3] and while his English imitators did attempt sympathetic characters this was somewhat foreign to the genre. The maker of characters observes from the outside and records the effect that this or that human specimen has upon him or the use which he intends to make of it. He is not a novelist of any kind and he neither knows nor cares about the inner motives and experiences which account for those foibles which are his stock-in-trade. Take, for example, the character of the 'shee-Puritan', or 'Shee-precise Hypocrite', in John Earle's *Micro-cosmographie*, who was born in about 1627:

> She is a Non-conformist in a close stomacher and ruffe of Geneva print, and her purity consists much in her linnen . . . Her devotion at the church is much in the turning up her ey, and turning downe the leaf in her book, when she heares named Chapter and Verse . . . She overflowes so with the Bible that she spills it upon every occasion, and will not cudgell her maydes w'houte Scripture. It is a question whether she is more troubled w'h the Divell or the Divell w'h her, she is alwaies challenging and dareing him, and her weapon is the Practise of piety.[4] Nothing angers her so much as that women must not preach . . .[5]

At one level, this character is not only irresistible (though Earle ends, 'I am weary of her') but accurately observed. We feel that we know the shee-Puritan and shall recognise her at once if we ever see her again. The turning up of the eye and the turning down of the leaf is as accurately observed as Earle's description of the sound inside St. Paul's Cathedral as 'a kind of still roar, or loud whisper'.[6] But at another level, Earle tells us little about his subject, less than he reveals of his own susceptibility to a chauvinistic convention. We cannot speak of his failure to inform us, since that was never his intention. Yet Earle's ironic eye is more tolerant and more like a camera than that of other character writers of his age. We may compare the character of 'A Puritane' as drawn by Sir Thomas Overbury and his collaborators:

> Ignorance and fat feed, are his founders; his nurses, railing, rabbies, and round breeches: his life is but a borrowed blast of wind; for betweene two religions, as betweene two doores, he is ever whistling. Truly whose child he is, is yet unknowne; for willingly his faith allowes no father . . . His greatest care is to contemne obedience, his last care to serve God handsomely and cleanly.

Another character, written some sixty years later, continues in the same vein:

> A Scoundrel Saint, of an Order without Founder, Vow, or Rule; for he will not swear, nor be tyed to any Thing, but his own Humour . . . His Profession is but a Kind of Winter-Religion; and the Original of it is as uncertain as the hatching of Woodcocks, for no Man can tell from whence it came.[7]

Although the second account, by Samuel Butler, purports to characterise not a Puritan but a Quaker, the two sketches have a close affinity: neither has the slightest descriptive value, and there is no mistaking the anxiety motivating both these vitriolic miniatures.

Similar limitations apply to those characters which were writen more sympathetically and even approvingly. John Geree's *The Character of an Old English Puritane* (1646) identifies a number of qualities and incorporates them into what purports to be a human being, 'the good old English Puritan', but one that has no more authenticity than John Bull or Uncle Sam. Equally, there is less than total authenticity and something other than descriptive realism in the many 'lives' of Puritan saints and worthies gathered, mostly from funeral sermons, by that English Plutarch (as he was called) Samuel Clarke, and themselves closer to characters than to biographies.[8] And this is a point of no small importance, since Clarke's narratives provided the principal inspiration and matter for William Haller's *The Rise of Puritanism* (1938), a book which was more innocent in respect of the polemical intentions and literary constraints controlling its sources than it ought to have been. To learn that John Carter of Belstead in Suffolk 'all the time of his housekeeping . . . used constantly at his Table a little wooden Salt, which with age was grown to be of a duskish black, which was much taken notice of by all Comers' is to be told something deceptively, or at least artfully, descriptive and circumstantial. And when the reader learns that Carter had 'a sharp wit, and was sweet, milde, affable, and pleasant in his conversation; yet were there not any of his most facetious passages, that did not savour of holiness', he needs to know that this statement is contrived according to a rule which requires contrasting qualities (in this case pleasant affability and severe gravity) to be balanced in a whole image of judicious moderation, truly Plutarchan. But are we meeting the real John Carter?[9] To discover a more credible clergyman we may have to travel forward in time as far as the mid-1800s and the anti-heroic figure of Amos Barton in George Eliot's *Scenes of Clerical Life*, who is no less real for being the figment of a novelist's imagination.

'This hath been the inside of my life', writes an obscure curate of Derby, and we prick up our ears. For early seventeenth-century writers are not supposed to use expressions like 'the inside of my life', still less to describe it to an audience, as this man, Richard Kilby, proceeded to do. In a book published in 1608 and called *The Burthen of a loaden conscience* he uncovered a life which was, according to his own account of it, counterfeit. He neither believed nor was capable of believing the religion which he was employed to teach. His life was one continual lie. 'I have no power to turne unto God.' If we knew only a little about Kilby, an entry or two in an ecclesiastical visitation or court book, we should have no hesitation in categorising him as a typical Puritan clergyman. His early career in Kent, which involved nonconformity, had been blighted by brushes with authority. But quite apart from the ultimate scandal of his infidelity (if true), should we describe as a 'Puritan' someone who, by his own confession, was so hopelessly addicted to 'companie keeping', spending far too much time in the pub, and who for reasons of poor health and depression often failed to prepare his sermons, which led to complaints and threatened his livelihood? With this depressive and obscure bachelor living with his landlady in Jacobean Derby we seem closer to the alienated world of Raskolnikov than to that of the typecast 'godly preacher'.[10]

But are we closer to reality? It is hard to say. Kilby published *The Burthen of a loaden conscience* anonymously and it was a publishing sensation, achieving a dozen editions by 1635. A sequel was promised in which the author undertook to reveal his identity, but only when the repentance which so persistently eluded him had been found. In due course, after prolonging the suspense by a spurious announcement of relief, later repudiated, Kilby wrote in 1618 the book called *Hallelu-iah: Praise yee the Lord, for the unburthening of a loaden conscience*, which contained fresh revelations of the inside of this wretched life, not much more encouraging than the first. The wary historian at this point may suspect that he is being taken for a ride, the kind of ride involved in the Elizabethan device of 'flyting', that is, a largely contrived literary controversy from which both sides stand to profit, a device by no means confined to the sixteenth century. Whether Kilby really revealed the inside of his life we shall never know.

By implication I am taking a tough and sceptical line about the possibility of describing the character of a Puritan from within. I know that it has been said often enough that the essence of Puritanism was a certain kind of intense religious experience, both painful and ecstatic, an internal spiritual dynamic associated with what it is now fashionable to call 'experimental Calvinism'.[11] As a general proposition this can hardly be faulted. It is another matter to be certain about the nature and quality of experience in a given individual. Of course we gain insight from such intensely personal testimonies as the diaries and autobiographies of Samuel Ward, Richard Rogers, Ralph Josselin and, above all, the New Englander Thomas Shepard, whose writings, suggests Michael McGiffert, admit the reader directly into the heart of a Puritan.[12] Professor Paul Seaver's friend Nehemiah Wallington cannot fail to reveal a good deal of the inside of his life in his copious and almost solipsistic writings.[13] In a less familiar journal written by the Somerset clothier William Leonard, grandfather of the politician Simonds D'Ewes, we find these words: 'These troubles have happened. No hap [that is, no accident] but a means that my God hath used that I might the better know my self', and we too come to know this man, a little. According to Max Weber, or rather to the less subtle Weberians, an Elizabethan clothier who was also a godly Puritan ought not to have died with unpaid debts of £700. But that was Leonard's 'hap'. 'I have strived to do and to gain, but it was not thy will, O Lord'. 'O God, deliver me out of this usury for thy name's sake, for it is a hell to a good conscience'.[14]

I cannot imagine how historians of this subject could manage without such sources, which often escape unwittingly and as it were naively from the conventions that otherwise determine their content and structure. (But Lady Margaret Hoby is careful never to escape![15]) When Ralph Josselin tells us, and he often does, about a certain sore place on his navel, I take this as evidence that he had a sore place on his navel, not that he felt himself to be under some kind of formal constraint to say so, although the point of reference, as with virtually every circumstance mentioned in the diary, is the doctrine of providence. But, as with Richard Kilby's highly disorganised life, Josselin's unguarded disclosures suggest a paradox, and a difficulty. If we were supplied with thousands of narrations resembling Josselin's, all equally idiosyncratic in their personal detail, how should we begin to construct out of them a general category called Puritan? Would it be sensible to try? The coherence of our concept of Puritanism depends upon knowing as little about particular Puritans as possible. It might disintegrate altogether if we knew everything. Historians of Puritanism sit in Plato's cave, describing not reality but those shadows of reality which are 'characters' and stereotypes.

Richard Parker, vicar of Dedham in Essex in the 1580s and minute clerk of the Dedham Conference, or 'Classis',[16] is a Puritan minister more familiar than most. We know not only about his nonconformity but about the depth of his pastoral commitment. He was anxious to resolve certain doubts about the observation of the Sabbath, and he asked his brethren 'what course a minister should take when disorders be risen up in a church' and yet the officers and other leading men of the parish did nothing about them. Was it necessary, he asked on another occasion, that a pastor should visit the homes of all his parishioners, however unresponsive they might be to his ministry? Perhaps there was more in that question that meets the eye. For Parker (like Kilby, a bachelor) was presently exposed as a man who had made indecent attempts on the chastity of a number of married women in the district, one of them living as close as the other half of his semi-detached, or duplex, vicarage. A local clothier and churchwarden told how he had walked with Parker in his garden, urging him to admit his fault; whereupon the vicar

> began to relent, and confessed, that for the attempt he would not deny, but for the fact, he never did, and that the Lord did know how sorrowful he had been for that his great oversight, desiring this examinate to stand his friend and consider his estate, being a young man, and that his credit once taken away he was utterly undone, showing himself very much grieved, with weeping eyes.

Does that evidence prove that Richard Parker of Dedham was not a Puritan because Puritans do not behave like that? Or that Puritans are not necessarily what they seem since Parker, who was a Puritan, did behave like that? Or does it simply inform us about one aberrant individual?[17]

Thomas Larkham belonged to a later generation. He was a New Englander of the 1630s who returned to England in the 1640s to serve as an army chaplain and as vicar of Tavistock in Devon. Larkham's Puritan credentials were ostensibly impeccable. He tells us that he had suffered 'in the time of the prelacy in almost all the courts in England', a typically hyperbolical statement. But the known facts of his early career are more ambivalent. His troubles pursued him across the Atlantic and were not all of the kind celebrated in Puritan hagiography. There was a violent quarrel with another minister, Hanserd Knollys, and talk of a bastard child. Back in England Larkham's adventures were a long-running soap opera of controversies. According to his perception of himself, he was a zealous man, striving to impose the discipline of a 'powerful' ministry on his godless parish. His diary contains the fervent outpourings we expect of such a document: 'Wonderfully hath the Lord been gracious to me, though I should never enjoy mercy more; I have unspeakable cause to be thankful.' But according to his enemies Larkham was a passionate, rancorous, foul-mouthed man who indulged in 'personal' preaching, that is, the practice of reviling named individuals from the pulpit in the hearing of great assemblies. And he alienated many members of his gathered congregation. To those who found that they had had enough and walked out, he was alleged to have shouted: 'Let them go to what church they will, we shall find dirt enough to cast after them'.[18]

We cannot say that this case was unique, only that the evidence is exceptionally copious, if contradictory. Susan Hardman Moore, who has carefully studied it, concludes: 'The truth about his ministry will never be known'. There would be little point in this instance in suggesting that Larkham was not some kind of Puritan. But whether that tells us very much about the objective circumstances in which the disharmonies occurred, or about his inability to get along with other human beings, is another matter. And it is both sides of the equation, not only what Larkham thought of his people but what they made of him, which must be understood, if only to gain some understanding of what it was that made Larkham a Puritan in the first place and progressively radicalised him. Who would not gladly exchange a hundred pages of Josselin's diary for half a dozen sheets of notes written about him by some of his Earls Colne parishioners? Since the pastoral capacity of a minister who reduced a parochial congregation of almost a thousand to a pious little 'society' of fewer than forty is less certain than the fact that he had a sore place on his navel.[19]

Thus far, some iconoclastic demythologising. But it would be pointless to react as the great American public reacted to scandalous revelations about the electronic evangelists Bakker and Swaggart, that is, to conclude, judgmentally and dismissively, that the Puritan religious experience was fraudulent. It would be pointless because the complexity of what we call the Puritan character included the nagging conviction of fraudulence, or at least of hypocrisy, on the part of the Puritan himself. Richard Kilby was unusual in the urge, however motivated, to dramatise publicly his wretched condition, probably not so in the condition itself. David Leverenz writes of the Puritan character in terms of 'ambivalence, anxiety, and contradiction' reflected in 'a private language of agonised doubt' complementing 'a public language of militant submission'. Thomas Shepard is the extreme case, his journal reverberating with such statements as 'I saw how I was without all sense as well as sight of God, estranged from the life of God'. 'I felt a wonderful cloud of darkness and atheism over my head'. Professor McGiffert comments that Shepard's suspicions of his own hypocrisy run through his journal 'like threads of fire'. And they were readily communicated to others. Giles Firmin reported meeting persons who 'could not be resolved that ever their faith was true because of that which he had written'.[20]

So the inside of Puritanism, insofar as we can see into it, is not so much discreditable as contradictory. McGiffert tells us that Shepard had no formal psychology of the emotions at his command and that his record of his own fluctuating feelings was 'anything but intellectually strict'. He only knew that he could not trust his own feelings. His own perception of his hypocrisy could have been hypocritical.[21]

Here I make no further effort to order that intrinsic disorder with psychological analysis of the Puritan character in its innerness but only to pursue a more limited if necessary question: Why do we call it a Puritan character? In the past I have argued,[22] perhaps somewhat perversely, that Jacobean Puritanism had no real existence, belonging in the eye of the beholder. Puritans did not call themselves Puritans but suffered the name as an objectionable stigma. In a situation dominated by Puritans there would have been no Puritans, or at least the word would not have been much used. If all the inhabitants of the Shropshire village of Eaton Constantine had been of his persuasion, Richard Baxter's father would not have been known as a Puritan. The fact that he was so branded is indicative of the uncomfortable conditions in which his singular lifestyle was lived out: he was the only inhabitant who chose to read his Bible rather than sit under the great dancing tree, which grew inconveniently outside his front door.[23] If references to Puritans become less frequent in some kinds of documents, that may be evidence not that Puritanism had been effectively stamped out but of the reverse, its growing prevalence. Yet a Puritanism which was no longer in contention, no longer setting itself against the stream, would cease to be in any very meaningful sense Puritanism. We might as well stop talking about it.

This relativist and nominalist argument is assisted by appreciation of the Humpty Dumpty world of religious parties and religious terminology which characterised the early years of the reign of Charles I. Humpty Dumpty connected power with making words mean what he wanted them to mean. So, evidently, did the Laudian-Arminian party in the Church of England. At the time of Charles I's accession and for a few years following, Puritanism was said by some to be a thing of the past.

Archbishop Abbot said that 'there is not . . . left any inconformable minister which appeareth' save two or three, and clearly he had in mind Puritanism in the historically justified and objectively definable sense of conscientious nonconformity in respect of the laws of the church, especially with regard to ceremonies.[24] So did the author of *A Discourse concerning Puritans* when he wrote in 1641 that 'there seemes now little remaining of Puritanisme, but the breathlesse carkas of it', even while he complained that 'this detested odious name of Puritan' was becoming ever more prevalent.[25]

These witnesses testify that there were such things as real Puritans but that they were becoming hard to find, like flies in the wintertime. There was little connection between their sort and the 'orthodox' who considered themselves to be pillars of a legally established reformed church and who were surprised and affronted to find themselves victims of the 'odious name'. It has become a useful piece of shorthand to talk of Jacobean Calvinist consensus,[26] an expression which needs clarification since the word *consensus* ought not to mean the universal appeal of Calvinist theology but only its dominance and need not imply the absence of differences of emphasis within a measure of consensus. But the ascendancy after about 1626 of the Arminian, or (better) anti-Calvinist, tendency represented a drastic U-turn, accompanied by the denigration of Calvinists, hitherto a kind of political as well as moral majority of the religious public, as Puritans. Sir Benjamin Rudyerd in a speech to the Long Parliament, which identified the religious opposition, called it 'their great work, their masterpiece', that all who professed 'our religion' were now branded as Puritans, as if they were 'the suspected party of the kingdom'. Francis Rous, who called 'the word Puritan' an 'essentiall engine' in the work of reconciling England and Rome, said that it was now the common word for 'an orthodox man'; it was what Arminians or papists called Protestants. By 1641 these were long-established commonplaces. Remarking in a parliamentary speech of 1586 that the traitor Babington had called two privy councillors 'Puritans', Job Throckmorton exclaimed: 'The Lorde send her Majestie stoare of such Puritanes.' William Prynne, noting in *Histrio-Mastix* that to condemn stage plays was 'one grand badge of a Puritan', reminded his readers that the Apostles and Fathers had also condemned them. 'Therefore they are arrant Puritans'.[27] According to *A Discourse concerning Puritans*, 'scarce any civill honest Protestant' could now avoid the aspersion.

> Thus by its latitude it strikes generally, by its contraction it pierces deeply, by
> its confused application it deceives invisibly. Small scruples first intitle mee to
> the name of Puritan, and then the Name of Puritan intitles me further to all
> mischiefe whatsoever.[28]

Admittedly more might be involved in the imputation of Puritanism
than mere sleight of hand, a polemical conjuring trick. Men were now
actually turned into, or back into, Puritans who had not previously or
always been Puritans. That is to say, they acquired or reacquired a sense
of indignant alienation which they had not manifested before the anti-
Calvinist innovations of the 1630s, just as some veterans of Elizabethan
Puritanism had effectively abandoned their Puritanism under James I.
Nicholas Bownd was a prominent Elizabethan activist. But in the altered
circumstances of the Jacobean peace he dedicated books to bishops and
told his own bishop of Norwich 'how readie we are, and shall be, to yeild
obedience to all your lordship's godly proceedings'.[29] Conversely, Henry
Burton, who lost his ears to Archbishop Laud's repression, had described
himself as 'orthodox' in 1626 and 'in one sense . . . no Puritan, for he is
conformable [and] none of the refractories, but doth both practise himselfe
and preach upon occasion in the defence of ecclesiasticall ceremonies,
and that very earnestly . . .' Burton even claimed to have repelled from
the Communion those who refused to receive it kneeling. But in his
autobiographical *Narration* (1643) he tells us how the undermining of 'the
true Protestant religion' by the new 'prelaticall party' caused him to 'fall
off from ceremonies' and presently from any respect for episcopacy itself,
for by now he was a hardened root-and-brancher and would soon be
an Independent. Thomas Shepard was called by Laud a 'nonconformable
man' but did not know why, since at the time he was, or so he claims, 'not
resolved either way, but was dark in those things'. Only after he had been
silenced did 'the Lord let me see into the evil of the English ceremonies'.[30]
So Burton and Shepard were actually turned into Puritans, not merely
designated as such.

But perhaps neither Burton nor Shepard was as innocent, or perhaps we
should say as passive, as he may have seemed. As an account of the revival
of militant Puritanism toward 1640, the nominalist-relativist approach
has seemed to its critics less than adequate.[31] To represent the Puritanism
which fed into the Civil War as simply reactive rather than active on its
own account is to turn the eye away from earlier provocations to which
Archbishop Laud and other anti-Calvinists were themselves reacting

and to disregard the convoluted complexity of the Puritan religious consciousness. The English religious scene was not disturbed for the first time in 1626 or 1633, and if talk of a Calvinist consensus suggests that, then the term had better be abandoned. So can we venture the further comment that to say that Puritanism was something which some people detected and detested in others is not to say that there was not something there to detect and detest? Surely we can, but it is not necessarily a very telling point, since in very many cases the essence of that *something* will be found to be nothing other than the evangelical Calvinist Protestantism which was prevalent in early seventeenth-century England as well as in other reformed communities of Western Europe, and which some of its opponents *chose* to describe and attack as Puritanism. It was not Puritanism until it was so described. John Geree's *Character of an old English Puritane* was refurbished in 1670 when a broadside was published under the title *The character of an old English Protestant; formerly called a puritan, now a non-conformist.*[32]

All attempts to distinguish this person, or that idea, or a certain practice or prejudice, as Puritan rather than otherwise are liable to fail, and the difficulty of finding a satisfactory and non-anachronistic term to take the place of *otherwise* is significant. There flourished in Jacobean conditions, especially among the clergy dominating what might be called the middle heights of the ecclesiastical economy, in leading London pulpits and important country and market-town livings, a phalanx of evangelical Calvinists whom it would not be very sensible to try to label as either Puritans or otherwise. Those who wrote books make an ABC beginning with golden-tongued Thomas Adams; Lewis Bayly (a bishop), whose *Practise of pietie* guided the steps of Earle's 'shee-Puritan'; Richard Bernard, plucked back from the brink of separatism by the great and the good of the Jacobean church, including the king's chaplain and editor, Bishop James Montague; and here we may include the young Henry Burton; Thomas Cooper, frequent preacher to the Virginia Company; and both the Downames, George and John, George an Irish bishop from 1616. That takes us through D; and eventually we should reach W with Samuel Ward, indeed both Samuel Wards, of Cambridge and of Ipswich; and William Whateley, the 'roaring boy' of Banbury whose 'stirring' ministry caused Thomas Shepard's father to move his household to the town; Andrew Willett and Thomas Wilson of Canterbury can bring up the rear. *Otherwise*, of course, has to mean, in some historians' books, *Anglican*, a term anachronistic for the seventeenth century but perhaps justified if we are speaking of Lancelot Andrewes or John Donne or even of George Herbert, with his unusual devotion to the particular, maternal genius of the 'British church'. But to debate whether this or that Jacobean cleric on our ABC list should be classified as Puritan or Anglican is futile. So too with their lay counterparts, those many readers of William Perkins. And in what sense was Perkins a Puritan?

In this field the fine art of taxonomy is misapplied, the ever greater refinement reflected in attempts to define Puritanism exactly, and within itself, actually counter-productive. The minute examination of inert specimens, pinned out on boards, the argument of their printed works carefully dissected, should be at least supplemented with more strenuous field studies, where the specimens can be observed alive and kicking. Here the natural historian of Puritanism will find that what matters is not what people were in themselves but what they were doing to each other and saying about each other and against each other. For even the taxonomical guidance provided by the contemporary literature is not really taxonomy at all but disguised polemic, part of the dynamic, stressful interaction which it is the historian's prime business to study. Like any naturalist, Giles Widdowes in *The Schysmatical Puritan* (Oxford 1630) defined Puritans in terms of 'genus' and 'species' and proceeded to construct a table containing no less than ten 'specific kinds' of Puritan nonconformist. That is significant, but not in the way that the historian supposes who says that 'according to Widdowes' there were ten kinds of Puritans; still less the more incompetent student of the subject who simply states that there were ten kinds of Puritans and quotes Widdowes as his authority. The 1641 *Discourse concerning Puritans* divides Puritans into four categories: Puritans in church policy; Puritans in religion; Puritans in state; and Puritans in morality — or 'Ethicall Puritan[s]'. But this is not proof that there were four kinds of Puritans. It is not even reliable evidence that contemporaries, all contemporaries, *thought* that there were four kinds.[33] What matters is not what was thought (and most thoughts are hidden from us) but what it was polemically advantageous to allege. The least of the concerns of such writers was to assist the objective understanding of the historians of a later generation.

So the term *Puritan* is to be studied with a certain suspicious reserve, and always in context — which can be heard as a plea for the same amount of attention to be paid to unprinted, social documentation as has been given to printed sermons and theological treatises. The kind of context I have in mind is that of the Wiltshire village where in 1624 the fun-loving daughter of a former churchwarden complained of her new vicar in the following terms: 'When once he . . . takes his green book in hand we shall have such a deal of bibble babble that I am weary to hear it, and I can then sit down in my seat and take a good nap'. 'We had a good parson here before but now we have a puritan . . . A plague or a pox in him that ever he did come hither'.[34] In a different setting, an archbishop of York said to a future archbishop of York: 'What . . . dost thou call me a papist? If I be a papist, thou be a puritan'.[35] Two leading churchmen, one of them archbishop of Canterbury, wrangled in similar terms in the presence of the king himself. Archbishop Abbot accused the Oxford divine John Howson, an early patron of Laud, of 'maine-tayning popery', or at least of all too rarely preaching against it. In retaliation, Howson alleged that the former primate, Richard Bancroft, had always 'held' Abbot for a Puritan.[36]

In this extraordinary series of exchanges we find James I, like some modern historians, desperately struggling to retain an objective, workable definition of Puritanism. When the name of a certain judge came up in discussion, the king remarked that he knew him to be a 'sowre puritan'. But when Howson suggested that Bishop Henry Robinson of Carlisle might be a Puritan, the king insisted that this could not be so. Robinson was a bishop and 'nowe noe puritan'. One can almost hear the matter-of-fact Scots voice: 'Na, na, he canna be a Puritan for he's a bishop forbye.' But before we accuse this most astute monarch of missing a trick, let us consider the possibility that James *chose* to mistake the point, just as at the Hampton Court Conference he pretended to misunderstand the moderate words of the leading Puritan spokesman (John Reynolds, lifelong friend of Bishop Robinson) as a demand for Presbyterianism, using them as a cue for his famous retort of 'no bishop, no king'. Puritans, like Catholics, were important parts of the stage scenery composing this king's worldview. If they had not existed it would have been necessary to invent them. For both Papists and Puritans in their pure, extreme forms defied his regal and divine authority. Either this was their only offence or it was the only one in which James took much interest, for he was tolerant of both Catholics and Puritans who moderated their opinions in this respect: he was in effect choosing to pretend that these moderates were not Catholics and Puritans. The Jesuits and high

Presbyterian Puritans were doubtless a menace, but a menace which enabled James to make the most of his affronted regality, just as he had earlier used the matter of witchcraft for a similar purpose, teaching in his *Daemonologie* that to know God adequately it was necessary also to know his adversary, the Devil.[37]

So such episodes are not to be taken as evidence that Archbishop Hutton of York or Archbishop Abbot of Canterbury were Puritans, only of the fact that it was useful (even if only momentarily useful) to call them that. It is the beginning of wisdom to appreciate that the utterance 'thou art a Puritan', 'supremely emotive and judgmental' as it was,[38] tells us as much, and perhaps more, about the utterer as about the party against whom the words were uttered. Or rather it tells us about both halves of a stressful relationship. Any historian who follows the celebrated dictum that he should read and read until he hears the voices of time speaking to him cannot disregard the word *Puritan*, which is an insistent, resonant voice. But his ear must be attuned to the conversational and especially the polemical settings into which the word obtrudes. This is merely a way of stating the truism that the historian studies not past reality but past perceptions of reality, of necessity more or less distorted, and that what comes out of his study are his own perceptions of those perceptions, no more distorted than he can help.

I believe that historians who keep eyes and ears open to the record of the 1560s to the 1620s will be able to come to this summary conclusion about what might be called Puritanism in the eye of the beholder: The term *Puritan* first came into use, as the 1641 *Discourse* and many other sources tell us, in the mid-1560s, in connection with the original controversies of the Elizabethan church about ceremonies and especially vestments, extending subsequently to larger questions of church discipline and government. But at this high controversial level, the stigma was applied intermittently, and interchangeably with other terms such as Precisian. Richard Bancroft, the most dedicated opponent the Elizabethan Puritans ever had, an archetypal Grand Inquisitor, never called them that. But the evidence of reported speech at a more popular level suggests that from at least the 1570s, and certainly toward 1580, *Puritan* was a gibe hurled, as it were, in the vernacular at all too evidently religious persons, Protestants, by their less obviously religious or crypto-Catholic neighbors: 'Oh say the scorning raylers, now this holy man will goe to heaven in a Hey barne, now these *Puritans* flocke together' (1583).[39] And it was in that kind of setting, rather than in learned ecclesiastical company, that the term mostly resided, for the next sixty years. In 1641 the author of *A Discourse concerning Puritans* thought it a recent development that this 'vile and scurrilous . . . licence of fiction and detraction', which had hitherto been heard only in 'Play-houses, Taverns, and Bordelloes', should be taken up in pulpits and in print.[40]

For reasons which have never been satisfactorily explored, and which have been discussed only in relation to the theatrical attack on Puritanism (beginning in the early 1590s),[41] this anxiety presently conveyed itself upwards into more polite circles and became a favorite topic of the newly sophisticated and brittle conversation of the later Elizabethan years, a subject for what Bishop William Barlow called *'Satyricall Invectives'*.[42] Perhaps this was symptomatic of a kind of secularisation, as the younger Elizabethan generation reacted against the Stoic religiosity of its elders.[43] That young-man-about-town John Manningham noted in his diary (1602) a number of anti-Puritan jokes in the form of neatly malicious definitions: 'A puritane is such a one as loves God with all his soule, but hates his neighbour with all his heart'.[44] Sir John Harington included similar items in his *Epigrams* (1615). Commonplace books contain verses with openings like the following:

> Long hath it vexed our learned age to scan
> Who rightly might be named a Puritan.[45]

Hence the archsophistication of the character of Malvolio, of whom Maria says, 'Marry, sir, sometimes he is a kind of puritan'.[46] The common theme running through much of this material is one of absurd hypocrisy, and it has a close affinity to the more developed matter of the characters, where the Theophrastan model requires the writer to begin definitionally, 'A Puritan *is* . . .'

The historical circumstances accounting for this hostile anxiety to know your enemy, but to know him in terms of a limited and consequently reassuring stereotype, can never be adequately known, although they are to some extent inferable from large numbers of conversational exchanges which could be more systematically collated than they have been so far. The literary and rhetorical circumstances are probably understood but they do not take us very far. The social-psychological circumstances favouring these sorts of verbal interaction have so far been neglected by historians, and to our loss, for they represent what we have to work on, our 'given'. Edwin Schur in *Labeling Deviant Behavior* (1971) provides an introduction to the concept and method of 'labeling', suggesting how our problem would be tackled by his kind of social scientist. In the early seventeenth century, Puritanism was perceived as no less perverse a form of deviance than the behavioural patterns to which the labels are applied within the scope of Schur's investigations: homosexuality; drug abuse; delinquency of various kinds; generally antisocial behavior. Moreover several of the working propositions of sociologists and social therapists who favour the 'labeling' approach manifestly extend to our subject. Walter Lippman has remarked: 'We do not first see, then define, we define first and then see'. Deviance is to a large extent 'created' through processes of social definition and stigmatisation. It is not so much an inherent quality of the person stigmatised as deviant, or even of his or her actions, as a description of behaviour which has been so labeled and stigmatised. 'Deviance is viewed not as a static entity but rather as a continuously shaped and reshaped *outcome* of dynamic processes of social interaction'. So Puritanism has to do with *process*, not *state*. St. Paul, a theologian, instructed his followers at Corinth (in effect): 'Become what you are.' Frank Tannenbaum, a sociologist, declares: 'The person becomes the thing he is described as being.' The critical variable, according to Kai Erikson, is not so much the subject labeled as the social audience, which may be defined as society at large, or as those individuals with whom the subject is in daily interaction.[47]

The theory of labeling, with its highly relativistic implication that deviance has a limited 'real' existence until attention is brought to bear on it, disturbs some other students of modern forms of deviance, who fear that it may discourage a realistic response to what are, after all, real problems. Drug abuse may arise through imputation, but the habit having been acquired has to be dealt with. A parallel historical case concerns the Ranters of the mid-seventeenth century, a subject brilliantly but somewhat perversely investigated by J.C. Davis in *Fear, Myth, and History* (1986), which Gerald Aylmer reviewed with an acidulated wit.[48] Can there be such a thing as smoke without fire? Can it be, as Davis has argued, that the Ranters never existed? Dr Aylmer drew our attention to Oliver Cromwell's nose, an object of the same order of evidential reality as Ralph Josselin's navel. If Cromwell had not in fact carried a nose of somewhat larger than ordinary proportions we should not have heard so much about it. There was some fire as well as smoke. The Ranters existed and did not have to be invented.

However, the applicability of the labeling theory to the subject of Puritanism seems by contrast to be virtually noncontroversial, and especially if we place it alongside the related Wittgensteinian concept of 'conflict games', as used by John Lofland in *Deviance and Identity* (1969).[49] In these 'games', opposing forces use wordplay to define situations and types of behaviour and to 'fix' the character of individuals. The early modern historian, inhabiting a culture in which *homo ludens* was still in his prime, is in a strong position to follow out these suggestive leads. For the circumstances in which the label *Puritan* was made to stick were ostensibly playful, 'pastimes' for the participants but serious and corrective in purpose and aggressive in expression. The setting resembles that of the skimmingtons or 'rough music' with which attention was drawn to incongruous marital unions, conspicuous domestic discord and other social deviations; the street theatre of shame included saucepans clashing, horns played aggressively, the derision of scatological contempt. According to the dictates of this repertoire, Puritans were mercilessly parodied in mocking rhymes and libels. In this society one neighbor could not invite another to accompany him to the sermon without risking the 'intollerable contempt' of being taken for 'a monster among men', 'an owl in the day time among the birds'.[50] He might be glad to get away with being called a Puritan.

Why this 'intollerable contempt'? And why contempt between two almost mythical constructs, Puritan and Anti-Puritan, which has lured social historians who suppose themselves to be dealing with reality into unrealistic and even false dichotomies? Twofold divisions between 'us' and 'them' reflect the most invidious and potentially the most destructive of all hostile situations. They also tend to be the most detached from reality, depending upon a gross oversimplification of the *complexio oppositorum* which is humankind. In the perception of Puritan divines, to dismiss the bulk of their flocks, as some did, as 'carnal', 'irreligious', and even 'wicked', as if they comprised a monolithic lump of undifferentiated evil, implies a blunting of pastoral sensitivity and the total abandonment of pastoral psychology. The great Richard Baxter, who knew better, divided his people at Kidderminster not into two crude categories of good and bad, nor even into the three preferred by Ralph Josselin at Earls Colne (the zealous and godly, the indifferent, the absent), but into no less than twelve types. Out of some eighteen hundred communicants he counted five hundred 'or perhaps somewhat more' who were rated 'serious Professors of religion . . . such as the vulgar call precise', or, as Baxter might have said but didn't, Puritans. At the other extreme he described some who gave themselves over 'to security and ungodliness'. Their irreligion consisted of a radical perversion of Calvinism. But between pure godliness and utter ungodliness, Baxter recognised many intermediate categories: those with 'tollerable knowledge' but who were nevertheless notorious sinners, drunkards or fornicators; an almost contrary type 'of more tractable dispositions' but who 'really know not what a Christian is', naive Pelagians who hoped to get to Heaven through the practice of social virtues. And both these were distinguished from others still 'of tollerable knowledge, and no Drunkards or Whoremongers' but who kept idle, tippling company and detested 'Strict Professors'.[51]

No doubt Baxter had motives of his own for drawing up this scheme, which like all exercises in typology must have done some violence to the teeming and infinite variety which was the population of the town of Kidderminster. But it was closer to life than the polemical analyses of John Darrell or Arthur Dent, who made a crude dichotomy between a godless majority, 'the prophane multitude', and a select remnant of 'sound, sincere, faithfull and zealous worshippers'. Dent thought that if the godless were sifted out and only the truly zealous left, 'I suppose we should not need the art of Arithmetick to number them'. 'I doubt they would walke very thinly in the streets, so as a man might easily tel them as they goe.' Darrell thought the true ratio of 'good' to 'naught' might prove to be one to nineteen in every twenty, while Shepard was prepared to believe that it was one in a thousand. William Perkins hit out against the Separatists in insisting that the Church of England was 'doubtless . . . God's cornfield . . . and we are the corn heap of God . . . But alas, the pure wheat how thin is it scattered?' For Perkins just two categories: Corn and chaff.[52]

The drastic dichotomising of society into two portions distributed in grossly unequal numbers is what we have to account for if we hope to understand both sides of the stressful relationship of which *Puritan* and other terms of pejorative stigmatisation were telling symptoms. This penchant for dichotomising is often described as an identifying feature of the Puritan mentality;[53] yet it was by no means a Puritan peculiarity but rather part and parcel of early modern thought and discourse. Recent studies of witch beliefs, by Stuart Clark, and of so-called atheism, by

Michael Hunter, have helpfully stressed the relevance of certain mental and rhetorical structures, highly characteristic of post-Renaissance discourse, for explaining the exaggerated dichotomies of the age. These were structures of binary opposition and of inversion. Thus obedience (as it might be manifested in children) was treated with reference to disobedience, patriarchy in terms of women on top, true religion in contrast to superstition. It would be a misreading of the contemporary literature on such subjects, however, to conclude that children were wholly out of hand, women dominant in the war of the genders, superstition rife. If anything this kind of evidence points in the opposite direction.[54]

Inversion as a formal principle was built into many of the rituals and group fantasies of popular culture, and its function was usually not disintegrative of existing institutions but rather collusive and affirmative. At a higher intellectual level, antithesis was the stuff of academic argument. The attention paid to 'atheism' as the most prevalent and threatening intellectual tendency of the age (Thomas Nashe reported that 'there is no sect now in England so scattered', and Richard Greenham thought that it was to be more feared than popery) seems to have borne no relation to the actual social incidence of what we should now recognise as atheism but had everything to do with the formidable forces in early seventeenth-century England making for theism. Similarly, the detailed attention paid to Antichrist is evidence of the pronounced Christocentrism of the age. One function of such drastic and (to our eyes) implausible dichotomies and inversions was to express in a pure and absolute form anxiety about disturbing and unwelcome tendencies, which may in reality have been weak and attenuated. Attitudes to popery, witchcraft and atheism are all examples of this procedure and were inferred from the most fragmentary and dubious of evidence. And so are attitudes to Puritanism and, for that matter, to what Archbishop Laud described as the 'great bugbear called Arminianism'.[55] This was a society which could not manage without its great bugbears. Dr Hunter has written: 'Real and exaggerated components were brought together into an idealised whole that we find distastefully artificial but which clearly served significant descriptive and prescriptive functions at the time, and coloured contemporary perceptions of reality'.[56]

The language and social imagery of binary opposition were nothing if not scriptural and consequently almost mandatory for religious discussion. As we read in Ecclesiasticus, chapter 42: 'All things are double, one against another'. One thinks of the words 'He that is not with me is against me'; of Christ's promises made to his 'little flock'; of the vision of the strait gate and narrow way 'and few there be that find it', contrasted with the broad gate leading to destruction. There are sheep, and there are goats. Even when the intention was that loyal and true-hearted Englishmen should stand as one against their foreign enemies, as John Foxe wrote 'in one ship together', the biblical rhetorical mode pitched the 'little flock of true Christians' against the deceptive might of the multitude, David alone (but for God) against Goliath. As John Norden wrote in *A Mirror for the Multitude* (1586): 'Let not custome or the multitude make you faine to followe their follie', the multitude signifying international popery, or Spain. 'From the beginning the church of God hath bin farre the least part of the worlde, the least part of everie countrey and kingdome: the least part of everie Citie, yea the least part of everie congregation.'[57] This was intended to encourage 'little England'. But later the topos became a weapon to divide England against itself, as Perkins revealed that the heap of good corn which was the English church was in truth a heap mostly of chaff, containing only 'few corns of wheat'. Thomas Cooper remarked in a London sermon: 'Oh how vaine . . . is theyr conceit, that dreame all shall be saved?' 'The number of his *Chosen* is a *little Flocke* in comparison of the *Cast-awayes*'.[58]

In the Bible, the division of righteous and unrighteous was eschatological. It would happen at the last day. Until then, the emergent wheat and the tares were hard to distinguish and were to be left to grow together. What tempted Puritans to begin the process of weeding here and now, at least in their social and pastoral assumptions and judgements, was presumably the perception, realistic enough, that as sincere and genuine rather than merely conformable Protestants they were thin on the ground (their ultra-religious way of life would nowadays be described as a sub-culture). This perception was reinforced by the internalisation within themselves as individuals and groups of the doctrine of saving grace by election, in itself a mental structure of binary discrimination when held, robustly, as a full and balanced doctrine of double predestination. Peter Lake comes close to the heart of the Puritan experience when he connects it with 'an extremely exalted view of the unity and mutuality of the community of the godly' and the urge to make that community real and visible.[59]

However, the Puritanism was not inherent in the godly community. It consisted in the tension between that community, the church in a gathered sense, and the church as the entire Christian nation. If those called Puritans had themselves made a clean mental break with the idea of a national, all-inclusive church, there would have been no tension. Separatists had made a hard and painful decision, drastic in its consequences. But the decision once made, there was little tension. Conversely, conformists, who readily identified the church with the whole baptised communicating population, and who agreed with Richard Hooker that church and commonwealth were virtually coterminous, felt no tension. The Puritans were those whose lives were strung between the contrary principles of inclusion and exclusion. George Widley proclaimed: 'Every hill is Sion, every river is Jordan, every countrie Jewry, every citie Jerusalem.' 'All must be compelled unto the true religion.' 'Wee are to inforce all unto the service of the true God'[60] The master principle, alone capable of taking the strain, was discipline. Without it, it was a matter of nagging uncertainty whether a true church existed in the English parishes. *An Admonition to the Parliament* (1572) proclaimed: 'We in England are so far off from having a church rightly reformed, according to the prescript of God's word, that as yet we are not come to the outward face of the same.' That *not* threatened to stretch the rope to breaking point. The authors thought again and altered the *not* to *scarce*: 'as yet we are scarce come to the outward face of the same'.[61]

As Dr Lake has helpfully suggested, virtually all the disputes between the Puritans and their opponents (which served to define and even to create Puritanism) can be reduced to the tension between the godly minority community, rendered partly visible as a kind of confessing church, and the church defined as the whole community, the territorial, or folk, church. In essence this was an argument about the visibility of the godly community and about its relationship to the English church as a whole. The point about the surplice, the cross in baptism, the ring in marriage, and other small ceremonies and customs was whether such things were to be conceded to those reconstructed papists who deserved no concessions at all, since their presence in the church was an offensive and essentially political contrivance. The major controversies about the constitution and government of the church can be read as an exegetical debate about New Testament ecclesiology, the meaning and force of certain texts. But more profoundly they had to do with how authority in the church related to membership, and indeed to the question of membership itself. The social, cultural and moral battles fought over the use of Sunday, contentions about maypoles, dancing and church ales, were waged to determine whether the godly minority community could impose its will on society.

To sum up these theoretical perspectives: Puritans were not different from Protestants. They were Protestants in a particular set of circumstances to which they actively contributed, but which were not of their choosing; or rather (since we see them to a great extent from the outside, even when we are seeing them through their own eyes) Puritans were Protestants as they were *perceived* in a particular set of circumstances.

And in practice? It is easier to trace the polemical polarities of early seventeenth-century English religious culture in principle than to follow them through on the ground. Richard Baxter wrote of 'the Warre ... in our streets' which was life-threatening and forced him out of Kidderminster.[62] But this was on the very eve of the Civil War itself, when the political atmosphere was highly charged. Rival religions in Jacobean England had not taken to cutting each other down in the streets. The gutters had not literally run with blood. This is worth our observation, since such things had happened almost routinely in France, in three decades of religious war. Hatred, it appears, never or very rarely reached that level, or if it did it was restrained by a combination of external law-enforcement processes and by internalised respect for the public peace. In 1572, a young man attempting to saw down a maypole in a Sussex village at eleven o'clock at night was shot in the neck and killed. He had walked from another village some miles away to do his work and so was a stranger. Otherwise, perhaps, such a thing would not have happened. Even so, the incident is outstanding, even unique.[63] And this degree of restraint, too, is not to be taken for granted, since the implications of the shared vision of godliness, which was of the essence of Puritanism, were absolute and drastic.

And here it is necessary to insist that the implications were especially drastic in those Puritan circles which drew back from the brink of ecclesiastical separation and so were, in that sense, moderate, insisting on the integrity of the public church and on the conscientious necessity of remaining in at least outward communion with it. The separatist ideologue Henry Ainsworth taught that the separated saints were to have no contact with the wicked in matters of religion. But in respect of all other occasions of life his casuistry was permissive. In such civil things as eating and drinking, or buying and selling, the saints were to converse with the wicked in peace. How else were they to live in Amsterdam?[64]

But in these circumstances their separation became a formality, not a way of life constantly practised. It was in Peter Lake's phrase, 'a fossilised act of commitment'.[65] This is the common experience of sects and cults which achieve a total or nearly total withdrawal from the rest of the world and no longer need to affirm their special identity by incessant acts of abstention and disapprobation. Among the so-called Plymouth Brethren, Open Brethren never touch alcohol, but the more drastically separated Exclusives are more relaxed in this respect and drink as a matter of course.

Among the nonseparated, the Puritans most properly speaking, these positions were exactly reversed. Their preachers taught that it was necessary to go to church and even to receive the sacrament alongside supposedly 'wicked' and 'irreligious' neighbours. The law required it, and St Paul writing to the Corinthians appeared to commend it. The situation was admittedly gravely deformed. The authorities ought to have separated out the ungodly and unworthy, as Abraham had sent Hagar and Ishmael into the wilderness. But if this was not done the remedy was not in the hands of private men. Thomas Hooker taught that the public congregation was like common pastures, open to every man's cattle. 'Suppose they that are in authority will not separate them . . . yet the saints of God should not abstain from the congregation. It is pitiful indeed, and the thing is troublesome and tedious to a gracious heart (and we must mourn for it), but being [so], it is not in my power; I must not abstain'.[66] 'Pitiful' this anomalous situation may have been, but it was also pragmatically advantageous. It enabled the Puritans for two or three generations to avoid the logical consequences of their own exclusive criterion of church membership. At its lowest and most practical level, it enabled Puritan incumbents to continue to collect their income in tithe from parishioners, perhaps the bulk of their parishioners, whom they mentally excluded from the Church in any meaningful sense.

But in all other respects, in the private occasions of life, and above all in 'the rule of sorting out company in private conversation'. the godly man not only could but must cut himself off from the ungodly. There were disturbing echoes here of the principles of the Anabaptists. Did this ethic of social shunning mean that bargains could be disowned, social and political obligations avoided, on the grounds that the other party to the transaction was ungodly, not of the household of faith? Should ordinary traffic with the wicked cease? No, came the regular reply. We must not be 'unnatural'. But when necessary duties were performed toward the carnally minded they were to be undertaken with a 'kind of mourning, and affliction for their sakes'. This seems to mean that while a godly wife could not refuse her ungodly husband his conjugal rights, she must on no account appear to enjoy it. As for unnecessary company keeping: avoid it.[67] This was to follow in the casuistical footsteps of the reformer Peter Martyr Vermigli, whose exposition of 1 Corinthians had been rendered into English in 1555 as *A Treatise of the Cohabitacyon of the faithfull with the unfaithfull.*

Nonseparated Puritans complained to separated correspondents in Amsterdam and elsewhere that the real martyrdom was theirs. They suffered for separating *within* the church, which was death, as it were, by a thousand cuts. They were, remarks Peter Lake, 'existentially if not legally' in the more exposed position.[68] It also seems likely that the need to maintain the sustained witness of social and cultural separation preserved a higher level of religious ardour in nonseparated circles than came to obtain in the little 'parlor' of Amsterdam—which may explain John Robinson's notorious concern, expressed in *A treatise of the lawfulnes of hearing of the Ministers in the Church of England* (1634), that the sermons of nonseparated Puritans should remain accessible to his people. Here, as Perry Miller discovered long ago, are the true title deeds of the New England Way, but not only of its ecclesiology, which Miller dismissed as an 'adroit . . . subterfuge', but of its spiritual experience, the credentials of a valid Christian identity.[69] That is as much as to say that if you removed that which Puritanism was pitched against, if you drew a curtain across the world so that it was no longer visible and apprehensible, Puritanism itself flickered and died. For it could not survive, had no existence, without contention. This, it may be, was the rationale of those dying flickers, the bitter internal disputes within the separated congregation at Amsterdam which have been explored by Michael Moody.[70] If there were no longer any enemies without it was necessary to reproduce them within. This may also have been the meaning of Thomas Larkham's tempestuous ministry.

Only with the maturing of a new social history which has been to school with anthropology and folklore do we begin to appreciate the potential consequences of the war declared by Puritans on the consensual social values characterised as 'good fellowship', and by the good fellows on Puritans. Pastimes were more than recreation. The alehouse was not peripheral. Good fellowship was social cement. As Keith Wrightson points out, these things were intended to excite sentiments necessary for the continuing life of the community, to give life to the social structure.[71] In justification of the contentious 'church ales' in Somerset, the bishop of the diocese reported in 1633 that they were valued by many of his clergy (significantly about half of them, the others being hostile) 'for the civilising of people, for their lawful recreations, for composing differences by meeting of friends, for increase of love and amity as being feasts of charity, for relief of the poor, the richer sort keeping then open house, and for many other reasons'.[72] But what was it to 'civilise' people? Puritans denounced such mechanisms and offered in their place a severe social discipline of external constraints, didactic instruction and self-control. If money was needed, to relieve the poor or to maintain the church fabric, it could be collected by the orderly and rational means of a rate, distributed among the inhabitants according to their means and ability to pay, by the vestry.

So the lines were drawn, in many communities. For as long as the outcome was uncertain, forces more or less evenly matched, the situation may have been threatening, even explosive. When the citizens of Chester were subjected to fines even for going to other towns to see plays (none was allowed in Chester), and when Mayor Henry Hardware physically smashed the most popular pageants and floats for the summer shows, they were not very pleased, no more content than the godly when, under a more indulgent mayor, some of these things came back.[73] Nor were many, perhaps most, people in Banbury delighted when countrymen coming into the pubs in town to spend their groats and to play at shovelboard were arrested and spent the night in the clink; or when a local innkeeper who was called out of church to attend to the needs of a customer was promptly seized by the constable. On that occasion, the entire congregation poured out into the churchyard and the innkeeper's wife, summoned by her children, came at the double, for all her seven months' pregnancy, a large stone in either hand. Presently the whole town was in uproar when the dominant, Puritan, faction of the governing body demolished the two famous market crosses for which Banbury is still famous, four centuries after their ritual destruction.[74]

Where such things happened there was spirited local resistance, a repetitive pattern of mocking rhymes and libels, anti-Puritan 'characters' again. Stratford-upon-Avon provides a good example, within three years of Shakespeare's death. In May 1619, a riotous 'confederacy', containing some of the late dramatist's kinsmen and friends, rallied around the town maypole, or 'summer-pole', to withstand the newly inducted and already unpopular vicar Thomas Wilson and his supporters, who included Shakespeare's highly respectable son-in-law, the physician John Hall. Among the sundry libels and mocking songs, 'A Satire to the Chief Rulers in the Synagogue of Stratford' announced:

> Stratford's a town that doth make a great shew,
> But yet it is governed but by a few:
> O Jesus Christ of Heaven,
> I think they are but seven;
> Puritants without doubt . . .[75]

Professor David Underdown has found evidence of what he calls states of 'moral panic', explosive episodes of cultural conflict, in a great many western towns in James I's reign: in Dorchester (1606), Wells (1607), Lyme Regis (1606–10), Wimborne Minister (1608), Weymouth (1618) and, we may add, Bridport (1614) — to travel no further west (or east) than Dorset and Somerset.[76] It is likely that comparative study of these explosions will reveal the sorts of regularities identified by students of iconoclasm in the continental Reformation or in eighteenth-century bread riots. Often they were short-lived episodes, succeeded in many cases by an unchallenged 'Puritan' ascendancy such as prevailed by the 1620s in Dorchester under its formidable patriarch John White, or in Banbury, a byword for Puritanism and a rich source of still more anti-Puritan jokes and characters. It was a Banbury cat which was hanged on Monday for killing a mouse on Sunday, and a Banbury man who in Jonson's *Bartholomew Fair* gave over his trade of baking because his Banbury cakes proved all too popular at 'bridals, maypoles, morrises and such profane feasts and meetings'.[77] Such was the transformation of English provincial life which is the real and still neglected story of the Reformation.

It would be a mistake to suppose that the only or chief cause of dissension in the local community was friction between the godly and the ungodly. Where the evidence makes it possible to investigate in microscopic detail, it is likely to emerge that patterns of conflict were more intricate than that. Shakespeare's Stratford was disturbed for many years, but apparently as much by Thomas Wilson's personality, his habit of 'grossly particularising in his Sermons' (like Thomas Larkham), as by his 'Puritanism'.[78] The work of Martin Ingram instructs us in the need to contextualise every kind of local dispute in a general pattern of 'small-scale tensions' and 'neighbourhood rivalries' that characterised local communities in this period.[79]

According to Professor Lawrence Stone, the early modern English village was 'filled with malice and hatred'. Can it really have been so? Dr Ingram is more cautious, but thinks it possible that parochial tensions were on the increase. Social historians have only recently begun to paddle in the shallow end of that reservoir which is the surviving evidence of malicious slander and verbal abuse, and the defensive legal actions which they provoked, 'complementary forms of aggression', 'a frogspawn mass of litigation'.[80] From this copious record it is clear that there was a formidable capacity for verbal violence indicative of deep hostility, that it was feared and resented to the extent that parties were prepared to venture their reputations and their limited financial resources to seek a remedy, and that deep-seated and long-running quarrels about other matters were often implied. But the evidence cannot be used to measure even approximately the level of resentment existing as a constant in this or that locality. And it may, paradoxically, be trying to tell us about a strong if sometimes frustrated disposition to maintain or restore the public peace.

So was provincial England at peace unless or until it was disturbed by some specific quarrel? Or, conversely, as Stone seems to think, were the inhabitants assumed to be enemies unless they happened to be friends, or to have made friends in those rites of passage which were marriage and godparenthood?[81] 'Face-to-face' communities present us with a contradiction. It was both necessary and perhaps very difficult to remain on good terms.

But Stone's notion of a Hobbesian state of endemic enmity is hard to reconcile with the expectations of the church and its local representatives, especially as they were annually demonstrated at the feast of Easter. As that season approached in the Kentish parish of Milton by Sittingbourne in about 1564, the minister, churchwardens, and principal parishioners, 'mynding to end all controversies betweene Warners wife and Wottons wife', called the parties together at one of their houses and after some exhortation and warning of the danger of being presented at the archbishop's visitation, succeeded in persuading the two women 'to be at an unytie and concord and each to forgeve other', with the happy consequence that Mrs Wotton shortly after agreed to receive communion 'as a Christian woman ought to do ... with divers other parishioners, which she did accordingly, declaring thereby her reconciliation'. In the same year at Benenden, in another part of Kent, the outcome of a similar exercise was less edifying. The wardens, sidesmen and other substantial men of the parish were summoned into church on a Wednesday afternoon to confront the archdeacon's official on visitation, 'and divers men also which had not received the holy communion were warned there to appere'. Among these offenders was one William Bigg, who explained that the reason why he had not received was some 'stryfe and trouble', 'jarring words' between him and a certain Gervase Morley. But far from proceeding to make peace with Morley, Bigg scandalised the whole company by continuing his quarrel in public. Bigg said to Morley, 'It is well knowne what thy wife is'. Morley replied, 'I pray the [e], what is my wife?' 'Mary, quod the said Bigg, she is a common scold'.[82]

These cases, though differing in their outcome, contain the same lesson. There was an expectation in the community, reinforced by the ecclesiastical authorities, that householders would take communion, at least on the annual and obligatory occasion of Easter. The inhibition on communion when not in a state of charity was taken seriously. Particular quarrels stood out like sore thumbs and invited the available mechanisms of reconciliation to be brought into play. If these processes normally prevailed, to the extent that a general, formal harmony was preserved, or at least seasonally patched up, it would show up all the more invidiously the antisocial principles of Puritans who refused to kneel with their neighbours or to drink with them afterwards in the alehouse.

There is, of course, another possibility. In some places, which were not the smallest or most compact places, which we may call back-to-back rather than face-to-face, the norm may have been one of social neutrality, in which people were careful not to invade one another's space and kept themselves to themselves, not even acknowledging one another in the street (the common 'salutations'), unless for some good reason. In such a privatised, secularised world, the cultures of 'good fellowship' and 'godly discipline' would have become equally redundant and would have found increasingly less occasion to conflict and collide. The absence of certain individuals from the alebench would go unremarked. Church ales and dances on the village green would be abandoned, giving way to patterns of what Keith Wrightson calls 'fragmented sociability',[83] not because Puritans opposed such things but because nobody could be bothered to make the arrangements or to raise the necessary funds. 'Festive fund-raising' was giving place to 'the growing bureaucratisation of parochial finances'.[84] As Max Weber has observed, in the iron cage of bureaucracy many things languish and die; among these is the 'Puritanism' which has helped in some measure to construct it.

6

Sects and the Evolution of Puritanism

The question of 'Puritanism and the evolution of sects' embodies a conventional teleology and one which is built into the standard historiography of 'Puritan' dissent and nonconformity. We begin with an ostensibly monolithic and almost unchallenged Catholic Church. We end with — shall we say? — California, a licensed and potentially limitless plurality of religious entities, both cults and sects. From this promised land there is, or so far has been, no return. Sir Nicholas Bacon (the father of Francis) expressed an Elizabethan fear that a certain train of undesirable events would determine that religion 'which of his own nature should be uniform, would against his nature have proved milliform, yea, in continuance nulliform.'[1] It was polemically conventional to proceed from the uniform through the milliform to the nulliform. The opposite course of events had not occurred to Bacon and is still less likely to coincide with our modern expectations. It is now impossible to believe that Christendom can lie in the future, except perhaps eschatologically. Progressive fissiparation, whether or not concluding in the 'nulliformity' projected by Bacon, is seen as virtually a law of Protestantism, somewhat resembling the biological law of evolution from simple to more complex forms: Bossuet subsumed in Darwin.

So far as the religious history of the English in the second half of the sixteenth century and the seventeenth is concerned, we move by a series of primary, secondary and tertiary processes from Protestantism through Puritanism to Separatism and Sectarianism. The strength of this version of the *longue durée* of post-Reformation religious history is that it is not only more or less true to what in fact happened but that it provides historical justification for all of the main religious interests concerned, as we find them institutionalised in the principal churches of the English-speaking world. Both Roman Catholics and those Anglicans who adhere to an essentially Catholic ecclesiology within the Church of England can exclaim, in effect, 'We told you so'. Sectarian anarchy is the inevitable outcome of the exercise of wilful and private religious judgment. As

Hilaire Belloc once wrote: 'The moral is, it is indeed,/ You must not monkey with the Creed'. Meanwhile, what used in England to be called 'free churchmen' have turned vices into virtues. From their side of the fence, they have agreed with high Anglicans that the principles of the Reformation have necessarily tended towards a radically decentralised and individualistic religious experience. So at least have reported Congregationalists, Baptists, and, *a fortiori*, Quakers. Presbyterians might have had a different tale to tell if they had not been gobbled up by, on the one hand, the rational dissent of Unitarianism, the brainchild of the eighteenth century, and on the other by Scottish and Scoto-Hibernian Presbyterianism, the legacy of nineteenth-century migration within the British Isles, a species not so much of nonconformity as of religious tribalism. What follows can be read as a kind of apology or lament for the lost tribe of the English Presbyterians.

Meanwhile, in another part of the forest, investigations of religion as a social 'factor', whether more or less Marxist or Weberian in their understanding of what that factor is and of how it operates, have added reinforcement to these ecclesiological and church-historical perspectives. Christopher Hill tells us that by some historically necessary process, compulsory communities in early modern England were giving way to voluntary communities, as parishes broke up into conventicles and house churches. These were the ecclesiological analogues and facilitators of proto-industrial units of production and capital accumulation.[2]

For the purpose of this essay it is necessary to note only in passing the suggestion of Richard Niebuhr and his disciples among religious sociologists that these centrifugal tendencies tend by a generational process to which most if not all sects are prone to give way to renewed centripetal forces which turn them into those denominations whose instinct it is to secure a new kind of *modus vivendi* with society and its majority values, a society which, in the case of the United States especially, became simultaneously pluralistic and consensual.[3] Nor is it necessary to become embroiled in the 'ecumenical' aspirations of many twentieth-century churchmen in the radical protestant tradition towards so-called 'Unitive Protestantism', motives arising in the perception of some critics of ecumenism from the pathological degeneration and even disintegration of once confident religious traditions, including the tradition of independency: for example, British Congregationalists swallowed up in something called the United Reformed Church.[4] The experience and fortunes of religious bodies in liberal, competitive and pluralistic conditions lie beyond the chronological scope of this essay.

What I want to suggest is that the conventional teleology of 'Puritans and the evolution of sects' tends to obscure, in the second half of the sixteenth century and the first half of the seventeenth, strong currents running in the opposite direction, from a relatively incoherent and disorganised sectarianism towards that version of 'unitive Protestantism' which English Puritanism in the rhetoric of its own apologetics aspired to be. An East Anglian minister published a book in the early years of the seventeenth century which claimed to contain the sum of that unitive divinity (in a thousand pages!), demonstrating 'in how many truths, that is in particulars above number, we do agree, teaching the same things from one and the same word, by one and the same Spirit, with a sweet consent, in comparison of those few things wherein the jugementes of some doe differ'.[5] It is not necessary to believe that this witness was telling the whole truth and nothing but the truth. But it is helpful to acknowledge that 'sweet consent' was a positive value for ministers in the Puritan tradition, which they not only sought but claimed, for understandable polemical reasons, actually to enjoy. It is also necessary to attach due importance to the insistence of the Puritan mainstream on the involuntary constraints imposed on private judgment by true belief. Richard Bernard of Worksop in Nottinghamshire and Batcombe in Somerset denounced among other errors of his time will-worship, defined as 'a voluntary worshipping of God in and by such means as man inventeth'. This led to schism, 'which is an uncharitable division, and an unlawfull separation from the true church of Christ . . . forsaking the fellowship of the Saints wilfully in a factiousness of spirit, making unlawfull assemblies within and among themselves'. 'We depart from this iniquity'.[6]

According to conventional perspectives, the first (if by no means the last) time that English-speaking religious history ran into the sectarian sand was in the mid-seventeenth century: the consequence of migration, revolution and civil war. In fact, the mid-seventeenth-century experience was not unprecedented. An earlier chapter is half forgotten, or consigned to somewhat marginal literatures on something called the Freewill Men of mid-Tudor England and on an Elizabethan phenomenon called the Family of Love. These movements are understood to have borne the same relation to 'orthodox' English Protestantism as continental Anabaptism to the 'magisterial' Reformation: conventional teleology again. Where the still older sectarian tradition of Lollardy fits in, whether it was indeed sectarian, or a tradition, and what it may have contributed to the Reformation on the one hand and to mid-sixteenth-century sectarianism on the other, are questions which continue to confuse historical discourse but need not detain us. Here we may only note that the Protestant version of history created by the sixteenth-century martyrologist John Foxe proposed an alternative teleology of Lollard sects as the progenitors of a national Protestant Church, a scenario with which some nineteenth-century Anglicans felt by no means comfortable.

What does concern us is that the Reformation and pre-Reformation chapters of sectarian history were separated from the revolutionary sects of the mid-seventeenth century by a hundred years in which sectarianism was evidently not rampant and which we may call the Puritan century. This major feature of the religious-historical landscape is obscured in the special pleading to establish the continuity of radical, centrifugal dissent to be found, for example, in Christopher Hill's essay 'From Lollards to Levellers', an argument which assimilates Puritanism itself to that continuum, at least to the extent of making it a Trojan horse with a bellyful of sects.[7] It is possible that what happened between the Lollards and the Levellers was the religious equivalent of one of those rivers in limestone country which run for half their course underground; and that part of that underground was the Puritan consciousness itself. The first is uncertain, the second contestable. What is more certain is the consolidation in the later sixteenth and early seventeenth centuries of centripetal Puritanism, 'radical' in a rather different sense, which assimilated and domesticated the sectarian tendency by a process which some would want to describe as the reception of Calvinism, others as routinisation, but those pursuing the studies represented in this conference as 'the rise of Puritanism'.

It is possible, if the unpredictability and arbitrariness of the historical process is accepted, to understand Puritanism as comprising a series of developments opposite to those which we tend to take for granted. The rise of Puritanism, if sustained and stabilised, could have meant not the triumph of pluralistic and eventually tolerant religious individualism, which William Haller thought was a historical paradox on the grand scale,[8] but the success of the opposite, unitive and intolerant. It would take a large book, or an anatomy of many books already written, to establish how and why the unitive and intolerant scenario proved implausible and impermanent. The most that I can hope to establish here, or at least to assert, is that Puritanism in its original intentions believed itself to be headed in a direction quite contrary to that implied in the phrase 'Puritanism and the evolution of sects'.

As a religious movement and as a godly community, Puritanism grew by subjecting scattered and disorganised elements to a process of church formation, albeit the formation of a church within the church. The means of formation were educational, which is to say catechising, preaching and sermon repetition, on which few disabling restrictions were placed by the larger church authorities, except temporally and locally; and collective disciplines which on the contrary were significantly restricted. It is possible to argue that the combination of unrestricted preaching and restricted discipline produced the unintended and unwanted result of sectarianism.

Let us assume, as most historians of the Reformation do, that English Protestantism succeeded and even in some sense grew out of the antecedent Lollard tradition. Lollards were relatively incoherent and disorganised, or at least localised.[9] It is not clear that they stood over against the late medieval church as a counter-church. Their principles, or at least their strategies, were not separatist but allowed a posture of outward confirmity and subterfuge and a measure of integration in the wider society. The first generation of Protestants differed from the last generation of Lollards not only in their solifidian theology, a matter noticed by all historians, but in their conviction that they constituted the true church, and this conviction must be articulated in separation from the false, popish church. This idea was shared by one of the earliest of the Protestant bishops, William Barlow, when he defined 'the trewe church of God' as 'where so ever ii or iii simple personnes as ii coblers or wevers were in company and elected in the name of God' and with the simple Cornish woman who told her own bishop that the true Church was 'not your popish Church' 'but where two or three are gathered together in the name of God'. A Kentish weaver said the same, and of course all three were merely elaborating Matthew 18:20. 'Come out from among them and separate yourselves', wrote the Essex curate William Tyms to 'all Gods faithfull sevants'.[10] That was 2 Corinthians 6:17. One result of this new and uncompromising separatism was the unprecedented holocaust of Mary's reign. But if the immediate consequences of the new Protestant ecclesiology were separatist, its longer-term implications were anti-separatist. There could be no separation from the true Church which had separated itself against the false. Gathered sect and universal church are, as Troeltsch perceived, congruous.

The enterprise of Protestant church-building involved a secondary process of separation from surviving elements of pre-Protestant dissent, insofar as these elements were not assimilated into 'orthodox' Protestantism. It is conventional to regard tendencies such as the so-called 'Free Will Men' of the 1540s and 1550s as breakaway sects. 'Anabaptist' was a term used somewhat promiscuously in the England of Edward VI. But in the perception of these heretics themselves, it was the Protestants with their unfamiliar, academic theology and 'clerkly' fluency who were the splitteres and sheep-stealers. The leading freewiller (and in all probability old Lollard) Henry Hart (we know a man of the same name with a Lollard past in Kent) was given to saying that 'all errors were brought in by learned men'; while the Somerset radical John Champneys claimed to speak for 'the electe unlearned people' in a book 'grossly compyled without any clearkly eloquence'.[11] The evidence for the penetration of radical dissent by orthodox Protestantism is necessarily elusive, but some of it will be found in the prison debates and martyr letters of the Marian persecution, and especially in the writings of the Coventry weaver John Careless, not himself a learned man but content to submit to learned evidence. Careless advised a fellow prisoner what he should say to his judges: 'I am a poor man without learning; but am commanded of God to follow the counsel of his constant preachers'. 'This kind of answer, my dear heart, it shall be best for you to make'.[12]

It remains an open question what happened to the English 'Anabaptists' after the accession of Elizabeth. The early 1560s saw a continuing polemic 'to enarm and fence the true Church of God againste the pestiferous sect of the free will men of our time', but this was not sustained and perhaps there was no need to keep it going. English 'Arminianism', when it took shape in the early seventeenth century, had no sense of any indebtedness to an earlier anti-predestinarian tradition, and of course the social and intellectual circumstances were very different.[13] There are three possibilities. The old heretics, or at least any effective leadership of the kind that Henry Hart seems to have exercised, may have been wiped out in the Marian persecution, in which case the Marian authorities did orthodox Protestantism an unintended good turn. Or they survived as a radical religious underground, to resurface in due course under new names, Christopher Hill's subterranean river. In the meantime, the Elizabethan Family of Love looks like a kind of residual category, the fag end of the old Lollard traditions: safe houses, covert ways, a *secretum vocabulum* and a cunning mixture of internal and external integration.[14] But the exceptionality of the Familists and (apparently) their very small numbers and spotty distribution point to the third possibility: that radical dissent was domesticated and re-educated within Elizabethan Protestantism and indeed Puritanism, which should be seen as a force making for integration rather than sectarian disintegration: the Careless model.

We should think of this as an ongoing process, a kind of acted-out version of John Coolidge's 'Pauline Renaissance in England': practical edification. The interface separating the learned preaching ministry and the unlearned, unpreaching but informed and even opinionated body of 'professors' is an area all but inaccessible to the historian of Puritanism, but the one which he most needs to understand. We catch stray glimpses of it in certain exchanges between the unseparated Puritan ministry in Elizabethan East Anglia and the Brownist movement, and especially in Robert Harrison's 'treatise of the church and the kingdome of Christ', written in about 1580 against the rector of Booton in Norfolk, Edward Fenton. Some might suppose, wrote Harrison, that Fenton was the spiritual father of the godly in his neighboured, 'manie in whome some good towardnes did appeare'. But in truth the children were more forward than their father and could be said to have begotten themselves 'by fruitfull edifying of gratious speach and godly conference, of whome you chalenge to yourself the honor of parentage'.[15] Harrison's attack on Fenton (and Harrison was himself a minister, or at least a Cambridge graduate and a schoolmaster) could have had no motive if Fenton and others like him were not successfully restraining the majority of the godly professors of the Norfolk parishes from the drastic step of Brownist schism. There were of course currents, probably less strong, running in the opposite direction. Thomas Wolsey, the third and most obscure member of the original Brownist troika, spent thirty years in jail as an incorrigible Separatist, advanced beyond Separatism to judaising extremes and, according to later testimony given by Stephen Offwood, 'perverted many zealous professors, of which I knewe twentie'. The twenty allegedly included none other than Henry Barrow, who would carry the torch forward into the next generation of Separatism.[16]

A second point is the logical counterpart of the first and may be more briefly stated. If Thomas Wolsey perverted as many as twenty zealous professors to schismatic Separatism, the bishops, and especially bishops like Edmund Freke of Norwich (whose episcopate coincided with the

Brownist episode) or John Aylmer of London, and above all Archbishop John Whitgift of Canterbury, perverted many more. Insofar as these authorities within the greater church frustrated the enterprise of lesser church formation, which is how we may characterise the enterprise of Puritanism and the counter-enterprise of 'Anglicanism', they encouraged rather than discouraged sectarian tendencies which the Puritans deplored. Admittedly most of the evidence to this effect reaches us from the protesting pens of the Puritans themselves (they would say that, wouldn't they?), but if biased it is also plausible.[17] Godly professors whose faith was simple and robust and who were not versed in the theory of adiaphora would be offended by the sight of their minister in a surplice, perhaps even physically repelled into illegal conventicles. A minister who was silenced for nonconformity might join them in their conventicles and could do little to prevent his people wandering off to find sustenance elsewhere. Consequently it became a paradoxial commonplace in the seventeenth century to say that the bishops were the greatest sect-makers.

The third point concerns the sustained polemical and practical resistance offered by mainstream Puritanism to what the Westminster divine Edward Staunton called 'England's incurable wound', Brownist Separatism. This resistance can be considered under three sub-headings, since it was mounted in published apologetics and polemics, in face-to-face confrontations and conferences with Separatists or those threatening to separate, and in the encouragement of covenanted religious meetings best described as semi-separatist and designed to satisfy the appetite for the intensity of godly fellowship and to make the invisible visible, short of actual schism from the wider, more diffuse parochial and national christian community. Antiseparatism, as a broad plank in the Puritan platform, could be considered under a fourth sub-heading which would take due account of the heavy emphasis placed in the Puritan biographical tradition on the relentless opposition offered by the old Puritan divines to the Separatists in the days before and leading into the Civil War. The biographical collections of Samuel Clarke have been formative of three centuries of Puritan and nonconformist historiography (and not least for William Haller), but they were originally intended for a Restoration readership. There were obvious polemical advantages post-1662 in drawing attention to the antiseparatist convictions of the 'old English Puritans' before 1640.[18] So this evidence may appear somewhat suspect.

There is no reason, however, to suspect Clarke and the preachers of the funeral sermons who provided him with his raw material of inventing a spurious tradition and pedigree. The titles of a large number of books published between the 1580s and the 1620s are no inventions: Stephen Bredwell's *Rasing of the foundations of Brownisme* (1588); Richard Alison's *A plaine confutation of a treatise of Brownisme* (1590); the early Henry Jacob (*A defence of the churches and ministery of Englande* (1599)); two books by Richard Bernard (*Christian advertisements and counsels of peace: also disswasions from Brownisme* (1609) and *Plaine evidences: the Church of England is apostolicall* (1610)); William Bradshaw's *The unreasonablenesse of the separation* (1614); and John Darrell's *Treatise of the Church written against those of the Separation, commonly called Brownists* (1617). It is significant that, with the exception of John Paget's *An arrow against the separation of the Brownists* (1618) (and Paget lived and ministered in frontier territory, in Amsterdam), these attacks were made not from the Presbyterian right (as it were) of the Puritan movement but by writers, including some of Perry Miller's so-called non-separating congregationalists, who were themselves, or had been, close to Separatism. Stephen Brachlow demonstrates that this was a very fine, if critically important, dividing line.[19]

One of the most uncompromising denunciations of separation came from the pen of a certain Randall Bate, an extremist in all respects but this, who died in prison as 'a glorious Martyr of Jesus Christ'. In what were posthumously described as his 'daily meditations', Bate asked whether it were fitting to be buried in churchyards? ('Answer: It seems no'.) and 'Whether it be not needfull to pull downe churches built for the honour of Idolls', that is, the parish churches, consecrated as they were to saints? ('Answer: it seems it is'.). Yet Bate, while professing to love them as persons, rebuked the Separatists for a blind zeal which was self-willed, even Satanic. 'Men must not separate till the Lord separate for gods people must follow the Lord, not goe before him'. 'This kind of separation obscures the good providence of god towards the land, which gives some liberty in his service, but with some paines, cost and other crosses, which usually accompany the pure worship of god. This is no small sin, to bereave the Lord of so great mercy in spirituall blessings, as he hath shewed towards our land'.[20] In Bate's perception, and it was a perception widely shared, what he called 'totall separation' (and it would be accurate to call Bate a semi-separatist) was a separation not from evil but from the great deal of good which was still to be found in the parish assemblies, to separate indeed from the true children of God. Like Henoch

Clapham, of whom more presently, Bate regarded this as an error of the right hand, which is to say the pardonable error of excessive zeal. But it was none the less an error, indeed a sin, which Clapham had diagnosed as the sin against the Holy Ghost.

A telling part of the anti-Separatist polemic was to insist that opponents of Separatism separated not from the Church but from notorious sins within the Church, sins which ranged from intolerable but discardable ceremonies to the moral contagion incurred in the course of unnecessary 'company keeping', so-called 'good fellowship' which was nothing of the kind. 'Though a corporall separation cannot be had, yet in spirit thou must separate thyself.' This was said to be the harder, more painful way. 'We suffer for separating within the Church.'[21]

In October 1605, one Margaret Browne of Slaughterford in Wiltshire found herself part of a group of weavers and their wives who were presented to the archdeacon for Brownism (not inappropriate in her case!) and 'going from the Church of England'. When Browne appeared in court, she alleged that she was now 'better perswaded and doth and will acknowledge her error'.[22] It is not unlikely that the pressure applied by the ecclesiastical tribunal itself, the danger in which Goodwife Browne stood, persuaded her to abandon her Brownism. But we must not discount the effects of a number of set-piece encounters between Separatists and Nonseparatists, some of them perhaps casual and opportunistic, others involving elaborate arrangements, in pulling back from the brink some of those for whose benefit they were staged. As it happens a conference of this kind had been held in Slaughterford a year before Browne and her accomplices appeared in court, and was connected with the well-publicised defection from Separatism of the minister Thomas White, as well as the conversion of a more obscure participant who having once thought the religion of the Separatists to be 'trew and right' subsequently discovered it to be 'false and erronious'.[23]

Looking back from New England in the 1640s, John Allin and Thomas Shepard recalled the tense atmosphere prevailing in some of these encounters: 'Yea, how many serious consultations with one another, and with the faithfull ministers, and other eminent servants of Christ have been taken about this worke is not unknowne to some.'[24] Some of these occasions were thoroughly ventilated in the controversial literature of Dissent, such as the meetings in the East Midlands which involved John Robinson, John Smyth, and Richard Bernard, John Cotton recalling how

Robinson 'resorted ... to many judicious divines in England for the clearing of the scruples, which inclined him to separation'.[25] Other episodes are known only from the records of the ecclesiastical courts (and doubtless most are not known at all). Such was a two- or three-day conference hastily convened in a vicarage in the village of Ash near Sandwich in East Kent, when two notorious Separatists from twenty-five miles away in the Weald were heard to be passing through.[26] 'The assertions of John Silliman of Aldwinkle in the county of Northampton delyvered to be examyned and answered'[27] were evidently connected with a similar occasion. These gatherings, essentially for the resolution of vexed and wounded consciences, were in a tradition which was well-established long before the reign of James I. It cost the troubled conscience long cross-country journeys, such as those undertaken by the many who came to Richard Greenham at Dry Drayton outside Cambridge with their problems. Soon Greenham moved to London, which may have made it easier for some. So it had been in Mary's reign when the husbandman Henry Orinel from Willingham in Cambridgeshire tramped to Colchester to confer with the future Familist missionary Christoph Vittels, was disturbed by what he heard, and promptly set off towards Oxford seeking further resolution from the Protestant bishops in prison.[28] Orinel's problem was not utterly different from that confronting radical Jacobean Puritans: what to do about the legal demands of the established Church. There has been a persistent tendency to underestimate the capacity of such people to make up their own minds on difficult religious problems, suitably assisted, or, where this has not been underestimated, to assume a radical conclusion to every such quest. (But apparently Orinel did later succumb to Familism.)

Another strategy of Puritan ministers concerned to find a prophylactic for the bacillus of separation was the semi-separated, semi-gathered group, the church within the church realised in private meetings of the godly minority. Such house meetings were so commonplace as to make it unlikely that they were always related to a perceived Separatist threat. Often they may have been unselfconscious, naive. But it is hard to tell. When the Essex preacher and diarist Richard Rogers brought together the super-saints of his parish, 'well-nigh twenty persons', to subscribe a special covenant among themselves, we do not know whether there was a separatist problem in Wethersfield to which this was a response.[29] Yet when Richard Bernard established a voluntary covenant among a hundred of his Worksop flock ('which covenant long since you have dissolved'), it was alleged by the Separatists Ainsworth and Robinson that he had done this 'only in policy, to keep your people from Mr Smyth'.[30] And John Cotton admitted to the same motivation when he wrote of the covenant which he had initiated among 'some scores of godly persons in Boston Lincolnshire', claiming that while this was 'defective', yet it was 'more than the old Non-conformity'.[31]

The fourth of my related points is that the debate between Separatism and Antiseparatism was conducted at the greatest intensity within the intelligences and consciences of individuals living very close to Stephen Brachlow's critically drawn, thin frontier. One Puritan has left it on record how 'this twenty years and more' he had 'sought out the truth through a world of controversies'. After reading the Scriptures, presumably the most relevant texts, 'not so little as fifty or threescore times', he could still find no justification for separation.[32] (But why then did he keep on searching?) The teleology of Puritanism to Sects encourages us to look for a progressive radicalisation in such tortured souls. But, as in this case, progress was often regress. So it was, after all, with the founding father of Separatism who gave it its name, Robert Browne: although historians more or less loyal to his memory have sought to dismiss the significance of his betrayals, making them a mere personal aberration, the actions of a man with diminished responsibility.[33] But Browne's case was not unique, not even all that singular. Witness Thomas White's thoroughly embittered *Discoverie of Brownisme* (1605), containing the memorable discovery: 'I thought . . .that they had been all saints, but I have found them all devils'.[34] Witness too the picaresque account of his adventures in Morocco and elsewhere recorded by the relapsed Brownist Peter Fairlambe, *The recantation of a Brownist, or a reformed Puritan* (1606).

The Separatist who, like Fairlambe, finished up in the arms of the bishops was perhaps the ultimate and arch-separatist, since he had separated against Separatism itself. One of these stormy petrels was Henoch Clapham, a failed poet turned preacher and biblical paraphraser who reached Separatism and the ancient congregation of Amsterdam by a checkered course, 'sometimes haled by this faction, sometimes pulled by that faction'. But presently Clapham had persuaded himself that Puritans, Separatists and Anabaptists were all 'flat Donatists'. He claims to have been converted to this view, like some precursor of John Henry Newman, by patristic study, presumably St Augustine. But we may suspect that, like Thomas White of Wiltshire, what got up his nose was the petty tyranny of Francis Johnson's Amsterdam 'parlour'. He recorded the caustic comment that 'tell the church' meant, in separatist circles, 'tell Tom Tyncker, tell Dick Cullier, tell Jone the Oyster Wench'. Soon Clapham discovered that the faith professed in the Church of England was so far true that to separate from it was equivalent to the sin against the Holy Ghost. This was awkward, since by now Clapham was ministering to a tiny splinter group of half a dozen who with him had broken away from Johnson's congregation. He asked his pathetic flock why they should turn aside 'as if there were no prophet but my selfe?' And yet something had happened between Clapham and those half dozen which it was hard to repudiate utterly. 'You and I have gone a warfare at our own charges.' There was, after all, no other destination for this prodigal than the established Church, which presently gave him a living in Kent. There he wrote two remarkable books, *Errour on the right hand* and *Errour on the left hand*, a series of recognisable portraits of the turbulent spirits of the age, taken from the safe and central ground of 'Mediocritie'.[35] Even as a reformed Anglican, Clapham's Anglicanism was not the same substance as the Anglicanism of the elder brother who had never left his father's house. Yet when it came to the crunch, Clapham and we cannot tell how many others found that the official Church with its patronage, the objective reassurance of its sacraments, its stability, had more to offer than Amsterdam.[36]

So it was that others drew back from the verge, like the Nottinghamshire minister Richard Bernard who confessed that he had been 'tossed by the present tempest' and, according to John Smyth, 'did acknowledge this truth wee now professe divers tymes and was upon the point of Separation with some of his people with him'. Instead, Bernard was persuaded by the great and the good of the Jacobean church to take on a new pastoral role of immense usefulness and great personal profit at Batcombe in Somerset.[37] Others strove to have it both ways. Henry Jacob wrote in 1611: 'for my part I never was nor am separate from all publike communion with the congregations of England'.[38] Much depended upon what was meant by 'all'. Such personal life histories made the religious history of early Stuart England. There are no such things as religious and social 'forces': only individuals, trying to be both consistent and safe in a set of inconsistent and unsafe circumstances.

The fifth and final point concerns 'conventicles'. Private religious meetings of the kind: formalised by Cotton in Boston and Bernard in Worksop and countless more informal meetings were called conventicles when they attracted the unfriendly attention of the authorities. Conventicle is a spectral term embracing at one extreme subversive, criminal conspiracies having nothing to do with religion, and at the other innocent religious gatherings without any subversive, criminal intent. Somewhere in the middle of this spectrum we find the religious conventicle which had, or was supposed to have, a subversive intent. That intent was to conduct religious proceedings contrary to the Act of Uniformity and, subsequently, to the Conventicle Acts. In the words of the Canons of 1604 they were secret meetings tending 'to the impeaching or depraving of the doctrine of the Church of England or of the Book of Common Prayer'. Bishop Bancroft's 1601 visitation of the diocese of London asked: 'Whether any within your parish do resort into barns, fields, woods, private houses, or to any extraordinary expositions of Scripture, or conferences together: or that be drawers or persuaders of others to any such schismatical conventicles?'[39]

In another chapter I have made the following observations.[40] Many, and for all that we know to the contrary most, frequenters of so-called 'conventicles', as practised within the early seventeenth-century Puritan mainstream, denied, or would have denied, that their meetings were conventicles in any criminal sense, which is as much as to say that they were not considered by those who frequented them to be separatist in intent. The standard 'conventicle' appears to have been held primarily for the purpose of sermon repetition, which consisted of confirmation in the ears and memories of the hearers of doctrine originally delivered in public sermons. A secondary activity may have been prayer. The Act of Uniformity of 1559 made illegal any form or act of public prayer conducted outside the liturgical forms and rubrics of the Prayer Book. It failed to define what was public prayer and presumably had no intention to inhibit private prayer. Puritans denied that their meetings for private prayer were public. In their perception, private religious duties were compatible with the public duties which the law required. In the words of the lawyer Roger Quatermayne : 'I did always think that publick duties did not make voyd private, but that both might stand with a Christian'. An earlier writer distinguished between 'godly societies and assemblies of the righteous' and the 'ordinary assemblies and meetings together at the house of prayer'.

Much of course depended upon the public-private distinction, upon who was making it and who was entitled to make it. The unrestricted, unlicensed voluntarism of private religious meetings might well have been thought incompatible with the kind of church-state that seventeenth-century England, as a civil society, aspired to be. Nevertheless the law, which was uninformative (before the eighteenth century) on the general subject of lawful and unlawful assembly, failed to define as unambiguously illegal the kind of private religious meeting often called a conventicle; although the 1664 Conventicle Act would later somewhat clarify the situation in terms of a certain number attending 'over and above those of the same household', a principle which served to turn an ostensibly legitimate private activity into an actually illegal public activity. I further argue that, however honest and limited their intentions, however far they may have been from claiming the status of separated and gathered churches for their conventicles, some conventiclers did tend, especially in particular historical circumstances, to grow into the gathered churches which, existentially and in the some sense, they already were. The long-lived religious society known as Broadmead Baptist Church Bristol, which grew from conventicle to gathered church in the course of the 1640s, is a case in point. But it was a protracted growth, the details of which were dependent at every point on arbitrary and unusual circumstances, nothing less than a revolution. The origins of many such churches, Congregational or Baptist, were more circumstantial than wholly intentional or predictable. Undue attention has been devoted to those conventicles which did so develop, to what we may call the Broadmead model, especially and for understandable reasons in histories written within and for these denominational traditions. The conventicle which never did become a gathered congregation, which I believe was the more typical conventicle, was necessarily ephemeral, leaving behind no formal record and attracting no historians.

This argument can be set in a model representation of the character and structures of English Christianity in the early seventeenth century, as accommodating and reconciling elements of compulsion and voluntarism, inclusion and exclusion, public obligations and private imperatives. Spontaneous expressions of these imperatives were integrated within the more permanent and legally prescribed structures of the church with varying degrees of majority-minority friction and tension. As Peter Lake has shown,[41] two very different ecclesiologies coexisted uneasily in post-Reformation England. In principle they may appear incompatible. But in practice they were not and there were good and pragmatic reasons why the conflict was not tidily resolved, either before 1640 or after 1660–1662. This coexistence of church-type and sect-type Christianity (to use the Troeltschian categories) was of the very essence of Elizabethan and Jacobean Puritanism but it was a longer-lasting and more universal phenomenon than Puritanism. There was something of this hybrid situation, not necessarily fraught with friction, in the interwoven history of parishes (which Christopher Hill calls 'compulsory communities') and voluntary religious fraternities, before the Reformation. And there was more of it in the history of successive versions of radical religious dissent, from the late fourteenth to the late seventeenth centuries. Studies have shown, especially the studies of rural dissent undertaken by Dr Margaret Spufford and her pupils, that these 'sects', Lollards, Familists, Baptists and Quakers, were not really sects at all in the full-blooded Troeltschian sense. In many unsuspected respects they were integrated in the wider local community, in which their leading male members, often men of some substance, assumed the public and semi-public functions appropriate to their economic and social standing.[42]

Dr Christopher Marsh has shown that the secret of the success of the Family of Love in certain villages of south Cambridgeshire, a success which seems to have consisted not only of surviving as a religious minority group in an ostensibly intolerant majority society but of conspicuous material prosperity, was a shrewd and advantageous strategy of both internal and external integration. The business they did with each other, the spiritual and material benefit cultivated by introversion and endogamy, by no means excluded 'normal' relationships with other villagers and parishioners, the taking on of functions and responsibilities proper to their status. Among the Familists, this strategy seems to have been finely tuned to ensure not sectarian growth, for that may never have been their ambition, but the perpetuation of a small religious elite which eventually, and unlike the Quakers, failed to transmit itself into the third and fourth generations and beyond. Among the Puritans, other strategies, in some ways more exclusive and socially rejectionist than those of the Family of Love, were destined to ensure that a religious minority could ensure the advantages, and take on the responsibilities, and the power, of a moral majority. In the event that strategy too failed, at least in Old England, and we are inclined to add 'of course'. But who is to say that that would have been the outcome if seventeenth-century history had taken another course? Puritanism and the evolution of sects; sects and the evolution of Puritanism; Separatism, Antiseparatism and Semi-separatism; integration or distintegration. All these tendencies had some parts of the historical process going for them. But none was invested with inevitability or irreversibility.

7

The English Conventicle

In the midst of the nervous excitement of the autumn of 1640 a Londoner called Roger Quatermayne, a Puritan and, as we might say, barrackroom lawyer, was investigated by Archbishop Laud and other privy councillors for the offence of holding religious meetings in circumstances which were politically as well as ecclesiastically suspect, since it was thought that Quatermayne and his friends had made treasonable contact with the Scottish army, then at war with its king and in occupation of English soil.[1] Quatermayne, charged with holding a *conventicle*, asked the archbishop to inform him 'what a Conventicle is'. Laud replied: 'Why, this is a Conventicle, . . . when ten or twelve or more or lesse meet together to pray, reade, preach, expound, this is a conventicle'. Laud's definition may appear uncontroversial, particularly if to his 'ten or twelve or more or less' is added the formula of the 1664 Conventicle Act, 'over and above those of the same Household'.[2] But Quatermayne objected: 'My Lord, I do not so understand it'.

Quatermayne's point was that private meetings held in a domestic setting for mutual edification were 'nothing but godly conference', not properly conventicles at all. He would have found many to agree with him, including the consistory of the Dutch church in London which in 1621 judged that by the laws of England members of their congregation who met with the pious purpose of bettering their religious knowledge did not constitute a conventicle, since a conventicle was an unlawful gathering openly defiant of the doctrine and government of the Church of England.[3] Many years later, Richard Baxter agreed in refuting the suggestion that such private meetings were schismatic. If held not 'in distaste' of the public meeting nor in opposition to it, but at a different hour and 'in subordination to the publique', they represented 'not a separated Church but as a part of the Church more diligent then the rest . . .'[4] However, Laud seems to have considered any private meeting as at least potentially schismatic, a doctrine to which Quatermayne took strong exception: 'I did always thinke that publick duties did not make voyd private, but that both might stand with a Christian.'[5] The difference between public and private duties was a familiar commonplace, and not only in the metropolis. As far away as Westmorland, and half a century before Quatermayne's appearance before the Privy Council, a preacher distinguished between 'two temples', both requiring the Christian's attention: 'publike assemblies' and 'godly societies': that is, 'ordinary assemblies and meetings together at the house of prayer', and 'godly societies and assemblies of the righteous'.[6]

The contention between Quatermayne and Laud — as to whether any small unauthorised religious meeting constituted a conventicle and whether it stood *ipso facto* condemned by that label — remained unresolved. Laud appealed to the Lord Chief Justice to confirm his definition but judges are better at asking learnedly naive questions about terms and entities than responding to them and the Lord Chief Justice 'answered nothing', or so Quatermayne alleged.[7] This was wise, and the wisdom was shared by the Restoration Conventicle Acts, which nowhere define what a conventicle is. The ambiguity underlying the Quatermayne–Laud exchange was rooted in English usage of the sixteenth and seventeenth centuries and has persisted in the vocabulary of historians. On the one hand, we encounter the neutral, non-pejorative definition of 'conventicle' offered in a glossary of 'hard English words' published in 1604: 'a little assemblie', evidently a little *religious* assembly since this was a religious glossary.[8] On the other hand a conventicle could mean an unlawful assembly, involving conspiracy, not necessarily religious at all. One might have a conventicle of highwaymen or of pickpockets. Holdsworth found in a late fourteenth-century source a conventicle of tenants banded together to resist certain demands of their lords, which suggests a medieval usage in the context of agrarian bargaining more or less equivalent to the early nineteenth-century 'combination': a conspiracy to deflect the laws of economics.[9] There is potential here for absurd errors. In the Staffordshire Quarter Sessions Rolls for 1586 we find the indictments of four individuals, three of them gentlemen, 'for unlawful and riotous assembly in conventicle in the highway at Fowtherley', leading to an assault on two individuals and battery upon a third. The same phrase, 'unlawful assembly in a conventicle' was used in conjunction with two other Staffordshire cases of assault and battery in 1587. The editor of these proceedings chose to detect in such cases what he called 'glimpses of the puritan movement' and he classified them under the heading of Protestant Dissent.[10]

This bizarre confusion need not detain us. It is not my purpose to argue that associations hitherto regarded as religious were in fact criminal conspiracies in disguise, still less to suggest that covens of criminals, denizens of the late Gamini Salgado's Elizabethan Underworld, were really prayer meetings which have received a bad press. All reference in what follows will be to conventicles in the common and religious sense. Dr Jim Sharpe, in his study of the Essex parish of Kelvedon Easterford, can demonstrate that not all the members of a particular conventicle were necessarily impeccable. Even visible saints could be guilty of sexual misdemeanours, drunkenness, theft and other offences against God and man.[11] But that is neither here nor there. Let us assume that these assemblies held for a conventionally religious purpose by persons who desired to appear conventionally religious were, in a conventional sense, religious assemblies. Were they as innocuous as Quatermayne insisted and were they generally so regarded, except in the perception of hardline prelates? If so, then pre-revolutionary England (as Dr Christopher Hill has characterised it), or at least pre-Laudian England, was a more open society than some historians have allowed.

The issue between Quatermayne and Laud cannot be resolved on a narrowly legal basis, although that is how we shall deal with it in the first instance. If we ask whether 'conventiclers' like Quatermayne intended to take part in activities which they knew to be incompatible with their responsibilities as baptised members of the established Church and subjects of its discipline the question moves publicly away from the law of the land and towards ecclesiology, and privately, for the individual, it adds to the matter of legal liability a further consideration of conscience. Either Quatermayne was in good faith or he was not. Some 'conventicles' were separatist, others not. A group meeting at Balsham and Strethall in Cambridgeshire in the 1570s persuaded first the Elizabethan Master of Peterhouse, Andrew Perne, and then, a little later, myself that their meetings were innocent. In fact we now know the men at Balsham to have been members of a radical sect of professional dissemblers, the Family of Love.[12] However, I shall argue that a historiographical bias has operated in favour of paying too much attention to conventicles the implications of which were schismatical and sectarian and too little to conventicles which were free of such connotations: which is as much as to say that the conventicle, as distinct from the gathered church to which it occasionally tended, has not been much studied. For this bias two explanations offer themselves: first, the dependence of historians on the record of various kinds of criminal procedure which would be wasting time on innocent, non-separatist conventicles; secondly, the preponderance (until recently) of denominational history which has quite naturally focused on the emergence from the conventicle, or from whatever other historical circumstances, of the fully gathered and separated church. So the annals of Broadmead Church Bristol, while preserving precious evidence of the origins of that society in more or less spontaneous and casual conventicles, encourage us to regard it as a natural progression for the conventicle to grow into a church, and diverts attention away from those conventicles — perhaps, though this can never be verified, the majority — which obstinately remained pumpkins and were never transformed by the magic wands of Mrs Dorothy Hazard of Broadmead or Archbishop Laud into Cinderella's coaches.[13] Conventicles, like other voluntary and relatively unstructured and discontinuous religious societies, lack the direct historiographical posterity which churches enjoy.

However, the historian who confines himself to the conscious and deliberate levels of human motivation and action is tying one hand behind his back. I shall also argue that beyond intentionality the English conventicle of the sixteenth and seventeenth centuries always had the potential to become, or give birth to, a separated and gathered church. There was and is a difficulty for actors and historians alike, of distinguishing clearly between voluntary societies within or alongside the Church and alternative or rival churches taking shape outside it and in total rejection of it. To claim an exclusivity in certain respects and for certain purposes, which self-selecting groups must do, devoting themselves to ends which are not those of mankind or even of the Church in general, may imply a claim to the general, absolute and ultimate exclusivity of the Church itself, especially where the ends in question are of an exalted moral and spiritual character and pursued in the context of a larger society which itself claims to be Christian and is suspicious of minority groups and hostile to the exclusive. Nevertheless it is not, I submit, a piece of pedantry but recognition of a debt which the historian owes to the past to insist that the rudderless drift of many a conventicle into separation was without deliberate intent, indeed directly contrary to intention, and principle. Edmund Wilson wrote a book called, *Apologies to the Iroquois*, the allbut extinct Indian tribe which had once inhabited New York City. Although I have never been a Presbyterian and am unlikely now to become one, what follows could be called 'Apologies to the Presbyterians', or to the long defunct aspirations of the Presbyterians of the first half of the seventeenth century, a world of human and religious experience and aspiration which we have lost.

The question must now be faced: were conventicles at risk under common law, a law which might have endangered a Jacobean association of, as it might be, anglers or bird-watchers? Or were they made illegal by particular statutes or canons? It would be a rash man who laid down the law of public assembly in England before the nineteenth century, if his life depended upon it.[14] Tudor and Stuart magistrates and constables were empowered to arrest and imprison anyone who presumed to play bowls, likewise those playing a variety of other unlawful games, 'already invented or hereafter to be invented'.[15] Bowls was a sociable game requiring the assembly of a number of players. But wherein lay the unlawfulness of unlawful games? Perhaps in the principle of playing for money,[16] perhaps in their attractiveness to the lower orders or in their lack of athletic and martial utility, not in the principle of assembly. William Hawkins, in his *Treatise of the Pleas of the Crown,* argued that such sporting diversions as bull-baiting, wrestling and the like were not unlawful: or at least the assemblies associated with them were not unlawful since they implied no intention to riot.[17] (Nowadays he would have to revise his opinion.) And what about assemblies for a religious purpose, commonly and significantly called religious *exercises?* When subjected to harrassment, religious people complained of a double standard. It was no crime for ten or twenty men to meet together in an alehouse and there lewdly misspend their time. 'All this is not harme: it is but good neighbourhood, it is no conventicle'. It was said on behalf of some Kentish ministers in 1584: 'If all manner of meetings for the bellie and pastimes . . . have their tolleration and allowance, must the meeting of mynisters at a sermon . . . be judged a conventicle?' While denying that he was a conventicler, Roger Quatermayne denounced a sporting assembly attended by a great crowd on the Sabbath as 'a fearfull conventicle'.[18] Here was a tension not so much in the law as in the interpretation of the law within the moral economy of the time, amounting to a contradiction. The classification of unlawful games was an exact, if arcane science. To repress those sociable offences which went with a pot of ale accorded with social mores which if not popular were increasingly dominant in provincial society. But it was the religious sociability of those godly persons who in their own eyes were the staunchest upholders of law and order which in the time of Archbishop Whitgift or Archbishop Laud seemed most at risk.[19] In 1639 a Cambridge shoemaker and his wife were told by the Court of High Commission that when a householder received a minister 'together with any company of men and women of other families' for the purpose of repeating a sermon, all those involved were to be accounted 'conventiclers and breakers of His Majesties Lawes Ecclesiasticale and the Constitution and Canons of the Church of England'. Like Quatermayne, the shoemaker's wife stoutly denied it. She had not heard and did not believe that such activities were unlawful. John Winthrop noted in his diary for 1624 that many were 'unjustly traduced for Conventicles'.[20]

There was no law which in the sixteenth and seventeenth centuries positively protected and in so doing defined a right of common assembly. Legally, no such right existed. But on the other hand the legal principle of *un*lawful assembly was very narrowly defined and glossed and would not be extended before the nineteenth century.[21] In defining unlawful assembly, legal commentators concerned themselves with motives and actions which were a potential extrapolation beyond the assembly: which is to say that the concept of unlawful assembly was connected with the concept of conspiracy and that in its turn to the twin principles of rout and riot. An unlawful assembly, by definition, was one which conspired to cause a riot. Those who were able to prove that this was not their intention were neither conspirators nor unlawfully assembled. For, according to Coke, the act of unlawful assembly cannot be perpetrated unless the purpose of assembly is illegal, while the action of a man to assemble his friends for the purpose of defending his property is specifically indulged by law: for, says Hawkins, following Sir Matthew Hale, 'a Man's House is looked upon as his Castle'.[22] Similarly, William Lambarde, while noting that statute law recognised a variety of 'conventicles', observed that they were all definable as such by virtue of a conspiracy to commit an indictable offence, whether to kill a man, or to corrupt the course of justice. '*Champeries*, also *Maintenances*, *Conspiracies*, *Confederacies* and giving of *Liveries* . . . be contained under the worde Conventicles', even if they contained no 'apparent shewe of Assembly against the Peace'.[23]

Until the later years of Elizabeth I it was not apparent that a private assembly of a man's friends held in his house for a religious purpose was unlawful, but nor was it positively lawful. It is significant that the succession of Conventicle Acts, beginning in 1593 and taken up in 1664 and 1670, are consistent with the common law of unlawful assembly in that they all allege some conspiratorial motive without which, or so it appears, there would have been no conventicle within the meaning of these acts. The Elizabethan statute 'to retain the Queen's subjects in obedience', came closest of all the conventicle acts to defining the religious motive of the conventicle as constituting an offence in itself, since the 'unlawful assemblies, conventicles or meetings' against which it legislated were said to be frequented by persons who obstinately refused to repair to church or who persuaded others to absent themselves. In 1664 and 1670 there is no mention of recusancy. However even in the 1593 statute the connection between a species of recusancy and conventicling is no more than an inference.[24]

In the eighteenth century it was said that 'the preamble of acts of parliament is the great window by which light is let in upon the sense of them',[25] and from the preamble to the 1593 Act and its parliamentary and wider context we know that the act was provoked by the discovery of the overtly schismatic and separatist congregation associated with the names of Henry Barrow, John Greenwood and John Penry, who all suffered execution on somewhat dubious grounds while the statute was in passage.[26] Similarly, those ecclesiastical canons of 1604 which addressed themselves to the subject of conventicles (nos 11, 71, 72 and 73) are capable of a specific and relatively narrow historical gloss in each case. Canon 11 intends to condemn outright Brownist and Barrowist separation. Canon 72, which outlaws solemn fasts held publicly or in private, together with 'prophecies or exercises in market towns or other places', also speaks of fasting and prayer to drive out devils, which suggests that the canon in its entirely arose from particular anxieties surrounding the case of John Darrell, the Puritan exorcist.[27] Canon 73 speaks of 'conventicles and secret meetings of priests and ministers', which makes it an echo of the Elizabethan classical movement. And by this canon such meetings are only judged unlawful if they 'tend to the impeaching or depraving of the doctrine of the church of England or of the Book of Common Prayer', or of any part of the established government and discipline of the English Church. So it is by no means as clear as Holdsworth supposed that by 1604 the holding of a conventicle, by which, according to Holdsworth, was meant any assembly for the exercise of religion in another manner than is allowed by the liturgy or practice of the Church of England, was made punishable. Nevertheless, there is evidence that in the perception of the architect of the Canons, Archbishop Bancroft, any privately conducted meetings for 'extraordinary expositions of Scripture or conferences together' stood condemned as 'schismatical conventicles'.[28]

When we reach the Conventicle Acts of the Restoration, 1664 and 1670, we find reference not to 'the exercise of religion in other manner than is allowed' but to 'any Assembly, Conventicle or Meeting under colour or pretence of any exercise of religion in other manner than is allowed . . .'[29] a phrase borrowed directly from the Elizabethan Act of 1593. Somewhat may hang upon what we understand by 'under colour or pretence of any exercise of Religion'. If 'exercise of Religion' is an expression properly attributed only to the authorised rites and ceremonies of the established Church (and *religio* had properly carried that limited sense for centuries) then any other, irregular practice of what was not properly religion at all could amount to a 'colour or pretence of religion', and the intention of these acts may have been simply to outlaw any religious exercise conducted outside the terms of the Act of Uniformity. A Cambridgeshire JP seems to have thought that this was the intention of the statute when he asked: 'If the liturgy bee said, question if itt bee a conventicle?'[30] Yet it appears more consistent with the internal logic of the statutes and of what we know of their context and origins to suppose that the phrase 'colour and pretence' hints at other illegal activities for which the religious exercises conducted in conventicles were thought to be a mere pretext and cover. For the title of the 1664 Act speaks of 'seditious conventicles' and it is aimed at 'seditious sectaries and other disloyal persons', who 'under pretence of Tender Consciences do at their Meetings contrive Insurrections, as late Experience hath shewed.' It would be hard indeed to exaggerte the impact of 'late Experience' on the post-1649 perception of religious dissent.

Admittedly, the mentality of the legislators may have found it difficult, unnecessary and even meaningless to distinguish between sedition and insurrection in a religious and in a civil sense. Nor do I suggest that local magistrates adhered to the strict terms of the Conventicle Acts, still less to what might appear to be their motivating spirit, in their summary and even arbitrary proceedings against all kinds of private religious meeting, even before the 1664 Act was passed. Nevertheless it is significant that in Parliament at least it was thought inappropriate to make conventicles criminal without connecting them in the public mind, however loosely, with such events as the regicide or Venner's Rising of 1661. In the two years intervening between the implementation of the Uniformity Act and the first Conventicle Act, the steps already being taken against dissenters in Lancashire seem to have been motivated by fear of a presbyterian rebellion, Booth's Rising in reverse. This alarm and the rumours which fuelled it are reflected in the correspondence of Sir Roger Bradshaigh, whose vigilance was desired by three other justices 'to prevent all future dangers which may accrew by the Presbyterians or other factions which tends to the disturbance of the peace and quiet of the Kingdom and the subvertion of his Majesties present Government.' As the Quaker Act of 1661 and its implementation suggest, Quakers were feared more than Presbyterians as insurrectionaries, and for reasons only indirectly 'religious': above all for their refusal to take the Oath of Allegiance and other oaths, refusing and inciting to refuse inferentially constituting the conspiratorial purpose for which Quaker 'conventicles' were assembled.[31] So it was as 'factious persons' that the frequenters of conventicles were targetted by the cavalier magistracy.

Knowing himself to be no 'factious person', the Lancashire minister, Adam Martindale, was resistant before the passing of the first Conventicle Act, to any imputation that private religious gatherings were necessarily 'conventicles'. 'For I knew they were not unlawfull by the law of God . . . and some particulars comprehended within their generall terms were confessedly neither against statute, common law, or the canons'. The statute of 1664 left the conscience of this doughty preacher of lawyer-like yeoman stock equally undisturbed. A posse of officers outside the locked doors of a private house in 'a dark corner of Bury parish' was ignored while Martindale calmly concluded an exercise of preaching and prayer. The reverend magistrate before whom he was taken expressed surprise that he should expose himself to the lash of the law for conventicling. 'I told him he was mistaken; it was no conventicle, either by statute, common, or canon law'. As for the first, there was no statute in form which defined it; and for the second, a conventicle, by common law had been defined by the lord chief justice as a meeting together to plot against the king and the state. 'And as for the canons, I told him there was onely two cases that were made conventicles by them, and this was neither, as I clearly proved'.[32] So far as I can tell, Martindale was substantially correct. But these things were almost as uncertain as they had been in the days of the Laud-Quatermayne encounter. In September 1662 Henry Newcome desisted from preaching but thought the domestic exercise of repeating sermons no offence. 'But the Justice told me it was'.[33]

Let us cease to pretend to be lawyers, or legal historians. What, leaving aside the tinctures of 'faction', 'sedition' or 'insurrection', was a conventicle?

Of what did it consist, in content and proceedings and in the perceptions of the participants? As I have already suggested, the subject has not been much explored phenomonologically. Even sources which are among the most familiar to seventeenth-century ecclesiastical historians have not been read with an eye to practice, or to terms and idioms; otherwise the historical literature would display a better sense of the language defining the religious culture of, for example, Protestant Lancashire in the time of Newcome and Martindale. Newcome maps out his spiritual odyssey and that of his people in such significant terms as the distinction between 'private days' and 'public days': that is, private or public days of preaching, prayer and fasting. Note these phrases: 'We had a day in public'; 'Oh what days were these!' 'We kept a private day in the house of Benjamin Brooke in Broughton'. Public is also used substantively of public worship, always called 'the public'. Compare the use of 'the public place' in the annals of Broadmead, Bristol, where the splendid fane of St Mary Redcliffe becomes simply 'Redclif publique place.' The ordinary and daily private devotion of the household or of the individuals who make it up are described by Newcome as 'duty' — 'family duty': 'Wee had sweet family duty'; 'Wee had pretty lively dutyes'. 'Duty' or 'duties' was supplemented by conference and 'repetition', of which more anon. Compare Oliver Heywood's account of his father's religious habits: 'Ever after that he associated himself with gods people, maintained days and dutys of fasting and prayer, conference, and other christian exercises'; 'many days of that nature in my fathers house'[34] Such was the rhythm and shape of the life pursued by those 'notable christians', known for an 'eminent profession of religion' in the north west. It was made up of regular 'exercises', together with monthly 'lectures by combination' or 'running exercises', and the less predictable funerals, always marked by two sermons punctuated by dinner.[35] It is in this cultural setting, and according to the authenticity of its own language of identification, that the so-called conventicle must be understood: as a species of religious activity associated by those undertaking it with the private domain: Quatermayne's 'private duties' which were not made void by 'public duties'.

Since the English conventicle was not an invention of the mid-seventeenth century, let us carry this kind of sensitivity back to what I take to be its earliest discernible origins, in the religious gatherings held in private houses in the fifteenth and early sixteenth centuries, uncovered by the ecclesiastical authorities and incriminated by association with

Wycliffite heresies held and propagated by so-called 'Lollards'. To encapsulate the history of the conventicle in terms of a continuity with its roots in Lollardy may seem to subscribe to Christopher Hill's theory of a more or less continuous and coherent tradition of radical dissent, 'from Lollards to Levellers'.[36] That is possible rather than proven or even proveable but it is not something which I wish to argue for on this occasion: rather that at the level of a somewhat low lowest common denominator there is a consistency of habit in the meeting together of a considerable number of 'friends' (in the sense of that word current in the period, that is, embracing kindred as well as unrelated neighbours) for a purpose both sociable and religious. The religious purpose which we happen to know about from the sources available to us was one of dissenting more or less radically from the received doctrine of the Church and orthodox religious practice, and of drawing spiritual sustenance from an alternative source, the Bible or parts of the Bible in the vernacular. It is possible that this tincture of heretical dissent is exaggerated in our sources, even planted there in some cases by the inquisitorial mind:[37] although it could be argued that it was only the critical edge of the heretical or semi-heretical mind which was capable of introducing an element of religious indoctrination and controversy into the idle gossip which might otherwise have accompanied the eating and drinking which was perhaps the chief business on such occasions. Not only their heterodoxy but the structural informality and wholly domestic setting of these gatherings distinguished them from more formal religious fraternities.

The question of Lollard belief enters the present argument only indirectly, for the subject of Lollardy has been discussed too exclusively in terms of belief, as if the thing consisted of a bundle or series of bundles of doctrine, carried about by obscure and in themselves unimportant human vectors. The basic *res* of Lollardy, what is available to handle, is not so much a body of beliefs as a corpus, or rather scattered detritus, of texts.[38] But what can be said about Lollardy as a social institution? It is important to insist that when Lollards met together, they met as a kind of conventicle, not as some kind of church.[39] It is more profitable to consider what Mrs Hawisia Moone of Loddon in Norfolk may have meant when, in the late 1420s, she confessed to having been 'right hoomly and prive' with nineteen named persons, four of them priests, 'and many others',[40] than to ask whether the Lollards celebrated the sacraments among themselves. Indeed the latter is probably a question badly put in respect of the later Lollards, since there is hardly enough evidence one way or the other to justify putting it, and to pose it at all is to imply that Lollardy constituted a counter-church with ministers, and that its meetings were 'church' occasions, perhaps conducted vaguely along the lines of a later nonconformist 'service'. Dr J.A.F. Thompson came close to implying as much when he wrote of 'the Lollard congregations' and 'the Lollard sect'.[41] We may well heed Dr Euan Cameron's warning about the lesson 'which the late medieval clergy could not learn, that heretics were not like another kind of public church, mirroring the official institution in every detail'.[42] These 'known men' and women comprised not a separate sect but a tendency within a church so comprehensive that it defied imagination to put oneself wholly outside it.[43] Mistress Alice Rowley of Coventry might boast that 'my beleve is bettur that thirs', but the self-defining elite of which she was part still went to church and behaved themselves there with exaggerated devotion.[44] At Amersham the local heretics were so dominant as to dare to demonstrate their contempt for the consecrated host. But it was in church that they conducted themselves in this fashion, and only after mass was over did they go off to their own conventicles.[45] This resembles Elizabethan Puritanism more than Elizabethan Separatism. There are elements of Wycliffite ecclesiology which point in the same direction, the *Lantern of Light* distinguishing between the church as 'a litil flock' of truly faithful souls and as a 'comyng togiddir of good and yvel in a place that is halowid' for sacraments, prayer and preaching; while denouncing the religious orders as 'private religion', 'our new fayned sectis', insisting that 'peple schulde drawe to parische churchis and here her service there.'[46]

If Lollardy was a kind of conventicle, it was also a kind of school, or a conventicle which functioned as a school, and the documents echo to the phrase 'schools of heresy'. Sir Thomas More complained of 'night schools', while a hundred years earlier Hawisia Moone had confessed to the frequent holding of 'scoles of heresie yn prive chambers and prive places of oures', in which she had 'herd, conceyved, learned and reported' errors and heresies.[47] The plurality of 'chambers and prive places' may be significant, for there is no need to suppose that the whole attention of those present in a house on such an occasion would have been concentrated on a single discourse or action. From later generations, Marian, Elizabethan, Jacobean,

Caroline, it is possible to collect examples of religious sociability which is distinctly fragmented (to borrow a phrase and concept from Dr Keith Wrightson.)[48] It was reported of those present in a house in Ash in East Kent in 1625, where a religious conference between separatists and non-separatists continued for two whole days, that many said nothing at all and 'some took not any notice at all'.[49]

What were the modes of instruction in a 'school of heresy'? We can distinguish between reading aloud and the recitation of passages of scripture, and the teaching of certain 'lessons', although some of the early sixteenth-century sources suggest that the latter was often a one-to-one tutorial exercise, not necessarily occurring in the context of a well-attended conventicle, or proceeding on its periphery. Of these two elements we can be confident. What is less clear is how far there may also have been religious conference, whether in the sense of the free exploration of religious topics or of the disputation of questions, and whether discussion would have proceeded syllogistically, or by means of biblical texts and precedents, or according to still more primitive mental and rhetorical principles. 'Questions' may have belonged to the realm not of idle curiosity but of conscience. In Mary's days it was conscience which drove the husbandman Henry Orinel from Willingham in Cambridgeshire to a brief and disturbing encounter with the Familist joiner Christopher Vittels in a Colchester inn and sent him on his way again to the more reliable counsel of the Protestant bishops imprisoned in Oxford.[50] 'Lessons' taught in Lollard and early Protestant circles seem to have been encapsulated in the memorable, aphoristic forms, whether scriptural in origin or 'popular', which Dr Cameron has described as the typical expression of the minds of the heretical mountaineers of the Vaudois in the same period.[51] John Foxe carefully described the prodigious evangelical learning of the cloth-workers of early Protestant Hadleigh according to a threefold formula. They had read the whole Bible through. They could recite many of Paul's Epistles by heart. And they were well able to supply 'a godly learned sentence in any matter of controversy'.[52]

That was a degree of erudition beyond anything attainable before the days of regular Protestant preaching and widespread literacy and Bible ownership, but one which may have grown out of earlier traditions, especially with respect to 'godly learned sentences', such as the sixty-

nine *mala dogmata* listed by the Lower House of Convocation in 1541.[53]
Assuming that we are justified in positing some continuity between
pre-Reformation 'schools of heresy' and post-Reformation conventicles,
a major difference would appear to lie in the greater dependence of the
latter on the public sermon and, indeed, on the person and authority
of the preacher, whether physically present or represented by the notes
of his sermons carried and deployed by the hearers. There were other
probable differences between the agenda of a typical early seventeenth-
century conventicle and its precursor: notably in the use of vocal prayer,
condemned in some Lollard sources as mere 'lip-labour',[54] and in psalm-
singing. But these seem to have been concomitants to the main function
of the domestic meetings of early Protestant generations which was
repetition: that is, repetition of sermons.

'Repetition' is among the more neglected words in the religious glossary
of the seventeenth century. Among the Elizabethan godly, neighbours
met to pray, or to listen to the New Testament or to readings from
Foxe's Book of Martyrs, but primarily to engage in repetition.[55] So it was
in Lady Margaret Hoby's model household at Hackness and in countless
humbler households.[56] It was said of the Norwich MP Sir John Hobart
that he was unwilling to let a sermon pass without also hearing it
repeated.[57] The 'supposed conventicle' against which the Puritan lawyer
Nicholas Fuller defended his clients Lord and Maunsell in a *cause célèbre*
of 1607 was a regular exercise of repetition. For it was the practice
of these Yarmouth shopkeepers on Sunday evenings to join with their
minister 'in repeating of the substance and heads of the sermons that
day made in the church'.[58] John Udall of Kingston on Thames supplies
a rationale for the practice: 'If one have missed the observation of this
or that point, another hath marked it, so that among them they may
bring away the whole, and so be edefied one by another'.[59] Such was
the practice around Manchester and generally in south-east Lancashire
and neighbouring parts of Cheshire in the mid-seventeenth century.[60]
In Baxter's Kidderminster, 'you might hear a hundred families singing
psalms or repeating sermons as you passed through them'.[61] In John
Angier's Denton there was repetition of the morning sermon both in
Angier's house and in the church 'to many people that stayed there', with
psalms sung before and after. This occupied the time until the afternoon
sermon, which in its turn was immediately repeated. On Monday nights

Angier's family repeated the sermon of the preceding Sunday morning, on Saturday nights the same day's afternoon sermon.[62]

The fact that the principal activity in 'meetings of the godly' was to repeat sermons heard in public earlier in the day is important in itself, the implications of the fact even more so. Repetition was akin to the process of catechising, in that sermons having been reduced in summary form to their 'heads' (it seems to have been a rare gift to memorise an entire sermon, verbatim)[63] were by repetition impressed, perhaps permanently, on the minds of the hearers. The Fifth Monarchist John Rogers later recorded the consequences of his adolescent exposure to this discipline in his superstitious habit of repeating sermons to himself in bed, as a kind of talisman to protect himself against the Devil while he slept, and according to a set plan. On Sunday night he would repeat the sermon heard that afternoon, on Monday a sermon heard the previous Sunday, on other nights sermons heard as much as ten years before.[64]

This was how that famous edifice 'the Puritan Mind' was erected and furnished. We may apply to repetition what has been said of the mental effects of catechisms: that those who listened to sermons and read the Bible did so with faculties trained by catechisms[65] — trained, that is, to arrange what they heard in formal rhetorical structures, a much more advanced facility than the tendency of earlier heretics and Protestants to reduce a sermon to one or two strikingly memorable and even scandalous pronouncements, prefaced by 'he hath heard it said that . . .' or 'that there was a saying in the country that . . .'[66] Mentally and rhetorically this was the very essence of what Dr Cameron has called 'the reformation of the heretics'.[67]

The gratification offered by the catechitical method may seem to us somewhat elusive, and our prejudice against a stultifying exercise tends to be reinforced by the accounts given by the radical spiritual autobiographers of the age — Quaker, Ranter, Muggletonian — of their subsequent emancipation from the truly vain repetitions of this religious culture. Richard Farnworth, for one, described a youth spent writing and repeating sermons 'and all this while I was but carnall and earthly, knowing nothing . . .'[68] However we should not ignore the fact that Henry Newcome employs a spiritually emotive language to describe the experiences of his own household as they perfected this art: 'Wee had repetition pretty lively' — 'very comfortable repetition and prayer'

— 'after supper wee had repetition pretty sweet'. In his diary for Sunday 11 May 1662, Newcome wrote: 'Now for mee comfort may come in at repetition, and to them that partake of it.' As for whole 'private days', Newcome noted that they were called by some 'soule fatning dayes', while Oliver Heywood wrote of 'a sweet melting heart-inlarging day'.[69]

But for the present purpose the importance of repetition lies chiefly in the link, the umbilical cord as it were, which it served to symbolise between the public assemblies and doctrine of the church and the exploration of religious knowledge and experience at a private and domestic level; and also between the trained and qualified professional, the minister, and his people. So long as lay participation in conventicles, whether or not a minister was present, was confined to the derivative exercise of repeating what had been uttered authoritatively from the pulpit, stopping short of an original exposition of the text, then there was no separatist implication, no claim that God was communicating in a directly inspirational manner with and through the minds and tongues of those gathered in private. This was the case even when the doctrine was carried back from other parishes by those who 'gadded' to sermons elsewhere for want of preaching at home or in pursuit of 'edification', a practice typical of Elizabethan lay Puritanism and yet not schismatic, neither in the perception of the gadders themselves nor according to some ecclesiastical lawyers.[70] And even within the separated world of the gathered sect, the same principle of dependence might prevail. In the Weald of Kent in 1627 we come across Margaret Adams, an old woman who trudged around with 'notes in papers' of the sermons of the separatist tallow chandler John Turner 'and where she commeth there she sheweth them'.[71] When defenders of the godly way of life spoke of their meetings as 'honest and lawful conventions'[72] and denied that they were conventicles in any pejorative sense, they meant that those participating were regular attenders at public worship who did not presume to utter original doctrine in their more private meetings.

By the same token, the moment at which a conventicle or private 'society' of Christians ceased (in these terms) to be an innocent and legally defensible annexe to the public assembly and became, in its own eyes, a separated and gathered church in its own right might coincide with the point at which the leaders of the group cast aside their sermon notes and depended upon their own relatively unaided capacity to expound directly from the biblical text. The *locus classicus* for this process of emancipation is the Baptist William Kiffen's *Remarkable Passages*, where we encounter a group of London apprentices (which included the future Leveller John Lilburne) which met at five in the morning, an hour before the lecture at one of their preferred London churches, to pray, communicate to one another what they had received from the Lord, 'or else to repeat some sermon which we had heard before'. But in the course of time they began to read a portion of Scripture and to speak from it 'what it pleased God to enable us'.[73] The annals of Broadmead, Bristol, record a similar progression, from informal meetings for repetition, 'repeating their notes to one another, whetting it on their hearts', to separation from the 'public places', with gifted 'brethren of the Church' taking on the ministry and 'carrying on the Meetings'. Significantly it was at this point that the separatist presumption of the group attracted public hostility with a riotous mob attacking their meeting place and complaining of the novelty of 'a Church with a Chimney in it.'[74]

This was a very thin line to cross, a tiny ditch, but a Rubicon nevertheless. Participants in a late Elizabethan Dover 'conventicle' protested that their meetings implied no intention 'to become singular' but were undertaken 'in the way of simplicitie'. Yet, with the best will in the world, and in all simplicity, 'singularity' could not always be avoided.[75] It was said of the early Bristol Separatists that in 1640 there were no more than five of them, and that like Abraham they went out 'not knowing where they went'.[76] No doubt in many cases the first steps into schism were taken blindfold, and as a series of more or less instinctive reactions to circumstances, although we should not underestimate the charismatic role in initiating a decisive separation of leaders like Dorothy Hazzard in Bristol; or Katherine Chidley in Bury St Edmunds, with her tiny nucleus of eight covenanting members.[77] Some of these emigrations into separatist dissent are well-documented and provide familiar paradigms in the history of nonconformity. Others are a matter of inference. We do not know who or what turned the godly of Cranbrook whose persons and 'private communion' their minister Robert Abbot had 'loved' and approved into incorrigible Brownists who rejected his ministry outright. Probably it was no single heresiarch, or Abbot would surely have named him in his book *A Trial of our Church Forsakers*, or in his correspondence with Sir Edward Dering.[78] But it is a reasonable inference that a large number of dissenting churches of late seventeenth-century Kent had come into being before 1662, many of them in the 1640s, and by some process which had transformed non-separated conventicles into fully gathered churches.[79]

The argument of the remainder of this essay proceeds along intentionally different lines from the time-honoured exercise of tracing the origins and development of 'The English Separatist Tradition', and establishing the proper genealogy of English, or American, Congregationalism.[80] There was, in the exceptional circumstances of the mid-seventeenth century political and ecclesiastical crisis, as, somewhat earlier, in the even more unusual environment of New England, a convergence of religious experience and practice upon elements and even the core and essence of the tradition of radical and exclusive dissent with which the argument *is* concerned, although it is fundamental to my purpose to insist that that convergence was as circumstantial and fortuitous as any great departures in human affairs can be. I refer to the coalescence of the 'Independency' of 'the Congregational Way'. At the heart of that emergent tradition was an ecclesiology, a settled and developed conviction that the national corporation calling itself the Church of England was not, as a body, a true Church of Christ, a title restricted to gathered and covenanted societies of 'visible saints'; although (according to all but the most far out of sectaries) the national parochial church might contain true Christians within it. We are not concerned with the theoretical formulation and elaboration of that proposition either, but only with some of the personal and collective circumstances and experiences which contributed to it.

Those who look for the beginnings of Separatism, as a principled and 'ideological' application of certain strongly discriminatory scriptural texts, rightly begin with the most drastic separation in all English religious history: the conviction of the first generation of lay Protestants, in all probability planted in their consciences by highly educated preachers, and subsequently brought to white heat in the Marian persecution, that they alone constituted the elect of Christ's little flock, the two or three gathered in his name.[81] 'Wherefore', wrote the Essex curate William Tyms 'to all God's faithfull servants', 'come out from among them and separate yourselves . . . and touch no unclean thing'. When the Londoner Gertrude Crockhay was told on her deathbed that unless she recanted and received the sacrament she could not be given Christian burial she exalted: 'Oh how happy am I that I shall not rise with them but against them!'[82] But here we are concerned with the post-1559 Protestant establishment, and with those situations in which a conscientious testimony was sustained against 'Anabaptist' Separatism and where there was no deliberate intention to contract the universality of the church into the petty sectarian particularity of the conventicle; and yet where this nevertheless tended, against all intentionality, to happen. In the broader context of Christian history, seen through Troeltschian spectacles, this was a poignant chapter in English seventeenth-century religious history, and one contained broadly within what was emergent as the Presbyterian wing of the Puritan tradition, or close to the indeterminate frontier dividing Presbyterianism from the Independency of the Congregational Way.

That we are able to observe this chapter in some intimate detail we owe to the habit of those ministers of the time who kept diaries or made autobiographies out of their experience. I refer to the first-person narratives of the Lancastrians, Thomas Newcome, Adam Martindale, Thomas Jolly and Oliver Heywood.[83] But the roots of this self-monitoring introspection grew in East Anglia and Essex, where Richard Rogers wrote the life of John Angier who came out of Dedham, where Rogers's formidable kinsman John Rogers ruled the Jacobean pulpit and was trained by John Cotton of Boston who was himself in debt to this tradition.[84] Newcome tells us that it was the diary of Samuel Ward of Sidney Sussex with its many frank disclosures which first inspired him: 'I thought it was a very brave thing . . .'[85]

The fullest as well as the bravest record of the Puritan conscience in action in this uncertain time, pitched somewhat between Presbyterianism and Independency, established church and gathered church, is the Diary of Ralph Josselin, vicar of Earls Colne near Colchester:[86] the Josselin who recalled how he was first drawn to the awesome challenge of the ministerial office: 'I confess my childhood was taken with ministers and I heard with delight and admiration and desire to imitate them from my youth, and would be acting in corners': words which are echoed in Newcome's Lancashire autobiography where we find a childhood 'attempting making English discourses sermonwise at vacant times . . . it being my ordinary play and office to act the minister among my play-fellows'.[87]

These narratives bring us into close contact with the professional Christian, striving through a lifetime of pastoral endeavour to retain and strengthen a sense of obligation to all God's people, to those afar off as well as those that were nigh. 'Have a care of the whole flock', Cromwell told Barebone's Parliament.[88] In the perception of ministers and preachers like these, voyaging together in a broad-bottomed and by now securely established Puritan tradition, the conventicle and its membership constituted that portion of a large and fluctuating parochial flock which was responsive to the gospel and willingly subject to its discipline, the kind of Christians described as 'conscionable', 'eminent', 'serious', 'the regenerate and truely religious christians', 'renowned christians'.[89] When Rogers of Wethersfield entered into a special covenant with a score of his people in 1588 he remarked that they did 'as farre exceed the common sort of them that professe the Gospell as the common professors do exceed them in religion which know not the Gospell',[90] those whose practice of religion was prodigious. In many of these little societies there seems to have been a female preponderance, explicable in terms of the special relationship often forged between preachers and anxious, self-deprecating Calvinist women, enduring what Oliver Heywood, describing his own mother, called their 'soul troubles'.[91] Whether they chose to or not, ministers in this tradition found that they had an exclusive relationship with these super-Christians which may have threatened their more general pastoral success. Adam Martindale, wrestling in conscience with the issues dividing the Presbyterian and Congregational tendencies in what he called 'that bustling year' of 1646, when both struggled in the womb like Jacob and Esau, wrote: 'I made no doubt of the truth of our English Churches, and consequently I thought they needed onely reformation, no new constitution, and that the congregationall way of gathering churches was the way to spoile many churches for the new making of one.' Yet Martindale was unable to fulfil his pastoral obligation to the entire parochial congregation, including the profane majority, especially since he lacked the power of discipline over those who stayed away from his ministrations. Of these he wrote that he was unlikely to see the faces of the tenth part of them.[92]

One way of defining a conventicle of the mid-seventeenth century would be to say that it consisted of faces which ministers like Martindale saw rather frequently, the inner fold of a scattered flock. And yet this little flock, with its intricate fabric of special intimacies, maintained a deeply conscientious abhorrence of separation and separatism. That abhorrence is deeply imprinted in the biographies of the famous ministers and eminent 'private christians' of this generation, which were derived from funeral sermons and built into substantial bodies of hagiographical ecclesiastical history by Samuel Clarke, minister of St Bennet Fink.[93] In the post-Restoration situation for which these 'lives' were adapted, anti-separatism served an obvious polemical purpose, yet there is no reason to doubt the authenticity of these convictions in their original, Jacobean context. Witness the anti-separatist polemics of Richard Bernard, John Darrell, William Bradshaw and many other ministers. Bradshaw wrote of the 'mistake' of supposing that non-conformists were 'all Brownists in heart', recalling 'how many Non-Conformists have written against Brownisme, as Maister Cartwright, Gifford, Hildersham, Darrell, Brightman, Ames, Paget etc'.[94] So Edmund Staunton was said to have declaimed against Separatism as England's 'incurable wound': 'It will never be well within the Church of God in this Nation so long as Christians are so prone to division and separation'. Arthur Hildersham was called 'the hammer of schismatics' and Thomas Taylor was credited with mightily confuting and reclaiming Brownists.[95] Thomas Gataker's life of Bradshaw ('and indeed to separatists he was ever very adverse') quotes him as declaiming in a public sermon: 'It is the great mercy of God toward us that we have no cause to seek the word in deserts and wildernesses, in woods and caves and desolate mountains, but such worthy edifices as these to assemble in, dedicated only to this use'. Even among Puritans more deeply alienated from the establishment than ministers of the mainstream we find the same aversion from what the radical Scot Alexander Leighton called the 'quicksands of Separation'.[96] Far from cherishing the parish churches as 'worthy edifices', Randall Bate, who died in a London prison in 1613, demanded their total destruction, as temples dedicated to idols. Yet no Jacobean Puritan denounced separatism more vehemently than Bate, insisting that the communion of the godly in private meetings must never lead to neglect of 'public meanes'. 'Men must not separate till the Lord separate'. 'This kind of separation obscures the good providence of God towards the land'. 'Make not the Church weak by your renting from it'.[97] When Archbishop Laud charged Roger Quatermayne with being 'the ring-leader of all the separatists', Quatermayne retorted that he was 'one of their greatest opposites'.[98]

We may find this insistence hard to understand, even incredible, and difficult to penetrate. Was the attitude of a Puritan like Bate to 'the public' comparable to our own rectitude in respect of civic duty, tax-paying, jury service and the like, and thus a *political* sentiment? Did the warmer feelings aroused in private meetings where there existed, in principle, no barriers or differences, no scandals not sought out and cauterised by mutual discipline, represent the substance of church fellowship, attendance on public duties and means their formal and empty shell? Perhaps, although twentieth-century Christians are almost disqualified from answering such a difficult question.

However, there was more than one form of separation. Jeremy Corderoy, no 'Separatist', in his *Warning for Worldlings* (1608) addressed himself to you, 'most deerely beloved brethren . . . who have separated your selves from other men, to set forth the glory of God'.[99] The Gloucestershire minister John Sprint wrote of separating *in the church*, that is, from its corruptions; and John Paget, minister of the unseparated English congregation in Amsterdam, recommended 'separation from known evils, but not from the Churches of Christ for evilles among them'. It was a commonplace among the unseparated that this kind of separation was more costly than the way taken by the Brownists. One such Puritan wrote to a friend in John Robinson's Leiden congregation and reproached him for not choosing to share 'the sharpe scourge of persecution' among 'our poor afflicted brethren'. Sprint wrote: 'We suffer for separating in the Church'.[100]

Whether this language referred to real persecution or was simply the metaphorical rhetoric of spiritual travail, unseparated Puritans practised, or at least preached, a drastic separation not only from 'known evils' and corrupt practices but from purportedly evil and corrupt persons, their neighbours. And here we confront three paradoxes which will complete the argument. As the popular Reformation progressed and put down social roots, as preaching became more prevalent and instructed Protestants more numerous, the conviction that true Christians — the 'better part' — were a mere remnant, 'the fewer part', whereas Christians 'in name only' comprised 'the greater part', seems to have grown in intensity and practical application. Jeremy Corderoy took it for granted that he lived in 'the last times', when 'corruption of manners shal most abound'.[101] John Darrell thought that nineteen parts out of twenty might prove to be 'naught', 'but the twentieth part good'.[102] This deeply pessimistic diagnosis was shared with Separatists, for whom the scandal of promiscuous church membership was the strongest of all imperatives to separate.[103] Yet antiseparatists or semi-separatists like Darrell or Richard Bernard (and this was the key to their ecclesiology) professed not to doubt that a little

leaven entitled the whole lump to the title of 'churches of the saints' 'in
the respect of the better part, though the fewer by many'. 'So we speake,
calling a heape of chaffe and wheate wheate onely, not naming the
chaffe . . .' In the parable of the tares, the field signified not the world
but the visible church, 'a mixt companie of good and bad' for which the
primitive church at Corinth was an apt model.[104]

The second paradox is that the semi-separatism or merely social
separatism advocated and, to an extent hard to measure, practised by
Jacobean Puritans was more starkly divisive in its consequences, more
prejudicial to consensual community values, than strict ecclesiastical
separatism. The separatist elder and ideologue Henry Ainsworth taught
that the saints were to have no communion with the wicked in matters
of religion, whereas his advice in respect of all other occasions of life was
relaxed and permissive. In civil affairs such as eating and drinking, buying
and selling, the saints were taught of God to converse with the wicked in
peace.[105] How else could the separated live in the foreign environment of
Amsterdam? But even in England a separatist might conduct himself with
tact and circumspection. The Wealden tallow chandler John Turner was
accounted by his neighbours 'a separatist from the Church of England' but
'yet in his dealinges was taken and reputed for an honest man'.[106] With the
non-separated Puritans, still living in the English parishes, the position
was exactly reversed. It was necessary to gather and even communicate
with the wicked and promiscuous multitude in the public exercises of
religion. The law required it. St Paul writing to the Corinthians positively
commended it. Those who had the authority to do so ought to separate
out the ungodly, as Hagar and Ishmael were put out of the the tent and
into the wilderness. But if the magistrate failed to do this — the only act
of separation which could be justified — there was no obvious remedy
for the private Christian. Thomas Hooker taught:

> 'Suppose they that are in authority will not separate them . . . yet the saints of
> God should not abstain from the congregation. It is pitiful indeed and the thing
> is troublesome and tedious to a gracious heart (and we must mourn for it) but
> being [so], it is not in my power; I must not abstain'.

However, in all private respects, 'familiar accompanying in private
conversation', the godly man not only could but must cut himself off. This
too was Paul's doctrine. 1 Corinthians 5:9–10. As a Carlisle preacher put
it in 1614: 'Though a corporall separation cannot be had, yet in spirit thou

must separate thyselfe'. 'Keepe thy selfe in the fresh aire'. 'Be no common companie keeper', wrote Richard Kilby of Derby. At Paul's Cross, William Crashawe's advice was the same: 'Wee must separate our selves from the wicked mans companie and societie, as far as lawfully and conveniently we may'. That was the true application of Jeremiah 51:11, forsaking Babel. Thomas Hooker's Chelmsford hearers were told: 'I can keep a man out of my house, but I cannot fling him out of the open congregation'.[107] As early as 1588 Stephen Bredwell had asked whether this principle undermined such fundamental social and political obligations as marriage, parenthood, civil obedience and commercial bargains. The answer was no. We must not be unnatural. But such necessary duties, when performed towards the carnal or wicked, must be undertaken with a 'kind of mourning and affliction for their sakes'.[108] In other words, a wife must not refuse her ungodly husband his conjugal rights. But she must not appear to enjoy it.

The conventicle, into which the godly withdrew from the 'company keeping' of what has been called the 'festive community',[109] no longer seems as innocuous as it did when we set out on this enquiry. Given the expectations and necessary conditions of a harmonious social existence in seventeenth-century England, it now looks thoroughly obnoxious. So we come to our third and final paradox, a familiar one which is so central to the traditional historiography of the Puritan Revolution that there will be no need to labour it. Just when the deep contradictions of Jacobean Puritanism should have been resolved in an all-embracing reformation, and when the spiritual resources built up in the conventicle ought to have been generally released to the church at large, almost the reverse happened. In the 1640s the church in the Puritan parish — or in some parishes known to us — effectively contracted to the limits of the conventicle which now came closer than ever before to detaching itself from the nominal Christianity of those outside its narrow walls. That is far from adequate as an account of the great diversity of ecclesiastical history in the period of the civil wars and Commonwealth. It also ignores the origins of powerful sectarian movements in the opportunities and opportunism of the time, which actively and willingly liberated forces and tendencies previously suppressed. I should not want to argue that the Quakers happened in a fit of absence of mind. But so far as the Puritan mainstream is concerned, the analogy of a great glacier advancing to engulf a whole landscape but then surprising itself by disintegrating and calving icebergs into a chilly sea seems apt.

Or so the precious autobiographical narratives suggest. Here we find on the one hand the imperialistic Puritan imperative, looking for nothing less than a general and national reformation, on the other the sense of a certain number, all too few, of 'serious Christians', those who are known for 'an eminent profession of religion', 'substantiall Christians of our societie'. Adam Martindale was attracted to a parish 'where there was a knot of good people'. 'Our society', whether in Martindale's Gorton or Jolly's Altham or Josselin's Colne was a choice but tiny fragment, almost lost to sight among the vastly more numerous ignorant and profane, Martindale remarking of his own large parish that 'the multitudes of the people would be dead, in all probability, ere we could goe once over them'.[110]

The crossroads was reached with the power now in principle within the grasp of many such ministers to apply stringent pastoral discipline, excluding from the sacrament all but the visibly worthy. In one direction the road led up from this crux to the sunny uplands of an effective discipline on Scottish lines, something far from impossible in some parts of south-east Lancashire. But in the other it ran steeply down into a cosy but insecure sectarian hollow. Mainstream Puritanism, having fought its way to the crossroads, hoped to find the high road but more often than not missed its way. Martindale's conditions of admission to the sacrament effectively restricted what in the north of England were called 'rightings' to 'serious christians', for he required communicants to use prayer and instruction in their families, to read the Bible and to sanctify the Lord's Day 'according to which rule (since the Reformation) we conceive we have walked and (God assisting) do intend to continue so'.[111] But who, in Lancashire, were 'we'? In Jolly's Altham, where this was called 'good order', the Lord's Supper was reserved for those who were worthy, that is, 'saints visible to the eye of rational charity'. These comprised 'the society of God's people', and baptism was made available only to the children of those who were now designated *members*, persons who had subscribed a church covenant. These were just twenty-nine persons, including fourteen women, representing only twenty of the 150 families which made up the parish. This gathered church within the church never numbered more than two or three dozen, and yet it retained the ambition of imposing a general reformation on the whole community, at the time of the major-generals offering to search out in their houses the nineteen out of twenty who never went to church. But in 1656 it was noted: 'No conversion work at Altham'. After St Bartholomew Day

1662 the little 'society' withdrew altogether from public worship and reverted to meeting in an alehouse, where, in 1667, Jolly preached to two women only.[112]

Josselin's diary tells a similar story of sectarian defeat snatched from the jaws of Puritan triumph, but with a less drastic and tidy conclusion. In Earls Colne the involuntary drift in a sectarian direction is first perceptible in 1645, when Josselin refers to house-hold meetings with those in spiritual affinity as 'conference with divers of my people', 'the society of divers loving friends' and 'the society of my friends', but when 'the society' had yet to become, as at Jolly's Altham, a formalised, covenanted membership. But in December 1646 Josselin and his intimates pitched upon a method and order for their meetings and met for the first time in Josselin's house.[113] On the face of it, these were 'lawful conventions' of a traditional type, and no threat or alternative to public church assemblies. But in the absence of the ecclesiastical courts and without any alternative form of credible parochial discipline, the assemblies were no longer very public. The sacrament of the Lord's Supper was already suspended (and remained in suspense for nine years), while in May 1647 Josselin noted that his congregation had grown 'very thinne . . . people seldom frequent hearing the word'.[114]

Meanwhile the small circle of 'the society', itself attended in August 1647 by 'very few', was threatened on the one hand by backwardness and indifference, on the other by the 'opinionative' who were insisting that only 'real saints . . . so farr as we can discerne' were to remain in fellowship. Although Josselin from time to time recorded 'comfortable' meetings and 'sweet' discourse, by the summer of 1648 (and with 'the Puritans' ostensibly triumphant what irony in this dating!) he doubted whether there was still work in Colne for him to do.[115] Sometimes it seemed that his 'friend of friends' and benefactor Mistress Mary Church, the source of 'loving and plentiful entertainment' for the society, was his only support. 'The Lord thins our town of christian people.' Moreover he had difficulty in securing his tithe income and probably doubted his right in conscience to collect it from parishioners who failed to come within his restrictive definition of 'christian people'. But the crisis passed thanks paradoxically to the death of Mistress Church, from whose estate Josselin benefited.[116]

In February 1651 the Lord's Supper was administered for the first time for many years, but only to 'such as in charity wee reckon to be disciples', some thirty-four persons. Although there was no covenanting, or none which Josselin recorded, it was on this deeply moving occasion that 'our society', now with formal procedures for admission, became, in effect, the Church in Earls Colne. A few weeks later the subject of conference was 'the practice of love mutually one to another', and in May there was another conference 'about the Saints mutually praying for one another'.[117] Yet in the 1650s Josselin continued to preach to 'sleepy hearers' and anyone else who cared to attend the larger, open and more diffuse congregation in church, where parishioners were still liable to insist in noisily disruptive fashion that their tithes and rates entitled them to a place.[118] Let us drop, for a moment, the convention which made such church attenders 'carnal' and irreligious. The population of Earls Colne was not far short of 900.[119] Large numbers of now nameless Christian people continued to claim their baptismal rights and to perform some of their duties, however vestigial, more or less regardless of developments which, in the eyes of a dominant but tiny minority, denied them all or most interest in it.

The Restoration found Josselin still secure as vicar of Colne, as, more surprisingly, did the Sundays following 24 August 1662, when 'great droves of people' flocked to hear him preach, doubtless attracted by the curiosity of the last beneficed nonconformist in that part of the country. Subsequently, congregations fell back to eighty or ninety.[120] But when the Lord's Supper was revived on Easter Day 1665 (the first Easter administration since the early 1640s) there were only twelve communicants, in 1669 twenty, in 1670 fourteen. On Easter Day 1674, Josselin wrote: 'Christs number at this sacrament. 6 men and 6 women and my selfe'. In 1679 'wee had 4 men. 12 women at sacrament'. As for conventicles, or meetings of 'the society' they had ceased, or at least are no longer mentioned by Josselin.[121]

It would make for a tidy conclusion to be able to say that by now roles were reversed. The conventicle had become the church, in the form of a tiny group of less than twenty communicants; whereas it was the open assembly of the parish church building which had become a peripheral and more or less casual audience of 'sleepy hearers'. Dissent was fully institutionalised, to endure for three centuries. But there is no neatly severed end to the strands of this rope, only a mass of loose and straggly threads. Josselin died in 1683, still vicar of Colne and so still charged with the cure of all its many souls. One loose end is old Henry Newcome,

deprived of his living and denied a public ministry but still taking himself
off to 'the public' in the first years of James II 'out of conscience of the
duty of public worship: and I bless God I met with something that did
me good'.[122] Another frayed thread is Adam Martindale, scrupulously and
'constantly' attending the sermons of the conformist who had supplanted
him and then following the old custom of repeating the sermons to
'an house full of parishioners of the devoutest sort' — who were kind
enough to say that they liked the sermons better in the repetition than
in the preaching.[123] The interacting themes of voluntary and involuntary
religion are an endless and never resolved counterpoint. Here we have
heard no more than a few bars of a theme explored elsewhere through
more variations than Diabelli inspired in Beethoven.

8

William Sancroft, 1617–1693: A Retiring Disposition in a Revolutionary Age

This essay does not aspire to be an account of William Sancroft's unusually well documented record as archbishop of Canterbury.[1] Rather it is an attempt to characterise and anatomise the man behind the career; and what a strange career! None of us can expect to be on the defeated side in a civil war, to suffer ten years of rustication and exile as a result; to see the cathedral of which we are dean (St Paul's no less) consumed by fire, and then to pore over the plans for its reconstruction with the architect, and that architect none other than Sir Christopher Wren; to crown a king, to be sent to the Tower by that same king, and then to see him deposed after a foreign invasion; and yet to remain loyal to that dethroned king. This was a life which at its flood commanded power in both church and state, potentially more state power than any other archbishop in post-Reformation history had exercised. And yet it ended in great privacy and obscurity, and had alway threatened so to end, a curious piece of wish-fulfilment. A twentieth-century bishop of Durham, on the ropes for his unorthodox beliefs, once declared: 'I am not of a retiring disposition.' But Sancroft was.

Alternatively, this essay might have had the title: 'From Fressingfield To Fressingfield'. The Suffolk village of Fressingfield, in the north east of the country, between Eye and Halesworth, was Sancroft's birthplace and also his deathplace; and, in between, a frequent resting place.[2] It was his Colombey les deux Eglises. This was high Suffolk, in Sancroft's phrase 'woodland country', a land of small properties and many cows. The family home, Ufford Hall, was a modest manor house, scarcely more than a large farmhouse. In childhood and youth, Sancroft shared it with his parents, to whom he was deeply attached, an elder brother and six sisters. This was his emotional anchor. In his forties, his bishop tried to marry him off, but neither Sancroft nor the unnamed lady, still less her family, were able to overcome 'invincible difficulties', so that the future archbishop's 'steddy resolution . . . never to marry' remained unshaken. When a sister married, a friend wrote: 'Well, you do not, but your sisters I see will, contribute to continue the species'.³

This resolute bachelor was married to his extended family, to which he returned, a dismissed archbishop of Canterbury, at the end of a long life. With the old place bursting at the seams, and at the age of seventy-four, Sancroft, an inveterate builder, proceeded to erect a new house at the bottom of the garden. But how he had always loved what he called 'the old tenement'! In earlier days, he had written to his brother, longing to hear the latest of 'the story of Fressingfield', 'the marvailes of your dairy, with the wooden looking glasses on the shelf'.⁴ A friend wrote from London to say that he would leave town tomorrow, 'could I find a Fressingfield amongst my relations'.⁵ The people mattered more than the place, and Sancroft expressed the usual ambivalance of his age towards rustic rudeness. Finding himself stranded at home in the exceptionally wet autumn of 1648, he wrote of living 'in Sloughland, in the midst of quicks and quagmires', 'the land of dirt'. He imagined himself in Ireland, or even in Venice, where at least he could have hired a gondola to convey him over the floods to visit the friends he had come to see. 'You might wonder such a country as this should be called high Suffolke.' "Tis so lewd a place . . . You might iustly wonder what detaines me heere so long."⁶ When Sancroft became archbishop, his nephew told his brother that nothing troubled his uncle more than having to refuse the many petitions made to him, 'and especially from Suffolke, from so many good friends there'. 'He had much ado to find employment for me'. But Sancroft made this nephew his steward.⁷

At the age of sixteen, Sancroft reached Emmanuel College Cambridge from the celebrated grammar school at Bury St Edmunds.⁸ In contrast to Archbishop Cranmer, about whom we know so little until middle life, Sancroft's compulsive record keeping, the habit of a lifetime, means that we even have some of his schoolboy exercises, a rare survival. 'William Sandcroft is my name and with my pen I writ the same and if my pen it had bin better I would have mended ons my letter'.⁹ The fact that Sancroft's uncle and namesake. William Sandcroft (as he is usually spelled), was master of Emmanuel at the time sufficiently explains the choice of this college for both William and his elder brother, Thomas. (Sancroft copied, and perhaps composed, an elegy 'upon the death of the only sonne of Mr D.

Sancroft Master of Emmanuel College in Cambridge'.)[10] Emmanuel in 1633 was the largest college in Cambridge in terms of student numbers and the most peculiar, distinguished by its reputation for puritan nonconformity, its unconventional chapel, its Calvinism; and by a statutory commitment to godly learning, which is to say, disapproval of learning for its own sake. In the mid-seventeenth century the college was to suffer a sea-change, of which the maturing William Sancroft was part. At the time that he became master, a correspondent contrasted 'the college as it is' with 'the college as it was'.[11] Sandcroft senior represented the college as it was, and had been chosen master to keep it that way. The puritan veteran, John Rogers of Dedham, wrote to him of 'the blessed Truthes that we have been trayned up in', another correspondent of 'your Nursery of Preachers', which the founder, Sir Walter Mildmay, had intended his college to be.[12]

The younger Sancroft owed less to his old-fashioned uncle than to his successor, the fourth master of Emmanuel, Richard Holdsworth.[13] He told Holdsworth: 'Your Counsell was both card and compasse . . . your favor the gale that fill'd my sails'. After Holdworth's death, Sancroft wrote that it was only the hope to live under his 'happy discipline', to receive his directions 'for study, for life, for all', that had kept him at Emmanuel.[14] Holdsworth was the author of some celebrated and enlightened 'Directions for Students in the Universitie'.[15] Sancroft applied these to himself in a set of good resolutions which laid out his disciplined programme for each day. 'Breakfasts are breakestudies. I'll abjure them; all but a draught of College beere and a morsell of bread'.[16]

Holdsworth was a moderate Calvinist, as was his friend Ralph Brownrigg, master of Pembroke Hall and, as bishop of Exeter, one of Sancroft's most supportive patrons. Where did Sancroft stand with respect to the Calvinism of his mentors and patrons, which in the Cambridge of the 1630s was hotly contested and under hostile political pressure?[17] His biographers, D'Oyly and Hutton, credited the future archbishop with the authorship of *Fur praedestinatus*, a satire which mounted a tendentious attack on Calvinism as equivalent to that dangerous antinomianism which was it perversion. The plot concerns a thief condemned to hang who is convinced that, regardless of his wicked life, he is predestined to salvation. The satire resembles that nineteenth-century masterpiece, James Hogg's *The Memoirs* and *Confessions of a Justified Sinner*. But the author of *Fur praedestinatus* was Dutch, and the tradition that Sancroft translated it from Dutch into Latin appears to be no older than the mid-eighteenth century, and is in all probability unfounded.[18] Yet of Sancroft's alienation from the Calvinism of the college 'as it was' there can be no doubt. A telling influence may have been his tutor, Ezekiel Wright, to whom Sancroft was devoted, and of whom there is evidence that he was part of the new tendency.[19]

However, in all of Sancroft's correspondence there is little evidence of absorption in controversial divinity, but much (in spite of Emmanuel's statutes) of a disinterested love of learning, in the tradition of Renaissance humanism. As a young fellow and tutor, building on Holdsworth's Directions, he advised a pupil that some authors should be treated as casual acquaintances, others entertained with 'some vacant howers in their company', but that others should be lasting friends: 'And these are the classical authors you mention', Virgil for poetry, Cicero for oratory, Tacitus and Livy for history. After a strenuous day engaged with Hebrew and Seneca's philosophy 'at last enters Horace . . . with his basket of flowers'.[20] Sancroft was upset on one occasion to find himself in Fressingfield having left behind 'my Horace'.[21]

In the early 1640s, three things were happening in the young Sancroft's world, occupying different areas of his consciousness. There was war with the Scots, and political turbulence in England. In September 1640 Sancroft was paying attention to the constitution, reading the Elizabethan Sir Thomas Smith's *De Republica Anglorum.* 'The newes heere is the rumour of a Parliament. I pray God make it true'.[22] A year later, Sancroft was being groomed for the fellowship which he would secure in 1642. But at the same time he was in emotional turmoil. Sancroft was in love with his room-mate ('chamberfellow' is the seventeenth-century term) Arthur Bownest, the only correspondent he ever addressed as 'thee', 'my onely friend, the better part of my soule'; and Arthur Bownest was dying of tuberculosis.[23]

Such special friendships were neither uncommon nor necessarily transgressive: witness John Donne and Sir Henry Wootton, or John Milton and Charles Diodati, for whom Milton wrote 'Epitaphium Damonis'.[24] The letters Sancroft and Bownest exchanged had been scripted by the masters of classical and Renaissance eloquence. 'Chambering' in college could naturally lead to profound friendships. Sancroft wrote to Bownest: 'I had once a colleague in my studies, with whom I could communicate, both my reading, and my doubts . . . But now, *solus, solitarius, privus, privatus*, I sitt alone'.[25]

But only rarely was such a relationship so passionately and yet prosaically recorded, and on both sides. Arthur's illness had taken him to his home in Hertfordshire, bringing the affair to a new intensity in the correspondence of separated lovers. Sancroft wrote from Fressingfield: 'I am heere in the bosome of my dear parents, in the embraces of my loving brothers and sisters, in the midst of my kinde freinds and acquaintance . . . and yett the absence of my Arthur takes from the lustre of them all, and oft times bemidnights my thoughts in a melancholy discontent.' Arthur wrote to 'Will': 'Thou art oftener in my thoughts then ever; thou art nearer mee then when I embraced thee'. 'Thou saiest thou lovest mee: good Will, repeat it againe and againe . . .' Will to Arthur: 'Oh lett me bosome thee, lett me preserve thee next my heart and give thee so large an interest there, that nothing may supplant thee'.[26]

The death of Arthur Bownest in May 1641 was a blow from which Sancroft may never have fully recovered. He turned to 2 Samuel 1.26: 'I am distressed for thee, my brother Jonathan, very pleasant hast thou been unto me; thy love to me was wonderful, surpassing the love of women'. To his father, almost a year later, he was lacking in the normal filial reserve: 'His converse was so sweet and so full of affection that methinks an university life hath not been so desirable since I lost him as before. Pardon this impertinency: I must needs break forth sometimes on which I spent so many thoughts'.[27]

Sancroft loathed war, preferrring 'the noble arts of peace and highest employment of a scholler.' At the height of the action in the series of engagements known as the Second Civil War, he wrote to a friend, deploring his friend's father's role in these events. There were better things to do with one's time than to fight one's way 'into petty towns [Colchester?] through our brethren's bowells'.[28]

But, from the outset, Sancroft was a royalist. So was Holdsworth, who was to lose his mastership and spend years in confinement for refusing the presbyterian Covenant; so was the deprived Bishop Brownrigg. But Sancroft's royalism and what we may call his Anglicanism were conspicuously fervent, leading him to repudiate for the remainder of his days both the religion and the politics of which his college was, or had been, a symbol. In the aftermath of the execution of Charles I, which he described as 'the Martyrdome of the best Protestant in these Kingdomes, and incomparably the best King upon earth, CHARLES, the Pious and the Glorious', he wrote bitterly: 'I looke upon that cursed Puritan faction as the ruine of the most glorious Church upon earth (in whose Faith I still live and hope to die)'. 'The black act is done, which all the world wonders at . . . The waters of the Ocean we swimme in cannot wash out the spotts of that blood, than which never any was shed with greater guilt, since the Sonne of God powred out his'. 'The Church heere will never rise againe, though the kingdome should'.[29]

Against the advice of Holdsworth, Sancroft would have nothing to do with Anthony Tuckney, who had replaced him as master, referring to the intruder as 'my continuing inconvenience'. It may well have been Tuckney, however, who protected Sancroft and his fellowship, using his considerable influence with the Westminster Assembly of Divines.[30] As he passively resisted first the National Covenant of 1644, and then, at the other end of the decade, the Enagement imposed as a test of loyalty to the newly-fledged English Republic, Sancroft modelled his conduct on the humble snail, just as he would in the circumstances of the next revolution, in 1688–89. Archbishop Sancroft's reaction to those later events was to sit in Lambeth Palace until thrown out, at nine o'clock at night. Now, in the 1640s, he continued to occupy his rooms in college, persisting in the quiet life of scholarship and teaching, hoping that he would not be noticed, but never secure. It is remarkable, and unusual, that this temperamental refusenik retained his fellowship for so long. In the hot summer of 1646, Sancroft was dangerously ill in London with what sounds like cholera, attended by Arthur Bownest's physician. 'London is very chargeable, a man cannot dye good cheape heere.' If only he could have been at Fressingfield! 'I am glad to heare you are all well there'. But in February 1649, very shortly after the king's execution, he lost his father, who was sixty-eight years of age.[31]

Sancroft was resisting not only the power of the state but that odd and much disputed statute which required a speedy advancement to the degree of Doctor of Divinity, to be followed by departure from Cambridge to a preaching and pastoral ministry in a parish, a path taken by several of his contemporaries. Sancroft had been ordained before 1641 (by whom? where?). But it would be 1662 before he would take his D.D., and he was a fellow of Emmanuel for nine years before his eviction in 1651, in 1644 and 1645 bursar, and from 1647 (the evidence is in the bursarial accounts) 'head lecturer'.[32]

Quiet flows the Don. But this quiet don wielded a razor-sharp pen. He wrote of 'the thing out of the North, the Covenant they call it'. When Holdsworth was deprived, he wrote: 'I had not thought they would have beheaded whole colleges at a blow'. ''Tis an experiment in the magistracy of cruelty farre beyond Caligula's wish.' (The Emperor Caligula had lopped off the head of Jupiter in the Capitol and had replaced it with his own.) In 1645, Sancroft wrote: 'I cannot look upon this bleeding kingdom, this dying church, with the same indifference as I would read the history of Japan or hear the affairs of China related.' In the aftermath of the regicide, and threatened with the Engagement, he told Brownrigg: 'When the Cedars fall and whole Lebanon shudders, who can be sensible that a poor shrub suffers?'[33]

Oliver Cromwell, 'his Mightinesse', Sancroft regarded with peculiar loathing.[34] In the early 1650s, there appeared from the press, anonymously, but dedicated to Brownrigg, a book destined to become a bestseller: *Modern policies, taken from Machiavel, Borgia and other choice authors by an eye-witness*. This was a satire on the cynical use of religious means to ruthless political ends. It consisted of a collection of Machiavellian principles, of which this was the first: 'The Politician must have the shadow of Religion, but the substance hurts'. 'There is no superstition in politics more odious, then to stand too much upon niceties and scruples.' The eighth principle concerned 'necessity'. 'It has been observed, that in all innovations and rebellions (which ordinarily have their rise from pretences of religion, or reformation, or both) the breach and neglect of laws have been authorised by that great patroness of illegal actions — necessity'. From this passage alone it is obvious that, in spite of all disclaimers about aiming at principles rather than persons ('I brand not persons but things'), Cromwell was 'the Politician' against whom *Modern policies* was targetted, the man who swam to his design through a sea of blood. Was Sancroft the author? The leading authority on Sancroft thinks not, the ascription resting on little more than his friendship with Bishop Brownrigg.[35] But almost forty years later, Sancroft would insist that there was 'no difference' between Cromwell and the Prince of Orange 'but that the one's name was Oliver, and the other William'.[36]

Sancroft spent years waiting to be thrown out of Emmanuel. In September 1650, he wrapped his viol in towels and tablecloths to be sent off to Suffolk, and began to shift his books. (Music was one of the country pleasures of Sancroft's large family and their friends.)[37] But it was not until Michaelmas 1651 that a newly-elected fellow knocked at the door and demanded possession of his rooms, forcing Sancroft to abandon a university which, as a colleague assured him, was 'up to the neck in rubbish (and what's Oxford then?)'.[38] Meanwhile, Sancroft's mind had turned and returned on the primitive theme of retreat into the wilderness. He had written to Holdsworth and to other victims of parliamentary harrassment variant versions of the same letter. Angels would minister to them 'as to the old Egyptian hermits', or to St John on Patmos. When the Covenant had threatened, in 1643, Sancroft had written: 'I am going forth, I know not whither: God, I hope, will provide me with a hiding place'.[39] (At this time, of course, he was not going forth, anywhere.) With the Engagement hanging over his head, he responded in theatrical terms to a gentleman who had made a bread-and-butter offer of a domestic chaplaincy. 'Were the Primitive Monkery retriv'd', he would become a monk in 'the utmost recesses and solitudes of the desert', 'in the homeliest cell', abandoning a world in which tyranny and atheism were triumphant.[40]

The desert was, of course, Fressingfield, where most of the next seven years were spent, punctuated by visits to London and valetudinarian excursions to Tunbridge Wells. As he left Cambridge, Sancroft wrote: 'I see nothing in life to be doted on: nothing in Death to be feared; and to endeavour the preservation of the one . . . and my preparation for the other, will be all the Employment I shall have in the country'.[41] There were further offers of chaplaincies in noble households, but Sancroft was in touch with exiled royalist groups and increasingly inclined to join them. Towards 1658, he was selling his books: a great atlas and his Ben Jonson and Rabelais. In September 1657, a friend wrote: 'Let others goe on ship-board to be knowne and heard of, you need not, neither can we spare you'.[42]

Almost immediately, Sancroft was gone. For more than a year he lived at Utrecht. But, having avoided domestic service yet again, this time with Charles I's daughter, the princess of Orange, he set out in the summer of 1659 for Italy, accompanied by his great friend Robert Gayer. In Geneva, the pair lodged in a house next door to Calvin's old address, and bought books. There followed visits to Padua (where Sancroft seems to have enrolled as a student), Venice and, finally and almost transgressively, Rome, where, in late May 1660, news arrived of the restoration of the monarchy. Sancroft took a leisurely journey home, via Paris, and was in London by October.[43]

In these wilderness years, Sancroft was well enough off, perhaps enjoying his share of the estate of his father. Robert Gayer's brother, an old pupil, died owing Sancroft £600 and left him an annuity of £60. The Gayers were the well-to-do sons of a former lord mayor of London. So as an exile and tourist Sancroft could afford to be generous, and on one occasion gave over a hundred crowns to the distinguished churchman and veteran of Charles I's days, John Cosin, who was starving in a Paris garret.[44]

That proved to be an excellent investment. With the Restoration, Cosin became bishop of Durham, invited Sancroft to preach at his consecration (Sancroft being his second choice for this office),[45] and then took him up to his diocese, where he was rewarded with a cathedral prebend and one of the richest parochial livings in all England, Houghton-le-Spring.[46] Sancroft was now in the fast lane of preferment, too busy for distant Fressingfield, and in particular busy with the revision of the Book of Common Prayer, which he saw through the press. In June 1663 he wrote that he had been home but once in seven years, which is to say, only once since returning from the Continent.[47] Bishop Gilbert Sheldon of London, the driving force behind the Restoration Church, warned Cosin that Sancroft was only on loan to Durham.[48] In August came election to the mastership of Emmanuel. This was not a free election. On his own admission, Sancroft knew almost no one in the college, 'my acquaintance being wholly worn out'. It was 'a new College, quite another thing from what I . . . left it'.[49] This was Sheldon's plan, and therefore the king's too. Sheldon wrote: 'Sir, the Church and University want your service in these parts'. Sancroft was soon a regular court preacher and chaplain in attendance.[50]

Sancroft had no wish to be master of his old college, or so he professed. 'There are many things that discourage me. I affect not an university life. I never had my health there. The Statutes are very odd and strict in point of residence, and otherwise'. 'Otherwise' meant money, the founder, Mildmay, having both fixed the master's stipend at an absurdly low figure and ruled against additional sources of income. 'The Mastership is not able to maintain itself'.[51] He was glad that there was now little left of 'that former singularity', but on the other hand he told his old tutor that what had also departed was 'that old genius and spirit of learning . . . that made it once so deservedly famous'.[52]

Sheldon and Charles II overcame Sancroft's reservations and brushed aside the college statutes, while the college found ways and means to

augment the stipend.[53] He became master, but retained both his Durham
prebend and his parish, and perhaps gained other things. The first master,
Laurence Chaderton, would have been appalled. But it was to prove a
momentous if brief mastership, into which Sancroft managed to squeeze
the vice-chancellorship. He was busy with an abortive revision of the
college statutes, and with plans for the new and more acceptable chapel
which Christopher Wren would design for him, and a new library too.
Long after he left Emmanuel, Sancroft would continue to be involved in
the chapel project as benefactor, fund-raiser and architectural consultant.
As late as 1688, with Wren's beautiful edifice complete, Sancroft was
responsible for the last touch, the altar-piece.[54] There was also a law-
suit of awesome complexity, in which the stakes were high: as high as
the library of 10,000 volumes (the largest private collection of books
in the England of its day) which Richard Holdsworth had left behind,
together with a most unsatisfactory will which forced Emmmanuel
and the university to compete for its possession. Eventually the matter
went to the arbitration of three bishops, who found for the university.
Holdsworth's books are to be found in the Cambridge University Library
to this day, the backbone of its early printed collections, but not as a
discrete collection 'to be distinguished from other books there', which
would have answered to Holdsworth's intentions (which Sancroft was
anxious to see respected, wheresoever the books might finish up) and as
the arbitrators had directed.[55]

By the time of this verdict, Sancroft had been made dean of York and,
within a matter of months, dean of St Paul's, the last dean to preside
over the ancient gothic pile of old St Paul's. This last appointment was so
far a foregone conclusion that the king appointed Sancroft within three
days of the old dean's death. Even before this promotion, a well-wisher
had written: 'The next step will be to a mitre'.[56] Only now, at the end of
1664, did Sancroft resign Houghton-le-Spring, although he retained his
prebend and would use the diocese of Durham as a lucrative nest-egg
for years to come. Presently there followed what the senior fellow called
'your unexpected and . . . unwelcome resignation' of Emmanuel, with the
Crown immediately intervening to mandate Sancroft's successor, John
Breton, in all probability on Sancroft's nomination. Just as well, wrote the
senior fellow. 'This I thinke was the onely way to preserve unity among
us . . . It is easier to obey then to chuse' — a good motto for England under
the Stuarts.[57]

Everyone knows what happened next, in 1665 and 1666. What we were taught at school to call 'the Great Plague', preceding 'the Great Fire', began to spread in June and July of 1665. Sancroft's part in this huge calamity was not heroic. He had arranged, on medical advice, a holiday at Tunbridge Wells, a regular habit, and, with the first news of infection, saw no reason to change his plans. On the contrary. The bishop of London wrote: 'Do not hasten back.' Nor did he. Soon Sancroft was being warned ('give me leave to discharge the part of a frend and to tell you what I hear') that he was one of the London clergy much censured for having deserted their posts. The money he had left behind for relief purposes could not begin to match the awesome scale of the tragedy. So it was that Sancroft, in Tunbridge Wells, heard from one of his staff at St Paul's: 'The increase of God's Judgments deads peoples hearts, that trading strangely ceaseth and bills of exchange are not accepted, so that they shutt up their shopps'. And from another residentiary, the future Archbishop John Tillotson, came this: 'Death stares us continually in the face in every infected person that passeth by us, in every coffin which is dayly and hourely carried along the streets.' The unburied dead lay in heaps. 'Johnson your bailliff was buried last night'.[58]

By late September, Sancroft had left Kent and was — where else? — at Fressingfield. On 20 September he wrote to Sir Robert Gayer: 'We were yesterday all together (seven couples and I the single eight), fifteen brothers and sisters, besides nephews and neeces'. (No doubt there was much music-making.) Home had been reached via Ewell (Ewell, Surrey or Ewell, Kent, where Emmanuel had property?), Fulham Palace (but not London), and Cambridge (where his coach and horses were left). Suffolk itself was full of plague, and Sancroft was afraid of having picked up the infection along the way. He would not budge from Fressingfield until it was safe to do so, although he tried to assure Bishop Henchman that he would return at once if summoned by him to do so.[59] But the carriers were no longer travelling between Suffolk and London, and Henchman never received his letter. It was not until December that he and Archbishop Sheldon knew whether Sancroft was alive or dead. In that month, the dean moved cautiously towards London, where he had duties to perform at Whitehall in January. But he skirted the city, stayed at Fulham, and, finding that the Court was still at Oxford, set off again in that direction. By the time he returned to London he had been absent from his deanery for seven or eight months.[60]

With 1666 we come to the Fire of London. It is one of the ironies of architectural history that in the months before the fire, and following Christopher Wren's return from overseas, there was a great debate about the future of London's cathedral, whether it should be patched up or substantially demolished to make way for a new edifice in 'true latin', the plans for which Wren already had in hand. Part of the old church was already clad in scaffolding, and the scaffolding would help the fire to spread. At a meeting at St Paul's on 27 August, attended and recorded by John Evelyn, one of the three 'surveyors of the repaires of Paules', it was agreed, against opposition, to adopt the more radical solution, capping the great central tower with 'a noble cupola'.[61] England was about to catch up with the architectural classicism of the Renaissance on the most heroic scale imaginable. Sancroft was present, and, we may assume, supportive.

But ten days later he was back at Fressingfield, where he wrote a letter on 6 September. The Great Fire had started on the night of 2 September, and on the 4th it had engulfed St Paul's. By the 6th, it was all over. And yet news of what a Durham correspondent called 'the reeke of the warming-pan from God' had yet to reach the fastnesses of high Suffolk. Sancroft wrote on the 6th: 'I intend about Michaelmas by God's permission to return to London.' Nor, on this occasion, did the dean 'hasten back'. When, on 17 September, a correspondent sent a description of the 'horrid spectacle' of the burned-out city and cathedral, it was to Fressingfield that he addressed his letter.[62] However, on 10 October Sancroft preached before the king in what remained of St Paul's, a suitably providentialist disquisition on 'the moral rickets' of the age, 'that swells and puffs up the Head, while the inner Man of the Heart wasts and dwindles'.[63]

We must all be grateful for the fact that Sancroft was dean of St Paul's in the months and years that followed. For he was an enthusiastic architect manqué, rather like Prince Charles, but with far greater creative opportunities. Back in 1650, he had asked to be sent Sir Henry Wootton's *Elements of Architecture*. From Durham in 1662, a friend had written: 'I wish you a large dividend, that may better enable you to build'; and another, in 1663: 'I believe you'l come downe with some ideas of building in your head; let them not be too vast'.[64] Now, besides building a new deanery, Sancroft supported Wren through thick and thin in the designing of the new St Paul's, writing in April 1669 to command his presence and assistance with all possible speed. 'You will think fit, I know, to bring with you the excellent Draught and Designs you formerly favour'd us with'.[65] Subsequently, we are told, nothing was done without Sancroft's presence, no materials bought, no accounts passed without him. He contributed generously to the building fund from his own purse. And in the year which followed the fire he carried through a radical overhaul of the system of accounting for receipts and disbursements.[66] *Si monumentum requiris, circumspice.* The St Paul's we know was as much a monument to Sancroft as to Wren. It is also the most concrete expression of the assertiveness of the Church of England of the 1670s and 1680s, and, so far as Sancroft's role in its creation was concerned, of a strange fusion of outward confidence and inner diffidence.

Archbishop Sheldon died on 6 November 1677. The reasons why Sancroft, who had already refused two bishoprics, succeeded Sheldon were much discussed by contemporaries, and therefore by historians; partly because this was to be no repetition of the catapulting of Sancroft into St Paul's. For almost two months, no decision was made. It has been suggested that Charles II had no idea whom to appoint, only that he didn't want another Sheldon, who had been given to throwing his considerable weight around.[67] The obvious candidate was the highly competent Henry Compton, bishop of London, to whom the chief minister of the day, Danby, had all but offered the job. But this, wrote a contemporary diarist, was 'a Newmarket trick'. The hostility of the Roman Catholic duke of York ruled Compton out as too Protestant. Moreover, he had in his care York's two Protestant daughters, the Princesses Mary and Anne. When our diarist wrote that Sancroft's 'leap' from a deanery to St Augustine's chair was 'to the dissatisfaction of many bishops', he may have meant to the dissatisfaction of Compton, for this diarist was chaplain and tutor to the two princesses. Sancroft may have appealed to the king because Charles II thought that the dean of St Paul's would not make a nuisance of himself, or even because the royal profligate acknowledged in Sancroft austere and admirable qualities. More to the point, perhaps, Sancroft was in good standing with the duke of York. Nevertheless it was, wrote Dr Edward Lake, 'contrary to the expectations of all the Court'. Perhaps so. But Cambridge was better informed. Within ten days of Sheldon's death, it was confidently reported in the coffee houses of the town that he would be replaced by Sancroft. The source of this information was the Court.[68]

A whole book on Sancroft would now embark on a full account of his archepiscopal stewardship of the Church.[69] I shall attempt no such thing, but move almost at once to the politics of Sancroft's undoing, and what these events may tell us about the strangeness of his inner life. Suffice it to say that Archbishop Sancroft resembled, in many ways, if in altered circumstances, Archbishop William Laud, with whose memory and literary remains he was preoccupied in his last illness.[70] His programme, too, was one of 'thorough'; of perserving, and enhancing, Anglican worship, piety and discipline; enforcing conformity (his motto might have been Luke 14.23 — 'compel them to come in'); strengthening the machinery of the church courts; raising clerical and pastoral standards; and above all restoring to a church impoverished at its grass roots the alienated revenues on which its pastoral success depended. Let one tiny detail suffice. Sancroft was much concerned that the feast of St Matthias (that somewhat marginal apostle whose recruitment to fill the vacancy created by Judas Iscariot may have been a rare mistake on the part of the Holy Spirit) should be celebrated on the correct day in leap years. He not only issued an order on the subject but wrote a book about it. St Matthias should be honoured not on 25 February but on 24 February, leap year or no leap year.[71]

And so we reach the climax and consequential anticlimax of this strange career, which was the reign of James II, and the Glorious Revolution which overtook it: which I must first place in context. The historian of the politics of religion in Restoration England confronts a scene and a sequence of events of a rich complexity.[72] Over a period of thirty eventful years, four teams were in competition for possession of a far from level playing field: the Stuart monarchy and its sustaining ministries; the Church of England; Protestant Dissent; and Roman Catholicism. Within themselves, the teams were neither united nor consistent, and both politics and alliances were inherently unstable, those of the established Church especially so. A crown at first sympathetic to, and then, with the duke of York's conversion, the failure of exclusion and his accession to the throne, committed to the advancement of Catholics, confronted a Protestant and virulently anti-Catholic nation, largely held in conforming obedience to the national Church, but containing a body of separated and partially separated Dissent, the extent of which was not accurately known.[73]

The policies towards dissenters of the Crown and ministry fluctuated between episodes of toleration, never, until 1689, supported by parliamentary law, indeed dependent upon an arbitrary power to suspend or dispense with the law, and bouts of repression. The Church contended with two religious enemies in Jesuitical popery and the dissenting 'fanatics', and deeply feared a third, atheism and mere irreligion, which the indulgence of Dissent would tend to license by undercutting ecclesiastical discipline. Sometimes, and especially in the period following York's coming out of the closet, and throughout his three-year reign, popery appeared to be the greatest menace; at other times, Dissent, especially as the political convulsions of 1678–81, called all too inadequately by historians the Exclusion Crisis,[74] threatened to drag the nation back into the 1640s, when king and Church had gone under together.

In the aftermath of this nasty scare, altar committed itself to throne, mitre to crown, as never before, and to the legitimate heir to the throne; and by no churchman more whole heartedly than William Sancroft, who had supplied the manuscript for the publication of a perfected text of that ultra-royalist manifesto, Sir Robert Filmer's *Patriarcha*, procured from Filmer's son.[75] Never were churches better attended, never so many communicants. Sancroft's correspondents in the dioceses assured him that organised Nonconformity was on the point of collapse. There was a strong reciprocity of interest. Francis Turner, the duke of York's Anglican chaplain, told Sancroft in 1681 that James 'places his hopes altogether upon that interest we call the Church of England, upon the Episcopal party, and mainly upon the Bishops themselves, your Grace especially'.[76] After 1681, Sancroft managed an Ecclesiastical Commission which ensured that only the staunchest royalists and, in effect, Tories, were elevated to bishoprics, a control over clerical preferments which was unprecedented.[77]

So long as there was no conflict between church principles and the doctrine of non-resistance and unswerving loyalty to the Stuart monarchy, all was set fair for a triumphalist Church of England that was much more than a figurehead for the politics and policies of the nascent Tory party. But with the accession of James II and the flagrantly pro-Catholic illegalities in which he was soon indulging, it became apparent that there was indeed a conflict of interest between these parties and principles. The royal instrument of coercive Anglicanism broke in the Church's hands, and, conversely, the king learned that he could not rely upon the Church after all. Both parties were more or less obliged to knock out from under them the best props that they had.

In 1643, the Long Parliament preacher Stephen Marshall had prophesied: 'And I suspect, in case the tables were turned and we had a king endeavouring to take down the bishops, . . . the world would hear another Divinity'.[78] And so it now proved. Sancroft, even Sancroft, committed to a private paper the unthinkable thought that in certain circumstances the Church might have to go it alone, preserving itself independent of the state.[79] Of the two loyalties in question, Sancroft in the last resort must needs prefer that which bound him to the Church. For the sixteenth-century religious historian who has strayed into the later seventeenth century, nothing is more striking that the churchly (rather than godly) rhetoric of Sancroft and other churchmen of his high persuasion. Sancroft had no reason to trust the civil power, which he had known to be at best unreliable and at worst malevolent. After the 1688 Revolution, William III would be to him 'L'Hombre, the Man Himself', Queen Mary 'the Great Woman'. At that time, James II, deposed and exiled, was still for Sancroft 'our Master'.[80] Having with his own hands placed the crown on that head, Sancroft would never be the man to take it off again.

Yet this was loyalty to James II as symbolic of the legitimate body politic, not devotion to James the man. Sancroft's obedience had been strained to breaking point, not only by James's betrayal of the Church, and by his use of arbitrary and illegal instruments, but by the threat he posed to the Protestant settlement. For this profoundly Anglian archbishop was also some kind of Protestant. On the eve of James's accession, he had written words which, no doubt intentionally, echoed those of the martyr bishops at the stake in the first Mary's reign: 'God hath, by the Reformation, kindled and set up a light in Christendom, which, I am fully persuaded, shall never be extinguished.'[81] Only the fact that Sancroft was a Protestant as well as a churchman can explain how it was that he drafted (even if he did not send) a letter to Princess Mary, who had written from Holland, putting out a feeler to the archbishop. Sancroft wrote that the greatest calamity to have befallen England after the murder of Charles I was that his sons had been driven out into foreign places where they had served other gods: which is to say, had been contaminated by Catholicism. 'The dreadful effects hereof we shall feel every moment, but must not (nay we can not) particularly expresse'. Not that loyalty to the sovereign, or to the royal family in the legal succession, could be in doubt. 'Yet it imbitters the very Comforts that are left us, it blasts all our present Joys'. The heart of the Church of England would surely break if it were not that God had caused 'some Dawn of Light to break forth unto us from the Eastern shore in the Constancy and good Affection of your Roial Highness and the excellent princ towards us'. He added: 'You have put new life into a dying old man'.[82] This was the closest that Sancroft came to issuing an invitation to the Oranges to intervene in English politics (but not, of course, to usurp the throne), and it was surprisingly close.

The watershed came for Sancroft in the summer of 1686, when he declined to serve on James II's Ecclesiastical Commision, an illegal engine for the advancement of the Catholic interest. This led to his removal from the Privy Council, exclusion from the Court, and the loss of all influence over preferments. Bishop Burnet's comment on the archbishop's behaviour at this juncture, although unfriendly, reveals the Sancroft we know. Sancroft, having refused to sit on the Commission, failed to absent himself 'with that vigour that became his post in going to the Court and declaring the reasons for which he could not come and sit among them'.[83] Henceforth, Sancroft was to be almost a prisoner at Lambeth House, mentally as well as physically detached from the scene of political action across the river, increasingly dependent upon the information and advice of that coming man, the courtier Francis Turner, now bishop of Ely and widely tipped to succeed him. Lambeth became Sancroft's own Patmos.

Presently, in May and June 1688, there was the occasion of more widespread passive resistance of James II, and specifically to his declaration of a general indulgence for both Catholic and Protestant dissenters. That was controversial enough in itself. But the indulgence was accompanied by the nearly inexplicable royal demand that it be announced from the pulpits first of the London churches and then nationwide, an order with which it was certain many, even most, of the clergy would refuse to comply, and against which the bishops protested. So arose the great affair of the Seven Bishops: Sancroft of Canterbury, Lloyd of St Asaph, Turner of Ely, Lake of Chichester, Ken of Bath and Wells, White of Peterborough, Trelawny of Bristol. ('And shall Trelawny die? Here's twenty thousand Cornishmen will know the reason why'.) *The Oxford Dictionary of the Christian Church* devotes twenty-three lines to the 'Trial of the Seven Bishops', compared with eighteen to the 'Seven Sacraments' and two and a half to the 'Seven Deadly Sins'.[84]

When the Seven Bishops petitioned the king to withdraw the Declaration, James II interpreted their intransigence as sedition. Traditionally, and thanks above all to Macaulay, the Seven Bishops have been seen as passive martyrs for England's constitutional liberties. It is more to the point that they were to a man Sancroftians and Yorkists, the very bishops who had master-minded the repressive Anglicanism and the Tory regime which James had so unwisely slighted. Their démarche was intended not so much to defend affronted liberty against the arbitrary use of power as to recover their very illiberal grasp of the rudder of church and state. Bishop Gilbert Burnet reported that it was understood in Europe that the issue was simply whether the king or the bishops were to be on top.[85]

As Macaulay himself might have put it, every schoolboy knows (or used to know) that when James confronted his bishops, he told them: 'This is a standard of rebellion!' and, looking particularly at his old chaplain, Turner of Ely: 'I did not expect this from you, especially from some of you'. Ken of Bath and Wells muttered: 'God's will be done'. The king: 'What's that? [what did you say?]', or, perhaps 'what's that?'[86] A sequence of dramatic scenes followed: committal to the Tower, upon the refusal of the bishops, as peers of the realm, to offer recognisances for their appearance, release on bail, the trial in Westminster Hall for seditious libel, and, finally, acquittal.

The Church of England now briefly enjoyed the greatest popularity in its entire history: witness the numerous copies still surviving, in oils and as prints, of the collective portrait of the Seven Bishops. When the bishops were merely released on bail, the bishop of Sodor and Man, who was carrying out confirmations in Kent on Sancroft's behalf, reported great jubilation as he confirmed thousands in three- and four-hour ceremonies.[87] With news of the acquittal, the city of Hereford (for example) went wild. 'Really', wrote an elderly correspondent, 'the noise of the bells and acclamations of the people have much disturbed mee, though pleasant'. He sent the archbishop 'a poore plaine Protestant present' of Herefordshire cider, bacon and beef. It was a time for presents all round. The heavy legal costs of the bishops included substantial financial rewards for the jurymen.[88]

But disaster lay in the very lap of triumph. In the aftermath of the trial, Sancroft girded his loins for a renewed application of Anglican thorough in the dioceses, and hoped that the king would be forced back into older and wiser courses. This was an abortive 'Anglican Revolution', which in the summer and autumn of 1688 might well have put power back into the hands of the Tories and Sancroftians, perhaps with an episcopal regency for James's new-born son.[89] It was not to be. As has been said, 'in ruining himself, James ruined his old friends and their policies'.[90] Soon William of Orange was stepping ashore at Torbay, publicly announcing that lords spiritual as well as temporal had invited his intervention. Now there were further encounters at Whitehall between king and bishops, with James demanding a 'Lord not I' denial from each prelate in turn. All gave it, even Compton of London, whose signature to the invitation is still to be seen.[91] But the king's position was now so parlous that, whatever he may privately have thought, he could only say: 'I believe you'. The bishops avoided publishing a statement of abhorrence of William's invasion. But Sancroft declared that he himself had offered no invitation, 'by word, writing or otherwise', and added that he believed he could say the same for all the bishops.[92]

In mid-December James fled from his capital, invalidating all processes of government as he went, or attempting to do so, and Sancroft became part of an emergency regime which filled a dangerous constitutional vacuum and tried to restore order to a riot-torn city.[93] But such was the archbishop's loyalist rectitude that he withdrew from this Commission when, in order to broaden its political base, it removed from a public pronouncement of its intentions a phrase referring to the king's return 'with honour and safety'. When the kind did return, and with that a brief episode of political near-normality, Sancroft rejoined the Commission.[94] But then came William's *coup d'état*, James's effective deposition, and, on 23 December 1688, final departure. This was a shock from which the public Sancroft never recovered, becoming the intensely private Sancroft of the last years.

While a Convention Parliament met and wrestled with the squaring of constitutional circles, Sancroft did and said almost nothing. He was repeatedly summoned over the river to take his seat in the Lords. On the second occasion, he made the usual excuses about ill health, age and the weather, noting that since he had been banished from the Court, two and a half years earlier, he had 'scarce ever stirr'd out of Doors, but when I was fore'd out' (a reference to his brief excursion to the Tower).[95] At no time in history was it more necessary for the archbishop of Canterbury to be politically active. But no archbishop has ever been more inactive than Sancroft at this critical moment, suggesting to some historians a kind of nervous collapse. In mid-January, it proved possible to hold a meeting of bishops and other magnates at Lambeth, attended and recorded by Evelyn.[96] But counsels were divided, and this was positively Sancroft's last appearance on any kind of public stage. Yet he still had almost five years to live.

If Sancroft's strange inertia was an embarrassment for the new regime, it dismayed friends and colleagues, Turner of Ely in particular, who is to be seen in the correspondence of the early months of 1689 looking desperately and all in vain for a lead. 'If your Grace will forgive me and my brother our unwelcome importunities yesterday', Turner wrote on 11 January, urging Sancroft to employ his unrivalled knowledge of formularies, canons and statutes to buttress the Church of England case against revolution. If only Sancroft could be persuaded to wait upon Orange to explain the position which the bishops had adopted, and the role which they would allow the prince to play![97] But it seems unlikely that the archbishop ever so much as set eyes on the man he ironically called the rising sun. Turner would soon write with some bitterness of this 'strange, obstinate passiveness'.[98] Turner was not at the end of his career and his life, and he had expected to be the next archbishop of Canterbury. But to be fair, his diplomacy was defeated not only by Sancroft's rigid obstinacy, but by a still greater loss of nerve on the part of James II, and the decisive ambitions of William of Orange, who was interested in nothing less than a share of the Crown.

Those who could not tolerate his ambitions and who refused the oath of loyalty to the new regime were the Non-Jurors, a schismatic Anglican sect with a long history ahead of it. It was the Sancroftians, the very core of the Anglican Church militant of the 1680s, who were now to follow their lost leader into the non-juring wilderness: five of the Seven Bishops: besides Sancroft himself, Ken of Bath and Wells, Lake of Chichester, Turner of Ely, and White of Peterborough, now joined by Frampton of Gloucester and Sancroft's especial friend, always addressed as 'brother', William Lloyd of Norwich. Their defection had profound consequences not only for the Church of England but for English Christianity more generally. For it is possible (to believe the spin later put on these events) that if they, and Sancroft in particular, had stayed on board, playing an active role in Parliament and Convocation, the revolution settlement would not have merely tolerated Protestant Dissent but would have accommodated the more moderate Dissenters, especially the Presbyterians, within a more broadly defined national Church. That was implicit in the greater measure of latitude and 'tenderness' which Sancroft's Church, assisted by more moderate churchmen and some of the leading Dissenters themselves, had improvised at the time of the trial of the Seven Bishops. The failure in 1689 of comprehension, the indirect rather than direct result of the non-juring schism, determined that from henceforth the Church of England, while remaining uniquely privileged and established, would forfeit the status of a truly national Church.[99] It was over such historically momentous events and determinations that Sancroft's career tracked its strange trajectory.

By March 1689, the crown had been offered to William and Mary and the oath of allegiance was pending, for Sancroft a sword of Damocles. He found reasons for absenting himself from the coronation, although summoned by the Earl Marshall to attend, 'all excuses set apart', and to 'perform such services as shall be required and belong to you'.[100] In the event, Bishop Compton stood in for the archbishop, and the iron in his soul must have nearly melted as he asked Sancroft for any books or papers on the subject of coronations which he might be willing to make available.[101] A deeply troubled Turner wrote to Sancroft from deepest Warwickshire, whither he had 'fled' (more from the riots in London than for political reasons), urgently seeing advice on how he should conduct himself. 'I beseech your Grace's Directions'.[102] Whether he received any seems doubtful.

The chancellor of the University of Cambridge chose this of all inconvenient moments to die, and the university to seize upon the already impotent Sancroft to succeed him. Sancroft insisted on his total ineligibility, aged and infirm as he was, and unable to do the university any good in high places. Nothing deterred, on 15 December 1688 the Regent House elected the archbishop 'by unanimous consent'. In vain Sancroft continued to protest his inability and unwillingness to assume and perform the office. On 16 January, the formalities of election were completed. Now in the perception of Cambridge he *was* their chancellor, whether he liked it or not. In late February, ignoring the deafening silence from Lambeth, the vice-chancellor sought the chancellor's advice on, of all matters, the reception of the new sovereigns, who were about to visit the university. Cambridge was neither pig-headed nor native. It was using Sancroft, cynically, as a stop-gap, to postpone the evil day of having to hold a real election, which would prove politically divisive and might cause incalculable damage. Only in March did the vice-chancellor concede that they would have to think of someone else, although 'at present no particular person is named or thought on'. Presently Cambridge thought upon a safe, if second-rate, candidate, Charles Seymour, sixth duke of Somerset, who would remain chancellor for the next sixty years: one of the more bizarre consequences of the Glorious Revolution.[103]

Knowing what we know, Sancroft's 'strange obstinate passiveness' as he stood at this crossroads of history is not unexpected. Just so had been his behaviour all of fifty and forty years before, faced first with the Covenant and then with the Engagement. In 1650 he had written: 'This makes me almost long to be displaced, that I may hide my head in some hole.'[104] Some such mood in 1689 made Sancroft deaf to the plea that, since 'all the treu members of the Church of England have their eyes now fixt upon you', he should seek an accommodation with the government; and no less deaf to the opposite advice that he should be an active and vocal leader in intransigence. A Devon clergyman addressed him as 'the admiration of the present age . . . Champion of Church of England Doctrine', even one of 'the great Confessors of the Christian Faith'. 'Proceed, pious Prelate, perswade our Clergy, command your sons to stick to the truths of our Church'.[105] But Sancroft was in no mood to persuade or command, and as for proceeding, there was now nowhere to proceed to but Fressingfield. He refused the oath, and, having drawn up a form of resignation, had no need of it, suffering first suspension and then, on 1 February 1690, deprivation, along with five other bishops and some four hundred clergy.[106]

There followed a long and embarrassing impasse while Sancroft continued to occupy Lambeth House, until they virtually had to carry him out, at nine o'clock at night.[107] Sancroft's friends have found this conduct no easier to explain or condone than his enemies, such as Bishop Burnet. Waiting for terminus, Sancroft sems to have spent his time filling his notebooks with all kinds of material in his tiny, close hand, including 'The Great Parliament Fart', a political satire on an incident in the parliament of 1607.[108] Was this a proper occupation for a great Confessor?

Such were the unpromising origins of the Non-Juring Church. One of Sancroft's few decisive acts in these last years, having delegated his archepiscopal powers and functions to his fellow Non-Juror and friend Bishop Lloyd of Norwich, was to sanction the perpetuation of hierarchy and orders in this profoundly schismatic and deeply orthodox body, the only battalion of the Church of England still in step.[109] (Sancroft has his successors in the Anglican Communion in the early twenty-first century.)

Sancroft and Lloyd of Norwich were in very regular correspondence, and these letters are our principal source for these final years. Without them we should not have known that Lloyd kept Sancroft's shrinking household supplied with soap — 'wash-balls' — and rather frequently. Were they really wash-balls, or was this a coded reference to something else? In 1691, the two deprived prelates shared a renewed interest in John Foxe's 'Book of Martyrs'.[110]

In late April of the same year, Sancroft told Lloyd how his namesake, Bishop William Lloyd of St Asaph (one of the seven bishops, now conformable to the new regime), came across to Lambeth, accompanied by the future Archbishop Tenison. His mission was to tell Sancroft about the new episcopal appointments, the men that he would be handing over to. 'I soon saw in the Bishop's solemn gravity what news he was big with; but staved him off for half an hour with common discourse, as brisk as I could contrive it. But at last, out it must come, and then I let him see that I knew more than he knew, or at least pretended to know'.[111] What Sancroft knew was that, for a second time in a row, the dean of St Paul's (Tillotson) had been named for Canterbury. Compton of London had been passed over again, the Rab Butler or Denis Healey of the Restoration and Revolutionary Church.

So Sancroft was a hermit with ears. And now his ears were deafened with the noise of carpenters 'putting up some of my luggage'. By late May 1691 he was effectively obstructing the consecration of his intended successor, defying an order made by Lloyd of St Asaph in the name of 'the Great Woman'.[112] On 31 May, Tilotson was consecrated. But Sancroft remained at Lambeth until the law and *force majeure* removed him in late June. It was only on 26 November that Tillotson moved in, the delay occasioned, as with some masters' lodges in Oxbridge nowadays, by the need for improvements, including the provision of suitable accommodation for his wife. Mrs Tillotson was the first spouse of an archbishop to have been seen at Lambeth for 116 years, and only the third in history. John Evelyn dined with Tillotson on December 28th 1691 and found him 'farr politer than the old man'.[113] But three years later Tillotson died, on the very day of the month on which Sancroft had been put out of Lambeth.

By late August 1691, and after six weeks lodged in the Temple, with almost no privacy,[114] Sancroft was safely back in Fressingfield. His Suffolk relations and friends had all been received, and would now stave off less welcome callers, including some spies. 'There is nothing that I regret the loss of but Lambeth Chapel and the company of a few friends'.[115] It was getting chilly, cold dews, cold mornings and evenings, and Sancroft, at the age of seventy-four, was building a new house, at the end of the avenue leading to the old family home. While the work went ahead, with the usual builders' delays ('my building goes on *piano piano*'), Sancroft with his servants and workmen were uncomfortably crammed into the old house with the family of his nephew, who was also his steward. His way of life was austere and consistent. He enjoyed a couple of cups of coffee and bread and butter with a pipe of tobacco for breakfast, some chicken or mutton at noon, and a glass of 'mum' (wheat beer) and a bit of bread at night. He never ventured beyond the bounds of the little estate. Sancroft allowed no ministrations from clergy who had taken the oath, not so much the saying of grace, but performed the divine office himself, praying 'for the king only' (not the two new joint sovereigns). Those not permitted to exercise their ministry in his presence included his own chaplains, William Needham and that industrious scholar and amanuensis, Henry Wharton.[116] Before Christmas 1691, he was told that the top London clergyman, William Sherlock, had been 'all along a spy amongst us', retailing the consultations of the non-juring group to the government. It was, of course, the politician, Turner of Ely, who had suggested that Sherlock should be party to their counsels, 'because he might be useful.' Having originally joined the Non-Jurors, Sherlock had defected and now succeeded Tillotson as dean of St Paul's, where Wren's massive labours continued.[117]

In April 1692, Sancroft was favoured with a visit from one of the most distinguished and politically active members of the emergent Non-Juring Church, Jeremy Collier. Collier was headed for St-Germain. Not knowing whether his words might not amount to misprision of treason, Sancroft 'desired him to let our Master know where I am, and in what condition: a very old infirm man, driven from my own house (and all that belongs to it) into the wilderness . . . confined to the poor house in which I was born'. Tactfully, Sancroft asked that he should not be compromised by receiving any commission from James II. Yet the king should believe that 'having lost all else, I will sooner lose my life too than quit my loyalty and my allegiance'; although he would not throw his life away foolishly and to no purpose, 'for thereby he would have one faithful subject fewer than he had before'. Collier was in and out of trouble and prison in 1692, and may never have reached St-Germain.[118]

Only in September 1692 was the new house fit for occupation. Sancroft shared it with a mere two or three servants, but knew that he would not be there for long. "'Tis not the first time that I have built, and left others to dwell there'. He was thinking of the deanery of St Paul's. In the summer of 1692, his mind had turned, as so often before, on the theme of retirement, the curious and recessive circularity of his life. 'I am old enough to look back forty years, and by comparing time and events to find that all is but *Vetus Fabula per novos Histriones* [the actors are different but the play is the same] . . . The comfort is that God is ever the same, wise and good, sits above, and does whatever pleases him: does it in his own manner too, and at his own time'.[119]

Now is the time to mention Sancroft the bookman, who made his London address his bookseller's, in Little Britain without Aldersgate and in Paul's Churchyard.[120] In these final months, large quantities of boks were on the move, most of them intended for Emmanuel. If history had gone differently, they would have stayed at Lambeth, to swell the library established by Archbishop Bancroft earlier in the century. John Evelyn saw the Lambeth books boxed up, and a little later one of Sancroft's chaplains was shown a roomful of books at Fressingfield which must have reached there, with whatever inconvenience to the family, in 1691. On 16 September 1693, ten weeks before the archbishop's death, the master of Emmanuel conveyed his thanks for 'the most valuable treasure of your Grace's books, just now lodged in our Library'.[121]

The five and a half thousand volumes now most honourably lodged in Emmanuel Library are a source of endless fascination, but also of puzzlement.[122] By no means all of Sancroft's books are there, so we can make nothing of the absence of the great English poets and playwrights: no Spenser, no Jonson, no Sidney, no Shakespeare (but some Donne);[123] no Holinshed either, and no Foxe's Book of Martyrs; Hooker's *Laws* incomplete. We know that it was Sancroft's intention to leave at Fressingfield 'a good Library for a gentleman', 'for the use of the family there', bequeathing to the college only 'the books of learning'. We also know that his failure to make a will (not a matter of negligence but reluctance to put his affairs into Tillotson's court, the Prerogative Court of Canterbury) was a cause of real difficulty, even if it meant that so much of his personal archive, through the happy fortunes of the market place, is to be found in the Bodleian Library.[124]

But the 'books of learning' are an extraordinarily eclectic collection. On the fourth shelf of Stack 16 we find continental works on witchcraft and demonology, Michaelis's *Pneumalogie ou discours des esprits* (Paris, 1587), Boguet's *Discours des sorciers* (Lyon, 1658), Serclier's *L'Antidemon historical: ou les sacrilèges, larcins, ruses et fraudes du prince des ténèbres* (Lyon, 1609).[125] These sit alongside *Segunda parte del ingenioso cavallero Don Quixote dela Mancha* (Brussels, 1616). There are sixteenth-century Italian play texts, such as *Il pastore fido tragicomedia*, and *Amore scolastico comedia*. Modern bibliographical scholarship may ask whether Sancroft took pleasure in the contents of such books, or merely collected them as some men collect inkstands or paperweights. There is an absence of telltale *marginalia* and *adversaria* (usually only Sancroft's careful notes on the flyleaf of composite volumes). But not all men are markers of their books. And surely he read and enjoyed his books: Witness many of his surviving notebooks, crammed with material transcribed from all over the place, including detailed observations about the locomotion of crabs and lobsters, 'dogs suffer from sea-sickness', and the evidence of fossil sea shells, far from the ocean, extracted from an Italian treatise.[126] (Why Sancroft should have felt compelled to make such lengthy transcripts out of books which he had on his shelves is a condundrum to which students of reading and commonplacing practices may have the solution.) We can be certain that Sancroft commanded the languages on which his enjoyment of foreign books depended. His Spanish grammar is heavily annotated, and he reflected ruefully on the intellectual ardours of learning Hebrew.[127]

The hermit of Fressingfield was thirsty for foreign news, and was regularly supplied with it by Sir Henry North.[128] Today would find him tuned to the BBC World Service. From his library, we know that he kept up his subscriptions to the learned foreign periodicals, such as *Bibliothèque universelle et historique*, and *Mercure historique et politique*. There is a run of twenty volumes of the Amsterdam *Journal des scavans*, running from 1666 to the year of Sancroft's death in 1693. In March 1693, he told

North: 'I pray, let Mr Berners be paid in the first place for the *Journal des Scavans*'.[129] There was no longer much money for such purposes.

The end was protracted and distressing. It began in the late summer of 1693 with a bad attack of malaria. Perhaps it had been wet again, in so-called high Suffolk. The severity of the 'fits' was mitigated by a resourceful pharmacopeia, although Sancroft was averse (for ideological reasons?) to quinine, the Spanish or 'Jesuit' bark, *cortex peruvianus*.[130] After a brief and deceptive remission, which led a foolish well-wisher to write on 17 November of God making him once more 'young and lusty as an eagle', Sancroft died between midnight and 1 a.m. on 24 November 1693. Like so many lifelong valetudinarians, he had lived to what for the time was a ripe old age. 'Many pious speeches and fervent prayers proceeded from him during his sickness, particularly he prayed with great zeal and affection for the k[ing] by name, for our persecuted and distressed Church, for her afflicted members.'

The strength of the Fressingfield connection had ensured that, on becoming archbishop, Sancroft had travelled to Suffolk to tell his friends how he wished to be buried, were he to die in country. The result is the tomb still to be seen, hard against the south-east wall of Fressingfield church, in the open air and looking towards the sunrise: unusual. Among other biblical sentiments inscribed, we may note: 'Naked he came forth, so naked he must return'.[131]

If no man is a hero to his own valet, a public figure who leaves behind as copious a personal record as Archbishop William Sancroft cannot expect to be canonised by biographers and historians. Sancroft's religion found such conventional and yet artificial expression that one is tempted to ask the inadmissible and certainly unanswerable question: was he truly (rather than only formally) religious? A certain vulnerable self-regard, manifested above all in the Plague Year, mitigates our admiration. And yet he was generous and imaginative in his generosity. And the virtue of consistency only became the vice of obstinacy in extreme circumstances.

Bishop Gilbert Burnet's character of Sancroft is not generous. Why should it have been? Sancroft had refused to consecrate Burnet, whom he had described as 'the great creature of the Prince of Orange'.[132] But nor was Burnet's portrait a poor likeness, certainly of the older Sancroft: 'He

was a man of solemn deportment, had a sullen gravity in his looks, and
was considerably learned. He had put on a monkish strictness, and lived
abstracted from much company'.[133] What Burnet failed to emphasise were
those attractive qualities which seem to have been almost universally
acknowledged by most of Sancroft's contemporaries. Among the many
hundreds of letters addressed to this monkish, abstracted, man, one looks
in vain for the poison pen. Unless he threw it away, and he seems to have
thrown nothing away, Sancroft never received any hate mail, not so much
as one hostile letter.

How do we reconcile Sancroft the power-broker, almost a beardless
ayatollah, with his retiring disposition? Sancroft and the Sancroftians
veered between St John's and Tertullian's alienation from earthly power
and Eusebius's glorification of the Emperor Constantine. St Augustine's
middle way eluded them.[134] One of Sancroft's sermons was on the text
Mark 11.31, where Jesus calls upon his flock to go into a desert place.
Sancroft says that he is not going to urge 'the old Eremeticall Life', since
he is addressing 'active persons'. Our Lord lived 'an active life'; 'and yet he
had his frequent temporary retreats too'.[135]

In September 2004 Lambeth Palace Library acquired a hitherto unknown exchange of letters
between Archbishop Sancroft and Thomas Sprat, bishop of Rochester. The letters reveal
that Sancroft could have been one of the victims of a conspiracy to incriminate Bishop Sprat
and other public figures in an invented association formed to restore James II to his throne.
In May 1692 Sprat had been arrested and his palace at Bromley searched. Sarah, duchess of
Marlborough, whose husband was also implicated, called this 'the flowerpot plot', since
the document, with its forged signatures, including Sancroft's, was planted in one of Bishop
Sprat's flowerpots. Fortunately the authorities failed to locate the fatal flowerpot. Sancroft
wrote: 'Had that cursed Association been found in the Flowerpot (& 'tis next to a Wonder
it was not;) Or had you made a weak defence; my Quarters here [scil., at Fressingfield] had
been beaten up too, my study ransackt by Messengers and Soldiers, & I myself hurried up
to London; so that notwithstanding my Innocence, the very Journey, the Attendance, & the
Imprisonment would in all probability effectually have destroied me, without any farther
prosecution. But blessed be God; our Soul is escaped, as a Bird out of the Snare of the Fowler:
The Snare is broken, & we are delivered'. The perpetrator of the 'plot', Robert Young, forger,
cheat and bigamist (D.N.B.), whose earlier escapades Sancroft had exposed, was pilloried
and imprisoned.[136]

Notes

Notes to Chapter 1 : Thomas Cranmer and the Truth

1. Jasper Ridley, *Thomas Cranmer* (Oxford, 1962); Diarmaid MacCulloch, *Thomas Cranmer: A Life* (New Haven and London, 1996).

2. *Miscellaneous Writings and Letters of Thomas Cranmer*, ed. J. E. Cox, Parker Society (Cambridge, 1846), p. 219; MacCulloch, *Thomas Cranmer*, pp. 21–22.

3. J. H. Nichols, ed., *Narratives of the Days of the Reformation*, Camden Society (London, 1859) prints the anonymous 'The Lyfe and Death of Thomas Cranmer, Late Archebushop of Caunterbury' (from British Library, MS Harley 417), which was the martyrologist John Foxe's principal source; and the account by Cranmer's secretary, Ralph Morrice (from Corpus Christi College, Cambridge, MS 128). So far as the anonymous life is concerned, MacCulloch (*Thomas Cranmer*, pp. 633–36) argues for the authorship of Stephen Nevinson. For Cranmer's total baldness and copious beard, 'covering his face with meruoilous grauitie', observed at his martyrdom, see John Foxe, *Actes and Monuments* (London, 1583), p. 1888.

4. *The life and Death of Cardinal Wolsey by George Cavendish*, ed. Richard S. Sylvester, Early English Text Society no. 243 (Oxford, 1959).

5. Foxe, *Actes and Monuments*, p. 1863.

6. *The Complete Works of St. Thomas More*, ii. ed. R. S. Sylvester (New Haven, 1963), p. 47; *Three Books of Polydore Vergil's English History*, ed. Sir Henry Ellis, Camden Society (London, 1844), p.227.

7. N. Sykes, E. C. Ratcliff and A. T. P. Williams, *Thomas Cranmer, 1489–1556: Three Commemorative Lectures delivered in Lambeth Palace* (London, 1956); P. N. Brooks, 'Cranmer Studies in the Wake of the Quatercentenary', *Historical Magazine of the Protestant Episcopal Church*, 31 (1962), pp. 365–74; P. Ayris and D. Selwyn, eds, *Thomas Cranmer: Churchman and Scholar* (Woodbridge, 1993).

8. Nichols, *Narratives*, pp. 219, 242.

9. MacCulloch, *Thomas Cranmer*, pp. 34–37. Peter Brooks in *Cranmer in Context*, pp. 18–22, provides evidence of Cranmer's possession and use of the 1524 Paris edition of Merlin's *Quatuor conciliorum generalium*, a source for the foundation prepared for the Henrician Reformation in the *Collectanea satis copiosa* of c. 1530, associated with Bishop Edward Fox,

who seems to have known only the later, 1530, edition of Merlin. See also D. G. Selwyn, *The Library of Thomas Cranmer* (Oxford, 1996), p. 63.

10. Nichols, *Narratives*, p. 252.

11. Cranmer to Thomas Cromwell, 15 August (1538), *Miscellaneous Writings of Cranmer*, p. 375.

12. *A Catechism Set Forth by Thomas Cranmer from the Nuremberg Catechism Translated into Latin by Justus Jonas*, ed. D. G. Selwyn (Appleford, 1978), p. 61.

13. *Writings and Disputations of Thomas Cranmer*, ed. J. E. Cox, Parker Society (Cambridge, 1844), p. 61.

14. P. N. Brooks, *Thomas Cranmer's Doctrine of the Eucharist: An Essay in Historical Development* (2nd edn, London, 1992).

15. *Miscellaneous Writings of Cranmer*, p. 566; Foxe, *Actes and Monuments*, p. 1887; MacCulloch, *Thomas Cranmer*, p. 603.

16. *Sermons of Hugh Latimer*, ed. G. E. Corrie, Parker Society (Cambridge, 1844), p. 487; *The History of the Church of England Compiled by the Venerable Bede*, trans. Thomas Stapleton (Antwerp, 1565), Epistle.

17. William Camden, *The History of the Most Renowned and Victorious Princess Elizabeth Late Queen of England*, abridged and ed. Wallace T. MacCaffrey (Chicago, 1970), p. 4.

18. Patrick Collinson, 'Truth and Legend: the Veracity of John Foxe's Book of Martyrs', in Patrick Collinson, *Elizabethans* (London and New York, 2003), pp. 151–77.

19. John Aylmer, *An harborowe for faithfull and trewe subiectes* ('at Strasborow' but *recte* London, 1559), sig. R1ᵛ.

20. Alastair Fox, *Thomas More: History and Providence* (Oxford, 1982); Alastair Fox, *Politics and Literature in the Reigns of Henry VII and Henry VIII* (Oxford, 1989), pp. 108–27; Judith H. Anderson, *Biographical Truth: the Representation of Historical Persons in Tudor-Stuart Writing* (New Haven, 1984), pp. 27–39, 75–109; *The Life and Death of Cardinal Wolsey*, pp. 3–4, 182–8.

21. Sir Philip Sidney, *An Apology for Poetry or the Defence of Poesy*, ed. G. Shepherd (London, 1965), p. 107.

22. *Prayers and Other Pieces of Thomas Becon*, ed. J. Ayre, Parker Society (Cambridge, 1844), p. 604.

23. Perez Zagorin, *Ways of Lying: Dissimulation, Persecution and Conformity in Early Modern Europe* (Cambridge, Massachusetts, 1990).

24. *The Works of John Jewel*, ed. J. Ayre, iv. Parker Society (Cambridge, 1850), p. 1167.

25. Nichols, *Narratives*, p. 249.

26. MacCulloch, *Thomas Cranmer*, pp. 25–32.

27. Brooks, *Thomas Cranmer's Doctrine of the Eucharist*, pp. 112, 141.

28. Dr Brooks gives a helpful and critical account of the long-running debate about Cranmer's eucharistic doctrine. But see, more recently, Diarmaid MacCulloch's penetrating and definitive account.

29. J. A. Muller, ed. *The Letters of Stephen Gardiner* (Westport, Connecticut, 1970), p. 330.
30. Ridley, *Thomas Cranmer*, p 12.
31. *The Obedience of a Christian Man* (1526), in *Doctrinal Treatises ... by William Tyndale*, ed. H. Walter, Parker Society (Cambridge, 1848).
32. Quoted, Gordon Rupp, *Six Makers of English Religion, 1500–1700* (London, 1957), p. 41.
33. Richard Rex, *Henry VIII and the English Reformation* (Basingstoke, 1993).
34. *The Remains of Archbishop Grindal*, ed. W. Nicholson, Parker Society (Cambridge, 1843), p. 379.
35. Brooks, 'Cranmer Studies', 365–74.
36. The latest accounts of the Prebendaries Plot are in Eamon Duffy, *The Stripping of the Altars: Traditional Religion in England c. 1400–c. 1580* (New Haven and London, 1992), pp. 433–42; MacCulloch, *Thomas Cranmer*, pp. 295–323; Ethan H. Shagan, *Popular Politics and the English Reformation* (Cambridge, 2003), chapter 6.
37. James M. Osborn, *Young Philip Sidney, 1572–1577* (New Haven and London, 1972), pp. 464–6.
38. E.M.W. Tillyard, *The Elizabethan World Picture* (London, 1943), pp. 13–14, 82–84. In the light of more recent scholarship, it is clear that Tillyard misattributed a didactic role to Shakespeare in the 'degree' speech in that play; and failed to detect either the uncertain note on which the speech and its reception ends, or the character of Ulysses, from whom one would hardly expect a sermon.
39. Patrick Collinson, 'Perne the Turncoat: An Elizabethan Reputation', in *Elizabethans*, pp. 179–217.
40. See the books, in the literary tradition of beast fables, written by the pioneering protestant physician and naturalist William Turner: *The huntyng & fyndyng out of the romishe fox* (Bonn, 1543); *The rescuynge of the romishe fox other wyse called the examination of the hunter deuised by steuen gardiner. The seconde course of the hunter at the romishe fox* (Bonn, 1545); *The huntyng of the romyshe vuolfe* (Emden, 1555?); *The hunting of the fox and the wolfe* (London, 1565). John Bale followed Turner's lead in a book subtitled *Yet a course at the romyshe foxe* (Antwerp, 1543); and Stephen Gardiner responded in *The examination of the hunter* (London, 1544). See Alec Ryrie, *The Gospel and Henry VIII: Evangelicals in the Early English Reformation* (Cambridge, 2003), pp. 106–7, 121.
41. Nichols, *Narratives*, pp. 254–59. The most famous refractions of Henry's trustful relationship with Cranmer occur in Shakespeare's *Henry VIII*, V. i and ii.
42. Matthew 10.16: 'Behold, I send you forth as sheep in the midst of wolves: be ye therefore wise as serpents, and harmless as doves.'
43. Selwyn, *A Catechism*. See also D. G. Selwyn, 'A Neglected Edition of Cranmer's Catechism', *Journal of Theological Studies*, new series 15 (1964), 76–91.

44. Selwyn, *A Catchism*, pp. 212 (introduction), 80 (text); Brian Cummings, *The Literary Culture of the Reformation: Grammar and Grace* (Oxford, 2002).
45. Brooks, *Thomas Cranmer's Doctrine of the Eucharist*, p. 38; MacCulloch, *Thomas Cranmer*, pp. 354–55, 379–83.
46. *A reporte of Maister Doctor Redmans answers to questions propounded him before his death concerning certaine poyntes of religion and now beyng with many in controversy* (London, 1551). A further account of Redman's death-bed confessions is contained in an undated letter from Thomas Lever to Roger Ascham: *Original Letters Relative to the English Reformation*, ed. H. Robinson, i, Parker Society (Cambridge, 1846), 150–52. The notorious difficulties surrounding this widely reported discussion are dealt with by Ashley Null in 'John Redman, the Gentle Ambler', in *Westminster Abbey Reformed, 1540–1640*, ed. C. S. Knighton and Richard Mortimer (Aldershot, 2003), pp. 38–74.
47. Brooks, *Thomas Cranmer's Doctrine of the Eucharist*, p.5.
48. Nichols, *Narratives*, p. 219.
49. *The Practice and Representation of Reading in England*, ed. James Raven, Helen Small and Naomi Tadmor (Cambridge, 1996); Lisa Jardine and Anthony Grafton, '"Studied for Action": How Gabriel Harvey Read his Livy', *Past and Present*, 129 (1990), pp.30–78; William H. Sherman, *John Dee: The Politics of Reading and Writing in the English Renaissance* (Amherst, 1995); Kevin Sharpe, *Reading Revolutions: The Politics of Reading in Early Modern England* (New Haven and London, 2000); Stephen N. Zwicker, 'Habits of Reading and Early Modern Literary Culture', in *The Cambridge History of Early Modern English Literature*, ed. David Loewenstein and Janel Mueller (Cambridge, 2002), pp. 170–98.
50. British Library, MSS Royal 7BXI and XII. Peter Brooks pioneered the use of the these *florilegia* in *Thomas Cranmer's Doctrine of the Eucharist*. Together with some collateral material in Lambeth Palace Library MS 1170, they have been more systematically exploited by Ashley Null, with particular reference to Cranmer's doctrine of repentance. (*Thomas Cranmer's Doctrine of Repentance: Renewing the Power to Love* (Oxford, 2000).)
51. On the reception and promotion of these continental divines in Edwardian England, see MacCulloch, *Thomas Cranmer*, extensively. On Melanchthon's absence from the scene, see B. L. Beer, 'Philip Melanchthon and the Cambridge Professorship', *Notes & Queries*, 232 (1987), p. 185; J. D. Alsop, 'Philip Melanchthon and England in 1553', ibid., new series, 37 (1990), 164–65. I owe these references to Professor MacCulloch.
52. E. C. Ratcliff, 'The Liturgical Work of Archbishop Cranmer', *Journal of Ecclesiastical History*, 7 (1956), 189–203.
53. John Hacket, *Scrinia Reserata* (London, 1693), ii, p. 103.
54. Patrick Collinson, *Archbishop Grindal, 1519–1583: The Struggle for a Reformed Church* (London, 1979), p. 67.
55. Collinson, 'Perne the Turncoat'; John Redman, *A compendious treatise called the complaint of grace* (London, 1556), preface and sig. Gii; Null, 'John Redman'; Richard Rex, *The Theology of John Fisher* (Cambridge, 1991).

56. Available in many nineteenth-century editions of the *Homilies* (evidence that they were still being read in church at that time); in Cranmer, *Miscellaneous Writings*, pp. 128–49; and in *English Reformers*, ed. T. H. L. Parker, Library of Christian Classics, 26 (London, 1966), pp. 253–86.

57. *A Necessary Doctrine and Erudition of a Christian Man*, ed. T. A. Lacey (London, 1895), pp. 144–45.

58. Cranmer, *Miscellaneous Writings*, pp. 338–39.

59. Ryrie, *The Gospel and Henry VIII*, pp. 243–47; Susan Wabuda, *Preaching During the English Reformation* (Cambridge, 2002); S. M. Wabuda, 'The Provision of Preaching during the Early English Reformation: With Special Reference to Itineration *c.* 1530 to 1547', unpublished Cambridge Ph.D. thesis, 1991, esp. 'Archbishop Cranmer's Patronage of Preachers', pp. 114–28.

60. Reference to PRO, SP. 1/115, fol. 89, establishes that Payne spoke of a thousand paternosters, not of a million, as Cranmer's Victorian editor mistakenly supposed.

61. Muller, *Letters of Stephen Gardiner*, p. 335.

62. Brooks, *Thomas Cranmer's Doctrine of the Eucharist*, pp. 141–43.

63. Ibid., pp. 146–47.

64. Rupp, *Six Makers*, p. 44.

65. One may compare the views of C.W. Dugmore in *The Mass and the English Reformers* (London, 1958) and in *The English Prayer Book*, 1549–1662, Alcuin Club (London, 1963), with those of Peter Brooks in *Thomas Cranmer's Doctrine of the Eucharist*, and with MacCulloch in *Thomas Cranmer*.

66. On Osiander, see David Steinmetz, *Reformers in the Wings* (Philadelphia, 1971), pp. 91–9; and the references Steinmetz supplies to the literature in German.

67. Printed in *Miscellaneous Writings*, pp. 203–11.

68. I have been helped on this point by Ashley Null.

69. Selwyn, *Catechism*, pp. 43–50 (introduction), 115 (text).

70. Cranmer, *Miscellaneous Writings*, p. 143.

71. Alister McGrath, *Iustitia Dei*, ii (Cambridge, 1986), chapter 8.

72. The Middelburg Prayer Book was reprinted by Peter Hall in *Reliquiae Liturgica: the Middelburg Prayer Book* (Bath, 1847).

73. MacCulloch, *Thomas Cranmer*, pp. 629–30.

74. J.S. Morrill, 'The Religious Context of the English Civil War', *Transactions of the Royal Historical Society*, fifth series, 34 (1984), 155–78; J.S. Morrill, 'The Attack on the Church of England in the Long Parliament, 1640–1642', in Derek Beales and Geoffrey Best, eds, *History, Society and the Churches: Essays in Honour of Owen Chadwick* (Cambridge, 1985), pp. 105–24. But note that MacCulloch thinks (*Thomas Cranmer*, p. 627) that 'the Prayer Book itself had attracted little open hostility during the course of the Civil War'. However, it was royalist perception of a threat to the Prayer Book, as well as to episcopacy, which made possible the necessary condition for any war: two sides.

75. John S. Coolidge, *The Pauline Renaissance in England: Puritanism and the Bible* (Oxford, 1970).
76. Foxe, *Actes and Monuments*, p. 1888.
77. Ibid.

Notes to Chapter 2 : Godly Preachers and Zealous Magistrates in Elizabethan East Anglia: The Roots of Dissent

1. John Bossy, 'The Character of Elizabethan Catholicism', *Past and Present*, 21 (1962), reprinted in T. Aston, ed., *Crists in Europe, 1500–1660'* (1965), pp. 247–69
2. Alan Everitt, *The Pattern of Rural Dissent: The Nineteenth Century* (Leicester, 1972), (and see the collection of his work in *Landscape and Community in England*, 1985); Margaret Spufford, *Contrasting Communities: English Villagers in the Sixteenth and Seventeenth Centuries* (Cambridge, 1974); Keith Wrightson and David Levine, *Poverty and Piety in an English Village: Terling, 1525–1700* (1979). See also David Underdown, *Revel, Riot and Rebellion: Popular Politics and Culture in England, 1603–1660* (Oxford, 1985); Martin Ingram, 'Religion, Communities and Moral Discipline in Late Sixteenth-and Seventeenth-Century England: Case Studies', in Kaspar von Greyerz, ed., *Religion and Society in Early Modern Europe, 1500–1800* (1984), pp. 177–93.
3. This, I know, is a contradiction in terms. The Suffolk Strict Baptists have no continuing city but a tabernacle or marquee in which their annual Association meetings are held, usually in some village setting: or so it ever was.
4. John Browne, *History of Congregationalism and Memorials of the Churches in Norfolk and Suffolk* (1877), pp. 544–45
5. Patrick Collinson, *The Birthpangs of Protestant England: Religious and Cultural Change in the Sixteenth and Seventeenth Centuries* (Basingstoke, 1988.)
6. See below, pp. 145–72. See also many of the essays in J. W. Martin, *Religious Radicals in Tudor England* (1989.)
7. Patrick Collinson, 'Towards a Broader Understanding of the Early Dissenting Tradition', in Patrick Collinson, *Godly People: Essays on Protestantism and Puritanism* (1983), pp. 527–62; and *The Religion of Protestants: The Church in English Society, 1559–1625* (Oxford, 1982), esp. chapter 6, 'Voluntary Religion: Its Forms and Tendencies'.
8. Patrick Collinson, 'The English Conventicle', below, and chapter 5 of *Birthpangs of Protestant England*, 'Wars of Religion'.
9. Peter Lake and Maria Dowling, eds., *Protestantism and the National Church in Sixteenth-Century England* (1987). Dr MacCulloch's remarks about the cuckoo in the nest are contained in his *The Later Reformation in England, 1547–1603* (2nd edn., Basingstoke, 2001.)
10. Diarmaid MacCulloch, 'Catholic and Puritan in Elizabethan Suffolk: A Country Community Polarises', *Archiv für Reformationsgeschichte*, 72 (1981), pp. 232–89; and *Suffolk and the Tudors: Politics and Religion in an English County, 1500–1600* (Oxford, 1986.)

11. Norman P. Tanner, ed., *Heresy Trials in the Diocese of Norwich, 1428–31*, Camden Society, 4th series 20 (1977).
12. British Library, MS Harley 421, fol. 18ʳ; John Strype, *Ecclesiastical Memorials* (Oxford, 1822), I.i. 122–23,
13. *The Acts and Monuments of John Foxe*, ed. S.R. Cattley (1837), iv, 642. On Bilney see most recently Greg Walker, 'Saint or Schemer? The 1527 Heresy Trial of Thomas Bilney Reconsidered', *Journal of Ecclesiastical History*, 40 (1989), 219–38.
14. *The Acts and Monuments of John Foxe*, iv, 766–67.
15. John Davis, *Heresy and the Reformation in the South East of England, 1520–1559'* (1983), pp. 116–17; and MacCulloch, *Suffolk and the Tudors*, pp. 178–79.
16. BL MS Harley 421, fols 140–1, 169–70, 216ᵛ. See, for example, the case against four men of Stoke by Nayland who affirmed, among other doctrine, that 'Christus non est deus et homo'; and the Haverhill butcher who said that he could not 'rede in Scripture that Baptisme shuld be a sacrament'. On the radical Marian martyrs of the Kentish Weald, see my essay, 'Truth and Legend: The Veracity of John Foxe's Book of Martyrs', in A. C. Duke and C. A. Tamse, eds., 'Clio's mirror: *historiography in Britain and the Netherlands*, viii (Zutphen, 1985), 31–54; reprinted, Patrick Collinson, *Elizabethans* (2003), pp. 151–77.
17. The problems of continuity and discontinuity, the crux of our understanding of Reformation processes at a local level, are investigated for another region, the West Country, in Robert Whiting, *The Blind Devotion of the People: Popular Religion and the English Reformation* (Cambridge, 1989).
18. MacCulloch, 'Catholic and Puritan', pp. 265–67; idem, *Suffolk and the Tudors*, pp. 189–90.
19. For Grindal, see Patrick Collinson, *Archbishop Grindal, 1519–1583: The Struggle for a Reformed Church* (1979); for Parkhurst, R.A. Houlbrooke, ed., *The Letter Book of John Parkhurst, Bishop of Notwich, Compiled during the Years 1571 to 1575'*, Norfolk Record Society, 43 (1974 and 1975), together with A.H. Smith, *County and Court: Government and Politics in Norfolk, 1558–1603* (Oxford, 1974), chapter 10; and MacCulloch, *Suffolk and the Tudors*, pp. 184–93; for Cox, Felicity Heal, 'The Bishops of Ely and their Diocese during the Reformation', (unpublished Cambridge Ph.D. thesis 1972) and her *Of Prelates and Princes: A Study of the Economic and Social Position of the Tudor Episcopate* (Cambridge, 1980). See also G.L. Blackman, 'The Career and Influence of Bishop Richard Cox, 1547–1581', (unpublished Cambridge Ph.D. thesis 1953) and E.J. Bourgeois II, 'A Ruling Elite: The Government of Cambridgeshire, circa 1524 to 1588', unpublished Cambridge Ph.D. thesis (1988).
20. Patrick Collinson, *The Elizabethan Puritan Movement* (1967) and *English Puritanism* (1983, revised 1987).
21. *Acts and Monuments of John Foxe*, vi, 767; viii, 556–57.
22. Collinson, *Elizabethan Puritan Movement*, pp. 202–5; Smith, *County and Court*, pp. 208–25.

23. MacCulloch, 'Catholic and Puritan', pp. 234–37; idem, *Suffolk and the Tudors*, pp. 193–95.
24. MacCulloch, *Suffolk and the Tudors*, passim; Patrick Collinson, 'Magistracy and Ministry: A Suffolk Miniature', in Collinson, *Godly People*, pp. 445–66; and *The Religion of Protestants*, pp. 153–64.
25. MacCulloch, 'Catholic and Puritan', pp. 237–40; idem *Suffolk and the Tudors*, pp. 195–97.
26. Alan Everitt, *Suffolk and the Great Rebellion, 1640–1660*, Suffolk Record Society, 3 (Ipswich, 1960), pp. 12, 16.
27. On Thetford, see my *Birthpangs of Protestant England*, p. 58, digesting material in Public Record Office, SP 12/155/11. On the Bury 'stirs', see MacCulloch, *Suffolk and the Tudors*, pp. 199–212; and earlier accounts in J.S. Cockburn, *A History of English Assizes, 1558–1714* (1972), pp. 199–206, Elliot Rose, *Cases of Conscience: Alternatives Open to Recusants and Puritans under Elizabeth I and James I* (Cambridge, 1975), pp. 158–68; Collinson, *Religion of Protestants*, pp. 153–64; and more fully in 'Puritanism and the Gentry in Suffolk, 1575–1585: A Case Study', chapter 9 of my unpublished London Ph.D. thesis, 'The Puritan Classical Movement in the reign of Elizabeth I' (1957).
28. Collinson, 'Puritan Classical Movement', pp. 123–26 and appendix B.
29. On Brown and Harrison and the original Brownists, see the sources published by L.H. Carlson. *The Writings of Robert Harrison and Robert Brown*, Elizabethan Nonconformist Texts, 2 (1953); and Albert Peel, *The Brownists in Norwich and Norfolk about 1580* (Cambridge, 1926); B.R. White, *The English Separatist Tradition: From the Marian Martyrs to the Pilgrim Fathers* (Oxford, 1971), pp. 44–66; Michael R. Watts, *The Dissenters: from the Reformation to the French Revolution* (Oxford, 1978), pp. 26–34.
30. Albert Peel, 'Congregational Martyrs at Bury St Edmunds: How Many? *Transactions of the Congregational Historical Society*, 15 (1946), 67–70.
31. Collinson, *Religion of Protestants*, p. 162.
32. British Library, MS Add. 38492, no. 63, fols 107–8.
33. Collinson, *Religion of Protestants*, p. 164. For Barrington, see William Hunt, *The Puritan Moment: The Coming of Revolution in an English County* (Cambridge MA., 1983) and *Barrington Family Letters, 1628–1632*, ed. Arthur Searle, Camden Society, 4th ser., 28 (1983).
34. Ernst Troelsch, *The Social Teaching of the Christian Churches*, tr. O. Wyon, 2 vols (1931).
35. William Burton, *Seven dialogues both pithie and profitable* (1606), sig. A2.
36. Collinson, *Religion of Protestants*, p. 153.
37. Ibid., pp. 119–20; idem, *Godly People*, pp. 449–50, 539.
38. Collinson, *Religion of Protestants*, p. 164.
39. W. Gurnall, *The Magistrates Portraiture* (1656), pp. 37–38, cited in MacCulloch, *Suffolk and the Tudors*.

40. Wrightson in Wrightson and Levine, *Poverty and Piety*, and in his unpublished Cambridge Ph.D. thesis, 'The Puritan Reformation of Manners, with Special Reference to the Counties of Lancashire and Essex, 1640–60' (1974); Hunt, *The Puritan Moment*.

41. Collinson, *Religion of Protestant*, pp. 158–59.

42. Thomas Rogers, *Miles Christianus* (1590), p. 17.

43. Bodleian Library, MS Tanner 68, fols. 41, 43, 54.

44. Browne, *History of Congregationalism*, pp. 393–95. For Mrs. Chidley, see Watts, *The Dissenters*, pp. 88–89, 96–99; and Robert Zaller and Richard L. Greaves, eds, *Biographical Dictionary of British Radicals in the Seventeenth Century*, i (Brighton, 1982), 139–40.

45. *Oliver Heywood's Life of John Angier of Denton*, ed. E. Axon, Chetham Society, new series 97, (1973), p. 50.

46. Quoted in Collinson, *Religion of Protestants*, p. 156.

47. Spufford, *Contrasting Communities*; Derek Plumb, The Social and Economic Spread of Rural Lollardy: A Reappraisal', in *Voluntary Religion*, 111–29; Christopher Marsh, "'A Gracelesse and Audacious Companie"? The Family of Love in the Parish of Balsham 1550–1630', ibid., 191–208.

48. Spufford, *Contrasting Communities*, p. 343. See also her polemical essay, 'Puritanism and Social Control', in Anthony Fletcher and John Stevenson, eds, *Order and Disorder in Early Modern England* (Cambridge, 1985), pp. 41–57.

49. Nick Alldridge, 'Loyalty and Identity in Chester Parishes, 1540–1640', in Susan Wright, ed., *Parish Church and People: Local Studies in Lay Religion, 1350–1750* (1988), pp. 85–124. For 'the social miracle', see John Bossy, *Christianity in the West, 1400–1700* (Oxford, 1985), chapter 4.

50. *Tracts ascribed to Richard Bancroft*, ed. Albert Peel (Cambridge, 1953), pp. 72–73.

51. For Carew's previous career at Hatfield Peverel, Essex, and the Ipswich parish of St Margaret's, see Collinson, *Elizabethan Puritan Movement*, pp. 340–41, 366.

52. Thomas Carew, *Certaine godly and necessarie semons* (1603).

53. Bezaleel Carter, *Christ his last will and John his legacy* (1621).

54. MacCulloch, *Suffolk and the Tudors*, p. 315.

55. Ibid, chapter 11.

56. Ibid., pp. 320–21.

57. David Cressy, *Coming Over: Migration and Communication between England and New England in the Seventeenth Century* (Cambridge, 1987); and further references in Dr Cressy's extensive bibliography.

58. Watts, *The Dissenters*, chapter 2; Geoffrey F. Nuttall, *Visible Saints: The Congregational Way, 1640–1660* (Oxford, 1957). I believe that the findings of G.F. Nuttall for Kent, published in 'Dissenting Churches in Kent before 1700', *Journal of Ecclesiastical History*, 14 (1963), could probably be extrapolated for East Anglia, so far as pre-Civil War roots were concerned.

59. Browne, *History of Congregationalism*, pp. 161, 297, 437.
60. Spufford, *Contrasting Communities*, pp. 233–38, 351, 329.
61. As argued particularly in 'The English Conventicle', below, pp. 145–72.
62. Anne Whiteman, ed., *The Compton Census of 1676: A Critical Edition* (Oxford, 1986); Spufford, *Contrasting Communities*, pp. 223–29.

Chapter 3 : Shepherds, Sheepdogs and Hirelings: The Pastoral Ministry in Post-Reformation England

1. Simon Harward, *Two godlie and learned sermons, preached at Manchester in Lancashire* (London, 1582), sig, Ciiij.
2. See the categories employed in the puritan 'Survey of the Ministry' carried out in various counties in 1584 and 1586. *The Seconde Parte of a Register*, ed. Albert Peel (Cambridge, 1915), ii. 88–184.
3. Cathedral Archives and Library, Canterbury, MSS X.11.2, fols 218–28, X. 11.9, fol. 103.
4. Patrick Collinson, 'Cranbrook and the Fletchers: Popular and Unpopular Religion in the Kentish Weald', in Collinson, *Godly People: Essays on English Protestantism and Puritanism* (London, 1983), p. 415; R.A. Christophers, 'Social and Educational Background of the Surrey Clergy, 1520–1620' (unpublished London PhD. thesis, 1975), pp.86–87.
5. Rosemary O'Day, *The English Clergy: the Emergence and Consolidation of a Profession, 1558–1642* (Leicester, 1979).
6. Patrick Collinson, *The Religion of Protestants: the Church in English Society, 1559–1625* (Oxford, 1982).
7. Helena Hajzyk, 'The Church in Lincolnshire, *c.* 1595–*c.* 1640' (unpublished Cambridge Ph.D. thesis, 1980), pp. 301–2. One of this minority, George Buddle, published *A short and plaine discourse fully containing the whole doctrine of evangelicall fastes* (London, 1609), a not conspicuously evangelical work which is concerned with fasting at Lent and other appropriate seasons of the Kalender, and which pays tribute to 'that good Hooker', 'worthy Hooker' (sigs, A2ᵛ–3).
8. *Luther's Meditations on the Gospels*, ed. Roland H. Bainton (London, 1963), pp. 98–99. Luther was preaching on John 10: 1–18.
9. (William Turner and John Bale), *The huntyng and fynding out of the romyshe foxe* (Basyll, 1543, i.e. Antwerp, 1544); William Turner, *The huntyng of the Romyshe vuolfe* (Emden, 1555 (?)); (William Turner), *The hunting of the fox and the wolfe, because they make havocke of the sheepe of Christ* (London , 1565). Instructing the people that it was not for them to decide whether or not to deliver the fleece (rents, tithes and other duties) to their masters, Thomas Lever said: 'It is magistrates dutyes, to consyder and note, whether they be theeves, or shepheardes, dogges, or wolfes that taketh the fleese.' *A sermon preached befroe the kynges maiestie* (1550), ed. E. Arber, *Thomas Lever, M.A., Sermons*, English Reprints (London, 1870), p. 86

10. For Haydocke, see Karl Josef Höltgen, 'The Reformation of Images and Some Jacobean Writers on Art', in *Functions of Literature: Essays Presented to Erwin Wolff on his Sixtieth Birthday* (Tübingen, 1984), pp. 138–46; Lucy Gent, *Picture and Poetry, 1560–1620* (London, 1981).

11. Samuel Crooke, *The ministeriall husbandry and building* (London, 1615), sigs A2ᵛ–3; Samuel Ward, *Jethros Iustice of Peace* (London, 1618), sig. A3ᵛ; Alexander Groose, *Deaths deliverance and Eliahs fiery chariot* (London, 1632), p. 24.

12. Collinson, 'Cranbrook and the Fletchers', p. 427.

13. Francis Parker, rector of Toynton St Peter and Lawrence Freeman, rector of Toynton All Saints (to the surrogate at Stamford?), c 1607, Lincoln Archives Office, MS COR/M/2, no. 32.

14. Jane Freeman, 'The Parish Ministry in the Diocese of Durham, c. 1570–1640' (unpublished Durham Ph.D. thesis, 1979), p. 387.

15. John Howson, *A second sermon, preached at Paules Crosse, the 21. of May, 1598* (London, 1598); Walter Balcanquall, *The honour of christian churches: and the necessitie of frequenting of divine service and publike prayers in them* (London, 1644), p. 23.

16. John Favour, *Antiquitie triumphing over novelties* (London, 1619), epistle.

17. *The Diary of Ralph Josselin, 1616–1683*, ed. Alan Macfarlane (Oxford, 1976); Alan Macfarlane, *The Family Life of Ralph Josselin, a Seventeenth-Century Clergyman: An Essay in Historical Anthropology* (Cambridge, 1970).

18. John Bossy, 'Blood and Baptism: Community and Christianity in Western Europe from the Fourteenth to the Sixteenth Centuries', *Sanctity and Secularity: The Church and the World, Studies in Church History*, ed. D. Baker, 10 (Oxford, 1973), 139; John Bossy, *Christianity in the West, 1400–1700* (Oxford, 1985), chapter 4.

19. See my *Religion of Protestants*, pp. 114–30. See also my 'Lectures by Combination: Structures and Characteristics of Church Life in 17th-Century England', in *Godly People*, pp. 467–98, and Ann Hughes, 'Thomas Dugard and his Circle in the 1630s: A "Parliamentary-Puritan"' Connexion?' *Historical Journal*, 29 (1986), 771–93.

20. J. McManners, *Death and the Enlightenment: Changing Attitudes to Death in Eighteenth-Century France* (Oxford, 1981), chapter 8. I am indebted to Dr Houlbrooke for an unpublished seminar paper on deathbeds, part of a study in progress on death in early modern England; and to Mr Christopher Marsh of Churchill College, Cambridge for sight of a so far unpublished paper on will-making.

21. Cathedral Archives and Library, Canterbury, MSS X. 10. 19, fols 229v–44ᵛ, X. 11.1, fols 225ᵛ–31ᵛ.

22. This reflects a mass of evidence in the series of deposition books from the Canterbury courts in Cathedral Archives and Library, Canterbury.

23. Cathedral Archives and Library, Canterbury, MS X. 10.17, fold 185–8ʳ.

24. *The Presbyterian Movement in the Reign of Queen Elizabeth as Illustrated by the Minute Book of the Dedham Classis, 1582–1589*, ed. R.G. Usher,

Camden third series, 8 (1905), pp. 27, 29, 39, 41, 47, 48, 49–50, 55–56, 71, 72, 73

25. This is still a neglected topic. But see my *Religion of Protestants*, pp. 118–19.

26. W. A. Pantin, *The English Church in the Fourteenth Century* (Cambridge, 1955), chapter 9, 'Manuals of Instruction for Parish Priests'.

27. Patrick Collinson, 'The Protestant Family', in my *The Birthpangs of Protestant England: Religious and Cultural Change in the Sixteenth and Seventeenth Centuries* (Basingstoke, 1988); Kathleen M. Davies, 'Continuity and Change in Literary Advice on Marriage', in *Marriage and Society: Studies in the Social History of Marriage*, ed. R. B. Outhwaite (London, 1981), pp. 58–80.

28. George Downame, *Two sermons, the one commending the ministerie in generall: the other defending the office of bishops in particular* (London, 1608), pp. 17–18, 25–26, 35–36.

29. Charles Richardson, *A workeman that needeth not to be ashamed: or the faithfull steward of Gods house: a sermon describing the duety of a godly minister, both in his doctrine and in his life* (London, 1616), p. 12.

30. Samuel Hieron, *The spirituall fishing: a sermon preached in Cambridge* (London, 1618), pp, 14–16, 22. See also Jerome Phillips, *The fisher-man: a sermon preached at a synode held at Southwell in Nottinghamshire* (London, 1623).

31. Downame, *Two sermons*, p. 27; Dering quoted in Patrick Collinson, 'A Mirror of Elizabethan Puritanism: The Life and Letters of "Godly Master Dering"', in *Godly People*, p. 299.

32. Pantin, *The English Church in the Fourteenth Century*, pp. 198–99.

33. Collinson, *Religion of Protestants*, pp. 85–86, 133–34.

34. Richard Bernard, *The faithfull shepherd: wholy in a manner transposed and made anew, and very much inlarged both with precepts and examples, to further young divines in the studie of divinitie. With the shepherds practise in the end* (London, 1621), pp. 3. 35–36, 98 et seq, 131–32, 159–355.

35. *The Works of George Herbert*, ed. F. E. Hutchinson (Oxford, 1941), pp. 244–45, 247–49, 236, 249–50, 257–59, 285–86.

36. I am indebted to Dr Eamon Duffy for making this point quite forcefully in discussion. The antagonism of Bolton and Bentham for commonplace neighbourly values (which may be less familiar than Gifford's writings) can be sampled in Bolton's *Some general directions for a comfortable walking with God* (London, 1638) and Bentham's *The saints societie* (London, 1636). This piece of Bentham's invective (pp. 167–68) is not untrypical: 'The pretty lispings and stammerings, the falls and stumblings, the unmannerly roguing, or whoring this man, that woman: the pretty pronunciation of this or that oath of their children shall not be forgotten: and then from these merrie Colloquies rake into the dunghill puddles of the true, or fained miscarriage of their neighbours, good or bad . . .'

37. *Works of Herbert*, p. 228.

38. However Benjamin Boyce in *The Theophrastan Character in England to 1642* (London, 1967), describes Herbert's treatise as a conduct book rather

than a 'character' and suggests that the word in the title was intended to have 'the ordinary, non-technical meaning' (p. 197). See also Heinz Bergner, ed., *English Character Writing* (Tübingen, 1971) and J. W. Smeed, *The Theophrastan Character: The History of a Literary Genre* (Oxford, 1985).

39. Collinson, *Religion of Protestants*, p.110.
40. Peter Lake, *Anglicans and Puritans? Presbyterian and English Conformist Thought from Whitgift to Hooker* (London, 1988), chapter 4, 'Richard Hooker'.
41. Stanley Fish, *The Living Temple: George Herbert and Catechising* (Berkeley, 1978); Joseph H. Summers, *George Herbert, His Religion and Art* (London and Cambridge, Massachusetts, 1954); Barbara K. Lewalski, *Protestant Poetics and the Seventeenth-Century Religious Lyric* (Princeton, 1979); John S. Coolidge, *The Pauline Renaissance in England: Puritanism and the Bible* (Oxford, 1970).
42. This view is explicit in the writings of Dr Christopher Haigh and implicit in the work of a number of other recent historians. The ultimate indebtedness of this negative assessment of Protestant ministry to the rich and subtle learning of Keith Thomas in *Religion and the Decline of Magic* (London, 1971) is, of course, very considerable. See Haigh, 'Introduction', 'The Recent Historiography of the English Reformation' and 'Anticlericalism and the English Reformation', all in *The English Reformation Revised*, ed. Christopher Haigh (Cambridge, 1987).
43. Christopher Haigh, 'The Church of England, the Catholics and the People', in *The Reign of Elizabeth I*, ed. Christopher Haigh (London, 1984), p. 213.
44. Samuel Clarke, *The Lives of Thirty-Two English Divines* (London, 1677), p.15.
45. Dr Parker is preparing an edition of John Rylands University Library Manchester, Rylands English MS 524, containing a collection of Greenham's casuistry compiled by Arthur Hildersham (?). Mr Carlson is engaged in a reconstitution of the population and society of Dry Drayton.
46. Thomas Settle, *A catechisme* (London, 1585), epistle.
47. Richard Greenham, *Grave counsels and godly observations*, in *Workes* (London, 1612), p.24.
48. George Gifford, *A sermon on the parable of the sower* (London, 1582); William Harrison, *The difference of hearers: or an exposition of the parable of the sower. Delivered in certaine sermons at Hyton in Lancashire* (London, 1614). On Harrison's sermons, see Christopher Haigh, 'Puritan Evangelism in the Reign of Elizabeth I', *English Historical Review*, 92 (1977), 30–58.
49. *Sermons by Hugh Latimer*, ed. G. E. Corrie (Cambridge, 1844), p. 155.
50. Dod quoted in Collinson, *Religion of Protestants*, p. 231; Bernard, *The faithfull shepherd*, pp. 98, 107.
51. Peter F. Jensen, 'The Life of Faith in the Teaching of Elizabethan Protestants' (unpublished Oxford D.Phil. thesis, 1979), p.29.
52. *Works of Herbert*, p. 256.

53. Richard Bernard, *Two twinnes or two parts of one portion of Scripture. I is of catechising. II of the Ministers maintenance* (London, 1613); *A double catechisme* (Cambridge, 1607); *The common catechisme* (London, 1630); *Good Christian looke to thy creede* (London, 1630).

54. Bernard, *The faithfull shepherd*, p. 100. Perkins's editor, William Crashawe, expressed himself in similar terms in what was evidently a commonplace, declaring that catechising was 'the life of preaching and such a meanes of knowledge as without it all preaching is to little purpose'. Quoted, Ian Green, '"For Children in Yeeres and Children in Understanding":The Emergence of the English Catechism under Elizabeth and the Early Stuarts', *Journal of Ecclesiastical History*, 37 (1986), 417.

55. Richard Kilby, *Hallelu-iah: Praise ye the Lord for the unburthening of a loaden conscience* (Cambridge, 1618), pp. 82–83.

56. Jensen, 'The Life of Faith', pp. 174–228; Green, 'The Emergence of the English Catechism', pp. 397–425.

57. See as examples of pessimistic pastoral perception Jeremy Corderoy, *A short dialogue, wherein is proved that no man can be saved without good workes* (Oxford, 1604), and Timothy Rogers, *The righteous mans evidence for Heaven, Or a treatise shewing how every one while he lives here may certainly know what shall become of him after his departure out of this life* (London, 1619).

58. Francis Inman, *A light unto the unlearned* (London, 1622), epistle; William Crashawe, *Milke for babe: or a North-country catechisme made plaine and easie, to the capacity of the simplest* (London, 1628); Samuel Hieron, *The doctrine of the beginning of Christ* (13th edn., London, 1626).

59. Preface by John Conant to Bernard's posthumously published *Thesaurus Biblicus* (London 1644), sig. A3ᵛ.

60. Bernard, *The faithfull shepherd*, pp. 102–3; Lyford quoted by Green, 'The Emergence of the English Catechism', p. 415.

61. Patrick Collinson, 'The English Conventicle', below, pp. 145–72.

62. Cathedral Archives and Library, Canterbury, MS X. 11.1, fols 229ʳ, 230ʳ.

63. Hajzyk, 'The Church in Lincolnshire', pp. 225–42. The episcopal hearings into the Williams case are documented in Lincoln Archives Office, MS Cj/12 (Episcopal Court Book, 1598–1600) with the cause papers in box 80/7.

64. Hajzyk, 'The Church in Lincolnshire', pp. 270–71. For the report of Bishop Neile's visitors, see my 'Lectures by Combination', p. 483, and references there. How exceptional the doctrinal storm in the little *pays* of Sleaford may have been remains uncertain. In 1595 Bishop Fletcher of London reported the clergy of Colchester and Maldon as 'at war with themselves, as well in matter of popular quarrels as points of doctrine'. (*H.M.C. Cal. Hatfield MSS* 5, p. 394.) See also Peter Gunter's *A sermon preached in the countie of Suffolke before the clergie and laytie for the discoverie and confutation of certaine strange, pernicious and hereticall positions publickly delivered herd and mainteyned touching justification by a certaine factious preacher*

of Wickham Market in the said countie, by which divers, especially of the vulgar, farre and neare, were greatly seduced (London, 1615). Dr Freeman writes of the diocese of Durham in the 1620s and 1630s: 'The unity in which they had previously lived . . . was destroyed by argument.' ('The Parish Ministry', pp. 408–17.)

65. This was affirmed by Nicholas Estwick in Bolton's funeral sermon. See *The life and death of M. Bolton*, published with *Mr Boltons last and learned worke of the foure last things* (London, 1639), pp. 18–19.

66. Anthony Cade, *Saint Paules agonie: A sermon preached at Leicester at the ordinary monthly lecture* (London, 1618), epistle.

67. For some evidence of Egerton's religious environment, see R. J. Acheson, 'Sion's Saint: John Turner of Sutton Valence', *Archaeologia Cantiana*, 99 (1983), 183–97.

68. Cathedral Archives and Library, Canterbury, MS X 10.20, fols 148ᵛ–62ᵛ, 211v–20r. However Mr Hudson's semon was perhaps not such an incoherent rigmarole as it was represented by his hearers. He seems to have been quoting from Sir Thomas More's *Dialogue Concerning Heresies* which includes the story of St Francis reacting to the sight of a young man kissing a girl by going down on his knees to thank God 'that charyte was not yet gone out of this wretched worlde'. Or did More and Hudson share a common source? (*The Complete Works of St. Thomas More*, vi, pt 2, ed. Thomas M. C. Lawler, Germain Marc'Hadour and Richard C. Marius (New Haven, 1981), 287.)

69. Cathedral Archives and Library, Canterbury, MS X. 10.11, fols 185ᵛ–8ᵛ.

70. *Paupers and Pig Killers:The Diary of William Holland a Somerset Parson, 1799–1818*, ed. Jack Ayres (London, 1986 edn), p. 118.

71. 'Articles presented by a preacher of London called John Feld', PRO, SP 12/164/11; another version in Dr Williams's Library, MS Morrice B 11, fols 94–96, calendared in *The Seconde Parte of a Register*, i, pp. 284–86 as 'Mr Feilde and Mr Egerton their tolleration'.

72. *A parte of a register* (Middelburg, 1593?), p. 317. See my *The Elizabethan Puritan Movement* (London and Berkeley, 1967), pp. 356–71 and, more fully, my unpublished London PhD. thesis, 'The Puritan Classical Movement in the Reign of Elizabeth I' (1957), pp. 716–54.

73. John Browne vicar of Loughborough to the chancellor of Lincoln Diocese, 22 July 1605; Lincoln Archives Office, MS COR/M/2, no.8.

74. Miss Judith Maltby has investigated a number of these cases from East Anglia and Huntingdonshire, evidently favouring the 'Prayer Book Anglican' thesis. (Information communicated in Oxford at a Colloquium for Local Reformation Studies, April 1980.) The case of Mr Gulliforde vicar of Wye in Kent, referred to twice above, appears to have been of the same order, with parishioners objecting to various pieces of 'puritan' practice, especially in the administration of the occasional offices. Since Wye probably had more recusants than any other parish in East Kent I tend to be strengthened in a rather different estimate of these complaints as indicative of the habits of church papists.

75. Lake, *Anglicans and Puritans*, p.164.

76. Freeman, 'The Parish Ministry', p.55.

77. Lake, *Anglicans and Puritans?*, chapter 4, 'Richard Hooker'.

78. Howson, *A second sermon*, pp. 39, 43–4; Balcanquall, *The honour of christian churches*, p. 22.

79. This was said in Barnstaple in the early 1580s by one of the supporters and offsiders of the radical minister Eusebius Paget, and in defiance of a faction of the town who had demanded the communion on Christmas Day. (Dr Williams's Library, MS Morrice B II, fol. 69$^\mathrm{v}$.)

80. Jeremy Boulton, 'The Limits of Formal Religion: Administration of Holy Communion in Late Elizabethan and Early Stuart London', *London Journal*, 10 (1984), 135–54.

81. John Randall, *Three and twentie sermons, or, catechisticall lectures upon the sacrament of the Lords Supper. Preached monthly before the communion* (London, 1630). pp. 3, 5.

82. Donald A. Spaeth, 'Common Prayer? Popular Observance of the Anglican Liturgy in Restoration Wiltshire', in *Parish Church and People: Local Studies in Lay Religion, 1350–1750*, ed. Susan Wright (London, 1988), pp. 125–51.

83. Cathedral Archives and Library, Canterbury, MS X. 10. 13, fold 24 et seq.

84. Collinson, *Religion of Protestants*, p. ix n. 2.

85. Gratia Johnson, household servant of Henry Hayward, butcher of Herne in Kent, gave evidence in July 1606 in the case of Butler contra Crumpe of how on a certain Sunday she 'made bold' to sit at the end of the pew in Herne church where Mother Crumbe and Butler's wife usually sat when Mother Crumpe came into church (late!) 'and sat her downe upon her knees in the same pewe . . . and when she arose from her kneeling she the said Susan Crompe set her selfe downe upon the seat . . .' (Cathedral Archives and Library, Canterbury, MS X. 11.10, fol. 8$^\mathrm{r}$.)

86. John Angier, *An helpe to better hearts, for better times: indeavoured in severall sermons preached in the year 1638* (London, 1647), p. 75.

87. Mark Byford's paper on William Sheppard of Heydon was communicated at the Colloquium for Local Reformation Studies held at Sheffield in April 1988 and will form part of his forthcoming Oxford doctoral dissertation on the Church and religion in Elizabethan Essex. I am most grateful to Mr Byford for allowing me to use his material on Sheppard.

88. Sheppard's 'Epitome' occupies fols 100$^\mathrm{r}$–3$^\mathrm{r}$ of the parish register of Heydon, Essex Record Office, MS D/P 135/1/1.

89. A similar pattern of charity is inferred in the will of John Gylderde, parson of Runwell, Essex, another celibate, made on 5 June 1551. The residue of Gylderde's estate was left to provide dowries for the poor maidens of the village and for 'mending of the most noisome highways about Runwell'. (Greater London Central Record Office, MS DL/C/357, fols 36–37.) I owe this reference to Mr Brett Usher.

90. This sermon, also entered in the parish register (fol. 57), proved a calamity for Sheppard, since in it he was moved by the occasion of the festival of

Christ's circumcision and naming as Jesus to exhort his parishioners, in 1581 of all years, to 'studye to be . . . true Jesuytts'.

91. George Carleton, *The Life and Death of Bernard Gilpin* (London, 1727 edn), pp. 29–31, 43–44, 91–92. Gilpin's confessional ambivalence, of which there is some evidence in the Life, is discussed by David Marcombe, 'Bernard Gilpin: Anatomy of an Elizabethan Legend', *Northern History*, 16 (1980).

92. Haigh, 'Anticlericalism and the English Reformation', *The English Reformation Revised*, pp. 73–74.

93. Freeman, 'The Parish Ministry', pp. 429, 438–39.

94. Ibid., pp. 418–19.

95. Collinson, 'Cranbrook and the Fletchers', p. 427.

96. Thomas Ballow rector of Belleau ('alias Helloe') to the surrogate of Stamford, 24 August 1609; Lincoln Archives Offices, MS COR/M/2, no. 39.

97. For example, the godly Richard Rothwell's daily routine was said to have consisted of mornings spent in study and afternoons 'going through his Parish and conferring with his people'. (Clarke, *Lives of Thirty-Two English Divines*, p. 70.)

98. Collinson, *Religion of Protestants'*, p. 106; Collinson, *Birthpangs of Protestant England*, pp. 67–68.

99. Freeman, 'The Parish Ministry', p. 384.

100. Cathedral Archives and Library, Canterbury, MS X. 11.9, fol. 18^r.

101. Patrick Collinson, ' "A Magazine of Religious Patterns": An Erasmian Topic Tranposed in English Protestantism', in *Godly People*, pp. 499–526.

102. Clarke, *Lives of Thirty-Two English Divines*, pp. 13, 59, 133–34, 171; Samuel Clarke, *The Lives and Deaths of Eminent Persons* (London, 1675), p. 461.

103. *The Works of Geoffery Chaucer*, ed. F. N. Robinson (Oxford, 1957 edn), pp. 21–22.

104. Ex inf. Mark Byford.

105. Freeman, 'The Parish Ministry', pp. 378–39.

106. Ibid., p. 377.

107. J. Sharpe, 'Defamation and Sexual Slander in Early Modern England: the Church Courts at York', Borthwick Papers, 58 (York, 1980); J. Sharpe, '"Such Disagreement betwyx Neighbours": Litigation and Human Relations in Early Modern England', in *Disputes and Settlement: Law and Human Relations in the West*, ed. John Bossy (Cambridge, 1983); Martin Ingram, *Church Courts, Sex and Marriage in England, 1570–1640* (Cambridge, 1987), pp. 292–319.

108. This follows the suggestions of Ingram, *Church Courts*.

109. John Bossy, 'The Social History of Confession in the Age of Reformation', *Transactions of the Royal Historical Society*, fifth series, 25 (1975), pp. 21–38.

110. Patrick Collinson, 'The Role of Women in the English Reformation Illustrated by the Life and Friendships of Anne Locke', in *Godly People*, pp. 273–87.

111. John Rylands University Library of Manchester, Rylands English MS 524.

112. Pantin, *English Church in the Fourteenth Century*, pp. 197, 209.

113. *Sermons and Remains of Hugh Latimer*, ed. G. E. Corrie, Parker Society (Cambridge, 1845), p. 180.

114. Thomas Cartwright, *Two very godly and comfortable letters* (1589), in *Cartwrightiana*, eds Albert Peel and Leland H. Carlson, Elizabethan Nonconformist Texts 1 (London, 1951), 88–105.

115. William Perkins, *Of the calling of the ministerie, two treatises, discribing the duties and dignities of their calling, delivered publickly in the Universitie of Cambridge* (London, 1605), pp. 28–29.

116. John Robinson, *Works*, ed. R. Ashton (1851), ii, 60

117. Anthony Sparrow, *A sermon concerning confession of sinnes, and the power of absolution* (London, 1637), p.17. Sparrow's sermon was reprinted in 1704.

118. Spaeth, 'Common Prayer?', pp. 125–51.

119. How polemical is shown by the judicious Hooker's autograph notes on the margins of the book written against him, *A christian letter.* 'How this asse runneth kicking up his heels as if a summerfly had stung him.' *Richard Hooker's Of the Laws of Ecclesiastical Polity: Attack and Response*, ed. John E. Booty, *Folger Library Edition of the Work of Richard Hooker*, iv (Cambridge, Massachusetts 1982), 42.

Chapter 4 : England and International Calvinism, 1558–1640 1

1. The occasion was the dedication of a literary work of seminal importance, the English version of the book of poems and emblems called *Het Theatre* (earlier printed in London in Dutch and French), translated by the young Edmund Spenser as *A Theatre . . . [of] Worldlings* (1569). See J. van Dorsten, *The Radical Arts: First Decade of an Elizabethan Renaissance* (Leiden and London, 1970), pp. 75–85. Van Dorsten suspects Noot of having been a member of the Family of Love.

2. W. B. Rye, *England as Seen by Foreigners in the Days of Elizabeth and James I* (1865), p. 70; British Library MS Add. 33271 fol. 15ᵛ. I am grateful to Professor G. R. Elton for helping with the dating of Bacon's speech, which was made in the House of Commons in Mary's last parliament.

3. Beza to Bullinger, 3 September (1566), *Correspondance de Théodore de Bèze*, vii (1566), ed. H. Meylan et al. (Geneva, 1973), no. 500; Beza to Bullinger, 29 July 1567, *Correspondance*, viii (1567) (Geneva, 1976), no. 566; Bullinger to Beza, 11 February 1568, *Correspondance*, ix (1568) (Geneva, 1978), no. 587.

4. Dewey D. Wallace Jr, *Puritans and Predestination* (Chapel Hill, North Carolina 1982).

5. The most recent account is A.D.M. Pettergree, 'The Strangers and their Churches in London, 1550–1580' (unpublished Oxford D. Phil. thesis, Oxford, 1983). See also P. Denis, 'Les Églises d'etrangers à Londres jusqu'á la mort de Calvin: de l'église de Jean Lasco à l'établissement du calvinisme' (unpubl. *mémoire de licence, Liège*, 1974); and Frederick A. Norwood, 'The Strangers' "Model Churches" in Sixteenth-Century England', in *Reformation*

Studies: Essays in Honor of R. H. Bainton, ed. F. H. Littell (Richmond, VA, 1962) and his *Strangers and Exiles: A History of Religious Refugees* (Nashville and New York, 1969), i, 263–308. The magisterial study is still Baron F. de Schickler, *Les églises du refuge en Angleterre,* 3 vols. (Paris, 1892). J. Lindeboom, *Austin Friars: History of the Dutch Reformed Church in London, 1550–1950,* English Tr. D. de Iongh (The Hague, 1950) is a slighter work.

6. Émile Doumergue, *Jean Calvin: Les hommes et les choses de son temps* (repr. Geneva, 1969), iii., appendix 5, 'Whittingham, le prétendu beau-frère de Calvin', pp. 666–75.

7. Beza to Bishop Edmund Grindal, 8 Mar. 1569, *Correspondance de Théodore de Beze,* x (1569), ed. A. Dufour et al. (Geneva, 1980), no. 658.

8. Full references for much of what follows will be found in my essay 'Calvinism with an Anglican Face', *Archbishop Grindal, 1519–1583: The Struggle for a Reformed Church* (1979), pp. 125–52.

9. *The Seconde Parte of a Register,* ed. A. Peel (Cambridge, 1915), i. 58.

10. P. Denis, ' Un combat aux frontières de l'orthodoxie: la controverse entre Acontius et Des Gallars sur la question du fondement et des circonstances de l' église', *Bulletin d' Humanisme et Renaissance,* 38 (1976), 55–72

11. This letter was suppressed in the 1575 edition. See P.G. Bietenholz, 'Limits to Intolerance: The Two Editions of Beza's *Epistolae Theologicae,* 1573', *Bulletin d' Humanisme et Renaissance,* 35 (1973), pp. 311–13.

12. Des Gallars to Grindal, 31 January (1569 or 1570) (preface to *Divi Irenaei Graeci scriptoris . . . libri quinque adversus portentosas haereses Valentini et aliorum* (Geneva, 1570), *Correspondance de Théodore de Bèze,* x, app. III, pp. 267–73. In dispensing the funds left for charity by their brother Robert Nowell, Alexander Nowell, dean of St Paul's and author of the standard catechism of the English Church, and Lawrence Nowell, dean of Lichfield, made payments to the most dissident of the learned strangers, Corro, Reina and the French theologian Peter Baro, as to impeccable Calvinists. (*The Spending of the Money of Robert Nowell,* ed. A. B. Grosart (London, 1877), pp. 62–65, 100–6.)

13. George Gifford, *A briefe discourse of certaine points of the religion which is among the common sort of christians which may bee termed the Countrie Divinitie* (1581).

14. J. A. van Dorsten, *Poets, Patrons, and Professors: Sir Philip Sidney, Daniel Rogers, and the Leiden Humanists* (Leiden, 1962); James M. Osborn, *Young Philip Sidney, 1572–1577* (New Haven, 1972); R.C. Strong and J.A. van Dorsten, *Leicester's Triumph* (Leiden, 1964).

15. This paragraph follows and quotes from S.L. Adams, 'The Protestant Cause: Religious Alliance with the European Calvinist Communities as a Political Issue in England, 1585–1630' (unpublished D. Phil. thesis, Oxford, 1973). I am grateful to Dr Adams for his permission to cite his thesis. See also his essays 'The Road to La Rochelle: English Foreign Policy and the Huguenots, 1610–1629', *Proceedings of the Huguenot Society of London,* 22 (1975),

414–29, and 'Foreign Policy and the Parliaments of 1621 and 1624', in *Faction and Parliament: Essays on Early Stuart History*, Kevin Sharpe (ed.) (Oxford, 1978), pp. 139–71.

16. *John Stubbe's Gaping Gulf*, ed. L.E. Berry (Washington, DC, 1968), p. 86.

17. To the references to be found in my essay 'The Elizabethan Puritans and the Foreign Reformed Churches in London', *Proceedings of the Huguenot Society of London*, 20 (1964), 528–55, repr. in Collinson, *Godly People*, pp. 245–72, add *The Spending of the Money of Robert Nowell*, pp. 62–65, 100–6.

18. Archives d'Etat, Geneva, Pièces Historiques 2066. See n.21 below.

19. Archives of the French Protestant Church of London, MS 194.

20. National Archives, SP 12/161/21.

21. The journal is in Archives d'Etat, Geneva, Pièces Historiques 2066. I am most grateful to Simon Adams for allowing me to use his transcript of this remarkable source, which he intends to publish. On Maillet's mission, see L. Cramer, *La seigneurie de Genève et la maison de Savoie de 1559 à 1603* (2 vols, Geneva and Paris, 1912) and in *Bulletin de la société d'histoire et d'archéologie de Genève*, 3 (1905), pp. 385–404. Part of a letter from Beza to Walsingham introducing Maillet is printed in Paul-F. Geisendorf, *Théodore de Bèze* (Geneva, 1967), p. 369.

22. 'Qui estoit cause que ceux qui estoyent tels, contribuyoient plus largement afin de n'estre suspects et de religion contraire.'

23. David Cressy, 'Binding the Nation: The Bonds of Association, 1584 and 1696', in *Tudor Rule and Revolution: Essays for G.R. Elton from his American Friends*, ed. Delloyd G. Gutha and John W. McKenna (Cambridge, 1982), pp. 217–34.

24. Patrick Collinson, *The Religion of Protestants* (Oxford, 1982), pp. 126–27; information supplied by Simon Adams.

25. National Archives, SP 14/4/8, SP 15/36/29. On the evolution of the procedures for conducting charitable collections or 'briefs' see C.J. Kitching, 'Fire Disasters and Fire Relief in Sixteenth-Century England: The Nantwich Fire of 1583', *Historical Research*, 54 (1981), 171–87.

26. *Secondé Parte of a Register*, ii, 58.

27. With what follows I have been helped by Dr O.P. Grell's unpublished doctoral dissertation (European University Institute, Florence, 1983): 'Austin Friars and the Puritan Revolution: The Dutch Church in London, 1603–1642', and in particular by ch. 5,: 'The Collections for the Palatinate'.

28. *Ecclesiae Londino-Batavae Archivum*, ed. J.H.Hessels, iii (Cambridge, 1897), no. 2239.

29. John Rushworth, *Historical Collections*, i (1862), 60–61; *Ecclesiae Londino-Batavae Archivum*, iii, no. 1805. See Marc L. Schwarz, 'Lord Saye and Sele's Objections to the Palatinate Benevolence of 1622: Some New Evidence and its Significance', *Albion*, 4 (1972), 12–22.

30. *Ecclesiae Londino-Batavae Archivum*, iii. nos 1985, 2100, 2239, 2262, 2263, 2276, 2281.

31. *Letters of John Davenport, Puritan Divine*, ed. I. M. Calder (New Haven, 1937), pp. 26–27, 29–30.

32. I.M. Calder, *Activities of the Puritan Faction of the Church of England, 1625–33* (1957); R.P. Stearns, *The Strenuous Puritan: Hugh Peter, 1598–1660* (Urbana, IL, 1954), pp. 34, 40; Frances Rose-Troup, *John White the Patriarch of Dorchester* (1930), pp. 43–44; A.P. Newton, *The Colonising Activities of the English Puritans* (New Haven, 1914); Valerie Pearl, *London and the Outbreak of the Puritan Revolution: City Government and National Politics, 1625–43* (Oxford, 1961), p. 179.

33. Grell, op. cit.

34. Samuel Clarke, *The Lives of Sundry Eminent Persons in this Later Age* (1683), ii, pp. 102–4.

35. *Cal. SP Dom. Charles I, 1627–1628*, 532; *Cal. SP Dom. Charles I, 1629–1631* 205; *Ecclesiae Londino-Batavae Archicum*, iii, nos. 1906, 2045, 2046.

36. Ibid., iii, scattered between nos 1851 and 2426. See especially no. 2191.

37. Grell, op. cit. The largest single contributor was apparently the Puritan civil lawyer Dr Henry Hawkins who in his will left £300 'to the distressed ministers of the disturbed protestant churches in Germanie' and an equivalent sum to the Feoffees for Impropriations, part of which was diverted to the Palatinate fund after the suppression of Feoffees, according to the terms of his will. William Gouge was an executor. (National Archives, HCA 1/32/1, fol. 90, cited by Grell; B.P. Levack, *The Civil Lawyers in England, 1603–1641* (Oxford, 1973), pp. 186–87, 237; *Ecclesiae Londino-Batavae Archivum*, iii, nos. 2158, 2160, 2179, 2267.)

38. *Puritan Manifestoes* ed. W.H. Frere and C.E. Douglas (1954 edn), p.19.

39. References for what follows will be found in my essay 'The Elizabethan Puritans and the Foreign Reformed Churches in London' already noted.

40. *Correspondance*, vii, nos 472, 476, 479, 500; viii, nos. 524, 534, 544, 547, 554, 557, 559, 560, 566, 573; ix, no. 615.

41. Thomas Sampson to Beza, 20 July 1567, *Correspondance*, viii, no, 565; Beza to Bullinger, 19 June 1566, *Correspondance*, vii, no. 476. A singularly unhelpful letter, as it transpired, was the one which Beza wrote to Grindal on 27 June 1566, which was pirated by the authors of the *Admonition*. (*Correspondance*, vii, no. 479; *Puritan Manifestoes*, pp. 43–55.)

42. Beza's dedication to Mildmay was dated 27 February 1570. (*Correspondance*, xi, no. 744.) For Beza and the *Admonition*, see Patrick Collinson, *The Elizabethan Puritan Movement* (1967), p. 121. Beza's later relations with the Church of England, and especially with Archbishop John Whitgift, are documented in John Strype, *Life of John Whitgift* (Oxford, 1822), ii, 105–6, 160–73, iii, 300–4.

43. *The Zurich Letters*, ed. H. Robinson, Parker Society, 52 (Cambridge, 1846), p. 291.

44. Grell, op. cit.

45. Quoted, Adams, 'The Protestant Cause', p.80

46. Commission of Bishop King to the Dutch congregations of London and Colchester, 9 August 1615; *Ecclesiae Londino-Batavae Archivum*, iii, no.

1758. For other references, see my 'The Elizabethan Puritans and the Foreign Reformed Churches in London'.

47. BL,MS Add. 4736, fol. 166ᵛ; R.M. Gillon, *John Davidson of Prestonpans* (1936), pp. 262–63; William Bradshaw, *A myld and just defence of certeyne arguments* (1606), p. 5.

48. I owe this careful phrase to an unpublished paper by Dr F.H. Shriver, 'The Character of Jacobean Anglicanism: Arminians, Calvinists and the Via Media'.

49. Thomas Rogers, *The Faith Doctrine and Religion Professed and Protected in the Realm of England*, (1607, repr. Parker Society, 40 (Cambridge, 1854)) was entitled in the original version of 1584, *The English creede, consenting with the true, auncient, catholique, and apostolique church.*

50. Wallace, *Puritans and Predestination*, pp. 16–17.

51. Norman Sykes, *The Church of England and Non-Episcopal Churches in the Sixteenth and Seventeenth Centuries: An Essay Towards the Historical Interpretation of the Anglican Tradition from Whitgift to Wake* (1949); idem, *Old Priest and New Presbyter* (1956).

52. Peter Lake, *Moderate Puritans and the Elizabethan Church* (Cambridge, 1982).

53. Collinson, *Elizabethan Puritan Movement*, p. 104; *The Works of John Whitgift*, ed. J. Ayre, i, Parker Society, 46 (Cambridge, 1851), 247–48, 436; H.C. Porter, *Reformation and Reaction in Tudor Cambridge* (Cambridge, 1958), pp. 359–60, 350–51.

54. *The Common Places of the most famous and renowned Divine Doctor Peter Martyr* (1583), Anthonie Marten's dedicatory epistle to Elizabeth I; David J. Keep, 'Theology as a Basis for Policy in the Elizabethan Church', in *The Materials Sources and Methods of Ecclesiastical History, Studies in Church History*, 11 ed. D. Baker (Oxford, 1975), 263–68, and Dr Keep's 1970 Sheffield Ph.D. thesis, 'Henry Bullinger and the Elizabethan Church'.

55. The prefaces to the following English editions of Luther, all printed by the Huguenot printer Vautrouiller, establish Foxe's prime responsibility for the whole enterprise: *A commentarie...upon the epistle to the Galatians* (1575); *A commentarie upon the fiftene psalms, called psalmi graduum* (1577); *A right comfortable treatise containing fourteene pointes of consolation for them that labour* (1578); *Special and chosen sermons* (1578).

56. C. M. Dent, *Protestant Reformers in Elizabethan Oxford* (Oxford, 1983) pp. 100–1.

57. Patrick Collinson, 'The Beginnings of English Sabbatarianism', in Collinson, *Godly People*, pp. 429–43.

58. Dent, *Protestant Reformers*, pp. 1–2, 91–102.

59. Amid a plethora of literature, two salient points: R.T. Kendall, *Calvin and English Calvinism to 1649* (Oxford, 1979); Perry Miller, *The New England Mind: The Seventeenth Century* (New York, 1939).

60. Kendall, *Calvin and English Calvinisim*, pp. 13–15.

61. Basil Hall, 'Calvin against the Calvinists', in G. Duffield (ed.), *John Calvin, Courtenay Studies in Reformation Theology*, 1 (Appleford, 1966),

19–37: B.G. Armstrong, *Calvinism and the Amyraut Heresy* (Madison, WI 1969); *The Work of William Perkins*, ed. I. Breward, The Courtenay Library of Reformation Classics, 3 (Appleford, 1970); Kendall, *Calvin and English Calvinism.*

62. Perry Miller misrepresented 'federal' theology as a radical departure from Calvinisim in *The New England Mind.* Among other critics, see Jens G. Moller, 'The Beginnings of Puritan Covenant Theology', *Journal of Ecclesiastical History*, 14 (1963), 46–67.

63. Jill Raitt, *The Eucharistic Theology of Theodore Beza: Development of the Reformed Doctrine* (Chambersburg, 1972); John S. Bray, *Theodore Beza's Doctrine of Predestination* (Nieuwkoop, 1975); Wallace, *Puritans and Predestination:* J.P. Donnelly, *Calvinism and Scholasticism in Vermigli's Doctrine of Man and Grace* (Leiden, 1976); C.J.M. Burchill, 'Girolamo Zanchi in Strasbourg, 1533–1563' unpublished Ph.D. thesis, Cambridge, 1980.

64. This is an evident weakness of Kendall's *Calvin and English Calvinism.*

65. A.W. Harrison, *Arminianism* (1937); N.R.N. Tyacke, 'Arminianism in England in Religion and Politics, 1604–1640 (unpublished D.Phil thesis, Oxford, 1968); N. Tyacke, 'Arminianism and English Culture', in A. C. Duke and C. A. Tamse, eds, *Britain and The Netherlands, Church and State since the Reformation* (The Hague, 1981), 94–117; Wallace, *Puritans and Predestination*, ch. 3 'The Arminian Controversies, 1610–1650'.

66. Six of Hemmingsen's works were published in English between 1569 and 1581 (*STC*, nos. 13057–68). See especially his *A learned and fruitful commentarie upon the epistle of James the Apostle* (1577) and *A postil or exposition of the Gospels* (edns 1569(2), 1574, 1578).

67. However, Dr Tyacke has voiced a caveat against the notion that Arminianism was 'a catch-all term of abuse', insisting that contemporaries had an exact sense of what it was ('Arminianism and English Culture', pp. 94–95).

68. Wallace, *Puritans and Predestination*, p. 101; Tyacke, 'Arminianism and English Culture', p.94.

69. Quoted by N.R.N. Tyacke, *History*, 69 (1984), 135. Compare Porter, *Reformation and Reaction in Tudor Cambridge* with Lake, *Moderate Puritans*, pp. 218–26, and with Wallace, *Puritans and Predestination*, pp. 66–68.

70. Tyacke, 'Arminianism in England'; idem 'Puritanism, Arminianism and Counter-Revolution', in Conrad Russell, ed., *The Origins of the English Civil War* (1973), pp. 119–43. On the complexities of the political and other motives for James's theological preference, which cannot be labelled simply 'Calvinist', see F.H. Shriver, 'Orthodoxy and Diplomacy'; Christopher Grayson, 'James I and the Religious Crisis in the United Provinces 1613–19'; and John Platt, 'Eirenical Anglicans at the Synod of Dort', in *Reform and Reformation: England and the Continent, c.1500–c.1750*, *Studies in Church History*, Subsidia 2, ed. D. Baker (1979), 195–219, 221–43.

71. Collinson, *The Religion of Protestants*, pp. 168–69; *Ecclesiae Londino-Batavae Archivum*, iii, p. 1414.

72. Tyacke, 'Puritanism, Arminianism and Counter-Revolution', pp. 121, 129.

73. Kevin Sharpe, 'Archbishop Laud and the University of Oxford', in *History and Imagination*, ed. Hugh Lloyd-Jones, Valerie Pearl and Blair Worden (London, 1981), pp. 146–64; Peter White, 'The Rise of Arminianism Reconsidered', *Past and Present*, 101 (1983), 34–54. I have benefited from discussing these issues with Dr F. H. Shriver.

74. Quoted, Collinson, *The Religion of Protestants*, pp. 82.

75. Platt, 'Eirenical Anglicans'; Bishop Lake's correspondence with Samuel Ward, Bodleian Library, MS Tanner 74, fols. 174, 190; for Lake, see Collinson, *The Religion of Protestants*, pp. 85–88.

76. I am indebted for several points to Dr Peter Lake's article, 'Calvinism in the English Church, 1570–1635', *Past and Present* 114 (1987), 32–76.

77. Quoted, R.G.Usher, *The Reconstruction of the English Church* (1910), ii, 165.

78. H.R. Trevor-Roper, *Archbishop Laud, 1573–1645* (1940), p. 376; William Prynne, *Canterburies Doome* (1646), pp. 391–93; *The Works of William Laud*, iv (Oxford 1584), 312–13; vi (Oxford, 1857), 417–18; vii (Oxford, 1860), 22, 126–27, 151. For what the queen of Bohemia thought of Laud's 'cold compliments', see *Cal. SP Dom.* 1634–1635, p. 509.

79. This relatively familiar aspect of the Laudian religious reaction is extensively documented in Hessels, *Ecclesiae Londino-Batavae Archivum*, and covered in Schickler's *Les églises du refuge*, Lindeboom's *Austin Friars*, and most recently by Dr Grell.

80. Quoted, Marc L. Schwarz, 'Lay Anglicanism and the Crisis of the English Church in the Early Seventeenth Century', *Albion* (1982), 2.

81. Information communicated by György E. Szönyi in a paper 'English Books in Hungary (1575–1714)'; Breward, *Work of Perkins*, pp. 106–7, 130

Chapter 5 : The Puritan Character : Polemics and Polarities in Early Seventeenth-Century English Culture

1. A.S.P. Woodhouse, ed. *Puritanism and Liberty: Being the Army Debates (1647–9)* (London 1938), p. 105.

2. Some of the more significant contributions to the debate since 1980 are contained in: Paul Christianson, 'Reformers and the Church of England under Elizabeth I and the Early Stuarts', *Journal of Ecclesiastical History*, 31 (1980), 463–82; Patrick Collinson, 'A Comment: Concerning the Name Puritan,' ibid., 483–88; Richard L. Greaves, *Society and Religion in Elizabethan England* (Minneapolis, 1981); Peter Lake, *Moderate Puritans and the Elizabethan Church* (Cambrige, 1982); Dewey D. Wallace, Jr. *Puritans and Predestination: NC, Grace in English Protestant Theology*, 1525–1695 (Chapel Hill, 1982); William Hunt, *The Puritan Moment: The Coming of Revolution in an English County* (Cambridge, MA, 1983); Michael G.

Finlayson, *Historians, Puritanism, and the English Revolution: The Religious Factor in English Politics before and after the Interregnum* (Toronto, 1983); Patrick Collinson, *English Puritanism* (London, 1983); Richard L. Greaves, 'The Puritan-Nonconformist Tradition in England, 1560–1700: Historiographical Reflctions,' *Albion*, 17 (1985), 449–86; Ann Hughes, *Politics, Society, and the Civil War in Warwickshire', 1620–1660* (Cambridge, 1987); Margo Todd, *Christian Humanism and the Puritan Social Order* (Cambridge, 1987); Peter Lake, *Anglicans and Puritans? Presbyterianism and English Conformist Thought from Whitgift to Hooker* (London, 1988).

3. Douglas Bush, *English Literature in the Earlier Seventeenth Century, 1600–1660* (Oxford, 1945), p. 197.

4. The reference is to the religious best-seller by Bishop Lewis Bayly, *The practise of pietie* (more than 50 licensed or pirated editions were issued between 1612 and 1640).

5. John Earle, *The Autograph Manuscript of 'Microcosmographie'* (Leeds, 1966), pp. 115–21; idem, *Microcosmographie* (London, 1628). The character, titled 'A shee-Puritan' in the manuscript, reappears as 'A Shee-precise Hypocrite' in the published work.

6. Earle, *Autograph Manuscript of 'Microcosmographie'*, p. 143.

7. Heinz Bergner, ed., *English Character-Writing* (Tübingen, 1971), pp. 21–22, 58–59. See also J.W. Smeed, *The Theophrastan 'Character': The History of a Literary Genre* (Oxford, 1985).

8. Patrick Collinson, '"A Magazine of Religious Patterns": An Erasmian Topic Tranposed in English Protestantism', in Patrick Collinson, *Godly People: Essays on English Protestantism and Puritanism* (London, 1983), pp. 499–525.

9. 'The Life and Death of Mr John Carter, Who died Anno Christi, 1634', in Samuel Clarke, *A Collection of the Lives of Ten Eminent Divines* (London, 1662), pp. 1–24, quotations on p. 8.

10. Richard Kilby, *Hallelu-iah: Praise yee the Lord, for the unburthening of a loaden conscience* (Cambridge, 1618), p. 28; Richard Kilby, *The Burthen of a loaden conscience* (Cambridge, 1608), pp. 2, 95.

11. R.T. Kendall, *Calvin and English Calvinism to 1649* (Oxford, 1979); P.G. Lake, 'Calvinism and the English Church, 1570–1635,' *Past and Present*, 114 (1987), 32–76, quotation on p. 75.

12. M.M. Knappen, ed., *Two Elizabethan Puritan Diaries, by Richard Rogers and Samuel Ward* (Chicago, 1933); Alan Macfarlane, ed., *The Diary of Ralph Josselin, 1616–1683* (London, 1976); Michael McGiffert, ed., *God's Plot: The Paradoxes of Puritan Piety; Being the Autobiography and Journal of Thomas Shepard* (Amherst, 1972).

13. Paul S. Seaver, *Wallington's World: A Puritan Artisan in Seventeenth-Century London* (Stanford, 1985). For further reflections on Wallington, based in part on material not used by Professor Seaver, see G.E. Aylmer, 'Collective Mentalities in Mid Seventeenth-Century England, i, The Puritan Outlook', *Transactions of the Royal Historical Society*, 5th series, 36 (1986), 21–24.

14. British Library, Harleian MS 70, fols 13^v, 54, 57^v, 9.
15. Dorothy M. Meads, ed., *Diary of Lady Margaret Hoby, 1599–1605* (London, 1930).
16. John Rylands University Library of Manchester, Rylands English MS. 874; printed (but incompletely and inaccurately) in Roland G. Usher, ed., *The Presbyterian Movement in the Reign of Queen Elizabeth as Illustrated by the Minute Book of the Dedham Classis', 1582–1589*, Camden, 3rd series, 8 (London, 1905).
17. Greater London Record Office, Liber Examinationum Testium ac Partium Principalium, 1586–1591, Marten vs. Parker; information kindly imparted by Mr Alan Pennie.
18. Susan Hardman [now Hardman Moore], 'Return Migration from New England to England, 1640–1660' (Ph.D. thesis, University of Kent at Canterbury, 1987), pp. 359–65. For additional information I am indebted to a typescript by Dr Hardman Moore 'The Mentality of a Reformer: The Case of Thomas Larkham (1602–1669)'.
19. Josselin's pastoral competence has been recently and indepedently challenged by Eamon Duffy, 'The Godly and the Multitude in Stuart England', *The Seventeenth Century*, 1 (1986), 38; and by Margaret Spufford, 'Can we count the "Godly" and the "Conformable" in the Seventeenth Century?', *Journal of Ecclesiastical History*, 36 (1985), 428–38. Josselin was not necessarily entirely at fault. Thomas Shepard, who was at Earls Colne before him, found it 'a most profane place' with only one inhabitant that had 'any godliness' about him. But Shepard, too, was an extreme pastoral pessimist. (McGifferet, ed., *God's Plot*, pp. 74, 48.)
20. David Leverenz, *The Language of Puritan Feeling: An Exploration in Literature, Psychology, and Social History* (New Brunswick, NJ, 1980), pp. ix, 4, 17; McGiffert, ed., *God's Plot*, pp. 98, 135, 18.
21. McGiffert, ed., *God's Plot*, pp. 24, 18.
22. Collinson, 'A Comment: Concerning the Name Puritan', 483–88; Collinson, *English Puritanism*. See also much of the argument of Patrick Collinson, *The Religion of Protestants: The Church in English Society, 1559–1625* (Oxford, 1982).
23. N.H. Keeble, ed., *The Autobiography of Richard Baxter*, abridged by J.M. Lloyd Thomas (London, 1974), p. 6.
24. Quoted in Nicholas Tyacke, *Anti-Calvinists: The Rise of English Arminianism, c. 1590–1640* (Oxford, 1987), p. 185. The context is supplied by Kenneth Fincham, 'Prelacy and Politics: Archbishop Abbot's Defence of Protestant Orthodoxy', *Bulletin of the Institute of Historical Research*, 61 (1988), 36–64.
25. [Henry Parker?], *A Discourse concerning Puritans* (London, 1641), pp. 37, 50.
26. The notion was launched by Nicholas Tyacke in a seminal essay, 'Puritanism, Arminianism, and Counter-Revolution', in Conrad Russell, ed., *The Origins*

of the English Civil War (London, 1973), pp. 119–43. See also Tyacke's *Anti-Calvinists* and my *Religion of Protestants*.

27. J.S. Morrill, *The Revolt of the Provinces: Conservatives and Radicals in the English Civil War, 1630–1650* (London, 1976), p. 153; Tyacke, *Anti-Calvinists*, p. 236; Pierpont Morgan Library, MS MA 276 (Philipps MS. 13891), p. 18; William Prynne, *Histrio-Mastix* (London, 1633), p. 799.

28. *A Discourse concerning Puritans*, p. 9.

29. Collinson, *Religion of Protestants*, p. 78.

30. Tyacke, *Anti-Calvinists*, p. 187; McGiffert, ed., *God's Plot*, pp. 48, 50.

31. See the critical comments of Peter Lake, 'Puritan Identities', *Journal of Ecclesiastical History*, 35 (1984), 112–23; Kenneth Fincham and Peter Lake, 'The Ecclesiastical Policy of King James I', *Journal of British Studies*, 24 (1985), 169–207; Greaves, 'The Puritan Nonconformist Tradition', 449–86.

32. I owe this point to an intervention by Professor J. Sears McGee at the seminar in the Clark Library.

33. Collinson, *English Puritanism*, pp. 10–11; *A Discourse concerning Puritans*, pp. 10, 49 [misnumbered 48]–50. For an application of the scheme of the *Discourse* to the needs of modern historiography, see Christopher Hill, *Society and Puritanism in Pre-Revolutionary England* (London, 1964). For an apt comment on Widdowes, see Tyacke, *Anti-Calvinists*, p. 81.

34. Martin Ingram, *Church Courts, Sex, and Marriage in England,1570–1640* (Cambridge, 1987), p. 121.

35. Quoted in Peter Lake, 'Matthew Hutton—A Puritan Bishop?', *History*, 64 (1979), 189.

36. Nicholas Cranfield and Kenneth Fincham, eds, 'John Howson's Answers to Archbishop Abbot's Accusations at his "Trial" before James I at Greenwich, 10 June 1615', *Camden Miscellany*, 29, Camden 4th series 34 (London, 1987), 319–41.

37. Cranfield and Fincham, eds 'John Howson's Answers to Archbishop Abbot's Accusations', 334, 333; Patrick Collinson, 'The Jacobean Religious Settlement: The Hampton Court Conference', in Howard Tomlinson, ed., *Before the English Civil War: Essays on Early Stuart Politics and Government* (London, 1983), pp. 27–51; Stuart Clark, 'King James's Daemonologie: Witchcraft and Kingship', in Sydney Anglo, ed., *The Damned Art: Essays in the Literature of Witchcraft* (London, 1977), pp. 156–81.

38. Hunt, *The Puritan Moment*, p. 145.

39. Bartimaeus Andrewes, *Certaine Verie worthie, godly and profitable Sermons* (London, 1583), p. 185.

40. *A Discourse concerning Puritans*, p. 2.

41. William P. Holden, *Anti-Puritan Satire, 1572–1642* (New Haven, 1954).

42. William Barlow, *The Eagle and the Body* (London, 1609), sig. B2ᵛ.

43. See Anthony Esler, *The Aspiring Mind of the Elizabethan Younger Generation* (Durham, 1966).

44. Robert Parker Sorlien, ed., *The Diary of John Manningham of the Middle Temple, 1602–1603* (Hanover, NH, 1976), p. 219; see also pp. 44, 77, 114, 124, 163.

45. All Souls College, Oxford, MS 185, fols 180v–81r.

46. *Twelfth Night*, act 2, scene 3.

47. Edwin M. Schur, *Labeling Deviant Behavior: Its Sociological Implications* (New York, 1971), quotations on pp. 40, 8, 10.

48. J.C. Davis, *Fear, Myth, and History: The Ranters and the Historians* (Cambridge, 1986); G.E. Aylmer' 'Did the Ranters Exist?', *Past and Present*, 117 (1987), 208–19.

49. John Lofland, *Deviance and Identity* (Englewood Cliffs, NJ, 1969).

50. Martin Ingram, 'Ridings, Rough Music and Mocking Rhymes in Early Modern England', in Barry Reay, ed., *Popular Culture in Seventeenth-Century England* (London, 1985), pp. 166–97; idem, 'Ridings, Rough Music, and the "Reform of Popular Culture" in Early Modern England', *Past and Present*, 105 (1984), 79–113; D.E. Underdown, 'The Taming of the Scold: The Enforcement of Patriarchal Authority in Early Modern England', in Anthony Fletcher and John Stevenson, eds, *Order and Disorder in Early Modern England* (Cambridge, 1985), pp. 116–36; Andrewes, *Sermons*, p. 185.

51. Duffy, 'The Godly and the Multitude', 38–40. Martin Ingram's comment (*Church Courts, Sex, and Marriage*, p. 94) is apt: 'The evidence from Wiltshire and elsewhere suggests that it is a mistake to overemphasise either the presence of "godly" groups or the existence of people largely indifferent to religion. Most people were located somewhere between these poles.' See the case of the Wiltshire village of Wylye, discussed by Dr Ingram, ibid., pp. 118–23. See also Martin Ingram, 'Religion, Communities, and Moral discipline in Late Sixteenth-and Early Seventeenth-Century England: Case Studies', in Kaspar von Greyerz, ed., *Religion and Society in Early Modern Europe, 1500–1800* (London, 1984), pp. 177–93.

52. Arthur Dent, *The Plaine Mans Path-way to Heaven* (London, 1601), p. 287; John Darrell, *A Treatise of The Church: Written against them of the Separation, commonly called Brownists* (London, 1617), 25 [misnumbered 23], 28–29; McGiffert, ed., *God's Plot*, p. 9; Ian Breward, ed., *The Work of William Perkins* (Appleford, 1970), p. 297.

53. Leverenz, *The Language of Puritan Feeling*, p. 27.

54. Stuart Clark, 'Inversion, Misrule, and the Meaning of Witchcraft', *Past and Present*, 87 (1980), 98–127; Michael Hunter, 'The Problem of "Atheism" in Early Modern England', *Transactions of the Royal Historical Society*, 5th series 35 (1985), 135–57; David Kunzle, 'World Upside Down: The Iconography of a European Broadsheet Type', in Barbara A. Babcock, ed., *The Reversible World: Symbolic Inversion in Art and Society* (Ithaca, NY, 1978) pp. 39–94.

55. J. Sears McGee, 'William Laud and the Outward Face of Religion', in Richard L. DeMolen, ed., *Leaders of the Reformation* (Selinsgrove, 1984), p. 341.

56. Hunter, 'The Problem of "Atheism" ', 156–57.

57. Foxe quoted in William Haller, *Foxe's Book of Martyrs and the Elect Nation* (London, 1963), p. 250; John Norden, *A Mirror For The Multitude* (London, 1586), pp. 34, 38–39.

58. Breward, ed., *The Work of Perkins*, p. 297; Thomas Cooper, *The Blessing of Japheth* (London, 1615), p. 31; Thomas Cooper, *The Cry and Revenge of Blood* (London, 1620), p. 4.

59. Peter Lake, 'William Bradshaw, Antichrist, and the Community of the Godly', *Journal of Ecclesiastical History*, 36 (1985), 570–89, quotation on p. 572; see also idem, 'Calvinism and the English Church'.

60. Quoted in Collinson, *Religion of Protestans*, p. 230.

61. Idem, *English Puritanism*, p. 17.

62. Richard Baxter, *A Holy Commonwealth* (London, 1659), p. 457.

63. Jeremy Goring, *Godly Exercises or the Devil's Dance? Puritanism and Popular Culture in Pre-Civil War England* (London, 1983), pp. 3, 23–24.

64. Henry Anisworth, *The communion of saints* (Amsterdam, 1607), p. 137.

65. Lake, 'William Bradshaw', 579.

66. George H. Williams et al. eds, *Thomas Hooker: Writings in England and Holland, 1626–1633* (Cambridge, MA, 1975), p. 110. But Hooker's son-in-law Thomas Shepard had decided by the early 1630s that 'mixed communion' in the use of the sacrament was wrong; that was one of his motives for migrating to New England (McGiffert, ed., *God's Plot*, p. 55).

67. Stephen Bredwell, *The Raising Of the Foundations of Brownisme* (London, 1588), pp. 39–40. For a rare example of 'unnatural' shunning, see Ingram, *Church Courts, Sex, and Marriage*, p. 251: at Melksham in Wiltshire in 1622 a pair of religious radicals, Henry Cheevers and Mary Banfield, made a written covenant to forsake their respective spouses and to live as man and wife, 'David and Jonathan'. They denounced their legitimate children as bastards because they were not 'converted to the faith and were not in the state of regeneration'.

68. Lake, 'William Bradshaw', 580. See also the references cited in Collinson, *Religion of Protestants*, p. 277.

69. Perry Miller, *Orthodoxy in Massachusetts, 1630–1650: A Genetic Study* (Cambridge, 1933), pp. 73–101, quotation on p.99.

70. Michael E. Moody, 'A Critical Edition of George Johnson's *A Discourse of Some Troubles and Excommunications in the Banished English Church at Amsterdam, 1603* (Ph.D. thesis, Claremont Graduate School, 1979).

71. Keith Wrightson, 'The Puritan Reformation of Manners, with Special Reference to the Counties of Lancashire and Essex, 1640–1660' (Ph.D. thesis, University of Cambridge, 1974).

72. *Calendar of State Papers, Domestic: Charles I, 1633–1634*, p. 275. See also Thomas G. Barnes, 'County Politics and a Puritan Cause Célèbre: Somerset Churchales, 1633', *Transactions of the Royal Historical Society*, 5th series 9 (1959), 103–22.

73. Lawrence M. Clopper, ed., *Chester*, Records of Early English Drama (Toronto, 1979), pp. 197–99, 234–36, 184, 104–5, 109–10.

74. National Archives, State Papers 12/223/47, 224/54, 55, 57, 58, 61, 65, 66; *Acts of the Privy Council of England* 17:202; National Archives, Star Chamber 5 B 31/4.

75. Edgar I. Fripp, *Shakespeare: Man and Artist* (London, 1938), ii, 838–45, quotations on 842, 841, 843. See also Hughes, *Politics, Society, and the Civil War in Warwickshire*, pp. 82–84.

76. David Underdown, *Revel, Riot, and Rebellion: Popular Politics and Culture in England, 1603–1660* (Oxford, 1985), pp. 44–72. Information on Bridport was kindly supplied by Mr John Perris of the History of Parliament Trust.

77. On Dorchester, see Frances Rose-Troup, *John White, the Patriarch of Dorchester (Dorset) and the Founder of Massachusetts, 1575–1648* (New York, 1930); and Collinson, *Religion of Protestants*, pp. 271–72. On Banbury, see the references supplied in note 72; idem, *Religion of Protestants*, pp. 145–46; and Ben Jonson's *Bartholomew Fair*, act 1, sc. 3.

78. Hughes, *Politics, Society, and the Civil War in Warwickshire*, pp. 82–84, quotation on 84.

79. Ingram, *Church Courts, Sex, and Marriage*, pp. 292, 356 and passim.

80. J.A. Sharpe, *Defamation and Sexual Slander in Early Modern England: The Church Courts at York* (York; Borthwick Institute of Historical Research, University of York, [1980?]); J.A. Sharpe, "'Such Disagreement betwyx Neighbours': Litigation and Human Relations in Early Modern England', in John Bossy ed., *Disputes and Settlements: Law and Human Relations in the West* (Cambridge, 1983), pp. 167–87; Ingram, *Church Courts, Sex, and Marriage*, pp. 171–88, 292–319, quotations on pp. 315, 175. Professor Stone's remark was made in *The Family, Sex, and Marriage in England, 1500–1800* (London, 1977), p. 98.

81. See John Bossy, 'Blood and Baptism: Kinship, Community, and Christianity in Western Europe from the Fourteenth to the Seventeenth Centuries', in Derek Baker, ed., *Sanctity and Secularity: The Church and the World*, Studies in Church History, 10, ed. D. Baker (Oxford: 1973), 129–43.

82. Cathedral Archives and Library, Canterbury, MSS x.10.11, fol. 47 and x. 10. 12, fol. 143.

83. Wrightson, 'Puritan Reformation of Manners'; and further exploration of these ideas in Keith Wrightson and David Levine, *Poverty and Piety in an English Village: Terling', 1525–1700* (New York, 1979). See also Ingram, *Church Courts, Sex, and Marriage*, passim, and his 'Religion, Communities, and Moral Discipline'.

84. Ingram, *Church Courts, Sex, and Marriage*, pp. 101–2.

Chapter 6 : Sects and the Evolution of Puritanism

1. *The Remains of Edmund Grindal*, ed. W. Nicholson, Parker Society (Cambridge, 1843), 471.

2. Christopher Hill, *Society and Puritanism in Pre-Revolutionary England* (London, 1966); especially the chapters called 'The Spiritualization of the Household' and 'Individuals and Communities'.

3. H. Richard Niebuhr, *The Social Sources of Denominationalism* (New York, 1929).

4. John T. McNeill, *Unitive Protestantism: The Ecumenical Spirit and its Persistent Expression* (London, 1964), but deriving from lectures delivered in Chicago in 1928; Ian Henderson, *Power Without Glory: A Study in Ecumenical Politics* (London, 1967). This book was provocatively dedicated 'to the good Christians in every denomination who do not care greatly whether there is one church or not'.

5. Robert Allen, *The doctrine of the gospel* (London, 1606), sigs *4–5.

6. Richard Bernard, *The good mans grace or his stay in all distresse* (London, 1621), sigs C3^v–4^v.

7. Christopher Hill, 'From Lollards to Levellers', in *The Collected Essays of Christopher Hill, ii, Religion and Politics in 17th Century England* (Brighton, 1986), 89–116. See Dr Hill's more recent uncertainty ('From Lollards to Levellers' having first appeared in 1978) whether there indeed was 'a continuity underground from Lollards via Anabaptism and Familism to the sectarians of the 1640s' (*Three British Revolutions, 1641, 1688, 1776*, ed. J.G.A. Pocock (Princeton, 1980), p. 114).

8. William Haller, *The Rise of Puritanism* (New York, 1938), and *Liberty and Reformation in the Puritan Revolution* (New York, 1955).

9. Richard G. Davies, 'Lollardy and Locality', *Transactions of the Royal Historical Society*, sixth series, I (1991), 191–212. But Professor Ann Hudson, as an authority on Wycliffite texts who is impressed with their endurance in the Lollard tradition, takes a rather different view in *The Premature Reformation: Wycliffite Texts and Lollard History* (Oxford, 1988).

10. 'Sermon of the Bishop of St. Davids 12 November 1536', BL Cotton MS Cleopatra E.V, fol. 415; *The Acts and Monuments of John Foxe*, ed. S.R. Cattley, viii (London, 1839), 499, 330, 118.

11. Henry Hart, *A godly newe short treatyse instructyng every parson: howe they should trade theyr lyves* (London, 1548); John Champneys, *The harvest is at hand. Wherein the tares shall be bound, and cast into the fyre and brent* (London, 1548). On the freewillers and other mid-Tudor radicals, see J. W. Martin, *Religious Radicals in Tudor England* (London and Ronceverte, West Virginia, 1989), which corrects the terminologically anachronistic I.B. Horst, *Radical Brethren: Anabaptism and the English Reformation to 1558* (Nieuwkoop, 1972).

12. *Acts and Monuments of John Foxe*, viii, 187–88.

13. The mid-Tudor freewillers are not mentioned at all in Peter White, *Predestination, Policy and Polemic: Conflict and Consensus in the English Church from the Reformation to the Civil War* (Cambridge, 1992).

14. Alastair Hamilton, *The Family of Love* (Cambridge, 1981); J. W. Martin, 'Elizabethan Familists and English Separatists' and other relevant essays in *Religious Radicals*; and, most recently and authoritatively, Christopher Marsh, 'The Family of Love in English Society, 1550–1630' (Cambridge Ph.D. thesis, 1992).

15. *The Writings of Robert Harrison and Robert Browne*, ed. A. Peel and L.H. Carlson, *Elizabethan Nonconformist Texts*, no. 2 (London, 1953), 26–69, and especially 52–53. Further light is shed on the background to Harrison's 'Treatise' in the exchanges between Harrison and a fellow Separatist Thomas Wolsey and Edward Fenton by Dr Michael Moody in an unpublished paper which he kindly allowed me to read: 'Thomas Wolsey: A Forgotten Founding Father of English Separatism and a "Judaiser." ' See also Dr Moody's article 'Trials and Travels of a Nonconformist Layman: The Spiritual Odyssey of Stephen Off-wood, 1564–c. 1635', *Church History*, 51 (1982), 157–171.

16. My source is Michael Moody's use of Stephen Offwood, *An advertisement to John Delecluse and Henry May the Elder* (Amsterdam?, 1633?).

17. See, for example, John Field's complaint to Anthony Gilby that the bishop's persecution had driven some into sectarian extremes, "as full of errors as opinion". (Field to Gilby, 4 August 1572, Cambridge University Library, MS Mm.I.43. pp. 443–44.) Cf. the Cambridgeshire ministers who told the Privy Council in 1584 that if they were deprived, their flocks would be corrupted by the local Familists: and the authors of a 'generall supplication' made to Parliament in 1586 who protested that the 'faithful ministers' were so far from schism that they "chieflie more than anie of those which laie this blame upon them have laboured with manie, and by Gods blessing prevailed with a number, to the keeping in the unitie of (the Church) such as otherwise would have departed from it." *The Seconde Parte of a Register*, ed. A. Peel (Cambridge, 1915), i, 229–30, ii, 81.

18. Patrick Collinson, 'A Magazine of Religious Patterns': An Erasmian Topic Transposed in English Protestantism', in *Godly People: Essays in English Protestantism and Puritanism* (London, 1983), pp. 499–525.

19. Stephen Brachlow, *The Communion of Saints: Radical Puritan and Separatist Ecclesiology 1570–1625* (Oxford, 1988). Among other antiseparatist works now lost, note the Gloucestershire minister John Sprint's *Considerations* and *Arguments* (both 1607), which were answered in Henry Ainsworth's *Counterpoyson* (Amsterdam, 1608), and a third book by Bernard, also answered by Ainsworth, *The separatists schisme.*

20. *Certain observations of that reverend, religious and faithfull servant of God, and glorious martyr of Iesus Christ, M. Randal Bate* (Amsterdam, c. 1625). See Stephen Foster, *Notes from the Caroline Underground: Alexander Leighton, the Puritan Triumvirate ard the Laudian Reaction to Nonconformity* (Hamden, Connecticut, 1978), pp. 23, 89

21. John Sprint, as quoted by Ainsworth in *Counterpoyson*, sig. A.

22. Wiltshire Record Office, MS D 3/4/2. I owe this reference to Dr Michael Moody.

23. Wiltshire Record Office, MS QS/GR/E 1604, fol. 148v, MS D 3/4/3 1607 (calendared in *HMC Report, Various Collections*, i, 76). I owe these references to Dr Moody and Dr Martin Ingram. See M.E. Reeves, 'Protestant

Nonconformity', in *The Victoria County History of Wilshire*, iii, 95–101. Light is shed on conferences in Wiltshire in Thomas White's *A discoverie of Brownisme* (London, 1605) and in Francis Johnson's *An inquirie and answer of Thomas White his discoverie of Brownisme* (Amsterdam, 1606).

24. J. Allin and T. Shepherd, *A defence of the answer* (London, 1648), p. 6. See also their *A defence of the nine positions* (London, 1645).
25. John Cotton, *The way of the congregational churches cleared* (London, 1648), p. 7. See also John Robinson, *A justification of separation* (Amsterdam, 1610), in *Works of John Robinson*, ed. R. Ashton (London, 1851), ii, 8, and Richard Bernard's account of conferences with John Smyth in *Christian advertisements* (London, 1608), pp. 30–37.
26. Kent Archives Office, Cathedral Archives and Library Canterbury, MS Z.4.4, fols 67v–9r.
27. Bodleian Library, Ashmolean MS 826, fols 223r–6v. I owe this reference to Dr Michael Moody. John Silliman is named as a convicted Separatist in National Archives, SP 38/6, s.v. 25 May 1599.
28. Samuel Clarke, *Lives of Thirty-two English Divines* (London, 1677), p. 15; John Rylands University Library Manchester, Rylands English MS 525; William Wilkinson, *A confutation of certain articles delivered unto the Familie of Love* (London, 1579), preface. Further information on Orinel will be found in Margaret Spufford, *Contrasting Communities: English Villagers in the Sixteenth and Seventeenth Centuries* (Cambridge, 1974), pp. 245–48, and in Christopher Marsh, 'The Family of Love'.
29. Richard Rogers, *Seven treatises containing such directions as is fathered out of the holie scriptures* (London, 1603), fold 477–95. The Wethersfield covenant was publicised in further editions of the *Seven treatises* in 1604, 1605, 1607, 1610, 1616, 1627 and 1630, suggesting that historians should also take account of what in crime reports is called 'the copycat factor'. See Collinson, *Godly People*, p. 545.
30. Henry Ainsworth, *A brief answer to Mr Bernards book intituled the separatists schisme* (part of his *Counterpoyson*), pp. 155–56; *Works of Robinson*, ii, 101. See also *The Works of John Smith*, ed. W.T, Whitney (Cambridge, 1915), ii, 334.
31. Cotton, *The way of the congregational churches cleared*, pt. 1, p. 20.
32. Michael E. Moody, 'Puritan Versus Separatist: A New Letter', *Journal of the United Reformed Church History Society*, 2 (1981), 243–45.
33. See Peel and Carlson's remarks in *Writings of Robert Harrison and Robert Browne*, pp. 4–5, glossing items in their bibliography, pp. 545–56.
34. White, *Discoverie of Brownisme*, p. 25.
35. This passage draws freely upon the following works of Clapham: *A briefe of the Bible drawne first into English poesy* (Edinburgh, 1596), *Bibliotheca theologica* (Amsterdam, 1597), *The syn against the Holy Ghost* (Amsterdam, 1598), *The discription of a true visible christian* (Amsterdam?, 1599), *Antidoton: Or a soveraigne remedie against schisme and heresie* (London,

NOTES TO PAGES 140–145

1600), *A manuell of the Bibles doctrine* (London, 1606), *Errour on the right hand* (London, 1608), *Errour on the left hand* (London, 1608).

36. For an account of what may have motivated rank-and-file Separatists in retreating from their schism to the established churches of England or the Netherlands, among them the desire to secure regular baptism for their children, see A.C. Carter, *The English Reformed Church in Amsterdam in the Seventeenth Century* (Amsterdam, 1964), pt 1, chap. 4, and A. C. Carter, 'John Robinson and the Dutch Reformed Church', in *Studies in Church History*, 3, ed. G. J. Cuming (Leiden, 1966), 232–41.

37. John Smyth, *Paralleles, censures, observations* (Middelburg, 1609), in *Works*, ii, 331 et seq; Richard Bernard, *Plaine evidences* (London, 1610); Kenneth Fincham, *Prelate as Pastor: The Episcopate of James I* (Oxford, 1990), pp. 193–94, 300–1.

38. Henry Jacob, *A declaration and plainer opening of certain points* (Middelburg, 1612), pp. 5–6.

39. *Elizabethan Episcopal Administration: An Essay in Sociology and Politics*, ed. W.P.M. Kennedy, iii. *Alcuin Club Collections*, no. 27 (Oxford, 1925), 350

40. See pp. 145–72 below.

41. Peter Lake, 'Presbyterianism, the Idea of a National Church and the Argument from Divine Right', in *Protestantism and the National Church in Sixteenth-Century England*, ed. P. Lake and M. Dowling (London, 1987), pp. 193–224.

42. D. J. Plumb, 'John Foxe and the Later Lollards of the Thames Valley' (Cambridge Ph.D. thesis, 1987), and his 'The Social and Economic Spread of Rural Lollardy: A Reappraisal', in *Voluntary Religion*, 111–129; Marsh, 'Family of Love'; William Stevenson, 'The Economic and Social Status of Protestant Sectarians in Huntingdonshire, Cambridgeshire and Bedfordshire 1650–1725' (Cambridge Ph.D. thesis, 1990). See also some of the contributions to *Religious Dissent in East Anglia*, ed. E. S. Leedham-Green, Cambridge Antiquarian Society (Cambridge, 1991).

Chapter 7 : The English Conventicle

1. Roger Quatermayne, *Quatermayns Conquest over Canterburies Court* (London, 1641), pp. 28–31. See Murray Tolmie, *The Triumph of the Saints: The Separate Churches of London, 1616–1649* (Cambridge 1977), pp. 30–31.

2. 16 Charles II c.4.

3. Guildhall Library, MS 7411/2, fol 42r. I owe this reference to Dr O.P. Grell.

4. Richard Baxter, *The saints everlasting rest* (London, 1650) pp. 290–91. I owe this reference to Dr Eamon Duffy.

5. Quatermayne, *Quatermayns conquest*, pp. 28–29.

6. Richard Leake, *Foure sermons* (London, 1599), p. 8.

7. Quatermayne, *Quatermayns conquest*, p. 29.

8. Robert Cawdrey, *A table alphabeticall, conteyning and teaching the true writing and understanding of hard usuall English wordes* (London, 1604).

9. W.S. Holdsworth, *A History of English Law* (3rd edn, London, 1923), iii, 204

10. *The Staffordshire Quarter Sessions Rolls, i, 1581–1589*, ed. S.A.H. Burne, William Salt Socy (Kendal, 1931) pp. xxxvi, 145, 153, 155.

11. J.A. Sharpe, 'Crime and Delinquency in an Essex Parish, 1600–1640', in *Crime in England, 1550–1800*, ed. J. S. Cockburn (London, 1977), pp. 106–7.

12. For Perne's mistake, see Inner Temple Library, MS Petyt 538.47, fols 492–93; for mine, *The Elizabethan Puritan Movement* (London, 1967), p. 379, *Godly People: Essays on English Protestantism and Puritanism* (London, 1983), p. 10. The record is put straight by Felicity Heal, 'The Family of Love and the Diocese of Ely', *Studies in Church History*, 9 pp. 217–18.

13. *The Records of a Church of Christ in Bristol, 1640–1687*, ed. Roger Hayden Bristol Record Society, 27 (Bristol, 1974).

14. I have followed William Hawkins, *A Treatise of the Pleas of the Crown*, (5th ed, 1771), Sir Matthew Hale, *Pleas of the Crown* (1707) and Holdsworth, *History of English Law* with some guidance from Dr John Stevenson.

15. William Lambarde, *Eirenarcha: or of the office of the Iustice of Peace* (London, 1592), p. 197. Cf. William Lambarde, *The duties of constables* (London, 1604), pp. 49–50, Michael Dalton, *The countrey Iustice* (London, 1619), p. 341.

16. James Balmford in *A short and plaine dialogue concerning the unlawfulness of playing at cards or tables, or any other game consisting in chance* (London, 1593), argues that these games 'must needes be somewhat evill, because they somewhat depend upon chance'. To win money at play was a kind of theft. (Sigs A4^v–6).

17. Hawkins, *Pleas of the Crown*, p. 157.

18. John Udall, *Two sermons of obedience to the gospell* (London, 1596), sig. I iiiij; *The Seconde Parte of a Register*, ed. A. Peel (Camrbidge 1915), i, 231; Quatermayne, *Quatermayns conquest*, p. 27.

19. Compare the argument of 'Magistracy and Ministry' in my *The Religion of Protestant: the Church in English Society, 1559–1625* (Oxford, 1982), pp. 141–88.

20. Bodleian Library, MS Tanner 65, no. 35. fols 67–76; Winthrop quoted in D.G. Allen, *In English Ways: The Movement and the Transformation of English Local Custom to Massachusetts Bay in the Seventeenth Century* (Chapel Hill, North Carolina, 1981), p. 181.

21. Holdsworth, *History of English Law*, viii, 327.

22. Hawkins, *Pleas of the Crown*, pp. 155–58; Hale, *Pleas of the Crown*, p. 137; Holdsworth, *History of English Law*, viii, 324–27.

23. Lambarde, *Eirenarcha*, pp. 177–78.

24. 35 Elizabeth I c. 1.

25. Richard Burn, *Ecclesiastical Law* (London, 1781), ii, 159.
26. J. E. Neale, *Elizabeth I and her Parliaments, 1584–1601* (London, 1957), pp. 280–97.
27. Collinson, *Elizabethan Puritan Movement*, pp. 437–38; Keith Thomas, *Religion and the Decline of Magic* (London, 1971), pp. 483–85.
28. Holdsworth, *History of English Law'*, vi, 198; *Elizabethan Episcopal Administration*, ed. W.P.M. Kennedy, Alcuin Club Collections, 27 (London, 1925), iii, 350.
29. 16 Charles II c. 4; 22, Charles II c. 1. It would be useful to trace the origin of this phrase. See Bishop Aylmer's visitation articles for London diocese of 1586: 'Whether any schoolmasters under pretence of catechising their scholars . . . do keep lectures, readings, or expositions in their houses. . .?' *Elizabethan Episcopal Administration*, iii, 205.
30. Bodleian Library, MS Rawlinson D 1136, p. 145. I am grateful to Mr Anthony Fletcher for supplying the reference and to Dr Kenneth Fincham for securing a transcript of Sir Thomas Schlater's Doubts in the 'Act for Conventicles.'
31. 'Sir Roger Bradshaigh's Letter-Book' (absit author), *Transactions of the Historic Society for Lancashire and Cheshire*, 63 (1912), 120–73; William C. Braithwaite, *The Second Period of Quakerism* (2nd edn, Cambridge, 1961), pp. 22–23.
32. *The Life of Adam Martindale Written by Himself*, ed R. Parkinson, Chetham Society, 4 (Manchester, 1845), 145, 194–95
33. *The Diary of the Rev. Henry Newcome*, ed. T. Heywood, Chetham Society, 17 (Manchester, 1849), 126n.
34. *The Autobiography of Henry Newcome M.A.*, ed R. Parkinson, Chetham Society, 26 (Manchester, 1852), i, 27, 34, 94; *Diary of Henry Newcome*, passim; *Records of a Church of Christ*, p. 85; *The Rev. Oliver Heywood B.A., 1630–1702: His Autobiography, Diaries (etc.)*, ed J. Horsfall Turner (Brighouse, 1882), i, 20.
35. Collinson, *Godly People*, pp. 486–87, 521 n98, 538–39.
36. Christopher Hill, 'From Lollards to Levellers', in *Rebels and their Causes: Essays in Honour of A.L. Morton*, ed. Maurice Cornforth (London, 1978), pp. 49–67, In a later essay 'A Bourgeois Revolution?', Dr Hill appears to hold a more open mind on 'whether or not there was a continuity underground from Lollards via Anabaptists and Familists to the sectaries of the 1640s'. *Three British Revolutions, 1641, 1688, 1776*, ed. J.G.A. Pocock (Princeton 1980), p. 114: Dr Hill's readers will detect in what follows critical refractions not only of this argument but of his brilliant essays 'The Spiritualization of the Household' and 'Individuals and Communities' in his *Society and Puritanism in Pre-Revolutionary England* (1964).
37. Anne Hudson, 'The Examination of Lollards', *Bulletin of the Institute of Historial Research*, 46 (1973) 145–59; J.A.F. Thompson, *The Later Lollards* (Oxford, 1965), p. 229.
38. Anne Hudson, ed., *Selections from English Wycliffite Writings* (Cambridge, 1978); Anne Hudson, ed., *English Wycliffite Sermons* (Oxford, 1983);

Anne Hudson, *Lollards and their Books* (London, 1985). Compare Margaret Aston's 'cultural' rather then textual approach in various essays in *Lollards and Reformers: Images and Literacy in Late Medieval Religion* (London, 1984).

39. But note also the contemporary term 'Lollardorum familia'; Hudson, *Selections*, p. 9.

40. *Heresy Trials in the Diocese of Norwich, 1428–31*, ed. Norman P. Tanner, Camden fourth series, 20 (1977), 140.

41. Thompson, *Later Lollards*, pp. 5, 72, 81, 241.

42. Euan Cameron, *The Reformation of the Heretics: The Waldenses of the Alps, 1480–1580* (Oxford, 1984), p. 261.

43. 'Euan Cameron, 'The "Godly Community" in the Theory and Practice of the European Reformation', in *Voluntary Religion: Studies in Church History*, 23, ed. W. J. Sheils and Diana Wood (Oxford, 1986), 131–53.

44. John Fines, 'Heresy Trials in the Diocese of Coventry and Lichfield, 1511–12, *Journal of Ecclesiastical History*, 13 (1962), 162; *The Acts and Monuments of John Foxe*, ed S.R. Cattley (London, 1837), iv, 558.

45. Ibid., 224–25.

46. Hudson, *Selections*, pp. 116–17.

47. *Heresy Trials*, 140. Cf. Thomas More, *A Dialogue Concerning Heretics: The Complete Works of St Thomas More*, vi, eds T.M.C. Lawler, G. Marc', hadour and R. C. Marius (New Haven, 1981), 240.

48. K. E. Wrightson, 'The Puritan Reformation of Manners: With Special Reference to the Counties of Lancashire and Essex, 1640–1660' (Cambridge Ph.D. thesis, 1974), p. 38.

49. Canterbury Cathedral Archives and Library, MS Z.4.4, fols 67^v–9^r. Other examples will be found in Miles Huggarde, *The displaying of the Protestantes* (London 1556), fols 121–5 (Marian); Sir Julius Caesar to Lord Burghley, 18 May 1584, BL, MS Lansdowne 157, no. 74, fol. 186 (Elizabethan); the High Commission case of James and Elizabeth Andrews of Cambridge, Bodleian Library, MS Tanner 65, no. 35, fols 67–76 (Caroline).

50. William Wilkinson, *A confutation of certaine articles delivered unto the Family of Love* (London, 1579), sigs iiii, Ai^r.

51. Cameron, *Reformation of the Heretics*, pp. 68–69.

52. *Acts and Monuments of Foxe*, vi (London, 1838), 677.

53. BL, MS Harleian MS 419, fols 117–22. Compare William Perkins's list of 'common opinions' (old-fashioned and popish) which his late Elizabethan catechism was designed to replace with acceptable and godly opinions. (*The foundation of Christian religion* (London, 1641), Preface 'to all ignorant people').

54. I owe this point to Dr Susan Brigden.

55. See my 'The Godly: Aspects of Popular Protestantism', in *Godly People*, pp. 1–17. *The locus classicus* for this type of religious culture is Sir Julius Caesar's description of a 'conventicle' in the Essex parish of Aythorp Roding, BL, MS Lansdowne 157, no. 74, fol 186.

56. *The Diary of Lady Margaret Hoby*, 1599–1601, ed. Dorothy M. Meads (London 1930).

57. John Collings, *A memorial for posteritie* (London, 1647), p. 21.

58. *The argument of Master Nicholas Fuller in the case of Thomas Lord and Maunsell, his clients* (London, 1607), p. 1.

59. Udall, *Two sermons*, sig I iiiij.

60. See the narratives of Thomas Newcome, Adam Martindale and Oliver Heywood, cited elsewhere in this essay.

61. Quoted in G.R. Cragg, *Puritanism in the Period of the Great Persecution, 1660–1688* (Cambridge, 1957), p. 140.

62. Oliver *Heywood's Life of John Angier of Denton*, ed. E. Axon, Chetham Society, new series, 97 (Manchester, 1937), 85.

63. But see Oliver Heywood's vignette of his brother-in-law Thomas Crampton: 'a man of stupendious memory, that I have heard him repeat a sermon almost verbatim, memoriter . . .' (*Oliver Heywood*, i, 36).

64. John Rogers, *Obel or Beth-shemesh* (London, 1653) p. 421. Oliver Heywood's mother related to him 'many passages' of sermons she had heard preached before she was married. (*Oliver Heywood*, p. 53).

65. Peter F. Jensen, 'The Life of Faith in the Teaching of Elizabethan Protestants' (Oxford D.Phil. thesis, 1979), p. 182.

66. A.G. Dickens gives examples in 'Heresy and the Origins of English Protestantism', in Dickens, *Reformation Studies* (London, 1982), pp. 378–79. See two collections of scandalous and heretical sayings culled from sermons in PRO, SP 1/113, fols 106–9, and BL, MS Cotton Cleopatra E. V, fol 397.

67. In the title of his study of the Waldenses of the Alps, already cited.

68. *The heart opened by Christ* (London, 1654), pp. 1–2. 'Forms of Religion without Life do not profit', we read in *The invisible power of God known in weakness with a Christian testimony of the experience and sufferings of Edward Brush aged ninety-one years* (London, 1695), p. 6.

69. *Diary of Henry Newcome*, pp. 14, 36, 41, 83; *Oliver Heywood*, i, 199. Cf. Humphrey Mills's recollection of Richard Sibbes's 'sweet soul-melting Gospel-sermons'. (Rogers, *Obel*, p. 410).

70. Collinson, *Religion of Protestants*, pp. 248–49.

71. Canterbury Cathedral Archives and Library, MS Z.4.4, fol 208. For Turner, see R. J. Acheson, 'Sion's Saint: John Turner of Sutton Valence', *Archaeologia Cantiana*, 99 (1983), 183–97.

72. The defensive phrase was used of meetings gathered in the Wealden town of Cranbrook in the mid 1570s by John Strowd. (Collinson, *Godly People*, p. 418.)

73. *Remarkable Passages in the Life of William Kiffin Written by Himself*, ed. William Orme (London, 1823), pp. 11–14.

74. *Records of a Church of Christ*, pp. 82, 85–86, 97.

75. Canterbury Cathedral Archives and Library, MS X.9.1, fol. 5. I owe this reference to Dr R.J. Acheson.

76. *Records of a Church of Christ*, pp. 88–89.

77. John Browne, *History of Congregationalism and the Memorials of the Churches in Norfolk and Suffolk* (London, 1877), pp. 393–95; G.F. Nuttall, *Visible Saints: The Congregational Way, 1640–1660* (Oxford, 1957) pp. 27–29, 52. Katherine Chidley was the author of *The iustification of the Independent Churches of Christ* (London, 1641).

78. Collinson, 'Cranbrook and the Fletchers: Popular and Unpopular Religion in the Kentish Weald', in *Godly People*, pp. 427–28.

79. G.F. Nuttall, 'Dissenting Churches in Kent before 1700', *Journal of Ecclesiastical History*, 14 (1963), 175–89.

80. Most recently, B.R. White, *The English Separatist Tradition: From the Marian Martyrs to the Pilgrim Fathers* (Oxford, 1971), and Michael R. Watts, *The Dissenters: from the Reformation to the French Revolution* (Oxford, 1978). For a fuller exploration and exposition of the contentious issues hinted at in this paragraph, see my essay 'Towards a Broader Understanding of the Early Dissenting Tradition', in *Godly People*, pp. 527–62.

81. See examples in *Acts and Monuments of Foxe* (London, 1839) viii, 330, 449. It was not some Lollard hedge-priest but Bishop William Barlow who in November 1536 preached that 'where so ever ii or iii simple persons as ii coblers or weavers were in company and elected in the name of God, that ther was the trewe Churches of God'. (BL, MS Cotton Cleopatra E.V, fol 415).

82. *Acts and Monuments of Foxe*, viii 118, 728.

83. References to Newcome, Martindale and Heywood earlier in this essay; add *The Note Book of the Rev. Thomas Jolly . . . Extracts from the Church Book of Altham and Wymondhouses*, ed. Henry Fishwick, Chetham Society, new series, 33 (Manchester, 1895), 120–21.

84. *Two Elizabethan Puritan Diaries by Richard Rogers and Samuel Ward*, ed. M.M. Knappen (Chicago, 1933); *Heywood's Life of Angier*.

85. *Autobiography of Newcome*, i, 14.

86. *The Diary of Ralph Josselin, 1616–1683*, ed Alan Macfarlane, Records of Social and Economic History, 3 (Oxford, 1976). See also Alan Macfarlane, *The Family Life of Ralph Josselin a Seventeenth-Century Clergyman: An Essay in Historical Anthropology* (Cambridge, 1970).

87. *Diary of Josselin*, p. 1; *Autobiography of Newcome*, p. 7. And cf. Heywood: 'When I was a little child I delighted in imitating preachers and acting that part among my playfellows.' *Oliver Heywood*, 1. 157.

88. W.C. Abbott, *The Writings and Speeches of Oliver Cromwell* (Cambridge, Massachusetts, 1947), iii, 62.

89. Richard Bernard, *The ready way to good works* (London, 1635), pp. 281, 311.

90. Richard Rogers, *Seaven treatises* (London, 1605), fol 478^r. Rogers insisted that their meetings were not conventicles 'for the disturbance of the state of the Church and peace thereof'.

91. *Oliver Heywood*, i, 42. See my 'The Role of Women in the English Reformation Illustrated by the Life and Friendships of Anne Locke', in *Godly People*, pp. 273–87.

92. *Life of Martindale*, pp. 61, 66–67.

93. Patrick Collinson, 'A Magazine of Religious Patterns' : An Erasmian Topic Transposed in English Protestantism', in *Godly People*, pp. 499–525.

94. William Bradshaw, *The unreasonablenesse of the separation* (London, 1614), preface. See also Richard Bernard, *Christian adverisements and counsels of peace: also disswasions from the Separatists schisme, commonly called Brownisme* (London, 1608), *Plaine evidences* (London, 1610); Henoch Clapham, *The syn against the Holy Ghost* (Amsterdam, 1598), *Antidoton: or a soveraigne remedie against schisme and heresie* (London, 1600), *Errour on the right hand, through a preposterous zeale* (London, 1608); John Darrell, *A treatise of the Church, written against them of the separation, commonly called Brownists* (London, 1617); Peter Fairlambe, *The recantation of a Brownist* (London, 1606); Henry Jacob, *A defence of the churches and ministery of Englande* (Middleburg, 1599), *A declaration and plaine opening of certaine points* (Middleburg, 1611); John Paget, *An arrow against the separation of the Brownists* (London, 1618). Particular interest attaches to the writings of the reverted Separatists, Clapham, Fairlambe and White, and to the polemics of Bernard, Bradshaw and Darrell, who had all spent time on the Separatist frontier. Jacob was a *complexio oppositorum*. But see the pronouncement in *A declaration and plaine opening*, p.5: 'Howsoever, as to the point of separation, for my part I never was, nor am separated from all publike communion with the congregations of England.'

95. Samuel Clarke, *The lives of sundry eminent persons in this latter age* (London, 1683), p. 170; Samuel Clarke, *A general martyrologie* (London, 1677), pp. 120, 126, 56–57; Samuel Clarke, *The Lives of two and twenty English divines* (London, 1660), p. 73.

96. Quoted in Stephen Foster, *Notes from the Caroline Underground*, Studies in British History and Culture, 6 (Hamden, Connecticut, 1978), p. 27.

97. *Certaine observations of that reverend religious and faithfull servant of God and glorious martyr of Iesus christ, M, Randal Bate* (Amsterdam, 1624?), pp. 177, 183–89. For Bate, see Foster, *Notes*, p. 89 n. 37.

98. Quatermayne, *Quatermayns conquest*, p. 18.

99. Jeremy Corderoy, *Warning for worldlings* (London, 1608), sig. A 10.

100. Collinson, *Religion of Protestants*, p. 277.

101. Jeremy Corderoy, *A short dialogue wherein is proved that no man can be saved without good works* (Oxford, 1604), epistle.

102. Darrell, *Treatise of the Church*, pp. 28–29.

103. Or so I would argue. But strictly speaking, the Separatist platform was laid by Henry Barrow in the form of a quadrilateral, of which the second plank was 'the profane and ungodlie people receved into and retayned in the bozom and bodie of ther churches'. Henry Barrow, 'Foure Causes of Separation', in *The Writings of Henry Barrow, 1587–1590*, ed. Leland H. Carlson, Elizabethan Nonconformist Texts, 3 (London, 1962), 54.

104. Bernard, *Christian advertisements*, p. 86; Stephen Bredwell, *The rasing of the foundation of Brownisme* (London, 1588) p. 20. See also Richard Alison, *A plaine confutation of a treatise of Brownisme* (London, 1590), pp. 12–13: 'In the visible Church of God there will be tares, yea untill the harvest: chaffe among the wheat, goates among the sheep, hypocrites among the true professors: nay to go further, Antichrist for a time sitting in the temple of God, and other monstrous men abiding in the Church, turning the grace of God into wantonnesse.'

105. Henry Ainsworth, *The communion of saints* (Amsterdam, 1607), p. 137.

106. Canterbury Cathedral Archives and Library, MS X.II. 16, fol 103ᵛ.

107. *Thomas Hooker: Writings in England and Holland, 1626–1633* ed. George H. Williams et al., Harvard Theological Studies, 28 (Cambridge Massachusetts, 1975), pp. 110–11; Bernard, *Christian advertisements*, p. 108; Lancelot Dawes, *Two sermons preached at the Assise holden at Carlisle* (Oxford, 1614) pp. 33–35, 38; Richard Kilby, *The burthen of a loaden conscience* (Cambridge, 1608) p. 95; William Crashawe, *The sermon preached at the Crosse Feb. xiiij 1607* (1608).

108. Bredwell, *The rasing of the foundations*, p. 39.

109. Wrightson, 'The Puritan Reformation of Manners', pp. 24–25.

110. *Life of Martindale*, pp. 133, 79, 122.

111. Ibid. p. 129.

112. *Note Book of Thomas Jolly*, pp. 120–21, 128, 133–34; Wrightson, 'The Puritan Reformation of Manners', p. 281.

113. *Diary of Josselin*, pp. 31, 33, 77–79, 81.

114. Ibid., pp. 77, 230, 516, 83.

115. Ibid., pp. 102, 105, 124, 126, 132, 235, 137–38.

116. Ibid., pp. 197, 127, 140, 134–35, 204–5, 210.

117. Ibid., pp. 235, 238, 244, 313.

118. Ibid., pp. 376–77.

119. Wrightson, 'The Puritan Reformation of Manners', p. 273.

120. *Diary of Josselin*, pp. 492, 505.

121. Ibid. pp. 516, 546, 553, 574, 621.

122. *Autobiography of Newcome*, ed Richard Parkinson, Chetham Society, 27 (Manchester, 1862), ii, 257.

123. *Life of Martindale*, p. 173.

Chapter 8: William Sancroft, 1617–1693: A Retiring Disposition in a Revolutionary Age

General Note on Sources: There is no modern biography of Archbishop Sancroft: indeed, apart from eleven columns contributed to the *DNB* by W.H. Hutton and their replacement in the *Oxford Dictionary of National Biography* (2004), only one biography in 300 years: the *Life of William Sancroft Archbishop of Canterbury*, published in 1821 by the vicar of Lambeth, George D'Oyly (2nd revised edition,

1840). D'Oyly printed many documents in extenso, from the Tanner MSS and elsewhere, but not with complete accuracy. Many of the relevant Tanner MSS are also printed in *Memorials of the Great Civil War in England from 1642 to 1652: Edited from Original Letters in the Bodleian Library*, ed. H. Carey, 2 vols (London, 1842). The 1965 Oxford D.Phil. thesis by the living authority on Sancroft, Robert Beddard ('William Sancroft as Archbishop of Canterbury, 1678–90') is not available for consultation in the Bodleian Library. But Dr Beddard has contributed a substantial article to the *Oxford Dictionary of National Biography* (hereinafter *ODNB*). On the other hand, the primary source which is Sancroft's personal archive is copious in the extreme, consisting of correspondence and other materials, to be found in scores of volumes of the Tanner MSS in Bodley (mainly copies in Sancroft's hand of his own letters). The Sancroft MSS in MS Rawlinson D, also in Bodley, comprise no less than one hundred and forty-five notebooks and commonplace books. In the British Library, Harleian MSS 3783, 3784 and 3785 consist mainly of letters to Sancroft. The Harleian material passed through the hands of Sancroft's chaplain, Henry Wharton. But the bulk of the papers was purchased from Sancroft's nephew and steward, William Sancroft, by Dr Thomas Tanner, bishop of St. Asaph, and by him bequeathed to the Bodleian Library. Sancroft appears to have hoarded the written detritus of a lifetime. The contents of the Tanner MSS range from schoolboy essays to the pro-forma notices sent to him from the Convention Parliament of 1689, requiring (in vain) his presence in the House of Lords. When, in the plague year of 1665, Sancroft reached his family home from London, he sat down to write (as he tells us) nine or ten letters. Most of these survive. The principal source for this essay, not always specifically cited, is Tanner, where Sancroft's outgoing letters are mostly filed in (inverse) chronological order; together with Harleian MSS 3783–3785. I have also used the Sancroft-Lloyd correspondence of the last years, since 1991 Lambeth Palace Library (LPL) MS 3894, or rather the transcripts of these letters made by Mrs Barbara Graebe of Fressingfield and deposited in the Emmanuel College Archives (ECA), MS COL.9.8. I have made only a few forays into the Sancroft MSS in Rawlinson D, which would be essential materials for anyone wanting to reconstruct more fully the formation and application of Sancroft's mind. Most of the 145 volumes contain something of note, including theological materials, sermon notes, and even 'extracts from Beaumont and Fletcher, Shakespeare, Sidney etc.' (MS Sancroft 29), Not all the notebooks are filled up. For example, MS Rawlinson D 816 consists of 436 pages, 'quorum multa vacua'; in fact only 66 pages have been put to use. But, given Sancroft's distinctively economical handwriting, others contain hundreds of thousands of words each. I have made a cursory inspection of Sancroft's books in Emmanuel College, schooled by Dr Sarah Bendall, and advised by Dr Arnold Hunt. I am grateful to the master and fellows of Emmanuel College for access to its library and archives, and for the invitation to give a lecture on Sancroft on the 300th anniversary of his death, which was the occasion for writing an earlier version of this essay. I am also in debt to Professor John Morrill and Dr Mark Goldie for their comments.

1. For that we must look to Dr Robert Beddard.
2. James Raven, 'The Sancrofts', *Suffolk Institute of Archaeology and Natural History*, 7 (1891), 68–76; Charles Boyce, 'The Family of William Sancroft, Archbishop of Canterbury', *Suffolk Institute of Archaeology and Natural History*, 20 (1930), 116–23; William Sancroft to William Dillingham, 29 September [1640], MS Tanner 467, no. 2, fol. 19.
3. William Sancroft to Bishop John Cosin of Durham (draft), 29 August 1661, MS Tanner 467, fol. 72; Cosin to Sancroft, 23 August, 3 September 1661, MS Harl. 3784, fols 29, 34; Ralph Widdrington to Sancroft, 16 February 1655(/6), MS Harl, 3783, fol. 99.
4. Willim Sancroft to his brother, Thomas Sancroft, 10 July 1650, MS Tanner 56, no. 114, fol. 216.
5. John Gayer to William Sancroft, 7 May 1655, MS Harl, 3783, fol. 128.
6. William Sancroft to Ralph Widdrington, 21 October 1648, MS Tanner 57, no. 201, fol. 384.
7. William Sancroft (the nephew) to Francis Sancroft, 21 January 1667(8), MS Tanner 40, no. 108, fol. 166. For evidence that Sancroft had carefully nurtured his nephew's career, see MS Tanner 45, fol. 216, MS Tanner 49, fols 98–99.
8. See, as a source of much of what immediately follows, Sarah Bendall, Christopher Brooke, Patrick Collinson, *A History of Emmanuel College Cambridge* (Woodbridge, 1999).
9. Rare but not unique. The schoolroom exercises of the royal princes, the future Edward VI and James I's elder son, Prince Henry, survive. MS Tanner 467 contains schoolboy essays in Latin; MS Sancroft 31 numerous sermon notes made by Sancroft, probably in his Suffolk schooldays. 'William Sandcroft is my name . . .' occurs on the flyleaf of Sancroft 31.
10. MS Tanner 465, no. 37, fol. 73^{v}. MS Sancroft 31 includes 200 folios of the sermons (64 in number) preached (in Emmanuel?) by William Sandcroft senior.
11. G(eorge) D(avenport) to William Sancroft, 15 January 1662(/3), MS Harl. 3784, fols 96–97.
12. John Rogers to William Sandcroft, 4 September n.y. (1634), MS Harl. 3783, fol. 52; John Ward to William Sandcroft, 19 October 1634, ibid., fol. 39.
13. Bendall, Brooke and Collinson, *A History of Emmanuel College*, pp. 224–26, 243–46; my article on Holdsworth in *ODNB*.
14. William Sancroft to Richard Holdsworth, 19 August, n.y., MS Tanner 61, no. 31, fol. 64^{v}; William Sancroft to Bishop Ralph Brownrigg, 24 August 1649, MS Tanner 56, no. 52, fol. 95.
15. *Emmanuel College Magazine*, 1 (1889), 4 (1892, 1893).
16. MS Sancroft 80, p. 3. This MS is 'in a pitiful state' and cannot be consulted. I am grateful to Dr Barker-Benfield and Mrs Mary Clapinson for supplying me with a partial transcript.
17. Nicholas Tyacke, *Anti-Calvinists: The Rise of English Arminianism, c. 1590–1640* (2nd revised edn., Oxford, 1990); Anthony Milton, *Catholic*

and Reformed: The Roman and Protestant Churches in English Protestant Thought, 1600–1640 (Cambridge, 1995); David M. Hoyle, '"Near Popery Yet No Popery": Theological Debates in Cambridge 1590–1644', unpublished Cambridge Ph.D. thesis, 1991; BL, MS Harl. 7019, 'Innovations in Religion and Abuses in Government in the University of Cambridge'. For the institutional context, see Victor Morgan, 'with a contribution by Christopher Brooke', *A History of the University of Cambridge*, ii (Cambridge, 2004).

18. *Fur praedestinatus: sive, dialogismus inter quendam ordinis praedicantium Calvinistam et furem* was printed in London in 1651. Wing's *STC, 1641–1700* attributes the work to Henricus Slatius, who was certainly the author of the Dutch original; and credits Sancroft with an English edition of 1658, *The predestinated thief* (*STC*, no. 563, unique copy at Dulwich College). D'Oyly, *Life of Sancroft* (p.41) writes that the book was 'so universally attributed' to Sancroft 'as scarcely to admit of any doubt.' But see Thomas Jackson, 'Archbishop Sancroft Not the Author of *The Predestinated Thief*', *Dr Williams's Library Pamphlets*, p. 403; Geoffrey F. Nuttall, 'Some Bibliographical Notes and Identifications', *Congregational Historical Society Transactions*, 16 (1949–51), 154–55. I owe these references to Nicholas Tyacke.

19. Bendall, Brooke, Collinson, *A History of Emmanuel College*, pp. 251–52.

20. William Sancroft to 'Jacobissimo suo' (James Bownest), 25 August 1645, MS Tanner 467, no, 16, fol. 60ᵛ.

21. William Sancroft to William Dillingham, 29 September [1640], ibid., no. 2, fol. 19.

22. Ibid.

23. The Sancroft-Bownest correspondence consists of twenty-eight items, eighteen letters from Sancroft to Bownest, ten from Bownest to Sancroft: MSS Tanner 65, nos. 2, 13, fols 2, 26, Tanner 67, nos. 13, 50, 68, 78, fols. 32, 125, 173, 191, Tanner 467, no. 3, fols 20, 23–36, 38, 40–42, 44–45, 47. That the bulk of the correspondence is to be found in Tanner 467, out of the chronological sequence of Sancroft's letters otherwise, may suggest recognition in the process of collation of the intimately private nature of the letters. There are also two letters from Sancroft to his father, reflecting on his loss, 27 May 1641, 4 April 1642: MSS Tanner 66, no. 39, fol. 97, Tanner 63, no. 2, fol. 3. Both are printed in D'Oyly, *Life of Sancroft*, pp. 9–11. There are also letters from Bownest's mother who, perhaps unlike his father, thoroughly approved of Sancroft. Her letter reporting her son's death is written on the verso of a letter to Arthur from Arthur Jackson, 'your loving brother', 10 July 1640. (MS Harl. 3783, fol. 56.)

24. *The Works of John Milton*, xii. *Miscellaneous Correspondence* (New York, 1936). I was greatly assisted by the late Jeremy Maule in my understanding of the formal contextualisation of the Sancroft-Bownest correspondence.

25. William Sancroft to Arthur Bownest, 13 August [1640], MS Tanner 467, fol. 35.

26. William Sancroft to Arthur Bownest, 7 September 1638, MS Tanner 67, no. 13, fol. 32; Arthur Bownest to Sancroft, undated, MS Tanner 65, no. 2, fol. 2; Bownest to Sancroft, 5 March, n.y., MS Tanner 467, fol. 47; Sancroft to Bownest, 3 September n.y., MS Tanner 467, no. 3, fol. 20 et seq.

27. D'Oyly, *Life of Sancroft*, pp. 9–11.

28. William Sancroft to William Bloys jun., 10 July 1648, MS Tanner 467, no. 13, fol. 57.

29. William Sancroft to his father, Francis Sancroft, 10 February 1649, MS Tanner 57, no. 269, fol. 525; William Sancroft to his brother, Thomas Sancroft, 10 July 1650, MS Tanner 56, no. 114 fol. 216. At some point Sancroft copied out the anti-puritan satire and character 'Who is a Puritan', beginning 'Long hath it vext our learned age to scan,/Who rightly might be term'd a Puritan'. (MS Tanner 465, no. 49, fol. 82.) There is another copy of these verses in All Souls College Oxford, MS 185, fols 180^v–81^r. Sancroft's notebooks also reveal an interest in Molière's *Tartuffe*, a significant resonance.

30. William Sancroft to his father, Francis Sancroft, 27 November 1648, MS Tanner 57, no. 229, fol. 431; *ODNB*, art. Sancroft. And when Sancroft became master in 1663, Tuckney wrote to congratulate him. (Tuckney to Sancroft, 26 March 1663, MS Tanner 47, no. 2, fol. 3.)

31. William Sancroft to his father, Francis Sancroft, 28 July, 4 August 1646, MS Tanner 60, nos. 117, 124, fols 226, 237; William Sancroft to Thomas Holdsworth, 20 February 1649, MS Tanner 57, no. 274, fol. 535. For the impact of the Covenant and the Engagement on the University, see J. Twigg, *The University of Cambridge and the English Revolution, 1625–1688* (Cambridge, 1990).

32. For the history of the Emmanuel statute *de mora sociorum* see Bendall, Brooke and Collinson, *A History of Emmanuel College*, pp. 26–29; for Sancroft's college offices, ECA, BUR.8.2.

33. Draft of William Sancroft to 'Mr Need', MS Tanner 62, no. 329, fol. 641; William Sancroft to Richard Holdsworth, 17 January 1645(/6), MS Tanner 61, no. 100, fol. 261; William Sancroft to Bishop Brownrigg (draft), 7 December 1650, MS Tanner 56, no. 128, fol. 238; William Sancroft to Richard Weller, 26 May 1645, MS Tanner 60, no. 82, fol. 161. And see William Sancroft to James Bownest, 25 August 1645, MS Tanner 465, fol. 60: The college 'is much like the statue in the Capitol, when the tyrant Caligula had lopt off Jupiters head and set on his own'.

34. William Sancroft to his brother, Thomas Sancroft, 10 July 1650, MS Tanner 56, no. 114, fol. 216.

35. There were editions in 1652, 1653(2), 1654, 1655, 1657 and (most significantly) 1690: *Wing STC.*, nos. 555–60. Quotations are from sigs. B3, B4, F3^v of the first edition and the Epistle to the 1654 edition. *Modern Policies* was included in an appendix to the second edition of D'Oyly's *Life of Sancroft* (pp. 421–64). But see *ODNB*, art. Sancroft. MS Sancroft 55 consists of 'Maxims and Sentences Belonging to State and Policy' complied by William

Sandcroft senior, with notes by William Sancroft. They are Polonius-like, much less mordant.

36. Robert Beddard, *A Kingdom Without a King: The Journal of the Provisional Government in the Revolution of 1688* (Oxford, 1988), p. 7.

37. William Sancroft to his brother, Thomas Sancroft, 18 September 1650, MS Tanner 56, no. 121, fol. 229. Sancroft wrote to his father, 27 November 1648: 'going to Mr North with my letter, found there some forty strangers in a roome listening to good voices, well manag'd, and a lute well strung'. (MS Tanner 57, no. 229, fol. 431). See C. Paman to Sancroft, 17 January 1650(/1): 'Mr North hoped to have enjoyed your company double, you and your Musick.' (MS Harl. 3783, fol. 81). Dr Richard Luckett informs me that Sancroft gave his viol to his friend Henry North when he was ejected from Lambeth. See *Roger North on Music*, ed. John Wilson (London, 1959), p. xxi n.; and the autobiography of Rogar North chapter 7, beginning: 'As to music, it was my fortune to be descended of a family where it was native.' (*Lives of the Norths*, ed. A. Jessop (London, 1890), pp. 67–88).

38. Bendall, Brooke, Collinson, *A History of Emmanuel College*, pp. 254–55; Samuel Dillingham to Sancroft, 17 July 1651, MS Tanner 54, no. 53, fol. 108.

39. Drafts of William Sancroft to Ezekiel Wright, n.d., William Sancroft to Richard Holdsworth, 1 December 1644, MS Tanner 61, nos 31, 83 fols 64, 201; draft of William Sancroft to 'Mr Need', n.d. (1643), MS Tanner 62, no. 329, fol. 641.

40. Sir Framlingham Gawdy to William Sancroft and Sancroft to Gawdy (draft), MS Tanner 56, no. 82, fol. 163.

41. William Sancroft to Thomas Holdsworth (draft), 6 September 1651, MS Tanner 55, no. 21, fol. 39.

42. Robert Beaumont to William Sancroft, n.d., MS Harl. 3783, fol. 126; a letter dated, from London, 7 September 1657, ibid., fol. 168; D'Oyly, *Life of Sancroft*, p. 56. For further information about Sancroft buying and selling books, see MS Harl. 3783, fol. 148.

43. There is much evidence relating to Sancroft's continental travels in MS Harl. 3783. See also MS Harl. 3784, fols 5, 9, D'Oyly, *Life of Sancroft*, pp. 56–65. The evidence of Sancrofts's Genevan address is in MS Harl. 3784, fol. 182.

44. Robert Gayer to William Sancroft, 19 December 1657, MS Harl. 3783, fol. 176; further details concerning this legacy and certain complications, ibid., fols 184, 185, 188, 192, 200; *ODNB.*, art. Sancroft; evidence of Sancroft's generosity to Cosin and of their friendship in MS Harl. 3783, fols 149–50, 238, 241–42, MS. Harl 3784, fols 27, 29, 34, MS Tanner 467, fol. 72. Cosin's letters to Sancroft are printed in *Correspondence of John Cosin*, i. Surtees Society 52 (1869), ii. Surtees Society 55 (1870).

45. William Sancroft, *A sermon in S. Peter's Westminster* (London, 1660). For evidence that Sancroft was *proxime accessit*, see *Correspondence of Cosin*, ii, 12–13.

46. Ibid., 21–22, 27–28.

47. William Sancroft to Ezekiel Wright, 17 June 1663, BL, MS Add. 5860, fols 140r–41ʳ (William Cole's transcript of a letter lent to him by Richard Farmer, master of Emmanuel, 1775–1797). There is another copy of this letter in ECA, COL.9.1A, pp. 222–23. See D'Oyly, *Life of Sancroft*, pp. 76–79. See *ODNB*, art Sancroft.

48. Bishop Gilbert Sheldon to Bishop Cosin, 3 September 1661, *Correspondence of Cosin*, ii, 25–26.

49. William Sancroft to Ezekiel Wright, 17 June 1663, BL MS Add 5860, fols 140ʳ–41ʳ; William Sancroft to his brother, Thomas Sancroft, 4 October 1662, MS Tanner 48, no. 28, fol. 52.

50. Bishop Sheldon to William Sancroft, 2 October 1662, MS Harl. 3784, fol. 77.

51. William Sancroft to his brother, Thomas Sancroft, 4 October 1662, MS Tanner 48, no. 28, fol. 52.

52. William Sancroft to Ezekiel Wright, 17 June 1663, BL, MS Add. 5860, fols 140ʳ–41ʳ.

53. Bishop Sheldon to William Sancroft, 20 September, 2 October 1662, MS. Harl 3784, fols 71, 77; Charles II to the Master and Fellows of Emmanuel College, 13 October 1662, ECA, COL.14.1, p. 70; William Sancroft to his brother, Thomas Sancroft, 4 October 1662, MS Tanner 48, no. 28, fol. 52. On 14 November 1662, Sancroft was assured that he would receive the next fellowship at Eton to fall vacant, 'such satisfaction as to Eton as will please you.' (MS Harl. 3784, fol. 82.)

54. Frank Stubbings, *Emmanuel College Chapel, 1677–1977* (Cambridge, 1977); Bendall, Brooke, Collinson, *A History of Emmanuel College Cambridge*, pp. 273–75; Morgan, *History of the University of Cambridge*, ii, 46–47.

55. J.C.T. Oates, *Cambridge University Library: A History From the Beginnings to the Copyright Act of Queen Anne* (Cambridge, 1986), pp. 314–26; Bendall, Brooke, Collinson, *A History of Emmanuel College Cambridge*, pp. 270–71.

56. Thomas Page to William Sancroft' 27 January 1664(/5), MS Harl. 3784, fol. 123; Bendall, Brooke, Collinson, *A History of Emmanuel College*, p. 270. Bishop Humphrey Henchman wrote to Sancroft on 22 October 1664, the day the dean, Dr Barwick, died: 'Tomorrow I attend at Whitehall in hope to obtayne that you may succeed.' By 25 October he was able to tell Sancroft that the king had agreed to his appointment. (MS Harl. 3784, fol. 190, 195, 197).

57. Bendall, Brooke, Collinson, *A History of Emmanuel College*, p. 272.

58. Bishop Henchman to William Sancroft, 9 July 1665, MS Harl. 3785, fol. 8; Dr Robert Barwick to Sancroft, 5 August 1665, ibid., fol. 26; Stephen Bing to Sancroft, 27 July 1665, ibid., fol. 20; John Tillotson to Sancroft, 15 August, 18 August, 14 September 1665, ibid., fols 31, 34, 35; *A History of St Paul's Cathedral and the Men Associated with it*, ed. W.R. Matthews and W.M. Atkins (London, 1957), pp. 177–78.

59. William Sancroft to Sir Robert Gayer, William Sancroft to Bishop Henchman, William Sancroft to Dr Pory, William Sancroft to George Davenport, all dated 20 September 1655, MSS Tanner 45, no. 17, fol. 28, Tanner 467, nos 7, 8, fols 50, 52.

60. Bishop Henchman to William Sancroft, 9 December 1665, MS Tanner 45, no. 28, fol. 47; William Sancroft to his brother, Thomas Sancroft, from Fulham, 1 January 1665(/6), MS Tanner 45, no. 30, fol. 53.

61. *The Diary of John Evelyn*, ed. E.S. De Beer (London, 1955), iii, 448–49; D'Oyly, *Life of Sancroft*, pp. 83–84. See more generally Matthews and Atkins, *A History of St Paul's Cathedral*; and, more recently, *St Paul's: The Cathedral Church of London, 604–2004*, ed. Derek Keene, Arthur Burns, Andrew Saint (New Haven and London, 2004).

62. Isaac Basire to William Sancroft, 10 October 1666, MS Harley 3785, fol 257; Thomas Flatman to William Sancroft, 17 September 1666, MS Tanner 45, no. 56, fol. 97.

63. William Sancroft, *Lex ignea: or the school of righteousness. A sermon preach'd before the king October 10 1666 at the solemn fast appointed for the late fire in London* (London, 1666). H.H. Milman's *Annals of St Paul's Cathedral* (2nd edn, London, 1869) observes (p. 386) that, in this sermon, Sancroft 'approaches sublimity'.

64. William Sancroft to his brother, Thomas Sancroft, 17 November 1650, MS Tanner 56, no. 125, fol. 234; George Davenport to William Sancroft, 22 July 1662, MS Harl. 3784, fol. 64; ibid., fol. 102.

65. William Sancroft to Christopher Wren, 25 April 1668, 2 July 1668, D'Oyly, *Life of Sancroft*, pp. 86–88.

66. Keene, Burns, Saint, *St Paul's*, pp. 67–69, 186–232, esp. pp. 223, 232, 419–20, 481, 488. The main chapter account-book for Michaelmas 1666 to Michaelmas 1667 is written entirely in Sancroft's hand.

67. Ronald Hutton, *Charles II, King of England, Scotland and Ireland* (Oxford, 1989), p. 341; ODNB, art. Sancroft.

68. Gilbert Burnet, *History of My Own Time: Part I. The Reign of Charles the Second*, ed. O. Airy, 2 vols. (Oxford, 1897, 1900), ii, 100; *Diary of Dr Edward Lake . . . in the Years 1677–1678*, ed. G.P. Elliott, in *Camden Miscellany*, i, Camden Society 39 (1847); Mark Goldie, 'Danby, the Bishops and the King', in *The Politics of Religion in Restoration England*, ed. Tim Harris, Paul Seaward, Mark Goldie (Oxford, 1990), p. 84; John Miller, *Charles II* (London, 1991), p. 305; John Spurr, *The Restoration Church of England, 1646–1689* (New Haven and London, 1991), p. 74; Henry Lee, from Emmanuel, to Richard Kidder, 19 November 1677, MS Tanner 40, no. 73, fol. 113. See D'Oyly's examination of the evidence, pp. 91–93.

69. It is to be hoped that Robert Beddard will publish such a book, the book of his Oxford D.Phil. thesis.

70. D'Oyly, *Life of Sancroft*, p. 306; DNB, art. Henry Wharton.

71. ODNB, art. Sancroft; William Sancroft, *The true time of keeping St Matthias day in leap-years: shewn in a familiar conference between a church-man*

and a dissenter (London, 1711). In my twenties, the years of my historical apprenticeship, this was the only fact that I knew about Archbishop Sancroft.

72. Spurr, *The Restoration Church of England*; Harris, Seaward, Goldie, *The Politics of Religion*.

73. Bishop Henry Compton's 'Census' was an attempt to measure the extent of both catholic and protestant dissent. See *The Compton Census of 1676*, Records of Social and Economic History, new series 10, ed. Anne Whiteman (London, 1986).

74. Jonathan Scott, *Algernon Sidney and the Restoration Crisis, 1677–1683* (Cambridge, 1991), part one, 'The Restoration Crisis'.

75. *Patriarcha and Other Political Works*, ed. Peter Laslett (Oxford, 1949), p. 45; Mark Goldie, 'The Political Thought of the Anglican Revolution', in Robert Beddard, ed., *The Revolution of 1688* (Oxford, 1991), pp. 165–66.

76. Spurr, *The Restoration Church of England*, p. 81.

77. R.A. Beddard, 'The Commission for Ecclesiastical Promotions, 1681–84: An Instrument of Tory Reaction', *Historical Journal*, 10 (1967), 11–40.

78. Quoted Patrick Collinson, *The Religion of Protestants: The Church in English Society, 1559–1625* (Oxford, 1982), p. 7.

79. Spurr, *The Restoration Church of England*, p. 7.

80. LPL, MS 3894, nos 16, 20, 27.

81. William Sancroft To Dr Covel at the Hague, 2 January 1684(/5), D'Oyly, *Life of Sancroft*, pp. 117–20.

82. Princess Mary to William Sancroft, 1 October 1687, MS Tanner 29, no. 55, fol. 77; draft of William Sancroft to Princess Mary, ibid., no. 72, fol. 111. D'Oyly (*Life of Sancroft*, p. 224n.) prints a letter from William Stanley, dated 26 May 1715, which establishes that Sancroft's letter was never sent, and alleges that he was 'glad' that he had not written to the princess.

83. *A Supplement to Burnet's History of My Own Time*, ed. H.C. Foxcroft (Oxford, 1902), p. 211; D'Oyly, *Life of Sancroft*, pp. 135–36.

84. G.V. Bennett, 'The Seven Bishops: A Reconsideration', in *Religious Motivation: Biographical and Sociological Problems for the Church Historian*, Studies in Church History 15, ed. Derek Baker (Oxford, 1978), 267–87.

85. Burnet, *History of My Own Time*, ii, 227.

86. D'Oyly, *Life of Sancroft*, pp. 160–62, from MS Tanner 28, nos. 31, 51, fols 38ᵛ–39ʳ, 64ʳ.

87. Bishop Bapt. Levinz of Sodor and Man to William Sancroft (from Canterbury), MS Tanner 28, no. 67, fol. 83. See also nos 57, 69, fols. 70, 85.

88. MS Tanner 28, nos 90 and 84, fols 117, 104; D'Oyly, *Life of Sancroft*, p. 186n.

89. Goldie, 'The political Thought of the Anglican Revolution'. And see Goldie, 'Danby, the Bishops and the King'; and Robert Beddard, 'The Guildhall Declaration of 11 December and the Counter-Revolution of the Loyalists', *Historical Journal*, 11 (1968), 403–20.

90. Bennett, 'The Seven Bishops', 286.

91. Beddard, *A Kingdom Without a King*, p. 12; Beddard, *The Revolution of 1688*, p. 1.

92. Archbishop Sancroft's account of the interview is in MS Tanner 28, no. 31, fol. 38 et seq. (inaccurately in D'Oyly, *Life of Sancroft*, pp. 217–23) and MS Tanner 28, no. 157, fol. 219 et seq. Further relations by various bishops, MS Tanner 28, nos 165, 166, 168, 221, fols 232, 233, 241, 318. On 3 November the archbishop averred 'upon my word' that he had not been party to the invitation. (D'Oyly, *Life of Sancroft*, p. 226.) His disavowal, 3 November 1688, is in MS Tanner 28, no. 159, fol. 224. See also Bishop Henry Compton to Sancroft, 6 November 1688, MS. Tanner 28, no. 161, fol. 227.

93. Beddard, *A Kingdom Without a King*; Beddard, *The Revolution of 1688*.

94. Beddard, *A Kingdom Without a King*, pp. 39, 50, 71–72, 74, 92.

95. Sancroft's reply to the marquess of Halifax's summons to attend the Convention Parliament (which followed Halifax's rebuke for his absence on 25 January 1689 (MS Tanner 28, no. 233, fol. 232)), MS Tanner 28, no. 257, fol. 366, written on the *verso* of the summons. It is clear from a second summons, dated 22 March 1689 (Sancroft's holograph response, dated 23 March, MS Tanner 28, no. 267, fol. 378) that this reply was never sent.

96. *The Diary of John Evelyn*, iv, 613–14; D'Oyly, *Life of Sancroft*, p. 254. However, according to Evelyn, the bishops were all of one mind: for a Regency, 'thereby to salve their Oathes, and so all publique matters to proceede in his Majesties [scil., James II's] name'.

97. Bishop Turner to William Sancroft, 11 January 1689, MS Tanner 28, no. 221, fols 318 et seq; D'Oyly, *Life of Sancroft*, pp. 252–54. Turner had drafted the address which he intended Sancroft and the other bishops to make to Orange. (MS Tanner 28, nos 222, 223, fols 319^v. 320.)

98. Bennett, 'The Seven Bishops', 287 n. 65. See also Beddard, *The Revolution of 1688*, p. 44; Beddard *A Kingdom Without a King*, pp. 121–22.

99. Norman Sykes, *William Wake Archbishop of Canterbury, 1657–1737* (Cambridge, 1957), i, 48–9; Norman Sykes, *From Sheldon to Secker: Aspects of English Church History, 1660–1768* (Cambridge, 1959), pp. 83–9, Spurr, *The Restoration Church of England*, pp. 103–4; *ODNB*, art Sancroft. And see *A vindication of the arch-bishop and several other bishops* (1690). But would Sancroft and the Sancroftians *really* have embraced the Presbyterians?

100. Tanner MS 28, no. 267, fol. 378.

101. Bishop Compton to William Sancroft, 'Wednesday noon', n.d. (1689), MS Tanner 27, no. 7, fol. 8.

102. Bishop Turner to William Sancroft from Leamington, Warwickshire, 20 March 1688(/9), MS Tanner 28, no. 261, fols 370–71.

103. D'Oyly, *Life of Sancroft*, pp. 238–44; William Sancroft to Dr Montague, master of Trinity College, 30 November 1688, MS Harl. 3785, fol. 275; John Covel to Sancroft, 15 December 1688, ibid., fol. 277; John Covel to Henry Paman, 17 December 1688, ibid., fol. 282; form of election, 16 January 1688(/9), ibid., fol. 280; John Covel to Sancroft, 23 February 1688(/9), ibid., fol. 284; John Covel to Sancroft, 1 March 1688(/9), MS Tanner 28, no. 255, fol. 364.

104. William Sancroft to his brother, Thomas Sancroft, 18 September 1650, MS Tanner 56, no. 121, fol. 229.
105. Anonymous letter to William Sancroft, 23 October 1689, MS Tanner 27, no. 65, fol. 89; Bishop Levinz of Sodor and Man to Sancroft, 18 November 1689, ibid., no. 74, fol. 99; Edmund Elys to Sancroft, n.d., MS Tanner 28, no. 258, fol. 367.
106. Form of resignation, MS Tanner 28, no. 254, fol. 363. See *ODNB*, art Sancroft.
107. William Sancroft to Sir Henry North, 28 January 1693, *Familiar Letters of Dr William Sancroft Late Archbishop of Canterbury to Mr North Afterwards Sir Henry North of Mildenhall Bart* (London, 1757), pp. 41–43. Bodleian Library, MS Rawlinson D 835, fol. 15, is the formal indictment against Sancroft for illegally occupying his houses at Lambeth and Croydon.
108. This libel/satire was printed in 1655 and 1658 as *Musarum deliciae and wit restor'd*. There are numerous MS. copies in existence. William Sancroft's transcript is in MS Sancroft 53, p. 53 seq. Other material in this volume dates it to c. 1689–92.
109. LPL, MS. 3894.
110. William Sancroft to Bishop Lloyd, 24 April 1691, LPL, MS 3894, no. 11; Bishop Lloyd to William Sancroft, 24 April 1691, MS Tanner 26, no. 58, fol. 82; Dr Thomas Gale to William Sancroft, 9 April 1691, ibid., no. 66, fol. 91.
111. William Sancroft to Bishop Lloyd, 24 April 1691, LPL, MS 3894, no. 11. Compton was still in the dark, and, according to Sancroft, was about to enter the Council Chamber when a friend told him what was happening and pulled him back.
112. William Sancroft to Bishop Lloyd, 29 April (1691), LPL, MS 3894, no. 13; D'Oyly, *Life of Sancroft*, pp. 274–75.
113. *The Diary of John Evelyn*, v. 80, 195–96.
114. 'A short account of Arch Bishop Sancroft from Mr Needham', ECA, COL.9.8; D'Oyly, *Life of Sancroft*, pp. 277–9.
115. William, Sancroft to Bishop Lloyd, 26 August 1691, LPL, MS 3894, no. 19.
116. 'A short account'; William Sancroft to Bishop Lloyd, 15 December 1691, LPL, MS 3894, no. 23; D'Oyly, *Life of Sancroft*, p. 313. And see also William Sancroft to Sir Henry North, 23 December 1691, *Familiar Letters*, pp. 21–26. When Bishop Cosin was ill in 1663, George Davenport told Sancroft: 'I think coffee hath done him much good', but that his physicians had advised him 'rather to drink tea.' (MS Harl. 3784, fol. 90.)
117. William Sancroft to Bishop Lloyd, 23 December (1691), LPL, MS 3894, no. 25.
118. LPL, MS 3894, no. 27; *ODNB*, art Collier.
119. William Sancroft to Bishop Lloyd, 8 June 1692, 27 September 1692, LPL, MS 3894, nos 29, 36; *A letter out of Suffolk to a friend in London giving some account of the last sickness and death of Dr William Sancroft*, 'by Mr [Thomas] Wagstaffe' (London, 1694), p. 25.

120. *The Correspondence of John Cosin*, ii, 12–13; Bishop Henchman to William Sancroft, n.d. (1665(/6)), MS Harl. 3785, fol. 88; George Davenport to William Sancroft, 2 and 5 January 1663, MS Harl. 3784, fols 90, 92–3.

121. *The Diary of John Evelyn*, v, 51–52; John Balderston to William Sancroft, 16 September 1693, MS Tanner 25, no. 59, fol. 89.

122. H.S. Bennett, 'Archbishop Sancroft's Library', *Emmanuel College Magazine*, 45 (1962–63), pp. 32–36; Bendall, Brooke, Collinson, *A History of Emmanuel College Cambridge*, pp. 281–82. A catalogue of Sancroft's library is in preparation, begun by Dr Sarah Bendall and continued by Dr Helen Carron. See Helen Carron, 'William Sancroft: A Seventeenth-Century Collector and his Library', *The Library*, 7th series, 1 (2000), 290–307.

123. But see transcripts from the English poets (including Milton's 'Let us with a gladsome mind', 'done [Sancroft notes] at fifteen years old') in MS Tanner 466; and much literary material transcribed in MS Sancroft 29. MS Sancroft 122 consists of 'A catalogue of my books in mine owne study', c. 700 volumes, together with three pages of book prices (fols 16^r–17^r).

124. D'Oyly, *Life of Sancroft*, p. 307; Bendall, Brooke, Collinson, *A History of Emmanuel College*, p. 282.

125. MS Sancroft 28 contains (pp. 405 et seq.) an account of the Salem witch trials, taken from a pamphlet published in London in 1693, the year of Sancroft's death.

126. MS Sancroft 28, pp. 195, 199.

127. Information imparted by Dr Arnold Hunt.

128. There are many letters to Sancroft from North in MS Tanner 25, dated 1692, mostly about the 'news'.

129. William Sancroft to Sir Henry North, 15 March 1692(/3), *Familiar Letters*, p. 39

130. Fiametta Rocco, *The Micraculous Fever-Tree: Malaria, Medicine and the Cure that Changed the World* (London, 2003). However, *A letter out of Suffolk* (pp. 29–30) suggests that Sancroft *did* take quinine, although it was the author himself, Thomas Wagstaffe, who seems to have acted as his physician, who had reported to Bishop Lloyd (10 September 1693) his reluctance to take it. (MS Tanner 25, no. 58, fol. 87.)

131. MS Tanner 25, no. 69, fol. 102; Dr Ralph Taylor to Anthony a Wood, 23 December 1693, ibid., no. 72, fol. 108; *A letter out of Suffolk*; D'Oyly, *Life of Sancroft*, p. 312.

132. R. A. Beddard, 'Bishop Cartwright's Death-Bed', *Bodleian Library Record*, 11 (1984), 222–23.

133. Burnet, *History of My Own Time*, ii, 100.

134. I owe this insight to Mark Goldie. See his 'The Political Thought of the Anglican Revolution', p. 134.

135. MS Sancroft 22, fol. 2.

136. The Sancroft-Sprat correspondence is reported in *Lambeth Palace Library Annual Review*, 2004. Sancroft's letter of 12 April 1693, which is quoted here, is reproduced in the *Review* in facsimile.

Index

A

beast fables, Protestant ....203 n. 40, 210 n. 9
Becon, Thomas 5
Beddard, Robert ....242, 248 n. 69
Bedell, William, bishop of Kilmore and Ardagh (1629–42) 37
Belleau, Leicestershire..68
Belstead, Suffolk...103
Bemerton, Wiltshire..55
Bendall, Sarah..242
Benenden, Kent 127
Bentham, Joseph ....55, 212 n. 36
Bernard, Richard, 54, 58–60, 111, 131, 137, 138, 139–40, 141, 165, 166–67, 232 n. 19, 240 n. 91; *Christian advertisements and counsels of peace*, 137, 240 n. 94; *The faithfull shepherd*, 54, 59; *Plaine evidences*, 240 n. 94; *The separatists schisme*..232 n. 19
Berne.. 92
Beza (de Bèze), Theodore, 75,77, 79, 88–89, 90, 91, 92, 94, 221 nn. 41, 42; *Epistolae*, 79; *Correspondance*, 88; *Tractatae theologicae*........................89
Bible, 9, 27, 46–47, 58, 119–20, 155, 169; Great Bible (1539), 9; Geneva Bible (1560), 35, 77; Psalm 23, 46–47; Isaiah 56.10, 47; Jeremiah 5, 11; Ecclesiastes 42, 119–20; Matthew 10.16, 203 n. 42, 18.20, 133, 21.13, 48; Mark 11.31, 200; Luke 10.2, 45, 14.23, 186, John, 10, 45, 46; 1 Corinthians 124; 1 Corinthians 5.9–10, 167, 6.17, 133
Bigg, William 128
Bildestone, Suffolk 40–41
Bilney, Thomas..29–30
Blackerby, Richard 52
Bodley, John....................................83, 85, 89, 90
Bohemia..86, 99
Boleyn, Queen Ann....................................5–6, 7
Bolton, Robert.....................55, 62, 212 n. 36, 215 n. 65
Bond of Association (1584) 83
Book of Common Prayer (1549, 1552, 1559), Anglican Liturgy, ...6–7, 14, 18–20, 22–23, 31, 50, 51, 63–66, 88, 95–96, 142, 151, 181, 205 n. 74, 215 n. 74
Booton, Northamptonshire................................. 135
Bossy, John 25, 40, 49, 51, 71
Boston, Lincolnshire 140, 141, 163
Boulton, Jeremy...65
Bownd, Nicholas, 36, 39, 110; *The doctrine of the Sabbath*................36
Bownest, Arthur..............................176–77, 178, 244 n. 23
Brachlow, Stephen 137
Bradshaigh, Sir Roger.......................................153
Bradshaw, William, 70, 90, 137, 168; *The unreasonablenesse of the separation*.. 137
Bredwell, Stephen, 187, 168; *Rasing of the foundations of Brownisme*..................137

C

D

E

F

H

L

M

Q

R

S

T

W

Y

Z